W9-BCI-309

EDUCATING EXCEPTIONAL CHILDREN

Ninth Edition

Editor

Karen L. Freiberg

University of Maryland, Baltimore

Dr. Karen Frieberg has an interdisciplinary educational and employment background in nursing, education, and developmental psychology. She received her B.S. from the State University of New York at Plattsburgh, her M.S. from Cornell University, and her Ph.D. from Syracuse University. She has worked as a school nurse, a pediatric nurse, a public health nurse for the Navajo Indians, an associate project director for a child development clinic, a researcher in several areas of child development, and a university professor. She is the author of an award-winning textbook, *Human Development: A Life-Span Approach,* which is now in its fourth edition. She is currently on the faculty at the University of Maryland, Baltimore County.

A Library of Information from the Public Press

Dushkin Publishing Group/Brown & Benchmark Publishers
Sluice Dock, Guilford, Connecticut 06437

The Annual Editions Series

ANNUAL EDITIONS is a series of over 65 volumes designed to provide the reader with convenient, low-cost access to a wide range of current, carefully selected articles from some of the most important magazines, newspapers, and journals published today. ANNUAL EDITIONS are updated on an annual basis through a continuous monitoring of over 300 periodical sources. All ANNUAL EDITIONS have a number of features that are designed to make them particularly useful, including topic guides, annotated tables of contents, unit overviews, and indexes. For the teacher using ANNUAL EDITIONS in the classroom, an Instructor's Resource Guide with test questions is available for each volume.

VOLUMES AVAILABLE

Abnormal Psychology
Adolescent Psychology
Africa
Aging
American Foreign Policy
American Government
American History, Pre-Civil War
American History, Post-Civil War
American Public Policy
Anthropology
Archaeology
Biopsychology
Business Ethics
Child Growth and Development
China
Comparative Politics
Computers in Education
Computers in Society
Criminal Justice
Criminology
Developing World
Deviant Behavior
Drugs, Society, and Behavior
Dying, Death, and Bereavement

Early Childhood Education
Economics
Educating Exceptional Children
Education
Educational Psychology
Environment
Geography
Global Issues
Health
Human Development
Human Resources
Human Sexuality
India and South Asia
International Business
Japan and the Pacific Rim
Latin America
Life Management
Macroeconomics
Management
Marketing
Marriage and Family
Mass Media
Microeconomics

Middle East and the
  Islamic World
Multicultural Education
Nutrition
Personal Growth and Behavior
Physical Anthropology
Psychology
Public Administration
Race and Ethnic Relations
Russia, the Eurasian Republics,
  and Central/Eastern Europe
Social Problems
Social Psychology
Sociology
State and Local Government
Urban Society
Western Civilization,
  Pre-Reformation
Western Civilization,
  Post-Reformation
Western Europe
World History, Pre-Modern
World History, Modern
World Politics

Cataloging in Publication Data
Main entry under title: Annual Editions: Educating exceptional children. 9/E.
        1. Exceptional children—Education—United States—Periodicals. 2.
Educational innovations—United States—Periodicals. I. Freiberg, Karen, *comp.* II.
Title: Educating exceptional children.
ISBN 0–697–36323–6   371.9′05   76–644171

© 1997 by Dushkin Publishing Group/Brown & Benchmark Publishers, Guilford, CT 06437

Copyright law prohibits the reproduction, storage, or transmission in any form by any means of any portion of this publication without the express written permission of Dushkin Publishing Group/Brown & Benchmark Publishers, and of the copyright holder (if different) of the part of the publication to be reproduced. The Guidelines for Classroom Copying endorsed by Congress explicitly state that unauthorized copying may not be used to create, to replace, or to substitute for anthologies, compilations, or collective works.

Annual Editions® is a Registered Trademark of Dushkin Publishing Group/
Brown & Benchmark Publishers, a Times Mirror Higher Education Group company.

Ninth Edition

Printed in the United States of America

Printed on Recycled Paper

371.9
E24f
1997

99-2203

3623653l

Editors/Advisory Board

Members of the Advisory Board are instrumental in the final selection of articles for each edition of ANNUAL EDITIONS. Their review of articles for content, level, currentness, and appropriateness provides critical direction to the editor and staff. We think that you will find their careful consideration well reflected in this volume.

EDITOR

Karen L. Freiberg
University of Maryland
Baltimore

ADVISORY BOARD

Liz Begley
Ithaca College

Glenna DeBrota
Butler University

Sheila Drake
Kansas Wesleyan University

Mark B. Goor
George Mason University

Donna L. Jacobs
Essex Community College

Roberta Lubinsky
SUNY College, Geneseo

Mack McCoulskey
Angelo State University

Sharon Merrill
Xavier University

Susan M. Munson
Duquesne University

Araceli M. Nicolas
Dickinson State University

Virginia L. Nimmo
Gustavus Adolphus College

Gael L. Ragle
Arizona State University

Christina Ramirez-Smith
Christopher Newport University

Arthur Rathgeber
Nipissing University

Marcia J. Reinholtz
Greensboro College

Joyce M. Smith
SUNY College, Oswego

Faith M. Stayer
Augusta College

Linda A. Svobodny
Moorhead State University

Ruth Thompson
Edinboro University

Kathleen S. Whittier
SUNY at Plattsburgh

Steve L. Williams
California State University
Hayward

Staff

Ian A. Nielsen, Publisher

EDITORIAL STAFF

Roberta Monaco, Developmental Editor
Addie Raucci, Administrative Editor
Cheryl Greenleaf, Permissions Editor
Deanna Herrschaft, Permissions Assistant
Diane Barker, Proofreader
Lisa Holmes-Doebrick, Program Coordinator

PRODUCTION STAFF

Brenda S. Filley, Production Manager
Charles Vitelli, Designer
Shawn Callahan, Graphics
Lara M. Johnson, Graphics
Laura Levine, Graphics
Mike Campbell, Graphics
Libra A. Cusack, Typesetting Supervisor
Juliana Arbo, Typesetter
Jane Jaegersen, Typesetter
Marie Lazauskas, Word Processor
Larry Killian, Copier Coordinator

To the Reader

In publishing ANNUAL EDITIONS we recognize the enormous role played by the magazines, newspapers, and journals of the *public press* in providing current, first-rate educational information in a broad spectrum of interest areas. Many of these articles are appropriate for students, researchers, and professionals seeking accurate, current material to help bridge the gap between principles and theories and the real world. These articles, however, become more useful for study when those of lasting value are carefully *collected, organized, indexed,* and *reproduced* in a *low-cost format,* which provides easy and permanent access when the material is needed. That is the role played by ANNUAL EDITIONS. Under the direction of each volume's *academic editor,* who is an expert in the subject area, and with the guidance of an *Advisory Board,* each year we seek to provide in each ANNUAL EDITION a current, well-balanced, carefully selected collection of the best of the public press for your study and enjoyment. We think that you will find this volume useful, and we hope that you will take a moment to let us know what you think.

When Bob Dole retired from the U.S. Senate in the summer of 1996, after 35 years of service, a reporter asked him what he thought his crowning achievement was. His answer: helping to pass the Individuals with Disabilities Education Act (IDEA). This anthology about the education of children with exceptional conditions would be entirely different if IDEA had not been enacted in the United States. IDEA has transformed not only the way we provide special education to individuals with disabilities but, more importantly, the way we think about these individuals and accept them in everyday activities.

IDEA (formerly known as the Education for All Handicapped Children Act) was passed in 1975 and has been amended three times. It now guarantees that infants born at risk of developing any disabilities can be assessed early and frequently. An individualized family service plan (IFSP) is mandated. The plan describes how the infant and his or her family will be followed from time of assessment until entrance in public school. IFSPs outline the many forms of early childhood interventions that will be provided, including at-home services and preschool services.

IDEA guarantees that every child with an exceptional condition enrolled in the public school educational system will be assessed and provided with an individualized education program (IEP). This program, to be updated every year, outlines all the interventions to be provided by the public school. It is designed collaboratively by parents, teachers, specialists in the area of the child's disabilities, and school administrators. All children with disabilities are guaranteed a free and appropriate education in the least restrictive environment. While this does not mean that every child

with a disability must be included in a regular education classroom, it has drastically changed special education. Most special education schools and many full-day special education classes have been discontinued in compliance with IDEA's call for "least restrictive environment" (LRE). Inclusive education for children with disabilities is the trend of the 1990s.

IDEA was amended in 1990 to mandate the provision of transitional services to all children with disabilities from the end of their public school education through age 21. An individualized transition plan (ITP) must be written to describe all of the interventions that will be provided to help the student move into the community and workforce with as much independence as possible.

This ninth edition of *Annual Editions: Educating Exceptional Children* includes articles explaining how the IDEA provisions are being implemented in all areas of special education. Selections have been made with an eye to conveying information, some personal experiences, and many practical suggestions for implementation.

To improve future editions of this anthology, please complete and return the postage-paid article rating form on the last page. Your suggestions are valued and appreciated.

Good luck in using this anthology to make your own and others' lives easier and more rewarding.

Karen Freiberg

Karen Freiberg
Editor

Contents

UNIT 1

Inclusive Education

Five articles present strategies for establishing positive interactions between students with and without special needs.

UNIT 2

Children with Learning Disabilities

Four selections address the assessment and special needs of students with learning disabilities.

The concepts in bold italics are developed in the article. For further expansion please refer to the Topic Guide and the Index.

WK 6

UNIT 3

Children with Mental Retardation

Four articles discuss concerns and strategies for providing optimal educational programs for students with mental retardation.

The concepts in bold italics are developed in the article. For further expansion please refer to the Topic Guide and the Index.

UNIT 4

Children with Behavioral Disorders and Autism

Four articles discuss the regular education initiative and ways to teach emotionally and behaviorally disordered students in mainstream classes.

UNIT 5

Children with Communication Disorders

Four selections discuss disorders of communication and suggest ways in which adults can assist students' learning and development in speech and language.

WK 6

The concepts in bold italics are developed in the article. For further expansion please refer to the Topic Guide and the Index.

UNIT 6

Children with Hearing Impairments

Three articles examine due process for the provision of special services for the hearing impaired and strategies for teaching hearing impaired children in regular education classes.

UNIT 7

Children with Visual Impairments

Three selections discuss the special needs of visually impaired and blind children from infancy through secondary school.

The concepts in bold italics are developed in the article. For further expansion please refer to the Topic Guide and the Index.

UNIT 8

Children with Physical and Health Impairments

Four articles examine the educational implications of medical treatments and physical impairments on children.

The concepts in bold italics are developed in the article. For further expansion please refer to the Topic Guide and the Index.

UNIT 9

Children with Special Gifts and Talents

Three articles examine the need for special services for gifted and talented students, assessment of giftedness, and ways to teach these students.

UNIT 10

Early Childhood Exceptionality

Three articles discuss the implementation of special services to infants and preschoolers with disabilities.

The concepts in bold italics are developed in the article. For further expansion please refer to the Topic Guide and the Index.

UNIT 11

Transition to Adulthood

Three articles examine the problems and issues regarding transitions within school or from school to the community and work force.

The concepts in bold italics are developed in the article. For further expansion please refer to the Topic Guide and the Index.

Topic Guide

This topic guide suggests how the selections in this book relate to topics of traditional concern to students and professionals involved with educating exceptional children. It is useful for locating articles that relate to each other for reading and research. The guide is arranged alphabetically according to topic. Articles may, of course, treat topics that do not appear in the topic guide. In turn, entries in the topic guide do not necessarily constitute a comprehensive listing of all the contents of each selection.

TOPIC AREA	KNOWLEDGE (These articles provide information about a handicap or about a special education concept.)	ATTITUDES (These articles contain personal experiences of exceptional persons or discussions about changing children's attitudes toward a handicap.)	TEACHING (These articles contain practical suggestions about how to apply special education principles to the teaching of exceptional children.)
Assessment	4. Restructuring the Participation of African-American Parents 19. Distinguishing Language Differences 32. Education of Gifted Students	7. Identifying Students' Instructional Needs 14. They Can But They Don't 15. Culturally Sensitive Disciplinarian	6. Is ADD Becoming a Desired Diagnosis? 21. Do You See What I Mean? 35. Putting Real-Life Skills into IEP/IFSPs
Behavioral Disorders	14. They Can But They Don't 17. Autism	15. Culturally Sensitive Disciplinarian 16. Variables Affecting the Reintegration Rate	6. Is ADD Becoming a Desired Diagnosis?
Childhood Exceptionality	10. Prenatal Drug Exposure 17. Autism 25. Preschool Orientation and Mobility 36. Physical Education Curriculum	18. Language Interaction Techniques 37. "Buddy Skills" for Preschoolers	33. Meeting the Needs of Gifted and Talented Preschoolers 35. Putting Real-Life Skills into IEP/IFSPs
Communication Disorders	17. Autism 19. Distinguishing Language Differences 20. Toward Defining Programs and Services	18. Language Interaction Techniques	21. Do You See What I Mean? 30. Creating Inclusionary Opportunities
Computers and Technology		23. Developing Independent and Responsible Behaviors	8. Adapting Textbooks for Children with Learning Disabilities
Cultural Diversity	15. Culturally Sensitive Disciplinarian 19. Distinguishing Language Differences 32. Education of Gifted Students	4. Restructuring the Participation of African-American Parents 31. Listening to Parents	20. Toward Defining Programs and Services
Family Impact	10. Prenatal Drug Exposure 23. Developing Independent and Responsible Behaviors	7. Identifying Students' Instructional Needs 12. What's Right for Rafael? 14. They Can But They Don't 31. Listening to Parents	5. Peer Education Partners 20. Toward Defining Programs and Services
Gifted and Talented	32. Education of Gifted Students	27. Success of Three Gifted Deaf-Blind Students 34. Gifted Girls in a Rural Community	33. Meeting the Needs of Gifted and Talented Preschoolers
Hearing Impairment	22. Roles of the Educational Interpreter	24. By June, . . . Jaime Will Have a Friend 27. Success of Three Gifted Deaf-Blind Students	23. Developing Independent and Responsible Behaviors 30. Creating Inclusionary Opportunities
Inclusive Education	1. Questions and Answers about Inclusion 11. Integrating Elementary Students 30. Creating Inclusionary Opportunities	2. What Do I Do Now? 3. Real Challenge of Inclusion 12. What's Right for Rafael? 24. By June, . . . Jaime Will Have a Friend	4. Restructuring the Participation of African-American Parents 5. Peer Education Partners 9. Mastery Learning 27. Success of Three Gifted Deaf-Blind Students

TOPIC AREA	KNOWLEDGE (These articles provide information about a handicap or about a special education concept.)	ATTITUDES (These articles contain personal experiences of exceptional persons or discussions about changing children's attitudes toward a handicap.)	TEACHING (These articles contain practical suggestions about how to apply special education principles to the teaching of exceptional children.)
Individualized Education Program (IEP) and Individualized Family Service Plan (IFSP)	3. Real Challenge of Inclusion 24. By June, . . . Jaime Will Have a Friend 35. Putting Real-Life Skills into IEP/IFSPs	20. Toward Defining Programs and Services 31. Listening to Parents	2. What Do I Do Now? 9. Mastery Learning 13. Helping Individuals with Severe Disabilities 29. HIV/AIDS Education for Students
Learning Disabilities	6. Is ADD Becoming a Desired Diagnosis?	7. Identifying Students' Instructional Needs	8. Adapting Textbooks for Children with Learning Disabilities 9. Mastery Learning
Legal Processes	1. Questions and Answers about Inclusion 25. Preschool Orientation and Mobility 32. Education of Gifted Students	3. Real Challenge of Inclusion 12. What's Right for Rafael?	22. Roles of the Educational Interpreter
Mental Retardation	10. Prenatal Drug Exposure 17. Autism	11. Integrating Elementary Students 12. What's Right for Rafael?	13. Helping Individuals with Severe Disabilities
Multiple Disabilities	10. Prenatal Drug Exposure 17. Autism	3. Real Challenge of Inclusion 11. Integrating Elementary Students	13. Helping Individuals with Severe Disabilities 24. By June, . . . Jaime Will Have a Friend 26. Teaching Choice-making Skills 30. Creating Inclusionary Opportunities
Physical and Health Impairments	28. Medical Treatment and Educational Problems in Children 29. HIV/AIDS Education for Students	31. Listening to Parents	30. Creating Inclusionary Opportunities
Transition to Adulthood	23. Developing Independent and Responsible Behaviors 39. Is a Functional Curriculum Approach Compatible?	38. What Do Students with Disabilities Tell Us?	40. Preparing Students for Transition
Visual Impairments	25. Preschool Orientation and Mobility	27. Success of Three Gifted Deaf-Blind Students	30. Creating Inclusionary Opportunities

Inclusive Education

Even as this overview is written, the laws and mandates for inclusion of children with exceptional conditions into regular education classrooms are changing. Canadian laws and U.S. laws about inclusive educational placements differ. Therefore, the safest and surest way to introduce this section is to state that public schools do have an obligation to serve children with exceptional conditions in as normal an educational environment as possible. The reality of inclusive education is that it is very difficult. It works well for some students with exceptionalities in some situations, and it works marginally for others.

Inclusion is based on the premise that all children, regardless of abilities, have the right to participate fully in natural settings within their communities. The school community is such a setting. For inclusion to succeed within a school, everyone must help become part of the solution: superintendent, principal, teachers, coaches, aides, ancillary staff, students, and parents and families of students. High-quality education for all students, regardless of abilities, requires good communication, open books, and collaboration. It is complicated to achieve. It requires sufficient monetary support as well as extraordinary human effort.

If students can learn and achieve better in inclusive programs, then the programs are well worth the effort. If students can only marginally succeed in inclusive education classrooms, some alternate solutions are necessary. Current laws do not require that every child be placed in a regular education classroom, but rather that every child be educated in the least restrictive environment. A continuum of placement options exists to maximize the goal of educating every child.

The first article included in this anthology gives a brief overview of U.S. Public Law 94-142 and the impact it has had since its passage in 1975. It discusses the regular education initiative (REI) philosophy of the 1980s, and the inclusion philosophy that has been dominant in the 1990s. The authors, Bonnie and John Greer, give carefully articulated answers to complex questions about the why, the who, and the when of inclusion and about the support structure underlying inclusive education. These simplified but clear-cut answers act as springboards from which students can express their own opinions, prejudgments, and comments on inclusion. In addition, the article addresses practical information for teachers, such as how to make inclusion work better.

The second unit article addresses how to make inclusion work. Drawing on two recent books on inclusion (*Inclusion: A Guide for Educators* [1996] by W. Stainback and S. Stainback, and *Creativity and Collaborative Learning: A Practical Guide to Empowering Students and Teachers* [1994] by J. Thousand, R. Villa, and A. Nevin), the author gives 10 practical recommendations for teachers. All educators who find themselves faced with the task of making their classroom a good learning environment for included children with varying abilities will benefit from these 10 suggestions. The article will also initiate discussions of a hypothetical nature, such as "If I have this student, then . . ." Such exercises can generate more creative solutions to the questions about how to include unique students with very individualized abilities in regular education classrooms.

The next essay provides the flip side of the record on inclusive education. Diane Ferguson is both an academician and the mother of a severely disabled son. She traces their journey through the wilderness of special educational placements. Ferguson challenges many of the as-

sumptions about students and education that seem to be embedded in our culture. Her efforts to untangle the Gordian knot of the reform initiatives will stimulate a great many questions about the pros and cons of segregation and integration. Ferguson writes critically about the possible social and political repercussions of inclusive education, and she calls for new tactics and new philosophies to truly accommodate the needs of diverse students in the educational system.

This unit has been balanced with the addition of a new article on family involvement in inclusive education. The success of inclusion necessitates that each person touched by the process feel a part of the solution. Parents who consider themselves out of the mainstream may need special encouragement to participate in the school planning processes. They should be included in assessment, placement decisions, and advocacy programs for their children.

The article "Peer Education Partners" (PEP) presents excellent details about implementing peer tutoring in inclusive education classrooms. This report on the benefits of PEP should help future teachers and child care workers give serious consideration to the involvement of children in each other's education. Similarities are discovered, abilities are highlighted, and an egalitarian climate is enhanced when PEP is implemented.

Looking Ahead: Challenge Questions

What can teachers do to ensure the best education possible for each child with an exceptionality who gets moved to a regular education classroom?

What can teachers do to ensure the best education possible for each child without an exceptionality who is enrolled in a regular education classroom?

Discuss whether children with exceptionalities are "irregular" even if they are in a "regular" classroom. Has inclusive education moved special education into a different setting? Is a restructuring needed? Explain.

How can all parents, including the culturally diverse, be helped to be active participants in their children's educational programs?

How can peer tutoring strengthen academic skills? What effects can it have on social and vocational skills?

Questions and Answers about Inclusion: What Every Teacher Should Know

BONNIE B. GREER and JOHN G. GREER

Bonnie B. Greer and John G. Greer are professors in the Department of Instruction and Curriculum Leadership, University of Memphis, Memphis, Tennessee.

Since the passage of the landmark Education for All Handicapped Children Act (Public Law 94-142) in 1975, the special education profession and the school community have been guided by the concept of the least restrictive environment. Whenever possible, children with disabilities must be, and to an ever-growing extent have been, educated with children who are not disabled. However, Public Law 94-142 also stipulates that a continuum of placement options, ranging from institutionalization to education in the regular class, be employed. Traditionally, children with mild learning problems have been mainstreamed into general education classes while those with more serious problems have been sent to the resource room, educated in self-contained classrooms, or placed outside the regular school environment.

In recent years, the continuum of placement has come under fire (Will 1986). The Regular Education Initiative (REI), a philosophy developed in the 1980s, envisioned a fundamental restructuring of the relationship between special and regular education. Proponents of the REI argued for the elimination of the special education eligibility process and the questioned practice of labeling children. Calling for close collaboration between regular and special education personnel, proponents sought to require that schools educate the majority of children with disabilities in the regular classroom.

Today, the inclusion movement is at the forefront of reform and has many of the same objectives as REI—with one very significant difference. Although some reformers continue to believe that the continuum of services and placement options must still be used for those children with the severest problems (Gersten and Woodward 1990; Jenkins, Pious, and Peterson 1988), many others in the inclusion movement demand that all children, regardless of their dis-

abilities or special needs, be educated in the regular class (Lipsky and Gartner 1991; Stainback and Stainback 1992). They consider it the right of every child to be included in all aspects of school life alongside their nondisabled peers. Thus, they advocate the elimination of the present dual system of regular education and "pullout" special education alternatives in favor of a more unified, coordinated, and inclusive system. Responsibilities for the planning, delivery, and evaluation of every child's instruction would be shared in a multidisciplinary, school-based setting. If it is fully implemented, inclusion, which is based on principles that have long guided the special education profession, will have a profound impact on virtually every teacher in America.

Why Is Inclusion Being Proposed?

Those people who are most vocal in their support of full inclusion cite their disenchantment with the current system. Despite a proliferation of "special" or "compensatory" programs developed over the years, the special education effort has had only limited success, with many serious and widely recognized shortcomings. Instructional results have been mixed, and no consensus exists as to the effectiveness of pullout programs (Madden and Slavin 1983; Wang, Reynolds, and Walberg 1986). At the same time, those children segregated from their peers in special classes are often stigmatized and suffer from low self–esteem (Guralnick and Groom 1988).

Other problems with the present system also exist. Children are only identified as needing special services after they have failed in the regular system and have been labeled. The screening procedures and eligibility requirements used in this process often exclude many children who need extra instructional support (Reynolds, Zetlin, and Wang 1993). Overall the dual system of regular and special education is commonly described as fragmented and poorly coordinated (Jenkins, Pious, and Peterson 1988). Believing that many children fall through the cracks, advocates of inclusion look to a single system that is responsible for teaching all children, regardless of their needs or level of

From *The Clearing House,* July/August 1995, pp. 339-342. © 1995 by the Helen Dwight Reid Educational Foundation. Reprinted by permission of Heldref Publications, 1319 Eighteenth Street, NW, Washington, DC 20036-1802.

functioning. They believe that education in the regular classroom, using individualized instruction as has long been characteristic of special education, will result in more effective and more socially appropriate education for all.

Who Are the Children Involved in Inclusion?

At the heart of the inclusion debate is the question, Which children would actually be placed in the regular class and spend most or all of their time with nondisabled same-age classmates? Most people agree that students with mild and moderate disabilities who are currently served in special education classrooms will be placed in the regular class. A small but articulate, vocal group is calling for the inclusion of even those children who are profoundly retarded or who have severe behavior disorders (Snell 1991; Stainback and Stainback 1992). The instructional needs of these children are very different from those of the average youngster. Those with mental retardation, for example, learn in very small steps and need large amounts of repetition to master new material. The teacher emphasizes basic skills rather than academics. It is not uncommon for students with severe behavior disorders to bite without warning, poke someone else's eyes, and engage in other extremely violent and aggressive behaviors. Various self-stimulatory or self-injurious behaviors are also common to this group of children. Obviously, these students would be highly disruptive to the routine found in most regular classrooms.

Those of a less-extreme position believe in retaining the continuum of placement options for limited numbers of children, but they also envision children with severe disabilities in the regular class. Children with severe cerebral palsy, for example, who are wheelchair bound, with significant paralysis and distorted speech, might be provided with current technology to augment their speech and allow them to participate in appropriate, though mediated, instructional activities. Growing numbers of parents and teachers are recognizing the moral, social, and academic justification for placing such children in a regular class.

Medically fragile children represent another issue. Many children with severe disabilities have concomitant medical problems that can be very restrictive and often life threatening. If these children are placed in the regular classroom, they could be exposed to a much higher risk of infection than that to which they are accustomed. Although many would undoubtedly benefit from socialization with nondisabled classmates, a case-by-case decision-making process would seem to be the only realistic approach. It would be important to consider any medical procedures the child may need each day and whether a teacher would be qualified to carry them out.

In any case, the future promises a regular classroom population that will be far more diverse than the typical one today. Some children with disabilities will learn at a much slower rate than other students. What they do learn, they will have difficulty retaining, and they will need help generalizing skills from one situation to another. The focus, for most, will be on learning skills necessary for participating in everyday living activities.

Is There Strong Support for Inclusion?

The philosophical support for inclusion is basically the same as that which led to the passage of PL 94–142. Three factors, common to both, are especially important:

1. The principle of normalization. Originating in Scandinavia in the early 1970s, normalization holds that those with disabilities should, to whatever degree possible, be allowed to participate in the routines, the activities, and the general lifestyles enjoyed by those who are not disabled.

2. The zero-reject policy. All children, regardless of the severity of their disabilities, must be provided a free and appropriate public education. Local systems can neither choose whom to serve nor turn away any child from needed services.

3. The idea of least restrictive environment. This approach has guided the actions of special educators for two decades. Inclusion represents the culmination of this principle.

Solid legal support for inclusion also exists. The cumulative effect of legislation and litigation over the past several decades has been to clearly establish the right of every child, regardless of disability, to be educated in classes with same-age peers whenever possible. With recent advances in adaptive technology and growing expertise in the individualization of instruction, regular class placement will be possible for many, if not most, children with severe disabilities.

When Will It Be Implemented?

In some areas of the country, inclusion has already been put into practice. Several states (e.g., Vermont, Colorado, Minnesota, and Oregon) have for years supported the placement of children with disabilities in the regular class, and many more have received federal funding to develop programs that promote inclusion (Alper and Ryndak 1992). Many school systems are now fully inclusive.

The literature contains an ever growing number of articles on inclusive classrooms, and many of them report successful experiences (Johnston 1994; Leister, Koonce, and Nisbet 1993). Nevertheless, relatively few focus on the placement of children who have severe or profound retardation or severe behavior disorders. More often, the regular class experiences of children with physical disabilities are reported. In any case, little empirical support for or against inclusion exists. Although advocates claim that existing instructional models and strategies would enable the immediate implementation of inclusion (Slavin and Stevens 1991; Wang and Walberg 1988), most experts are more cautious. Pointing to the difficulties schools already have in handling the diversity of student needs, they argue that such a fundamental restructuring of American education cannot begin until there is a sound empirical basis for decision making.

1. INCLUSIVE EDUCATION

How Will the Classroom Teacher's Role Change?

With the implementation of inclusion, the role of the regular classroom teacher will change dramatically. If children with disabilities are no longer pulled out for special instruction and related services, teachers will provide those forms of assistance in the regular classroom. This change will require close collaboration between the special education teacher and other professionals who will need to work with these children. Drawing on the regular teacher's expertise in content and curriculum sequence and the special education teacher's understanding of disabilities and different learning strategies, the two professionals together can adapt instruction to the individual needs of their students. Common planning and shared decision making will therefore replace the relatively independent role played by many teachers today. Furthermore, teachers must work together to encourage peer acceptance of and tolerance for individual differences. They also must have similar behavior management strategies and enforce classroom rules consistently. In the inclusive classroom, the regular teacher must be as involved with the problems of children with disabilities as is the special educator.

Will It Work?

Changing the place of instruction is more easily accomplished than changing the nature of student–teacher interactions, which are complicated by myriad instructional variables. To work, inclusion will need a highly coordinated effort from all involved. Merging the talents and resources of regular and special educators will require a partnership in which all involved are committed to a common goal.

At present, there is no consensus in the educational community. Many, if not most, teachers, from regular classrooms and special education, are not strongly opposed to the current system. The main push for full inclusion has come from a relatively small group of parents and professionals. Concerned primarily with the instructional and social–emotional needs of children with severe disabilities, they are well organized and articulate their position with great zeal. They have already had a very significant impact on state and federal policies and have heavily influenced the positions taken by important professional organizations.

Inclusion, of course, is not the only agenda facing American education. As our preeminence in commerce, industry, and science is being eclipsed by other countries, it is widely agreed that the American school curriculum must be more rigorous and challenging, with greater emphasis on math, science, and foreign language. Balancing those demands for greater academic rigor with the challenges represented by inclusion is a daunting task for the regular classroom teacher as well as everyone else in the profession. To design an educational system that more effectively meets the needs of all children, we must find a process for consensus building. Open dialogue is a prerequisite to sound

decision making. The increasingly emotional rhetoric now characterizing the debate must be replaced with a more reasoned, constructive exchange of ideas. Until now largely restricted to the special education literature, with few regular educators participating, the debate is lacking a key ingredient. Because the ultimate success or failure of inclusion will depend on the commitment and willingness of the regular classroom teachers to put it into practice, their input in its design is absolutely critical. It is incumbent on all educators to become meaningfully involved—through professional organizations, local groups, state agencies, and representative government—in the process of shaping the future of American education.

REFERENCES

Alper, S., and D. L. Ryndak. 1992. Educating students with severe handicaps in regular classes. *Elementary School Journal* 92(3): 373–87.

Gartner, A., and D. K. Lipsky. 1987. Beyond special education: Toward a quality system for all students. *Harvard Educational Review* 57:367–95.

Gersten, R., and J. Woodward. 1990. Rethinking the Regular Education Initiative: Focus on the classroom teacher. *Remedial and Special* streamed and specialized classrooms: A comparative analysis. *Exceptional Children* 54:415–25.

Jenkins, J. R., C. G. Pious, and D. L. Peterson. 1988. Categorical programs for remedial and handicapped students: Issues of validity. *Exceptional Children* 55:147–58.

Johnston, W. F. 1994. How to educate all the students together. *Schools in the Middle* (May):9–14.

Leister, C., D. Koonce, and S. Nisbet. 1993. Best practices for preschool programs: An update on inclusive settings. *Day Care and Early Education* (Winter):9–12.

Lipsky, D. K., and A. Gartner. 1991. Restructuring for quality. In *The Regular Education Initiative: Alternative perspectives on concepts, issues and models*, edited by J. W. Lloyd, A. C. Repp, and N. N. Singh, 43–56. Sycamore, Ill.: Sycamore.

Madden, N. A., and R. E. Slavin. 1983. Mainstreaming students with mild handicaps: Academic and social outcomes. *Review of Educational Research* 53:519–69.

Reynolds, M. C., A. G. Zetlin, and M. C. Wang. 1993. 20/20 analysis: Taking a close look at the margins. *Exceptional Children* 59:294–300.

Slavin, R. E., and R. J. Stevens. 1991. Cooperative learning and mainstreaming. In *The Regular Education Initiative: Alternative perspectives on concepts, issues, and models*, edited by J. W. Lloyd, A. C. Repp, and N. N. Singh, 177–81. Sycamore, Ill.: Sycamore.

Snell, M. E. 1991. Schools are for all kids: The importance of integration for students with severe disabilities and their peers. In *The Regular Education Initiative: Alternative perspectives on concepts, issues and models*, edited by J. W. Lloyd, A. C. Repp, and N. N. Singh, 133–48. Sycamore, Ill.: Sycamore.

Stainback, S., and W. Stainback. 1992. *Curriculum considerations in inclusive classrooms: Facilitating learning for all students.* Baltimore: Paul Brookes.

Wang, M. C., M. C. Reynolds, and H. J. Walberg. 1986. Rethinking special education. *Educational Leadership* 55(2):128–37.

Wang, M. C., and H. J. Walberg. 1988. Four fallacies of segregation. *Exceptional Children* 55:128–37.

Will, M. C. 1986. Educating children with learning problems: A shared responsibility. *Exceptional Children* 52:411–15.

SUGGESTED RESOURCES

Fuchs, D., and L. S. Fuchs. 1994. Inclusive schools movement and the radicalization of special education reform. *Exceptional Children* 60:294–309.

This article examines the inclusive schools movement and cautions against the increasingly strident rhetoric that characterizes the debate. Critical of some positions taken by advocates of full inclusion, the authors call for more open and meaningful dialogue with general education.

Giangreco, M. F., R. Dennis, C. Cloninger, S. Edelman, and R. Schattman. 1993. "I've counted Jon": Transformational experiences of teachers educating students with disabilities. *Exceptional Children* 59:359–72.

This article describes the experiences of over thirty general education teachers who have had a child with severe disabilities in their classrooms.

Horner, H. H., S. J. Diemer, and K. C. Brazeau. 1992. Educational support for students with severe problem behaviors in Oregon: A descriptive analysis from the 1987–1988 school year. *Journal of the Association for Persons with Severe Handicaps (JASH)* 17:154–69.

Because Oregon has been identified as a leader in maintaining students with severe disabilities in the regular school environment, the authors used a survey to examine what placement options were used there with children with severe behavior problems.

Kauffman, J. M. 1993. How we might achieve the radical reform of special education. *Exceptional Children* 60:6–16.

While recognizing the current pressures for change in special education, the author of this article calls for decisions to be made on the basis of careful empirical investigation. He cautions against fashionable actions and fanaticism.

Rainforth, B., J. York, and C. MacDonald. 1992. *Collaborative teams for students with severe disabilities: Integrating therapy and educational services.* Baltimore: Paul H. Brookes.

Anticipating the placement of students with severe disabilities in the regular classroom, the authors examine strategies for collaborative teamwork and the delivery of therapy and related services.

Villa, R., J. Thousand, W. Stainback, and S. Stainback, eds. 1992. *Restructuring for caring and effective education.* Baltimore: Paul H. Brookes.

The authors critique current special education strategies and find them seriously inadequate. They emphasize the need for the inclusion of all children, regardless of the type and severity of their disabilities, in the regular education setting and argue for reform now.

What Do I Do Now?
A Teacher's Guide to Including Students with Disabilities

Michael F. Giangreco

Michael F. Giangreco is Research Assistant Professor, The University of Vermont, College of Education and Social Services, 499C Waterman Building, Burlington, VT 05405-0160.

Teachers who successfully teach students without disabilities have the skills to successfully teach students with disabilities. Here are 10 recommendations to guide you.

As students with disabilities are increasingly being placed in general education classrooms, teachers are asking many legitimate questions about what to do about their instruction and how to do it. For the past seven years, I've consulted with teachers, administrators, support personnel, and families who are grappling with these concerns. I've also joined with colleagues in conducting 12 research studies at some of these schools. The following suggestions are concrete actions to consider as you pursue success for both students with disabilities and their classmates.

1. Get a Little Help from Your Friends

No one expects teachers to know all the specialized information about every disability, or to do everything that may be necessary for a student with disabilities.

Thus, in schools where students with disabilities are successful in general education classes, teams usually collaborate on individualized educational programs. Team members often include the student and his or her parents, general educators, special educators, para-educators, and support staff, such as speech and language pathologists, and physical therapists. And don't forget: each classroom includes some 20–30 students who are creative and energetic sources of ideas, inspiration, and assistance.

Although teamwork is crucial, look out for some common problems. When groups become unnecessarily large and schedule too many meetings without clear purposes or outcomes, communication and decision making get complicated and may overwhelm families. Further, a group is not necessarily a team, particularly if each specialist has his or her own goals. The real team shares a single set of goals that team members pursue in a coordinated way.

2. Welcome the Student in Your Classroom

Welcoming the student with disabilities may seem like a simple thing to do, and it is. But you'd be surprised how often it doesn't happen. It can be devastating for such a student (or any student) to feel as if he or she must earn the right to belong by meeting an arbitrary standard that invariably differs from school to school.

Remember, too, that your students look to you as their primary adult model during the school day. What do you want to model for them about similarities and differences, change, diversity, individuality, and caring?

So when children with disabilities come to your classroom, talk with them, walk with them, encourage them, joke with them, and teach them. By your actions, show all your students that the child with disabilities is an important member of your class and, by extension, of society.

3. Be the Teacher of All the Students

When a student with disabilities is placed in a general education class, a common practice is for the teacher to function primarily as a host rather than a teacher. Many busy teachers actually embrace this notion because it means someone else is responsible for that student. Many teachers, in fact, think of these students as the responsibility of the special education teacher or para-educator.

Merely hosting a student with disabilities, however, doesn't work

From *Educational Leadership*, February 1996, pp. 56-59. © 1996 by Michael F. Giangreco. Reprinted by permission.

very well (Giangreco et al. 1992). Inevitably, these other professionals will work with the student, and the "host" will end up knowing very little about the student's educational program or progress. This perpetuates a lack of responsibility for the student's education and often places important curricular and instructional decisions in the hands of hardworking, but possibly underqualified, paraprofessionals.

Be flexible, but don't allow yourself to be relegated to the role of an outsider in your own classroom. Remember that teachers who successfully teach students without disabilities have the skills to successfully teach students with disabilities (Giangreco et al. 1995).

4. Make Sure Everyone Belongs to the Classroom Community

How, where, when, and with whom students spend their time is a major determinant of their affiliations and status in the classroom (Stainback and Stainback 1996). Too often, students with disabilities are placed with mainstream students, but take part in different activities and have different schedules from their peers. These practices inhibit learning with and from classmates, and may contribute to social isolation.

To ensure that students with disabilities are part of what's happening in class, seat them with their classmates, and at the same kind of desk, not on the fringe of the class.

Make sure, too, that the student participates in the same activities as the rest of the class, even though his or her goals may be different. If the class is writing a journal, the student with a disability should be creating a journal, even if it's in a nonwritten form. If you assign students homework, assign it to this student at an appropriate level. In like manner, if the class does a science experiment, so should this student. Although individualization and supports may be necessary, the student's daily schedule should allow ample opportunities to learn, socialize, and work with classmates.

5. Clarify Shared Expectations with Team Members

One of the most common sources of anxiety for classroom teachers is not understanding what other team members expect them to teach. "Do I teach this student most of or all of what

THE PRESENCE OF A student with disabilities may simply highlight the need to use more active and participatory approaches.

I'm teaching the other students?" Sometimes the answer will be yes, sometimes no. In either case, team members must agree on what the student should learn and who will teach it.

To do this, the team should identify a few of the student's learning priorities, as well as a larger set of learning outcomes as part of a broad educational program. Doing so will clarify which parts of the general curriculum the student will be expected to pursue and may include learning outcomes that are not typically part of the general program.

Many students with disabilities also need supports to participate in class. These supports should be distinguished from learning outcomes. If the supports are inadvertently identified as learning outcomes, the educational program may be unnecessarily passive.

Finally, on a one- or two-page program-at-a-glance, summarize the educational program, including, for example, priority learning outcomes, additional learning outcomes, and necessary supports (Giangreco et al. 1993). This concise list will help the team plan and schedule, serve as a reminder of the student's individual needs, and help you communicate those needs to teachers in special areas, such as art, music, and physical education. By clarifying what the team expects the student to learn,

you set the stage for a productive school year.

6. Adapt Activities to the Student's Needs

When the educational needs of a student with disabilities differ from those of the majority of the class, teachers often question the appropriateness of the placement. It's fair to ask, for example, why an 11-year-old functioning at a 2nd grade level is placed in a 6th grade class.

The answer is that such a student can still have a successful educational experience. In fact, many schools are purposely developing multigrade classrooms, where teachers accommodate students with a wide range of abilities.

When a student's needs differ from other members of the class, it is important to have options for including that student in activities with classmates. In some cases, the student requires instructional accommodations to achieve learning outcomes within the same curriculum area as his or her classmates, but at a different level.

The student might need to learn, for example, different vocabulary words, math problems, or science concepts. Or the student may be pursuing learning outcomes from different curriculum areas. For example, during a science activity, the student could be learning communication, literacy, or socialization skills, while the rest of the class focuses on science.

7. Provide Active and Participatory Learning Experiences

I've heard teachers of students with disabilities say, "He wouldn't get much out of being in that class because the teacher does a lot of lecturing, and uses worksheets and paper-and-pencil tests." My first reaction is, "You're right, that situation doesn't seem to match the students's needs." But then I wonder, Is this educational approach also a mismatch for students without disability labels?

Considering the diversity of learning styles, educators are increasingly questioning whether passive, didactic approaches meet their

TEACHERS CAN BECOME BETTER ADVOCATES for their students and themselves by becoming informed consumers of support services.

students' needs. Activity-based learning, on the other hand, is well suited to a wide range of students. The presence of a student with disabilities may simply highlight the need to use more active and participatory approaches, such as individual or cooperative projects and use of art media, drama, experiments, field study, computers, research, educational games, multimedia projects, or choral responding (Thousand et al. 1994). Interesting, motivating activities carry an added bonus—they encourage positive social behaviors, and can diminish behavior problems.

8. Adapt Classroom Arrangements, Materials, and Strategies

Alternate teaching methods or other adaptations may be necessary. For example, if a group lecture isn't working, try cooperative groups, computer-assisted instruction, or peer tutoring. Or make your instruction more precise and deliberate.

Adaptations may be as basic as considering a different way for a student to respond if he or she has difficulty speaking or writing, or re-arranging the chairs for more proximity to peers or access to competent modeling.

You may also have to adapt materials. A student with visual impairments may need tactile or auditory cues. A student with physical disabilities may require materials that are larger or easier to manipulate. And a student who is easily bored or distracted may do better with materials that are in line with his or her interests.

Rely on the whole team and the class to assist with adaptation ideas.

9. Make Sure Support Services Help

Having many support service personnel involved with students can be a help or a hindrance. Ideally, the support staff will be competent and collaborative, making sure that what they do prevents disruptions and negative effects on students' social relationships and educational programs. They will get to know the students and classroom routines, and also understand the teacher's ideas and concerns.

Teachers can become better advocates for their students and themselves by becoming informed consumers of support services. Learn to ask good questions. Be assertive if you are being asked to do something that doesn't make sense to you. Be as explicit as you can be about what type of support you need. Sometimes you may need particular information, materials, or someone to demonstrate a technique. Other times, you may need someone with whom to exchange ideas or just validate that you are headed in the right direction.

10. Evaluate Your Teaching

We commonly judge our teaching by our students' achievements. Although you may evaluate students with disabilities in some of the same ways as you do other students (for example, through written tests, reports, or projects), some students will need alternative assessment, such as portfolios adapted to their needs.

Often it is erroneously assumed that if students get good grades, that will translate into future educational, professional, and personal success. This is a dangerous assumption for any student, but particularly for those with disabilities. Although traditional tests and evaluations may provide certain types of information, they won't predict the impact of your teaching on the student's post-school life. Unfortunately, far too many graduates with disabilities are plagued by unemployment, health problems, loneliness, or isolation—despite their glowing school progress reports.

We need to continually evaluate whether students are applying their achievements to real life, by looking at the effects on their physical and emotional health, personal growth, and positive social relationships; and at their ability to communicate, advocate for themselves, make informed choices, contribute to the community, and increasingly access places and activities that are personally meaningful. The aim is to ensure that our teaching will make a real difference in our students' lives.

UNFORTUNATELY, FAR TOO MANY GRADUATES with disabilities are plagued by unemployment, despite their glowing school progress reports.

References

Giangreco, M., D. Baumgart, and M.B. Doyle. (1995). "How Inclusion Can Facilitate Teaching and Learning." *Intervention in School and Clinic* 30, 5: 273–278.

Giangreco, M., C. J. Cloninger, and V. Iverson. (1993). *Choosing Options and Accommodations for Children: A Guide to Planning Inclusive Education.* Baltimore: Brookes.

Giangreco, M., R. Dennis, C. Cloninger, S. Edelman, and R Schattman. (1992). "I've Counted Jon': Transformational Experiences of Teachers Educating Students with Disabilities." *Exceptional Children* 59: 359–372.

Stainback, W., and S. Stainback. (1996). *Inclusion: A Guide for Educators.* Baltimore: Brookes.

Thousand, J., R. Villa, and A. Nevin. (1994). *Creativity and Collaborative Learning: A Practical Guide to Empowering Students and Teachers.* Baltimore: Brookes.

The Real Challenge of Inclusion
Confessions of a 'Rabid Inclusionist'

DIANNE L. FERGUSON

The new challenge of inclusion is to create schools in which our day-to-day efforts no longer assume that a particular text, activity, or teaching mode will "work" to support any particular student's learning, Ms. Ferguson avers.

Illustration by John Berry

ABOUT A YEAR ago, a colleague told me that my work was constrained by the fact that "everyone" thought I was a "rabid inclusionist." I was not exactly sure what he meant by "rabid inclusionist" or how he and others had arrived at the conclusion that I was one. I also found it somewhat ironic to be so labeled since I had been feeling uncomfortable with the arguments and rhetoric of both the anti-inclusionists and, increasingly, many of the inclusionists. My own efforts to figure out how to achieve "inclusion" — at least as I understood it — were causing me to question many of the assumptions and arguments of both groups.

In this article, I wish to trace the journey that led me to a different understanding of inclusion. I'll also describe the challenges I now face — and that I think

---

DIANNE L. FERGUSON is an associate professor in the College of Education, University of Oregon, Eugene.

From *Phi Delta Kappan*, December 1995, pp. 281-287. © 1995 by Phi Delta Kappa, Inc. Reprinted by permission.

we all face — in trying to improve our schools.

The Limits of Our Reforms

Despite our best efforts, it was clear to my husband and me that even the possibility of "mainstreaming" was not open to our son Ian. Although mainstreaming had been a goal of the effort to change the delivery of special education services since the late 1960s, the debates never extended to a consideration of students with severe disabilities. Indeed, it was only the "zero reject" provisions of the Education for All Handicapped Children Act (P.L. 94-142) in 1974 that afforded our son the opportunity to attend school at all — albeit a separate special education school some 20 miles and two towns away from our home. What that landmark legislation did not change, however, were underlying assumptions about schooling for students designated as "disabled."

Since special education emerged as a separate part of public education in the decades spanning the turn of the century, the fundamental assumptions about students and learning shared by both "general" and "special" educators have not changed much. Despite periodic challenges, these assumptions have become so embedded in the culture and processes of schools that they are treated more as self-evident "truths" than as assumptions. School personnel, the families of schoolchildren, and even students themselves unquestionably believe:

• that students are responsible for their own learning;

• that, when students don't learn, there is something wrong with them; and

• that the job of the schools is to determine what's wrong with as much precision as possible, so that students can be directed to the tracks, curricula, teachers, and classrooms that match their learning-ability profiles.

Even our efforts to "integrate" and later to "include" students with severe disabilities in general education failed to challenge these fundamental assumptions. Indeed, these special education reform initiatives have served more to reinforce them.

Unlike mainstreaming, which was grounded in debate about where best to provide the alternative curricular and instructional offerings that students with disabilities need, the reform initiatives of integration and later of inclusion drew much more heavily on social and political discourse. From a democratic perspective, every child has a right to a public education. For those moderately and severely disabled students who had previously been excluded from schooling on the ground that they were too disabled to benefit, the application of a civil rights framework gave them the same status as any minority group that was widely disenfranchised and discriminated against.[1] The essential message of integration was to remediate social discrimination (not so much learning deficits) by ending stigmatizing and discriminatory exclusion.

We sought this more "normalized" schooling experience for Ian, advocating actively for placement in a typical public school rather than in a separate school. Unfortunately, the efforts of professional educators to balance the right of students to be educated with the still unchallenged and highly individualized deficit/remediation model of disability most often resulted in the delivery of educational services along some continuum of locations, each matched to the constellation of services believed to "fit" the identified type and amount of student deficit and disability.

For someone like our son, with multiple and severe disabilities, the result was self-contained classrooms that afforded only the briefest contact with nondisabled students. The integrationists' promise that the mainstream would tolerate and perhaps even incorporate more differences in abilities remained largely unfulfilled. Even when some students found themselves integrated into general education classrooms, they often did not reap the promised rewards of full membership.

Yet we could see the promise of something else. Ian's first experience in a *public* school was when he was about 10. He was assigned to a new self-contained classroom for "severely and profoundly handicapped" students. This new classroom was located in the "physically handicapped school," where all students with physical disabilities were assigned because the building had long ago been made accessible, unlike most other school buildings in town.

Because we hoped he would have some involvement with nondisabled peers, we lobbied the school administration for a policy that permitted two kinds of "mainstreaming": one kind for students who could learn alongside their peers with some extra teaching help and another kind for students like Ian, who could not learn the same things but might benefit by learning other things. It took months of discussion, but finally the grade 5 class down the hall from Ian's self-contained room invited him to join it for the "free" times during the day when students got to pick their own games and activities. The teacher was skeptical but willing and sent students to collect him for some part of nearly every day.

One day a small group of students invited Ian to join them in a Parcheesi game. Of course, he had no experience with the game and probably didn't grasp much of it. It could be argued, I suppose, that his lessons (at the separate school and class) on picking things up and putting them into cans offered him some ability to participate, but he would not be just another player like the other fifth-graders. The students, with no adult intervention, solved this participation problem by making him the official emptier of the cup of dice for all the players — something he could not only do, but relished. His role was critical to the game, and he got lots of opportunities to participate, since he was needed to begin every player's turn.

Ian's experience in Parcheesi expanded over the year to include some integration in music, lunch, and recess with these same students. More important were the lessons his participation began to teach us about the possibilities of integration that we and others had not yet fully explored, especially regarding the ways that learning, participation, and membership can mean different things for very different children in the same situation.

However it was being implemented, integration also contained a critical flaw in logic: in order to be "integrated" one must first be segregated. This simple point led to the first calls for inclusion. According to this new initiative, all students should simply be included, by right, in the opportunities and responsibilities of public schooling. Like integration, however, these early notions of inclusion focused primarily on students with moderate to severe disabilities who most often were placed along the continuum of service environments furthest from general education classrooms.

Unfortunately, neither integration nor inclusion offered much practical guidance to teachers who were engaged in the daily dynamics of teaching and learning in classrooms with these diverse students. The focus on the right to access did not provide clear direction for achieving learning outcomes in general education settings. Essentially, both of these reform efforts challenged the logic of attaching services to places — in effect challenged the idea of a continuum of services. However, the absence of clear directions for how services would be delivered instead and the lack of information about what impact such a change might have on general education led some proponents to emphasize the importance of social rather than learning outcomes, especially for students with severe disabilities.[2] This emphasis on social outcomes certainly did nothing to end the debates.

Inclusion as 'Pretty Good' Integration

The inclusion initiative has generated a wide range of outcomes — some exciting and productive, others problematic and unsatisfying. As our son finished his official schooling and began his challenging journey to adult life, he enjoyed some quite successful experiences, one as a real member of a high school drama class, though he was still officially assigned to a self-contained classroom.[3] Not only did he learn to "fly," trusting others to lift him up and toss him in the air (not an easy thing for someone who has little control over his body), but he also memorized lines and delivered them during exams, learned to interact more comfortably and spontaneously with classmates and teachers, and began using more and different vocal inflections than had ever before characterized his admittedly limited verbal communications. Classmates, puzzled and perhaps put off by him at the beginning of the year, creatively incorporated him into enough of their improvisations and activities to be able to nominate him at the end of the year not only as one of the students who had shown progress, but also as one who showed promise as an actor. He didn't garner enough votes to win the title, but that he was nominated at all showed the drama teacher "how much [the other students] came to see him as a *member* of the class."

Ian's experiences in drama class helped me begin to understand more fully that *learning* membership was the most important dimension of inclusion and that it was an extraordinarily complex phenomenon, especially within classrooms.[4] It also prompted me to question other bits of the conventional wisdom about inclusion: Is inclusion all about place? Must it be full time? Is it okay for learning to take second priority to socialization and friendship? Does one always have to be traded

for the other? Will students learn things that they can use and that will make a difference in their lives? Who will teach, and what will happen to special educators? And so on.

A three-year research effort followed, during which I learned a good deal about what inclusion is and isn't. Perhaps the most troubling realization was that — even when students were assigned to general education classrooms and spent most (or even all) of their time there with various kinds of special education supports — their participation often fell short of the kind of social and learning membership that most proponents of inclusion envision and that Ian achieved in that one drama class. Even to casual observers, some students seemed set apart — immediately recognizable as different — not so much because of any particular impairment or disability but because of what they were doing, with whom, and how.

During the years of our research, my colleagues and I saw students walking through hallways with clipboard-bearing adults "attached" to them or sitting apart in classrooms with an adult hovering over them showing them how to use books and papers unlike any others in the class. Often these "Velcroed" adults were easily identifiable as "special education" teachers because the students called them by their first names while using the more formal Ms. or Mr. to refer to the general education teacher. The included students seemed *in*, but not *of*, the class. Indeed, we observed teachers who referred to particular students as "my inclusion student." It seemed to us that these students were caught inside a bubble that teachers didn't seem to notice but that nonetheless succeeded in keeping other students and teachers at a distance.

We also saw other students "fitting in," following the routines, and looking more or less like other students. But their participation seemed hollow. They *looked* like they were doing social studies or math, but it seemed more a "going through the motions" than a real learning engagement. Maybe they were learning in the sense of remembering things, but, we wondered, did they know what they were learning? Or why? Or whether they would use this learning in their lives outside of school?

Even the protection of an individualized education program (IEP) — a key component of P.L. 94-142 and now of the updated Individuals with Disabilities Education Act (IDEA) — seemed yet one more barrier to real membership. Special

education teachers became "teachers without classrooms," plying their skills in many places, following carefully designed and complicated schedules that deployed support personnel in the form of classroom assistants to teach, manage, and assist the "inclusion students" so that they could meet the goals and objectives of their IEPs. Classroom teachers struggled to understand how to "bond" with their new students.

Even more challenging was how to negotiate teaching. The peripatetic special educator usually remained primarily responsible for writing IEPs that only distantly related to the classroom teacher's curriculum and teaching plans. At the same time the general educator would strive to assume "ownership" of the shared student's teaching, often by following the instructions of the special educator. Special educators who were successful at moving out of their separate classrooms struggled with the sheer logistics of teaching their stu-

> *In trying to change everything, inclusion all too often seems to be leaving everything the same. But in a new place.*

dents in so many different places. They also struggled with whether they were teachers of students or teachers of other teachers. And some wondered what would happen to them if the general educators ever "learned how" to include students without help.

Bursting Bubbles

Gradually I came to see these examples and the experiences that have been detailed elsewhere as problematic for everyone precisely because they failed to challenge underlying assumptions about student learning differences.[5] Too much inclusion as implemented by special education seems to succeed primarily in relocating "special" education to the general education classroom along with all the special materials, specially trained adults, and special curriculum and teaching techniques. The overriding assumptions remain unchanged and clearly communicated.

• These "inclusion" students are "irregular," even though they are in "regular" classrooms.

• They need "special" stuff that the "regular" teacher is neither competent nor approved to provide.

• The "special" educator is the officially designated provider of these "special" things.

In trying to change everything, inclusion all too often seems to be leaving everything the same. But in a new place.

My colleagues and I also saw lots of examples of things that did not remain the same, examples like my son's experience in drama class. The challenge was to try to understand what made these experiences different.

Gradually I began to realize that, if inclusion is ever to mean more than pretty good integration, we special educators will have to change our tactics. To resolve the debates about roles, ownership, accountability, student learning achievements, the meaningfulness of IEPs, and the achievement of genuine student membership in the regular classroom, we must begin with the *majority* perspective and build the tools and strategies for achieving inclusion from the center out rather than from the most exceptional student in. Devising and defining inclusion to be about students with severe disabilities — indeed, any disabilities — seems increasingly wrongheaded to me and quite possibly doomed to fail. It can only continue to focus everyone's attention on a small number of students and a small number of student differences, rather than on the whole group of students with their various abilities and needs.

Inclusion isn't about eliminating the continuum of placements[6] or even just about eliminating some locations on the continuum,[7] though that will be one result. Nor is it about discontinuing the services that used to be attached to the various points on that continuum.[8] Instead, a more *systemic* inclusion — one that merges the reform and restructuring efforts of general education with special education inclusion — will disassociate the delivery of supports from *places* and make the full continuum of supports available to the full range of students. A more systemic inclusion will replace old practices (which presumed a relationship between ability, service, and place of delivery) with new kinds of practice (in which groups of teachers work together to provide learning supports for all students).

Inclusion isn't about time either. Another continuing debate involves whether "all" students should spend "all" of their time in general education classrooms.[9] One form of this discussion relies largely on extreme examples of "inappropriate" students: "Do you really mean that the student in a coma should be in a general education classroom? What about the student who holds a teacher hostage at knife point?" Other forms of this argument seek to emphasize the inappropriateness of the general education classroom for some students: "Without one-to-one specialized instruction the student will not learn and his or her future will be sacrificed." Another version of the same argument points out that the resources of the general education classroom are already limited, and the addition of resource-hungry students will only further reduce what is available for regular education students.

Of course these arguments fail to note that labeled students are not always the most resource-hungry students. Indeed, when some students join general education classrooms, their need for resources diminishes. In other instances, the labeled student can bring additional resources that can be shared to other classmates' benefit. These arguments also fail to note that the teaching in self-contained settings, as well as the resource management, can sometimes be uninspired, ordinary, and ineffective. Consider how many students with IEPs end up with exactly the same goals and objectives from year to year.

Like the debates about place, debates about time miss the point and overlook the opportunity of a shift from special education inclusion to more systemic inclusion. *Every* child should have the opportunity to learn in lots of different places — in small groups and large, in classrooms, in hallways, in libraries, and in a wide variety of community locations. For some parts of their schooling, some students might spend more time than others in some settings. Still, the greater the number and variety of students learning in various locations with more varied approaches and innovations, the less likely that any student will be disadvantaged by not "qualifying" for some kind of attention, support, or assistance. If all students work in a variety of school and community places, the likelihood that any particular students will be stigmatized because of their learning needs, interests, and preferences will be eliminated. All students will benefit from such variety in teaching approaches, locations, and supports.

The Real Challenge of Inclusion

Coming to understand the limits of inclusion as articulated by special educators was only part of my journey. I also had to spend time in general education classrooms, listening to teachers and trying to understand their struggles and efforts to change, to help me see the limits of general education as well. The general education environment, organized as it still is according to the bell curve logic of labeling and grouping by ability, may never be accommodating enough to achieve the goals of inclusion, even if special educators and their special ideas, materials, and techniques become less "special" and separate.

It seems to me that the lesson to be learned from special education's inclusion initiative is that the real challenge is a lot harder and more complicated than we thought. Neither special nor general education alone has either the capacity or the vision to challenge and change the deep-rooted assumptions that separate and track children and youths according to presumptions about ability, achievement, and eventual social contribution. Meaningful change will require nothing less than a joint effort to reinvent schools to be more accommodating to all dimensions of human diversity. It will also require that the purposes and processes of these reinvented schools be organized not so much to make sure that students learn and develop on the basis of their own abilities and talents, but rather to make sure that all children are prepared to participate in the benefits of their communities so that others in that community care enough about what happens to them to value them as members.[10]

My own journey toward challenging these assumptions was greatly assisted by the faculty of one of the elementary schools in our research study on inclusion. Most of our research had really centered on the perspectives of special educators. While we talked with many other people in the schools, our access had always been through the special educator who was trying to move out into the school. Finally, however, we began to shift our attention to the *whole* school through the eyes of *all* its members. For me, it was a shift from *special education research* to *educational research* that also happened to "include" special education teachers and students. I began to learn the language of schooling, became able to "talk education" rather than just talk special education, and sought that same bilingualism for my students and colleagues through a series of reframed research and demonstration projects.

Learning about various reform agendas within education that support and facilitate systemic inclusion enormously reassured and encouraged me, and I have begun to refocus my efforts toward nurturing them. For example, in response to the changing demands of work and community life in the 21st century, some initiatives within general education reform and restructuring are focusing on students' understanding and use of their own learning rather than on whether or not they can recall information during tests. Employers and community leaders want citizens who are active learners and collaborators as well as individuals who possess the personal confidence and ability to contribute to a changing society.[11]

In response to these broader social demands, teachers at all levels of schooling are trying to rethink curriculum. They are

> *No longer must the opportunity to participate in life wait until some standard of "normalcy" is reached.*

looking for ways to help students develop habits of learning that will serve them long after formal schooling ends. In pursuit of this goal, they are moving from seeking to cover a large number of "facts" to exploring in more depth a smaller number of topics of interest and relevance to students.[12] An important aspect of this curriculum shift is that not all students will learn exactly the same things, even within the same lesson or activity.

These changes in general education are being pursued because of increasing social complexity and student diversity. Educators are less and less confident that learning one standard, "official" curriculum will help students achieve the kind of competence they need to lead satisfactory lives. Greater numbers of educators are concerned not so much that some bit of content knowledge is learned, but rather that students use their learning in ways that make a difference in their lives outside of school. The difficulty in making this happen in classrooms is that students bring with them all manner of differences that teachers must take into consideration. These include different abilities, of course, but also different interests, different family lifestyles, and different preferences about schools and learning. Students' linguistic backgrounds, socioeconomic status, and cultural heritage must also be considered when making curriculum and teaching decisions. Finally, some students have different ways of thinking and knowing — sometimes emphasizing language, sometimes motor learning, sometimes artistic intelligence, and so on.[13]

To general education teachers who are experimenting with these kinds of curricular and teaching reforms, students with official disabilities become different in degree rather than in type. Tailoring the learning event for them might require adjustments or supports not needed by some other students. But the essential process remains the same for all. Fear of "watering down" the official curriculum remains only for those classrooms that have not responded to the need for more systemic reform of curriculum and teaching. Classrooms and teachers seriously engaged in preparing students for the future have already expanded and enriched the curriculum to respond both to the demands for broader student outcomes and to the different interests, purposes, and abilities of each student.

A New Inclusion Initiative

These are just a few of the ongoing discussions within general education. There are many more. Some, like the pressure to articulate new national standards and benchmarks, are less clearly supportive of student diversity. Reform initiatives are emerging from all parts of the system — from the efforts of small groups of teachers to those of state and federal policy makers. Often these various pressures for change contradict one another, but in the

end all will have to be accommodated, understood, and transformed into a single whole.

Changing schools at all, never mind actually *improving* them, is an extraordinarily complex and arduous task. Public education is like a web: each strand touches many others, depending upon as well as providing support for the entire structure. Any change, even a small one, ripples through the web, sometimes strengthening, sometimes weakening the whole. When many things change at once, it is a time of both great risk and great energy.

Public education is in just such an exciting period of change. Perhaps for the first time, changes in all parts of the system can begin to converge. My own journey to understand inclusion has led me to propose my own definition of inclusion:

> Inclusion is a process of meshing general and special education reform initiatives and strategies in order to achieve a unified system of public education that incorporates all children and youths as active, fully participating members of the school community; that views diversity as the norm; and that ensures a high-quality education for each student by providing meaningful curriculum, effective teaching, and necessary supports for each student.

Perhaps there are "rabid inclusionists," foaming at the mouth over some specific change and having but little awareness of the challenge their agenda represents to fundamental assumptions. I suppose that there are also "rabid separatists," just as fanatically insisting on preserving the present system and similarly unaware of the fundamental assumptions that influence their positions.

My own journey led me to a different destination. It led me to take the risk of admitting that I have changed my mind about many things. (Perhaps it would be more accurate to say that I have not so much "changed" my mind as "clarified" and expanded my thinking.) I am still an advocate for inclusion, but now I understand it to mean much more than I believed it meant when I first began to study and experience it through my son. As I and others who share this broader understanding work to create genuinely inclusive schools, we will be encouraging people in schools, on every strand of the complex web, to change in three directions.

The first shift involves moving away from schools that are structured and organized according to ability and toward schools that are structured around student diversity and that accommodate many different ways of organizing students for learning. This shift will also require teachers with different abilities and talents to work together to create a wide array of learning opportunities.[14]

The second shift involves moving away from teaching approaches that emphasize the teacher as disseminator of content that students must retain and toward approaches that emphasize the role of the learner in creating knowledge, competence, and the ability to pursue further learning. There is a good deal of literature that seeks to blend various theories of teaching and learning into flexible and creative approaches that will accomplish these ends. The strength of these approaches is that they begin with an appreciation of student differences that can be stretched comfortably to incorporate the differences of disability and the effective teaching technology created by special educators.[15]

The third shift involves changing our view of the schools' role from one of providing educational *services* to one of providing educational *supports* for learning. This shift will occur naturally as a consequence of the changes in teaching demanded by diversity. Valuing diversity and difference, rather than trying to change or diminish it so that everyone fits some ideal of similarity, leads to the realization that we can *support* students in their efforts to become active members of their communities. No longer must the opportunity to participate in life wait until some standard of "normalcy" or similarity is reached. A focus on the support of learning also encourages a shift from viewing difference or disability in terms of individual limitations to a focus on environmental constraints. Perhaps the most important feature of support as a concept for schooling is that it is grounded in the perspective of the person receiving it, not the person providing it.[16]

The new challenge of inclusion is to create schools in which our day-to-day efforts no longer assume that a particular text, activity, or teaching mode will "work" to support any particular student's learning. Typical classrooms will include students with more and more kinds of differences. The learning enterprise of reinvented *inclusive* schools will be a constant conversation involving students, teachers, other school personnel, families, and community members, all working to construct learning, to document accomplishments, and to adjust supports. About this kind of inclusion I can be very rabid indeed.

1. John Gliedman and William Roth, *The Unexpected Minority: Handicapped Children in America* (New York: Harcourt Brace Jovanovich, 1980).

2. Jeff Strully and Cindy Strully, "Friendship as an Educational Goal," in Susan Stainback, William Stainback, and Marsha Forest, eds., *Educating All Students in the Mainstream of Regular Education* (Baltimore: Paul H. Brookes, 1989), pp. 59-68.

3. Dianne L. Ferguson et al., "Figuring Out What to Do with Grownups: How Teachers Make Inclusion 'Work' for Students with Disabilities," *Journal of the Association for Persons with Severe Handicaps*, vol. 17, 1993, pp. 218-26.

4. Dianne L. Ferguson, "Is Communication Really the Point? Some Thoughts on Interventions and Membership," *Mental Retardation*, vol. 32, no. 1, 1994, pp. 7-18.

5. Dianne L. Ferguson, Christopher Willis, and Gwen Meyer, "Widening the Stream: Ways to Think About Including Exceptions in Schools," in Donna H. Lear and Fredda Brown, eds., *People with Disabilities Who Challenge the System* (Baltimore: Paul H. Brookes, forthcoming); and Dianne L. Ferguson and Gwen Meyer, "Creating Together the Tools to Reinvent Schools," in Michael Berres, Peter Knoblock, Dianne L. Ferguson, and Connie Woods, eds., *Restructuring Schools for All Children* (New York: Teachers College Press, forthcoming).

6. Michael Giangreco et al., " 'I've Counted on Jon': Transformational Experiences of Teachers Educating Students with Disabilities," *Exceptional Children*, vol. 59, 1993, pp. 359-72; and Marlene Pugach and Stephen Lilly, "Reconceptualizing Support Services for Classroom Teachers: Implications for Teacher Education," *Journal of Teacher Education*, vol. 35, no. 5, 1984, pp. 48-55.

7. Russell Gersten and John Woodward, "Rethinking the Regular Education Initiative: Focus on the Classroom Teacher," *Remedial and Special Education*, vol. 11, no. 3, 1990, pp. 7-16.

8. Douglas Fuchs and Lynn S. Fuchs, "Inclusive Schools Movement and the Radicalization of Special Education Reform," *Exceptional Children*, vol. 60, 1994, pp. 294-309.

9. Lou Brown et al., "How Much Time Should Students with Severe Intellectual Disabilities Spend in Regular Education Classrooms and Elsewhere?," *Journal of the Association of Persons with Severe Handicaps*, vol. 16, 1991, pp. 39-47; and William Stainback, Susan Stainback, and Jeanette S. Moravec, "Using Curriculum to Build Inclusive Classrooms," in Susan Stainback and William Stainback, eds., *Curriculum Considerations in Inclusive Classrooms: Facilitating Learning for All Students* (Baltimore: Paul H. Brookes, 1992), pp. 65-84.

10. Dianne L Ferguson, "Bursting Bubbles: Marrying General and Special Education Reforms," in Berres, Knoblock, Ferguson, and Woods, op. cit.; and Terry Astuto et al., *Roots of Reform: Challenging the Assumptions That Control Change in Education* (Bloomington, Ind.: Phi Delta Kappa Educational Foundation, 1994).

11. See, for example, Anthony D. Carnevale, Leila J. Gainer, and Ann S. Meltzer, *The Essential Skills Employers Want* (San Francisco: Jossey-Bass, 1990).

12. David T. Conley, *Roadmap to Restructuring: Policies, Practices, and the Emerging Visions of Schooling* (Eugene: ERIC Clearinghouse on Educational Management, University of Oregon, 1993); Robin Fogarty, "Ten Ways to Integrate Curriculum," *Educational Leadership*, October 1991, pp. 61-65; Jacqueline G. Brooks and Martin Brooks, *In Search of Understanding: The Case for Constructivist Classrooms* (Alexandria, Va.: Association for Supervision and Curriculum Development, 1993); Nel Noddings, "Excellence as a Guide to Educational Conversations," *Teachers College Record*, vol. 94, 1993, pp. 730-43; Theodore Sizer, *Horace's School: Redesigning the American School* (Boston: Houghton Mifflin, 1992); and Grant Wiggins, "The Futility of Trying to Teach Everything of Importance," *Educational Leadership*, November 1989, pp. 44-59.

13. Thomas Armstrong, *Multiple Intelligences in the Classroom* (Alexandria, Va.: Association for Supervision and Curriculum Development, 1994); Howard Gardner, *Multiple Intelligences: The Theory in Practice* (New York: Basic Books, 1993); and Gaea Leinhardt, "What Research on Learning Tells Us About Teaching," *Educational Leadership*, April 1992, pp. 20-25.

14. Linda Darling-Hammond, "Reframing the School Reform Agenda: Developing Capacity for School Transformation," *Phi Delta Kappan*, June 1993, pp. 753-61; Jeannie Oakes and Martin Lipton, "Detracking Schools: Early Lessons from the Field," *Phi Delta Kappan*, February 1992, pp. 448-54; and Thomas M. Skrtic, *Behind Special Education: A Critical Analysis of Professional Culture and School Organization* (Denver: Love Publishing, 1991).

15. Conley, op. cit.; Robin Fogarty, *The Mindful School: How to Integrate the Curricula* (Palatine, Ill.: IRI/Skylight Publishing, 1991); Brooks and Brooks, op. cit.; Nel Noddings, *The Challenge to Care in Schools* (New York: Teachers College Press, 1992); Sizer, op. cit.; and Wiggins, op. cit.

16. Philip M. Ferguson et al., "Supported Community Life: Disability Policy and the Renewal of Mediating Structures," *Journal of Disability Policy*, vol. 1, no. 1, 1990, pp. 9-35; and Michael W. Smull and G. Thomas Bellamy, "Community Services for Adults with Disabilities: Policy Challenges in the Emerging Support Paradigm," in Luanna Meyer, Charles A. Peck, and Lou Brown, eds., *Critical Issues in the Lives of People with Severe Disabilities* (Baltimore: Paul H. Brookes, 1991), pp. 527-36.

Restructuring the Participation of African-American Parents in Special Education

BETH HARRY
University of Maryland

ABSTRACT: *Two traditions have combined to contribute to a form of discourse that is detrimental to the participation of African-American parents in special education procedures: first, a deficit view of African-American families and, second, the deficit view of children's learning difficulties on which P.L. 94-142 is based. These deficit views, together with the focus by many professional educators on legal compliance rather than collaboration, have cast parents in the role of consent-giver in a grossly asymmetrical form of discourse, with power residing mostly with professionals. Four specific parental roles—including parents in assessment, placement, policymaking, and advocacy—would restore the balance of power in parent-professional discourse. Future research should focus on the documentation of egalitarian participation structures for African-American parents and on action-oriented ethnographic studies.*

BETH HARRY (CEC MD Federation) is an Assistant Professor in the Department of Special Education at the University of Maryland, College Park.

☐ This article is concerned with the balance of power between special education professionals and African-American parents. Although it is true that the question of power is central to any consideration of parent-professional discourse in education (Gliedman & Roth, 1980), interactions with African-American parents are marked by certain crucial historical dimensions. Further, the role of this group of parents is particularly important because their children continue to be designated as students with disabilities in disproportionately high numbers (U.S. Department of Education, 1989).

The literature on parent participation in special education shows that this group of parents exhibits a pattern of relatively low participation and that teachers often interpret this pattern to mean that such parents are uninterested in their children's educational careers (Lynch & Stein,

1987; Marion, 1981; Sullivan, 1980). However, despite the potentially undermining influence of poverty and detrimental urban environments on traditional values, the belief that many parents do not care what happens to their children in school runs contrary to what is known about African-American family life and the values placed on education (Billingsley, 1968; Harry, Allen, & McLaughlin, 1992; Hill, 1971; Marion, 1981).

First, I present an overview of what is known about special education professionals' interaction with African-American parents; second, an examination of two sets of beliefs that underlie this form of discourse; and, third, some proposals for changing the implicit and explicit rules on which this discourse is structured. I posit that the structure of African-American parents' participation reflects two dominant traditions in professional thought: first, the deficit view of African-American families on which compensatory education practices have been based, and, second, the medical model on which special education is based and the resulting deficit view of African-American children that has been prom-

From *Exceptional Children*, October/November 1992, pp. 123-131. © 1992 by The Council for Exceptional Children. Reprinted by permission.

ulgated by continued misassessment and miseducation.

I use the term *discourse* to refer to the entire body of communication practices between parents and special education systems. In this sense, the concept includes not only written and oral communication, but the metamessages conveyed by the way the process of discourse is structured—how, when, where, by whom, and in what sequence information is conveyed (Bowers & Flinders, 1990). This framing of discourse reflects the power and value attributed to various parties and thus determines the type of social interaction that will occur.

Two acknowledgments are important in focusing on African-American parents: first, the impact of the discourse described is likely to be greater for parents of low income or limited formal education, because these factors are known to limit parents' ability to be influential in school systems (Lareau, 1989); second, many aspects of the discussion may also apply to other people of color who have traditionally been placed in subordinate positions within the larger society (Ogbu, 1978). Indeed, in recognition of certain commonalities among cultural minority groups of color in the United States, I will extrapolate from literature on these groups wherever appropriate.

AFRICAN-AMERICAN PARENTS AS PARTNERS IN SPECIAL EDUCATION

It might be argued that African-American parents simply represent one strand in a pattern of largely passive parental participation in special education generally (for a comprehensive review, see Turnbull & Turnbull, 1990). However, Lynch and Stein (1987) found that African-American and Mexican-American parents' levels of information and participation were significantly lower than that of their white counterparts. Other studies, delineating specific factors that limit the involvement of low-income, African-American parents, have revealed a picture of extreme alienation and markedly low awareness of rights and procedures (Cassidy, 1988; Lowry, 1983; Sullivan, 1980). There are four common interpretations of these patterns: trust, parental apathy, logistical constraints or stressful life circumstances, and parents' disagreement with special education classifications. These interpretations focus on difficulties seen as "belonging" to the parents themselves.

Attitudes and Behavior of Parents

The question of trust is crucial. As a classic example of an indigenous minority group that has historically been ascribed castelike status (Ogbu, 1978), African Americans have an intense awareness of the conflict between the democratic norms of their society and the actual distribution of power. Marion (1981) and Siddle-Walker (1991) have emphasized that the trust of African-American parents, whose attitude to schools was traditionally very supportive, was substantially undermined by the rejecting ethos of desegregated, traditionally white schools after the U.S. Supreme Court's 1954 decision in *Brown v. Board of Education*. This mistrust has been exacerbated by parents' awareness of the overrepresentation of African-American youth in special education programs (Marion, 1981).

The second interpretation is that African-American parents are apathetic. It is commonly heard in professional settings that "these parents just don't care about their children." In a study by Lynch and Stein (1987), teachers cited parental apathy as a source of noninvolvement. Can it be that African-American parents, or other minority parents similarly maligned, have somehow become the exceptions to a rule universally accepted as axiomatic, that is, that parents care about their children? Or perhaps those who exclaim thus really mean to say that they think poor parents of color do not value education, a notion that was promoted by the literature on so-called "cultural deprivation" in the 1960s (Deutsch, 1967; Reissman, 1962).

Researchers must investigate the meaning behind behavior that appears to suggest lack of parental interest. Qualitative methods, such as informal, open-ended interviewing and participant observation, are particularly well suited to this kind of inquiry. For example, in a recent study of another low-status group (low-income Puerto Rican-American parents, the majority of whom also happened to be black), recurrent, unstructured interviews revealed that what was interpreted by professionals as disinterest or apathy was a mask for parents' mistrust and their consequent withdrawal from participation (Harry, 1992).

A third trend in the literature is the observation that logistical constraints and stressful life circumstances act as a significant deterrent to low-income African-American parents' participation in special education matters (Cassidy, 1988; Lowry, 1983; Lynch & Stein, 1987; Marion, 1981; Nazarro & Portundo, 1981). Lowry's investigation of the barriers to participation among inner-city, low-income, black families documented an expressed sense of isolation and helplessness and concluded that parents "appeared to be apathetic and disinterested when in reality they were overwhelmed" (p. 58). Similarly, Cassidy (1988) found that problems with scheduling, transportation, and knowledge of the individualized educational program (IEP) process were the three greatest deterrents to African-American parents' participation. A related finding was that African-American parents' low level of knowledge regarding their rights and special education procedures may be yet another reason for their low involvement (Cassidy, 1988).

Finally, African-American parents' disagreement with special education classifications may contribute to communication difficulties with professionals. It is a common professional comment that many parents "deny" the validity of a diagnosis of disability, in particular, mental retardation. Indeed, the literature on parents' views of labeling continues to show that milder, less stigmatizing labels are more acceptable to parents (Barsch, 1961; Harry et al., 1992; Smith, Osborne, Crim, & Rhu, 1986; Wolfensberger & Kurtz, 1974).

The objections of African-American families, however, have been specifically targeted at social and cultural biases in the assessment process (Marion, 1981; Mercer, 1972). Moreover, low-income, African-American parents' disagreement with school classifications may reflect a wider acceptance of divergent patterns of development than is tolerated by schools. Even when parents agree that a child's development is delayed relative to others in the family, they may not consider this "disabling" if they do not expect it to prevent the child from achieving personal and economic independence. As a result of the historically limited range of occupations available to African Americans, expectations for their children are likely to include unskilled jobs, for which a high level of educational achievement is not deemed necessary. Further, parents whose own success in school was limited may not expect to send their children to school already prepared for reading and writing; they may consider this the school's job. Thus, a judgment based on middle-class norms of earlier acquisition of academic skills would probably not be shared by parents.

The concern about differential levels of preparation for school is not merely a peculiarity of the parental perspective. Indeed, this concern is at the heart of the dilemma concerning assessment of students from cultural minority backgrounds. It is now widely acknowledged that current assessment approaches and tools are inadequate to the task of accurately evaluating the learning difficulties of students whose homes and communities differ substantially from school expectations (Cummins, 1986; Neisser, 1986). The cultural heterogeneity, as well as the socioeconomic inequities of U.S. society, make it impossible for responsible professionals to rely solely on information from current standardized assessment approaches (Cummins, 1989; Ginsburg, 1986). Cummins (1989) and Harry (1992) have called for a recognition that parents' input is as important as that of professionals—indeed, a recognition that poverty and limited formal education are not equivalent to limited intelligence or common sense.

The foregoing interpretations of African-American parents' low participation are all based on statements about parents. We must ask what the role of professional behavior is in this pattern.

Attitudes and Behavior of Professionals

Three studies have investigated the actual detrimental patterns of inappropriate professional interaction with parents from diverse cultural backgrounds. Two studies focused on Hispanic populations, but their findings regarding the dynamics of parent-professional interaction are instructive in illustrating how professionals can "frame" (Bowers & Flinders, 1990) both the content and extent of discourse to exclude, rather than include, parents.

In a survey of 355 students referred for psychological services in an urban school system, Tomlinson, Acker, Cantor, and Lindborg (1977) found that professionals initiated significantly fewer contacts with parents of minority students, the majority of whom were African American, and offered a narrower range of services to minority as compared to majority parents. Bennett (1988), using a microethnographic analysis of parent-professional discourse, demonstrated that professional behavior succeeded in placing Hispanic parents "in a stance of noninvolvement" (p. 127). For example, by defining what was and was not legitimate content to be included in a child's IEP, professionals excluded a mother's concern with the effects of classroom structure on her child's behavior. Harry (1992) found that the use of formal, impersonal channels of communication, with an emphasis on written materials, not only failed to inform, but actually alienated low-income Puerto Rican parents. On the other hand, Harry's study also demonstrated the converse, that when professionals framed discourse in terms of personal interactions and placed parents at the center of the information-sharing process, parents demonstrated the ability to be effective advocates for their children.

Perhaps most important to this discussion is that professionals and parents alike buy into a structure that reflects shared values detrimental to parents and their children. Mehan, Hartwick, and Meihls' (1986) microethnographic analysis of decision making in special education makes the crucial point that the structure of discourse in conferences reflects three essential assumptions of special education theory and practice: (a) the superiority of technical/theoretical knowledge over common-sense knowledge; (b) the greater importance accorded information given by higher ranking personnel in the school organization; and (c) the power of professionals to define what may and may not be discussed (see also Bennett, 1988).

This tacit negotiation of structures of discourse is no less than a statement of a shared ideology which, according to Cherryholmes (1988), "intertwines with power as individuals accept, believe, and internalize explanations and justifications for the asymmetries of their social world" (p. 5). Though advocacy training aims to teach parents to reject rather than accept these asymmetries, professionals hold the power to change such beliefs far more quickly and effectively than do low-income parents. However, professionals' unwillingness to do so is the logical outcome of certain basic assumptions in American educational philosophy and in the framework of special education itself.

TRADITIONS INFLUENCING PROFESSIONAL INTERACTION WITH AFRICAN-AMERICAN PARENTS

The issue underlying parent-participation patterns is power. I contend that a combination of two traditions has disempowered many African-American parents: a tradition of cultural-deficit theories regarding African-American family life, and the medical model on which the Education for All Handicapped Children Act (EHA), Public Law 94-142, is based.

Parent Education, Parent Participation, and Cultural-Deficit Theory

Current mandates for parental participation in schools are a logical culmination of a century-old movement toward the improvement of parenting practices and the growth of parental influence in schools (Schlossman, 1983). Parent education and parent participation tend to be presented as a joint endeavor, proffering the betterment of students' educational progress as a common goal. But parental education and participation actually reflect opposite sides of the same coin. The notion of parent education presumes the desirability of improving some weakness in existing parenting skills whereas the notion of parent participation assumes that parents have something positive to contribute. Thus, educators have often linked the two, believing that many parents lack the knowledge and skills that are recognized and valued by the school. Educators further assume that it is necessary to educate parents in the needed practices, to enable them to make a useful contribution.

This combination has had particular implications for African-American families, since the notion of parent education took on a somewhat different meaning with the introduction of the federal antipoverty programs in the 1960s. Until that time, the movement had been concerned primarily with the inculcation by middle-class parents of modern child-rearing techniques derived from the behavioral sciences (Schlossman, 1983). The advent of the antipoverty movement, however, framed the notion of parent education

in terms of remediating what were seen as the cultural deficits inherent in poor, minority families (Haskins & Adams, 1983; Loasa, 1983). African-American families, in particular, were the target of the "tangle of pathology" image evoked by the much-quoted Moynihan report (U.S. Department of Labor, 1965). The twin goals of parent education and parent participation became cornerstones of compensatory education programs such as Head Start and Follow Through, which made funding contingent on unprecedented levels of parental participation in both policymaking and implementation (Haskins & Adams, 1983).

My argument is that, as long as professionals believe that low-income, minority parents must be "trained" and "educated" in appropriate parenting before their participation can be valued, attempts to alter the balance of power are undermined by lack of respect for differing parenting styles. It is not that parent education is never appropriate or helpful, but that it must be offered in culturally appropriate ways (Linn, 1990) and that professionals must be willing to negotiate with parents from a posture of cultural reciprocity (Harry & Kalyanpur, 1991).

Parent Education, Parent Participation, and Disability Theory

For parents of children with disabilities, the need for both parent education and participation is expected to be even greater. Yet, despite an explicit mandate for parental participation under P.L. 94-142, participation rates in special education are much lower than those reported for Head Start and other compensatory education programs. This brings us to the tradition most directly impacting parent-professional interaction in special education—the tradition of a pathological model of disability.

The mandate for parental participation in special education differs from compensatory education in that the former is cast within the framework of a medical model in which children with presumed deficits are identified, assessed, and treated by experts who are, in the course of their duties, required to gain the consent and participation of parents. This is a very different milieu than that of a compensatory education program, in which children are voluntarily enrolled, and parents are afforded a variety of influential roles.

Indeed, there is an inherent conflict between the medical-model/expert-treatment framework within which P.L. 94-142 operates and its mandate for consultation with parents. The positivistic assumptions of the law, driven by the charge to classify children by their deficits, results in the categorical framing of parent-professional discourse: It is the job of professionals to determine whether students have, or do not have, disabilities; and it is the job of parents to agree or disagree with professionals' findings and recommendations. When an educational system imbued with a deficit view of African-American families is combined with a deficit view of students with learning difficulties, the low involvement of the parents should come as no surprise. Parents' mistrust, disagreement, and competing priorities outlined earlier in this article are only one side of the picture.

It might be argued that the view of African-American families as pathological has been rejected by social scientists (Ginsburg, 1986; Wright, Saleeby, Watts, & Lecca, 1983), but it is common knowledge that such beliefs are still alive and well in the world of mainstream America. A widespread view of low-income, African-American families as entrenched in destructive forms of ghetto life has been promoted and perpetuated by the media and offers school personnel a further excuse not to interact with families from such neighborhoods. Many mainstream teachers reflect the society's pervasive fears of African-American neighborhoods and culture generally. Notwithstanding the existence of some crime-ridden areas in large urban centers, most African Americans know that their homes and families are not only safe but loving. How can mainstream professionals be brought to share this knowledge?

TOWARDS A RESTRUCTURING OF POWER

I have argued that the framework for parental participation is inextricably bound to two sets of attitudes that accord African-American parents particularly low status in the decision-making process. What we need is a restructuring of discourse to radically alter the balance of power between African-American parents and professionals.

The word *power* is used here in the sense defined by Cherryholmes (1988), "to refer to relations among individuals or groups based on social, political, and material asymmetries by which some people are indulged and rewarded and others negatively sanctioned and deprived" (p. 5). The current state of discourse in special education reflects an imbalance of power: The difficulties that seem to "belong" to parents, as well as the attitudes and behavior of professionals, combine to produce a form of discourse in which power is loaded on the side of professionals.

Professionals must ask whether participation is cast mainly in a framework of mere consent or whether it is conceived in terms of a dialogue whose purpose is to discern the true nature of children's learning difficulties in school. In other words, do professionals really believe that low-income, African-American parents have something to contribute to the school's understanding of children who are having difficulty? Or do we assume that professional efforts constitute the only legitimate source of opinion, and that the role of parents is to give permission for professional activities and automatic approval to professional decisions?

Unless parent-professional interactions are based on dialogue, professionals may view themselves or the system as the source of truth—and they may cast parents' interaction within an adversarial framework. In this atmosphere, parents find that they must either passively cooperate or take a stance of confrontation. Indeed, the legalistic framing of parent-professional discourse in special education, with its many documents and rituals, is known to be particularly intimidating to African-American parents (Marion, 1979). Many parents, rather than engage in challenging the school system, react by withdrawing from interaction, creating informal avenues for communication, or limiting their areas of interaction to those where they are more comfortable (Harry et al., 1992).

Developing New Roles For Parents

At present, essentially two roles are offered to parents: consent-giver and educational planner. The first of these is actually all that is required for legal compliance with P.L. 94-142. To be in compliance, most professionals make some attempt to see that parents are informed about processes and placement in order to ensure their consent. The second role occurs, in theory at least, when parents collaborate with the teacher in planning a child's IEP; and the regulations require that parents be invited to a conference for this purpose. Despite numerous exhortations to professionals regarding informed consent (e.g., Marion, 1979; Shevin, 1983; Turnbull & Turnbull, 1990), all attempts in the research to ascertain minority parents' level of awareness of this procedure have revealed exceedingly low awareness of either the planning event or the document that records it (Connery, 1987; Harry, 1992; Lynch & Stein, 1987; Sharp, 1983). I would conclude that the only role consistently applied to parents is that of consent-giver. The following are new parental roles that need to be developed.

Parents as Assessors. Parental participation in the actual assessment procedure should constitute the first step in a restructuring of communication. One possible reason for parents' low participation in and awareness of the IEP planning process may be the lateness of the invitation. By the time the IEP is to be developed, professionals have already established power and legitimacy by excluding parents from the assessment process. It is true that a thorough assessment is expected to include a social history given by the parent, and that state-of-the-art theory strongly recommends preevaluation, family-focused assessment. However, in practice, this is often either ignored, or implemented in such a way as to require parents simply to respond to constructs predetermined and presented by professionals.

One of the earliest and best known parent accounts, Park's *The Siege* (1967), tells of a parent's frustration at not being allowed to engage her autistic daughter in play that she knew would have demonstrated a much wider range of the child's behavior than could possibly be elicited by strangers, no matter how skilled. More than 20 years later, low-income, African-American parents are telling the same story (Harry et al., 1992). The exclusion of parents from the assessment process can be particularly devastating for such populations because of misunderstandings of children's behavior, which can result from the traditional deficit views held by many professionals. Further, most psychologists and speech and language therapists are unlikely to be familiar with African-American culture and, therefore, have difficulty interpreting the meaning of children's nonverbal, linguistic, and social behavior.

Precedent for such inclusion of parents has been documented in several exemplary projects funded by the Handicapped Children's Early Education Program (HCEEP), (Karnes, Linnemeyer, & Myles, 1983). By designating parents as part of the official assessment team, professional special educators can go a long way in altering—or even eradicating—the assumption that professionals have a monopoly on knowledge.

Parents as Presenters of Reports. At the time of the placement conference, parents, already members of the team, would be expected to present a report. This report would constitute an official document, to be entered into the record and taken into account in decision making, along with the professional reports. This official parental role would not only increase the value that professionals place on parental input, but this role would signal to parents that their input is not only valued but needed.

To include parental input as valued—and necessary—in the placement process would constitute radically different practice from the current situation, where parents may be told that it is "OK" if they cannot come to a conference since the decisions will be sent to them in the mail (Harry et al., 1992). If parents do attend placement conferences where it is evident that their presence is not influential, why should they continue to attend, especially if attending may mean feeling uncomfortable or intimidated, or, on a more practical level, losing a morning's pay or a day's leave?

The latter point brings us to a much-quoted concern in the literature: the difficulties low-income parents have with scheduling of conferences. Is it too much to ask that, where necessary, conferences be held after working hours, and that parents be polled well beforehand regarding the best times for the scheduling of conferences? Once more, although the latter suggestions have been made in parent-communication models (see Marion, 1981; Turnbull & Turnbull, 1990), it is doubtful that they are widely practiced. The same applies to concerns about child care and transportation. Such concerns are examples of the "material asymmetries" referred to by Cherryholmes (1988), which affect the balance of power.

Parents as Policymakers. Under the EHA, the only policymaking role provided by parents is membership on Parent Advisory Committees (PACs). These are usually advisory to the local educational agency (LEA), and therefore tend to be concerned with matters considerably removed from individual schools or communities. I strongly recommend school-based, advisory parent bodies for special education programs, as well as active recruitment of parents as teachers' aides. These roles are well established in compensatory education programs such as Follow Through. In these programs, particularly high parental involvement has been attributed to the requirements that (a) more than 50% of the PAC be low-income parents; (b) these members be elected by their peers, rather than appointed; and (c) parental involvement be carefully monitored and documented (Keesling & Melaragno, 1983).

These observations should serve as guidelines for the development of PACs in special education. If each school with a special education program had an active parent group that elected its own representatives on a school-based advisory committee, professionals would be forced to share power with parents. Such a group could also support professionals by taking responsibility for following up parent contacts, providing parents with support at IEP conferences, and generally boosting parent participation in special education events.

Parents as Advocates and Peer Supports. Parent groups serving within schools in both policy-making and support roles can also initiate parent-to-parent advocacy activities, such as those supported by federal funds under P.L. 98-199 (Ziegler, 1988). These could be promoted through existing Chapter 1 liaison activities in individual schools. Professionals may fear that such efforts would become yet another of their responsibilities, but this need not be so. Were schools to reconstruct parents' roles to offer parents meaningful input in the assessment, placement, and remediation of their children, parents would most likely develop a sense of competence and would want to share their learning with other parents.

Research Needs

We need more research regarding parent-professional discourse, particularly for special education settings. Further delineation of how the structure of discourse serves to disempower African-American parents will strengthen the case for radical alteration of these patterns. What we need the most, however, is documentation of genuine attempts at egalitarian forms of discourse with African-American parents. The process of parental empowerment has been documented with low-income, Spanish-speaking families, who, like African Americans, are at a considerable disadvantage in dealing with school systems (Ada, 1988; Delgado-Gaitan, 1990; Harry, 1992). In Delgado-Gaitan's study, the researcher combined the role of ethnographic researcher with that of catalyst in the empowerment of families.

We need qualitative, intervention-oriented research that investigates ways to alter the discourse of power between professionals and low-income, African-American families. Many professionals in the field genuinely want to contribute to the empowerment of African-American parents, but are constrained by deep-seated and pervasive myths about the nature of African-American family and community life and about the presumed cognitive, linguistic, and social deficits of African-American children. Researchers should seek out professionals who are willing to engage in constructive investigations of how their practice can be changed. Until professionals actually see African-American parents functioning as effective advocates for their children, the myth of the apathetic and incompetent African-American parent will survive.

REFERENCES

Ada, A. F. (1988). The Pajaro Valley experience. In T. Skutnabb-Kangas & J. Cummins (Eds.), *Minority education: From shame to struggle* (pp. 223-238). Clevedon, England: Multilingual Matters.

Barsch, R. H. (1961). Explanations offered by parents and siblings of brain-damaged children. *Exceptional Children, 27,* 286-291.

Bennett, A. T. (1988). Gateways to powerlessness: Incorporating Hispanic deaf children and families into formal schooling. *Disability, Handicap & Society, 3*(2), 119-151.

Billingsley, A. (1968). *Black families in White America.* Englewood Cliffs, NJ: Prentice-Hall.

Bowers, C. A., & Flinders, D. J. (1990). *Responsive teaching: An ecological approach to classroom patterns of language, culture, and thought.* New York: Teachers College Press.

Cassidy, E. (1988). *Reaching and involving Black parents of handicapped children in their child's education program.* Lansing, MI: CAUSE Inc. (ERIC Document Reproduction Service No. Ed 302 982)

Cherryholmes, C. H. (1988). *Power and criticism: Poststructural investigations in education.* New York: Teachers College Press.

Connery, A. R. (1987). *A description and comparison of Native American and Anglo parents' knowledge of their handicapped children's rights.* Unpublished doctoral dissertation, Northern Arizona University, Flagstaff.

Cummins, J. (1986). Empowering minority students: A framework for intervention. *Harvard Educational Review, 56,* 18-36.

Cummins, J. (1989). Institutionalized racism and the assessment of minority children. In R. J. Samuda & S. L. Kong (Eds.), *Assessment and placement of minority students* (pp. 95-198). Toronto: C. J. Hogrefe.

Delgado-Gaitan, C. (1990). *Literacy for empowerment.* New York: Falmer Press.

Deutsch, M. (1967). The disadvantaged child and the learning process. In M. Deutsch (Ed.), *The disadvantaged child.* New York: Basic Books.

Ginsburg, H. P. (1986). The myth of the deprived child: New thoughts on poor children. In U. Neisser (Ed.), *The school achievement of minority children: New perspectives* (pp. 169-189). Hillsdale, NJ: Lawrence Erlbaum.

Gliedman, J., & Roth, W. (1980). *The unexpected minority: Handicapped children in America.* New York: Harcourt Brace Jovanovich.

Harry, B. (1992). *Cultural diversity, families, and the special education system: Communication and empowerment.* New York: Teachers College Press.

Harry, B., Allen, N., & McLaughlin, M. (1992, April). *Communication versus compliance: Working with African American parents in special education.* Paper presented at the annual meeting of the American Educational Research Association, San Francisco.

Harry, B., & Kalyanpur, M. (1991). *A posture of reciprocity: Towards a model of collaborative interaction with culturally diverse families in special education.* Manuscript submitted for publication.

Haskins, R., & Adams, D. (1983). Parent education and public policy: Synthesis and recommendations. In R. Haskins & D. Adams (Eds.), *Parent education and public policy* (pp. 346-373). Norwood, NJ: Ablex.

Hill, R. B. (1971). *The strengths of Black families.* New York: Emerson Hall.

Karnes, M. B., Linnemeyer, S. A., & Myles, G. (1983). Programs for parents of handicapped children. In R. Haskins & D. Adams (Eds.), *Parent education and public policy* (pp. 181-210). Norwood, NJ: Ablex.

Keesling, J. W., & Melaragno, R. J. (1983). Parent participation in federal education programs: Findings from the federal programs survey phase of the study of parental involvement. In R. Haskins & D. Adams (Eds.), *Parent education and public policy* (pp. 230-256). Norwood, NJ: Ablex.

Laosa, L. (1983). Parent education, cultural pluralism, and public policy: The uncertain connection. In R. Haskins & D. Adams (Eds.), *Parent education and public policy* (pp. 331-345). Norwood, NJ: Ablex.

Lareau, A. (1989). *Home advantage: Social class and parental intervention in elementary education.* New York: Falmer Press.

Linn, E. (1990, Spring). Parent involvement programs: A review of selected models. *Equity Coalition, 1*(2), pp. 10-15.

Lowry, M. S. (1983). *Obstacles to parental involvement: A study of barriers to participation in the edu-*

cational process faced by Black, low-income, inner-city parents of handicapped children. Washington, DC: Office for Special Education & Rehabilitation Services. (ERIC Document Reproduction Service No. ED 244 487)

Lynch, E. W., & Stein, R. (1987). Parent participation by ethnicity: A comparison of Hispanic, Black and Anglo families. *Exceptional Children, 54,* 105-111.

Marion, R. (1979). Minority parent involvement in the IEP process: A systematic model approach. *Focus on Exceptional Children, 10*(8), 1-16.

Marion, R. (1981). *Educators, parents and exceptional children.* Rockville, MD: Aspen.

Mehan, H., Hartwick, A., & Meihls, J. L. (1986). *Handicapping the handicapped: Decision-making in students' educational careers.* Stanford, CA: Stanford University Press.

Mercer, J. R. (1972, February). *Sociocultural factors in the educational evaluation of Black and Chicano children.* Paper presented at the 10th Annual Conference on Civil and Human Rights of Educators and Students, Washington, DC.

Nazarro, J. N., & Portundo, M. W. (1981). *Understanding where children are coming from.* Reston, VA: Council for Exceptional Children. (ERIC Document Reproduction Service. ED 199 993)

Neisser, U. (1986). New answers to an old question. In U. Neisser (Ed.), *The school achievement of minority children: New perspectives* (pp. 1-18). Hillsdale, NJ: Lawrence Erlbaum.

Ogbu, J. (1978). *Minority education and caste: The American system in cross-cultural perspective.* San Francisco: Academic Press.

Park, C. (1967). *The siege: The first eight years of an autistic child.* Boston: Little, Brown.

Reissman, F. (1962). *The culturally deprived child.* New York: Harper & Row.

Schlossman, S. L. (1983). The formative era in American parent education: Overview and interpretation. In R. Haskins & D. Adams (Eds.), *Parent education and public policy* (pp. 7-39). Norwood, NJ: Ablex.

Sharp, E.Y. (1983). *Analysis of determinants impacting on educational services of handicapped Papago students.* Tucson: University of Arizona, College of Education. (ERIC Document Reproduction Service No. ED 239 468)

Shevin, M. (1983). Meaningful parental involvement in long-range educational planning for disabled children. *Education and Training of the Mentally Retarded, 18,* 17-21.

Siddle-Walker, E. (1991, February). *Separate but equal: A case study of "good" pre-integration schooling for African-American children.* Paper presented at the meeting of the Center for Urban Ethnography, Philadelphia.

Smith, R. W., Osborne, L. T., Crim, D., & Rhu, A. H. (1986). Labeling theory as applied to learning disabilities: Findings and policy suggestions. *Journal of Learning Disabilities, 19*(4), 195-202.

Sullivan, O. T. (1980). *Meeting the needs of low-income families with handicapped children.* Washington, DC: U.S. Department of Health and Welfare, National Institute of Education. (ERIC Document Reproduction Service No. ED 201 091)

Tomlinson, J. R., Acker, N. Canter, A., & Lindborg, S. (1977). Minority status, sex and school psychological services. *Psychology in the Schools, 14*(4), 456-460.

Turnbull, A. P., & Turnbull, H. R. (1990) *Families, professionals and exceptionality* (2nd ed.). Columbus, OH: Merrill.

U.S. Department of Education, Office for Civil Rights. (1989). *1989 elementary and secondary schools civil rights survey: National summaries.* Washington, DC: DBS Corporation.

U.S. Department of Labor. (1965). *The Negro family: The case for national action.* Washington, DC: U.S. Government Printing Office.

Wolfensberger, W., & Kurtz, R. A. (1974). Use of retardation-related diagnostic and prescriptive labels by parents of retarded children. *Journal of Special Education, 8*(2), 131-142.

Wright, R., Saleeby, D., Watts, T. D., & Lecca, P. J. (1983). *Transcultural perspectives in the human services.* Springfield, IL: Charles C Thomas.

Ziegler, M. (1988). Parent to parent support: A federal program. *Family Resource Coalition Report, 7*(2), 8-9.

PEER EDUCATION PARTNERS

A PROGRAM FOR LEARNING AND WORKING TOGETHER

Louise Fulton, Christopher LeRoy, Martha L. Pinckney, and Tim Weekley

Louise Fulton (CEC Chapter #530), Professor of Education and Director, California Transition Center, California State University, San Bernardino. Christopher LeRoy, Transition Program Manager, San Bernardino Unified School District, California. Martha L. Pinckney, Principal, and Tim Weekley, Teacher, Hillside University Demonstration School, San Bernardino, California.

"He acts like he doesn't know how to do something, but he really does."

This comment was made by Erika, a fourth grader at Hillside University Demonstration School participating in the Peer Education Program (PEP). PEP is a future-oriented program that gives typical fourth-, fifth-, and sixth-grade students opportunities to share activities with peers who have intensive needs. This program is a powerful tool for teachers in the 1990s, who must bring together core academic courses and the skills needed for living, learning, and working in future community environments.

This article describes how PEP provides mutually beneficial experiences for students as they learn, work, and play together. Teachers, parents, and students believe that PEP participants have shown gains in social, academic, and career vocational skills. More important, they have developed positive attitudes toward themselves and others that cross home, school, and community environments.

PROGRAM OVERVIEW

PEP has been a collaborative effort from the beginning. The program was initially motivated by a mainstreaming model described by Almond, Rodgers, and Krug (1979) and by other research and development reported in the literature (Brown et al., 1979; Sailor et al., 1989; Voeltz, 1980). Development and field testing of PEP occurred during the 1988–1989 school year. Initially the PEP planning committee, composed of regular and special educators, parents, two school principals, a program specialist, and a university professor, met many times to develop the model and procedures. These efforts resulted in joint problem solving and shared ownership of the program as well as the development of the *PEP Handbook*. The handbook, which includes all PEP procedures, forms, and handouts, has been useful for replicating PEP at other school sites.

PEP was originally conceived as a special education effort; however, the program thrust changed early in the developmental stages. Discussions at planning committee meetings revealed a need to emphasize academic, social, and vocational benefits for all students. This was viewed as an important means for capturing the interest of teachers and parents as well as for providing beneficial experiences for students in the regular education program.

During the final 6 weeks of the 1989–1990 school year, 16 students participated in PEP as student leaders. Three were from grade 6, four from grade 5, and nine from grade 4. These students were assigned to their partners by the PEP supervising teacher, who teaches students with severe disabilities at Hillside School. PEP leaders worked with seven of the classroom partners on reading, math, art, physical education, and computer skills. The disabilities among these first- and second-grade students included Down syndrome and severe cognitive or behavioral disorders.

PROCEDURES

Establishment of the PEP program at Hillside followed a step-by-step procedure now being implemented at five other school sites. In order to replicate the PEP model, the following sequence of activities is suggested:

1. Obtain administrative support and schedule an overview of the PEP program at the potential school site. Review the *PEP Handbook* and show slides or a videotape of typical PEP activities.
2. Identify a PEP coordinating teacher, who begins by establishing an implementation schedule.
3. Schedule a PEP School Awareness Day. Typical activities include classroom visits by individuals with disabilities, a poster contest with an appropriate one-school/community-for-all theme, and films or other activities depicting normalized experiences of individuals with a variety of disabilities.
4. Have special educators develop specific descriptions of jobs, which are advertised in conspicuous spots around the school.
5. Have interested students obtain job applications from their teachers. The students complete and submit the application forms with signatures from parents, teachers, and the principal.
6. Interview all student applicants for available PEP leader positions, and give them constructive feedback about their interviews and skills.
7. Following consideration of interviews and teacher recommenda-

tions, "hire" PEP leaders for the 6-week experience. Have the PEP leaders complete the pre-PEP survey form.

8. Conduct weekly PEP training sessions for 4 weeks. Training components specified in the *PEP Handbook* include (a) job procedures, forms, expectations, and reports; (b) development of job skills; (c) terminology, specific techniques, and behavior management; and (d) procedures and expectations for daily journal writing.

9. Establish schedules for student workers in consultation with the teachers and the students. Continue hiring PEP leaders as needed to work on specific volunteer jobs for 6 weeks. These jobs entail 30-minute sessions 3 to 5 days a week for a period of 6 weeks. Students participate in weekly conferences with the supervising teacher. Using the PEP progress conference form provides a forum for both the teacher and the student to talk about progress, successes, and areas of needed skill improvement.

10. At the end of 6 weeks, complete a final post-PEP survey. Interested students must then reapply for their current position or a different job.

11. Organize a social activity for students to enjoy, and recognize them at a school awards assembly for leadership and work success.

12. Make sure that all teacher and parent surveys are completed as a means to increase participation and gain input for program improvement.

BENEFITS OF PEP

"When we practiced math and reading together we both learned."

This typical comment was made by a fifth grader at the post-PEP interview. It supports the premise that student participants benefit academically and socially regardless of whether they are tutors or tutees (Jenkins & Jenkins, 1982; Osguthorpe & Scruggs, 1986). Moreover, cross-age peer education programs such as PEP provide a means for maximizing resources. Levin, Glass, and Meister (1984) found such programs to be more cost effective and successful in improving academic skills than reducing class size or increasing instructional time.

Vocational experiences are also emphasized in the PEP program. The PEP leader assists a fellow student with core academic and social skills while working at jobs with titles such as "Reading Friend," "Art Partner," "Playground Pal," "Library Friend," "PE Pal," "Computer Buddy," "Community Helper," and "Math Mentor." While "on the job," students learn or improve vocational skills such as punctuality, dependability, self-initiative, problem solving, leadership, and work evaluation. They also develop confidence in themselves as leaders among their peers. This job-oriented recruitment and participation of students has been highly motivating, with 60 students requesting interviews for the first 9 positions.

Students in the special education classroom also have been enthusiastic about PEP. This result is consistent with the findings of Kohl, Moses, and Stettner-Eaton (1983) who reported increased motivation among special education students who participated in learning activities with their general education peers.

"It's not just helping somebody. It's learning to work together"; "I learned not to 'blow up' but to keep trying to help him"; and "In the beginning Matt had to follow along with his fingers and count bears. Now he can count." In these comments two sixth graders summarized their feelings about PEP and how the program combines academic, social, and vocational experiences for lessons in learning together.

Students in the PEP program also have demonstrated significant growth in positive attitudes toward individuals with disabilities, as expressed in the following comments: "If you believe in someone they believe in themselves"; "When you get to know Sara she doesn't seem disabled"; and "If Joshua says no, just be patient and he'll do it."

The rich environment encouraged by the PEP program allows typical students to gain positive experiences with students who have special educational needs. These experiences have immediate and potential long-term implications. Fenrick and Petersen (1984) found an increase in positive attitudes toward students with severe disabilities following 7 weeks of peer tutoring. Stainback and Stainback (1982) reported that students participating in integrated school activities expressed positive feelings about their experiences and a desire to continue such experiences. Short-term interac-

tions may reach beyond the school to future living and working environments as PEP leaders grow to assume other roles in the school and community. The students' mutual enjoyment of the experience is evidenced in Josie's statement: "Natalie used to not jump rope. Now we jump rope together."

PEP encourages partnerships that begin with an assigned task but may develop into sustained friendships. Kishi (1985) noted that friendships develop from peer tutoring as well as special friends programs. The philosophy of PEP has been to emphasize reciprocal activities that move beyond tutorial partnerships to mutual relationships of personal choice. As one PEP student commented, "I want to be a PEP leader next year 'cause I want to be Sarah's partner." Another said, "I want to be with Adam again."

EVALUATION

Program evaluation procedures were incorporated early. The PEP planning committee wanted to know the opinions of students, parents, and teachers toward the program. Evaluation data were gathered in five ways.

First, PEP leaders completed a pre- and postparticipation survey. Prior to participation, students were asked to respond to the following four questions: What do you feel a student with a disability can learn? In what activities do you feel the student could participate? How could you help the student? What could you learn from the experience? Student responses were scored with points given for key expressions reflecting attitude, expectation, self-contribution, and self-benefit. Their individual comments also helped in identifying areas of strength as well as topics to discuss with the students throughout the next 6 weeks.

At the end of 6 weeks of employment, a post-PEP survey was given. Comparisons of pre- and post-PEP participation responses revealed positive changes in expectations and attitudes of PEP leaders toward their peers with special educational needs. In addition, all PEP leaders asked to reapply for a PEP position. Lindy summed it up when she said, "They can learn anything if they just try hard."

Second, PEP leader growth was examined at weekly progress conferences with the PEP supervising teacher. Topics included discussions about successes and areas of needed improvement in dependability, attitude, praise giving, helpfulness, and overall quality of work.

Third, at the end of each semester PEP leaders were interviewed and asked to talk about what they learned, what they taught, and what methods they used. According to Gracie, "I learned to use reverse psychology. When Carl doesn't want to work at the computer I tell him he doesn't have to. Then he wants to." Another student explained, "I was able to teach him more math than he knew." Arzebet described his teaching techniques by saying, "I tell Chris he's doing a good job, and it seems to make him feel good inside." Linda summarized her approach by saying, "I just make up games. Sometimes she already knew. I just helped her try."

Fourth, the students with special needs were observed for changes in socialization as well as progress in the tutored academic areas. PEP peers developed enhanced social confidence. With PEP intervention, these students began to initiate peer interactions more frequently, and they exhibited greater choice in selecting friends and activities.

Improvement in academic skills among the students with special needs was also documented. Progress in language arts was assessed by pre-post measures, with rewarding results. For example, students showed gains in reading, with three of the seven moving from preprimer to first grade level in 1 year. Similar results were recorded in mathematics, with several students moving from rote counting to simple addition. When asked about her teaching success, Michelle replied, "In the beginning he used his fingers to count bears. Now he can add."

Finally, parents and teachers were surveyed to gain their opinions and input. The program achieved 100% parental approval, with all parents supporting their child's continued participation. One of the most significant measures of the program's effectiveness was evidenced in the following comments by parents: "I think it's wonderful that Josie can help another child and at the same time help herself"; "It increases the children's understanding of each other"; "Summer is now talking about making a career of teaching." Teachers also were supportive in their comments and felt the program was well organized and beneficial. Valuable suggestions and input from parents and teachers are being incorporated into the program for continued improvement.

These suggestions included preparing an instructional video that outlined program procedures and depicted PEP student instructional sessions. Both parents and teachers suggested that such a video would be useful at implementation sites and for sharing the program at PTA meetings. Both parents and students indicated a need for the PEP program to continue at the middle school. Parents and teachers strongly approved of the 6-week periods with 30-minute sessions as ideal time frames. Finally, several teachers and parents asked that the number of PEP sessions in regular classrooms be increased.

CONCLUSION

The PEP program is but one model for increasing peer interaction while at the same time strengthening academic, social, and vocational skills among elementary school students. One of the greatest benefits of the program has been the positive attitude and cooperative spirit of the entire campus in assisting with its implementation. This spirit of partnership can only stand to benefit all children as they continue to learn, play, and work together in current and future environments.

REFERENCES

Almond, P., Rodgers, S., & Krug, S. (1979). A model for including elementary students in the severely handicapped classroom. *TEACHING Exceptional Children, 11*(4), 135–139.

Brown, L., Branston, M., Hamre-Nietupski, Johnson, E, Wilcox, B., & Gruenewald, L. (1979). A rationale for comprehensive longitudinal interactions between severely handicapped students and non-handicapped students and other citizens. *AAESPH Review, 4*(1), 3–14.

Fenrick, N., & Petersen, T. (1984). Developing positive changes in attitudes toward moderately/severely handicapped students through a peer tutoring program. *Education and Training of the Mentally Retarded, 19*,(2), 83–90.

Jenkins, J., & Jenkins, I. (1982). *Cross-age and peer tutoring.* Reston, VA: The Council for Exceptional Children.

Kishi, G. (1985, December). *Long-term effects of a social interaction program between non-handicapped and severely handicapped children.* Paper presented at the 12th annual conference of the Association for Persons with Severe Handicaps, Boston.

Kohl, E., Moses, L., & Stettner-Eaton, B. (1983). The results of teaching fifth graders to be instructional trainers with students who are severely handicapped. *Journal of Association for Persons with Severe Handicaps, 8*(4), 32–40.

Levin, H., Glass, G., & Meister, G. (1984). *Cost effectiveness of four educational interventions.* Stanford, CA: Stanford University Institute for Research on Education, Finance, and Governance.

Osguthorpe, R., & Scruggs, T. (1986). Special education students as tutors: A review and analysis. *RASE, 7*(4), 15–26.

Sailor, W., Anderson, J., Halvorsen, A., Doering, K., Filler, J., & Goetz, L. (1989). *The comprehensive local school.* Baltimore: Paul H. Brookes.

Stainback, W., & Stainback, S. (1982). Nonhandicapped students' perceptions of severely handicapped students. *Education and Training of the Mentally Retarded, 17,* 177–182.

Voeltz, L. (1980). Special friends in Hawaii. *Education Unlimited, 2,* 10–11.

For information about the PEP Handbook contact, California Transition Center, California State University San Bernardino, 5500 University Parkway, San Bernardino, CA 92407, 909/880-5495.

Children with Learning Disabilities

The passage of Public Law 94-142 in 1975 radically altered the nature of special education in the United States. Its mandate that all children be educated in the least restrictive environment (LRE) called into question not only the placement of children with learning disabilities in special schools or special classes, but also the accuracy of assessments of children as learning disabled (LD). The passage of amendments to this law in 1986 and 1990 and the renaming of the law as the Individuals with Disabilities Education Act (IDEA) furthered the movement away from special educational programs toward regular education classes, especially for children with mild disabilities.

Learning disabilities encompass a wide range of difficulties. There is no one accepted definition of an LD. To a large extent, exclusionary definitions help clarify the nature of LDs. They are not mental retardation. They are not deficiencies in any of the sensory systems (vision, hearing, taste, touch, smell, kinesthetics, vestibular sensation). They are not problems associated with health or physical mobility. They are not emotional or behavior disorders. They are not disabilities with speech or language. They can be assessed as true LDs if there is a discrepancy between the child's ability to learn and his or her actual learning.

IDEA's strong emphasis on a free and appropriate educational placement for every child with a disability has forced schools to be more cautious about all assessments and labeling. Increasing numbers of children are now being assessed as LD who once might have been labeled mentally retarded or disabled by speech, language, emotions, behavior, or one of the senses. A child with an LD can concurrently have a disability in any of these other areas, but if this occurs, both the LD and the other disability(ies) must be addressed in an individualized education program (IEP) designed especially for that unique child.

The two most commonly assessed learning disabilities are attention deficit hyperactive disorder (ADHD) and dyslexia. Both of these terms are often viewed as "umbrella" labels. They often encompass more disabilities than a strict use of their diagnostic criteria would merit.

LDs are usually diagnosed in the United States using the American Psychiatric Association's *Diagnostic and Statistical Manual of Mental Disorders* (4th edition). It divides LDs into academic skills disorders (reading disorders, mathematics disorders, and disorders of written expression) and ADHD. The National Joint Committee for Learning Disabilities (NJCLD) stresses that LDs are heterogeneous and separates specific problems related to the acquisition and use of listening, speaking, reading, writing, reasoning, or mathematical abilities.

The causes of LDs are unknown. Usually some central nervous system dysfunctions are believed to underlie the disabilities, even if their existence cannot be demonstrated with current diagnostic equipment. Other suspected causes include genetic inheritance and environmental factors such as poor nutrition or exposure to toxic agents.

This unit on learning disabilities addresses both the successes and frustrations of assessing and educating children with LDs. The first article in the section speaks to the question of who should be assessed as ADHD, and why. Almost half of all children with exceptionalities are labeled LD. A large percentage of these are assessed as ADHD. About 5 percent of U.S. children have labels of ADD (attention deficit disorder) or ADHD. Is this legitimate? The authors of the article question whether all hyperactivity is a result of central nervous system dysfunction and attention deficits. Are some ADHD children simply undersocialized? If the diagnosis is legitimate, should aberrant behavior be excused? The authors argue for ADHD education, including behavioral education and lessons on responsible conduct.

The next unit article advocates collaborative work between the school and the family to maximize the individualized educational program of each child with an LD. It presents a list of components to be designed into the school's instructional environment and another list of components to be encouraged as part of the support-for-learning environment at home. It also outlines a process for implementing school-home collaboration successfully.

The third essay on LDs appeals to the needs of regular education teachers who have students with heterogeneous forms of LD included in their classrooms. It discusses the specific requirement for adaptation of textbooks to maximize the IEPs for each student. Content area text-books can be modified in multiple ways, most of which are costly and time-consuming. Ruth Lynn Meese suggests simpler alternatives: altering instructional procedures and teaching students to help themselves in the reading process. She emphasizes finding the simplest adaptation that will meet the needs of both the LD student and the teacher.

The last article in this unit presents the mastery learning theory of Benjamin Bloom. Bloom studied individuals who had been very successful in a variety of fields, with special attention to what contributed to their early motivations and potential for achievement. He applied his findings to practical suggestions for enhancing the learning environment for children with special needs. This article summarizes some of Bloom's suggestions for mastery learning. It defines mastery learning, describes how it works, discusses Bloom's corrective activities, and outlines the process of instruction under mastery learning. Programs that have incorporated this strategy have documented impressive gains in student learning. Results of these programs are presented also.

Looking Ahead: Challenge Questions

What is attention deficit hyperactive disorder (ADHD)? Why do some experts believe it is being overdiagnosed in our contemporary culture? Discuss whether the diagnosis absolves a child from learning responsible behaviors.

How can learning environments be assessed to maximize the education of a child with LDs? If environments are found deficient, what interventions will mutually benefit the student, the parents, and the classroom teacher?

How can textbooks be adapted for students with LDs in inclusive educational settings? What else can be done to help students with LDs use content area textbooks?

What is mastery learning? How can it be incorporated into the regular education classroom environment to help at-risk students with LDs?

Is Attention Deficit Disorder Becoming A Desired Diagnosis?

RICHARD W. SMELTER, BRADLEY W. RASCH, JAN FLEMING, PAT NAZOS, AND SHARON BARANOWSKI

Professionals who serve children must exercise due caution when labeling children as suffering from ADD or ADHD, the authors warn. Likewise, those who work in schools should refrain from implying that such a diagnosis absolves the child from all responsibility for his or her behavior in the school setting.

IN CASE anyone has failed to notice, we live in a society that is rapidly being transformed. We all know about changes involving science, technology, and even human demographics. But many of us tend to overlook large changes taking place in the arena of social interaction, the often subtle manner in which individuals relate to

RICHARD W. SMELTER is principal of Manteno Elementary School and director of curriculum for Manteno Community Unit School District 5, Manteno, Ill. BRADLEY W. RASCH is a school psychologist in Marquardt School District 15, Glendale Heights, Ill., where JAN FLEMING is a teacher of the learning disabled and behaviorally disordered, PAT NAZOS is a school nurse, and SHARON BARANOWSKI is a school social worker.

one another. Sometimes, however, these interactions are not subtle at all and can lead to anxiety and conflict. When that happens, the disputants might resolve their own differences, or they might seek professional help.

We also live in an age in which people seem preoccupied with finding an underlying cause for everything, especially in the areas of medical science and human behavior. Year after year, the medical profession forges ahead, offering the public new hope, potential cures, and new diagnoses. Transplant this focus on underlying causes into psychology, and we have a corresponding focus on new rationales for behavior.

Over the past decade or so, rationales have become very important to our modern theories of social interaction. Almost overnight, or so it seems, terms such as "guilty," "responsible," "liable," "self-control," and a plethora of others have become passé, their use denoting the speaker as some type of ultraconservative reactionary. The use of some other terms, however, is on the rise; one hears more and more of "disorders," "afflictions," "dysfunctions," and "shared responsibility."

We suggest that in the current atmosphere of acceptance and explanation it is far easier to feel good about one's negative behaviors than it was 50 years ago. Doing a "bad" thing implies responsibility and guilt, as well as the need for some punitive action on the part of one's social peers. But having a "dysfunction" carries no such social stigma; instead, it evokes sympathy, feelings of compassion, and a genuine desire to help the transgressor.

From this, we suggest, comes the natural propensity of individuals to seek to escape from societal censure by claiming the role of victim as opposed to that of victimizer.

We can sense this change in the news every day. Bank robbers do not simply want an easy road to wealth; they are suffering from some type of compulsive behavior. Rapists are not sadistic opportunists with no sense of right and wrong; they have deep-seated doubts of their own sexuality, probably caused by some sort of abuse that we can ascribe to their parents or caretakers. We have seen the logical extension of all this: patricide and matricide and the hacking off of members of a spouse's body are acceptable behaviors, as long as you can document that you have been the recipient of abuse. The list of negative behaviors that we as a society hold people responsible for is shrinking year by year, while the list of negative behaviors we ascribe to "affliction" grows ever longer.

We are all susceptible to this need to avoid blame; it is not confined to the criminal element. Indeed, it stems from a natural, human desire to be well-thought-of. This is not lost on the children in our schools or on their parents. Like the rest of us, they read the papers and watch the news on television. They are aware that in the contemporary social landscape placing blame on others is becoming politically incorrect. This social change is particularly appealing when Johnny comes home with yet another detention slip or when Sally throws her book across the classroom after being told to sit still.

If misbehaviors persist, Johnny and

From *Phi Delta Kappan*, February 1996, pp. 429-432. © 1996 by Phi Delta Kappa, Inc. Reprinted by permission.

Sally will eventually be labeled "discipline problems" and will be suspended for insubordination. All too often such an action sparks a mad dash to the doctor's or psychologist's office in order to see if the verdict "discipline problem" can be tempered somewhat by the discovery of some hidden malady. Lo and behold, the child emerges from this visit with a diagnosis of Attention Deficit Disorder (ADD) or Attention Deficit Hyperactivity Disorder (ADHD).

Whose Needs Are Being Met?

The rush to label schoolchildren as suffering from ADD or ADHD has reached nearly epidemic proportions. Currently, between 3% and 5% of U.S. students (1.35 million to 2.25 million children) have been diagnosed as having ADD.[1] Is it time to investigate why this is happening? Perhaps there is more than one patient making the trip to the doctor's office: the child with the discipline problem *and* the child's parents. After all, there is no definitive test for the disorder and no agreed-upon etiology. There are no blood tests to be run, no x-rays to be taken. It would seem, at least on the surface, that people generally enjoy being told by their physician that they have a clean bill of health and have nothing wrong with them; why, then, do parents wish to come away with a diagnosis of ADD for their child?

The answer, of course, is that the diagnosis meets the needs of the parents more than it does those of the child. Almost at once, the parents feel relieved of some real or perceived pressures from educators, grandparents, and family friends. Having been unable to "control" the behavior of their children, they can now assign the control to Ritalin or some other drug. They are thus almost magically transformed into model parents. "I can't control you, son, but I have fulfilled my role as a parent by finding out what's 'wrong' with you."

School personnel often feed into parents' desire for a medical diagnosis by holding off on any contemplated "behaviorally disordered" classification and by directly or indirectly encouraging parents to seek "medication." In short, all the adults seem happy that some "dysfunction" has been discovered — exactly the opposite of what our normal reaction would be if our doctors discovered any other malady.

In addition, a parent may be less than effective in some areas of parenting. Denial of this shortcoming on the part of parents is natural and to be expected. These parents may seek the ADD diagnosis because it lets them off the hook, so to speak. It focuses attention on the child and on getting a prescription filled and thus demands no alteration of parents' behaviors or even any serious examination of them. The child now has a "medical condition" that has "nothing" to do with the child's upbringing. However, no parental introspection leads to no change in expectations or in conditions in the home. In this way, a diagnosis of ADD may not offset extremely negative conditions in a child's home that might best be served by the intervention of a social worker.

We are not questioning a physician's or psychologist's diagnosis of ADD. But we are suggesting that such a diagnosis be part of a total, wide-ranging investigation as to the conditions in which the child lives.

We have also noted that there is seldom, if ever, any reluctance on the part of the parents of ADD children to tell anyone within earshot that their child suffers from ADD. Sympathy is the usual reward for such utterances, and everyone likes sympathy. It is also a good statement to run by one's next-door neighbor the next time Bobby climbs over the fence and tramples the flower bed. We mustn't be too "hard" on the boy. After all, he's afflicted with ADD.

Popular magazines, television shows, and other media continually bombard parents with information on ADD. Many of these sources of information portray the disorder in such a way that virtually any youngster could be so classified. At one time or another, all children exhibit socially unacceptable behaviors; that is part of the maturation process. Anyone — even we professionals — can become hyperactive or distractible when forced to sit through a boring lecture or two. Going on a "shopping spree" is certainly a type of "impulsive" behavior. Yet when we give in to such an impulse, we don't immediately classify ourselves as ADD.

To further complicate the issue, parents with very low incomes generally qualify for increased Medicaid or Supplemental Social Security Income benefits if their child is diagnosed as afflicted with ADD or ADHD. Does this offer an additional incentive to have one's child diagnosed thus? Are there individuals in this world who would encourage their children to "act up" in order to obtain more money?

Who Else Is 'Off the Hook'?

Children are often more sophisticated than we give them credit for being. In this whole process, they are aware of what is going on. They are aware that the adults have found them difficult to handle. They are aware that conventional controls have not sufficed, and they are capable of working to sabotage the goals of those who would control them. Even if correctly labeled as ADD, the thinly veiled message that the child receives upon diagnosis is that he or she is somehow less responsible for his or her actions than the minute before the diagnosis was given.

Great care must be taken lest this awareness become an excuse for every disruption under the sun. The fact that a child is taking Ritalin does not afford him a license to affect other students at school in negative ways. A diagnosis of ADD is not an excuse to hit other children or to sneer at the teacher. Distractibility and hyperactivity are more closely associated with involuntary behaviors; waiting for another student after school in order to beat him up is most definitely a planned and voluntary action and should not be argued away by the aggressor's ADD classification.

Physicians and psychologists with ADD patients should exercise due caution when counseling the parents of afflicted children. Certain negative behaviors can be explained and even excused by a diagnosis of ADD, while others cannot. We must not lower our expectations for children because of the ADD diagnosis, or they will most certainly meet these lowered expectations. Lowered expectations can do great harm to a child. Given the fact that etiology and diagnosis are, at bottom, educated guesswork, this lowering of expectations for a child is not acceptable. Physicians should keep in close touch with the child's school in order to monitor the effect that the medication is having.

It is also unreasonable for school administrators to expect teachers to accommodate any type of aberrant behavior under the ADD umbrella. This distorts the ADD diagnosis, for ADD is not synonymous with "behaviorally disordered." Therefore, children who are classified as ADD may also be considered for a special education evaluation if it is thought that their behaviors are beyond the realm of the ADD or ADHD spectrum.

Classroom teachers have the added responsibility of conveying to ADD students that, now that they are receiving help with their affliction, expectations for their classroom behavior will rise. After all, that is the purpose of medicating an ADD child:

to bring that child into the circle of what is considered "normative" behavior. (And let us not forget that any sociologist can tell us that our definitions of "normative" often change dramatically from generation to generation.)

Adult counseling must also be a component of any ADD treatment. Children are experts at making excuses, and we do not want to give them the message that their classification as ADD or their being on medication affords them some added excuse whenever they get into trouble. We have to preserve the rights of the afflicted child's peers as well as the rights of the afflicted child. Physicians, psychologists, school officials, and teachers have an obligation to the child and the child's parents to explain that the classification of ADD or ADHD is not a license to get away with

al aberrations in children (and in adults, for that matter) seem to rise in societies whenever there is general disagreement as to whether or not people should be held responsible for socially unacceptable behaviors. In this context, it is interesting to note the experience of modern Russia when compared to that of the Soviet Union. Russian police report that Moscow is being infested by elements of organized crime, something it did not experience under the Communist Party dictatorship. We are not here advocating police states or schools run as such, but it is curious to note how many people formerly had more control over themselves.

Now we are faced with an affliction that is based mainly on conjecture and that is becoming increasingly popular in a society that is becoming increasingly conflict-

patient from paying the price for poor behavior at school.

We feel the need to conclude with a statement that is highly controversial and that, consequently, is seldom uttered: all children are not educable in the conventional sense, that is, within the walls of the school. Children are not interchangeable parts on a conveyor belt on a production line.

This does not necessarily mean that there is anything "wrong" with the children who do not conform; they may simply hate school. Adults tend to stick to tasks they dislike (sometimes for entire careers) because they have more self-control than children and because they deem the rewards worth the distaste of the job. Children, being children, shun that which they find boring or distasteful, and their attention starts

---

THE CLASSIFICATION OF ADD OR ADHD IS NOT A LICENSE TO GET AWAY WITH ANYTHING, BUT RATHER AN EXPLANATION THAT WILL LEAD TO LEGITIMATE HELP.

---

anything, but rather an explanation that may lead to legitimate help for the child in question.

An Edifice Built on Shifting Sand

We need to continually point out the facts that there is no concrete proof that the condition known as Attention Deficit Disorder even exists and that diagnosing the affliction remains more an art than a science. Moreover, the affliction seems to have no physiological basis. Although some correlation has been noted between fevers in early childhood and ADD, no causal connection has been proved, and the symptoms of ADD may be indicative of many other disorders, including a wide range of behavioral disorders.

When an etiology is not agreed on, when a definitive test is not available, and when only the efficacy of treatment seems to validate the initial diagnosis, then research typically abounds. But in the case of ADD, this has not held true. Clearly, more research is called for in order to determine whether a definitive test or series of tests is possible.

We also wish to point out that behavior-

ed with regard to differentiating between right and wrong. In an age in which discipline in the schools was strictly enforced, such afflictions or alleged afflictions were unknown. Children were, perhaps correctly and perhaps incorrectly, simply referred to as "discipline problems" and dealt with as such. It is probably safe to assume that, if we as a society continue to have problems deciding what one should or should not be held accountable for, we can expect to see a rise in the number of classified dysfunctions.

Simply stated, if excuses are courted and deliberately sought, then there will be no end of excuses available. This will be all the more lamentable if yet a further excuse for greater dysfunctional behavior lies embedded within each new excuse, leading to further diagnosis, more excuses, and so on.

To build a great medical/psychological edifice on such shifting sand seems ill-advised. It would behoove educators and the medical and psychological professions alike to downplay the diagnosis of ADD, the potential benefits of medication, and the insulation that such diagnosis affords the

to wander. In short, not every human action (or lack of action) that is not identical to the actions of the majority can be attributed to some affliction. Such different behavior might just be the product of human choice. We must, therefore, be somewhat skeptical about ADD-classified children who, when removed from the classroom setting, magically lose their ADD symptoms.

The professions that serve these children, from the school to the doctor's office, must exercise due caution when labeling children as suffering from ADD or ADHD. Likewise, those of us who work in schools should refrain from implying that the diagnosis of ADD or ADHD absolves the child from all responsibility for his or her behavior in the school setting. In the reality of the workaday world, the individual is expected to cope with society to a greater degree than society is expected to cope with the individual. Children with negative social behaviors get classified and treated; adults get fired or arrested.

1. *Children with ADD: A Shared Responsibility* (New York: Council for Exceptional Children, 1992), p. 7.

Identifying Students' Instructional Needs in the Context of Classroom and Home Environments

James E. Ysseldyke

Sandra Christenson

Joseph F. Kovaleski

James E. Ysseldyke (CEC Chapter #367), Professor, and **Sandra Christenson**, Associate Professor, Department of Educational Psychology, University of Minnesota, Minneapolis. **Joseph F. Kovaleski** (CEC Chapter #65), Director, Instructional Support System of Pennsylvania, East Petersburg, Pennsylvania.

Teachers refer students to intervention assistance teams or related services personnel because they want a change for the student, other students, and themselves. Quite simply, teachers want instructionally relevant information and helpful strategies for teaching the referred student. An excellent and scientific way to determine the referred student's needs is to ascertain whether specific instructional factors correlating with academic achievement are present or absent in the student's instructional environments. The key word in the previous sentence is "correlating." Teachers are not determinants of students' achievement, but they are facilitators of achievement.

Increasingly, teachers and diagnostic personnel are recognizing the importance of assessing student performance and learning outcomes in the context of classroom and home environments (cf. Ysseldyke & Christenson, 1987). Such recognition is leading to new approaches to identifying students' instructional needs. These approaches focus not only on assessing a learner and his or her characteristics but also on learning and the learning context. These new approaches are prescriptive rather than descriptive, and are used to specify the instructional needs of individual students in the context of the surroundings in which learning occurs.

The belief that diagnostic personnel ought to assess the learning environment in addition to assessing the learner is based on the belief that student performance in school is a function of an interaction between the student and the learning or instructional environment. Instructional environments are those contexts in which learning takes place: the schools and homes.

Ysseldyke and Christenson (1993) have developed a system, The Instructional Environment System-II (TIES-II), to provide a framework for assessing instructional environments. They identified 12 instructional and 5 home-support-for-learning components that are critical to consider when assessing learning environments (see Table 1). When instructional environments are assessed using systems like TIES-II, professionals are given essential information for preferral intervention, instructional consultation, intervention assistance, and collaborative intervention planning. Among other premises, such assessment practices are based on the assumptions that: (a) complex diagnostic procedures are not necessary to make a relevant instructional change and (b) assessment should be focused on collecting instructionally relevant information. Information necessary for instructional planning is gathered in classrooms (where problems and concerns typically arise) on variables that teachers can change (like skill level, participation, success rate, and task completion rate).

Steps in the collaborative intervention planning process are shown in

From *Teaching Exceptional Children*, Vol. 26, No. 3, Spring 1994, pp. 37-41. © 1994 by The Council for Exceptional Children. Reprinted by permission.

Figure 1. When teachers encounter difficulty with a student, they describe their concerns by differentiating between actual and desired student performance. They provide for the team's use of information on instructional needs. Team members gather information on the classroom instructional environment by observation, teacher interview, and student interview. Team members (teams must always include the teacher) meet to identify instructional needs and discuss how instruction will be planned, managed, delivered, and evaluated. Team members may also use a parent interview/survey form to document the presence and importance of specific home-support-for-learning components. They use the information obtained to identify ways to involve the student's parent(s) or guardian, and invite parents' assistance.

Team members brainstorm ways to intervene with students. Classroom-based assessment (e.g., curriculum-based assessment, observation, interviewing) is critical to framing the problem and developing the intervention. Practice has shown that brainstorming per se is a waste of time and can lead to ineffective interventions. More effective interventions are developed if the brainstorming is based on a good classroom-based assessment. For example, the classroom-based assessment might point to the need for the student to engage in more relevant practice. The brainstorming then is on alternative ways to provide relevant practice in school and at home, rather than on a broad-based listing of all known strategies. Team members share resources and discuss ways they can work together to implement the selected intervention(s). Throughout the intervention planning process the focus is on intervention and the use of instructionally relevant information to make a change. Questions and/or information tangential to the design of an intervention are temporarily tabled. This is essential to design an intervention expediently. Without this, it is easy for teams to discuss, discuss, and discuss—something the authors have referred to as "admiring the problem."

A Practical Example

The following case description is an example of the use of an analysis of the classroom environment to plan for a student's instructional needs. It assumes that the classroom teacher has access to an intervention assistance team (IAT) providing support in the regular classroom and a resource for use in planning interventions (e.g., Algozzine & Ysseldyke, 1992).

A Request for Assistance

Michael, a third grader, has been identified by his teacher as having difficulty in reading and classroom behavior. His teacher reports that Michael reads in a halting, word-by-word manner and does not connect discourse. He appears to be interested in getting through a passage without regard to its meaning and does not use reading as a skill to obtain information. The teacher is using the beginning 3rd-grade book with Michael and the other members of the lowest reading group. In addition, the teacher has noted that Michael leaves many assignments unfinished, bothers other students, is overactive, and has difficulty attending to task.

Michael's teacher has requested the help of her school's IAT. The IAT has been trained to assist teachers by closely analyzing the instructional environment in the classroom as well as the student's skills in meeting the demands of that setting. In the course of their work with each teacher, various team members thoroughly interview the teacher, the parents, and the student about the presenting problems. Other members conduct classroom observations and curriculum-based assessment in the area of concern. The IAT uses the Instructional Environment System (Ysseldyke & Christenson, 1993) as a framework to organize their work with each student. After selecting the interventions based on their assessment, the IAT assists the teacher in implementing the interventions and carefully monitors the student's response to determine their effectiveness.

In Michael's case, the IAT found Michael's classroom to have a highly positive learning climate. His teacher is lively and presents all of her lessons in an interesting and enthusiastic manner. While the instructional level was appropriate for most of the students in the class, Michael was unable to keep up. The kinds of feedback that worked with other students in the class did not result in improved performance for Michael. And, the team learned that Michael's parents are supportive but are bewildered by what to do about Michael's school problems. They report that Michael is happy at home and has lots of friends in the neighborhood. However, nightly homework time is a stressful event for Michael and his parents.

As a result of their work with Michael, his teacher, and his parents, the IAT has identified three areas of support for Michael: instructional match, evaluation and feedback, and home support. Each has direct relation to instructional interventions that are appropriate.

Instructional Match

Using curriculum-based assessment of Michael's reading, the IATs found that his average oral reading fluency in third-grade material was 16 words per minute (wpm) with seven errors per minute (epm), or about 70% known material. According to curriculum-based assessment guidelines (e.g., Gickling & Thompson, 1985; Shinn, 1989), Michael was working at a frustrational level in his material. He hesitated over many words and displayed no strategies to "unlock" unknown words. He understood little of what he read. While the other students were reading, Michael looked around the room. When presented with other language arts materials based on the third-grade reader (e.g., seatwork), Michael was on task about 40% of the time and finished only about 25% of the work. Interestingly, the IAT found that during math activities Michael's on-task behavior was around 80% and his task completion 95%. Michael was assessed to be working at an instructional level in math.

The IAT hypothesized that Michael's reading and behavior problems could be traced to his frustration in reading, in

Table 1. Instructional-Environment and Home-Support-for-Learning Components

Instructional-Environment Components

Instructional Match: The student's needs are assessed accurately, and instruction is matched appropriately to the results of the instructional diagnosis.

Teacher Expectations: There are realistic, yet high expectations for both the amount and accuracy of work to be completed by the student, and these are communicated clearly to the student.

Classroom Environment: The classroom management techniques used are effective for this student; there is a positive, supportive classroom atmosphere; and time is used productively.

Instructional Presentation: Instruction is presented in a clear and effective manner; directions contain sufficient information for this student to understand what kinds of behaviors or skills are to be demonstrated; and the student's understanding is checked.

Cognitive Emphasis: Thinking skills and learning strategies for completing assignments are communicated explicitly to the student.

Motivational Strategies: Effective strategies for heightening student interest and effort are used with the student.

Relevant Practice: The student is given adequate opportunity to practice with appropriate materials and a high success rate. Classroom tasks are clearly important to achieving instructional goals.

Informed Feedback: The student receives relatively immediate and specific information on his or her performance or behavior; when the student makes mistakes, correction is provided.

Academic Engaged Time: The student is actively engaged in responding to academic content; the teacher monitors the extent to which the student is actively engaged and redirects the student when the student is unengaged.

Adaptive Instruction: The curriculum is modified within reason to accommodate the student's unique and specific instructional needs.

Progress Evaluation: There is direct, frequent measurement of the student's progress toward completion of instructional objectives; data on the student's performance and progress are used to plan future instruction.

Student Understanding: The student demonstrates an accurate understanding of what is to be done in the classroom.

Home-Support-for-Learning Components

Expectations and Attributions: High, realistic expectations about school work are communicated to the child, and the value of effort and working hard in school is emphasized.

Discipline Orientation: There is an authoritative, not permissive or authoritarian, approach to discipline and the child is monitored and supervised by adults.

Home Effective Environment: The parent-child relationship is generally positive and supportive.

Parent Participation: There is an educative home environment, and others participate in the child's schooling, at home and/or at school.

Structure for Learning: Organization and daily routines facilitate the completion of schoolwork and the child's academic learning is supported.

Note: Adapted from *The Instructional Environment System–II* by J. Ysseldyke and S. L. Christenson, 1993, Longmont, CO: Sopris West. Copyright 1993. Reprinted by permission.

that his behavior problems were not as evident in other subjects nor in the home. In consultation with the classroom teacher, the IAT planned to implement strategies for improving Michael's pool of known words through a drill sandwich technique (Gickling & Thompson, 1985; Shapiro, 1992). This technique allows for a systematic presentation of new words along with a structured procedure to ensure adequate repetitions of new learnings. Relevant practice of this newly learned material would be provided by reading the new words in a variety of print contexts. Michael would also be taught to self-monitor his comprehension of reading passages as a further check on passage difficulty. The IAT also assisted his teacher in adapting other tasks (e.g., Huck, Myers, & Wilson, 1989) to maximize engaged time by ensuring that all materials were at his instructional level.

Ongoing Monitoring and Feedback

Once the classroom-based interventions were planned, it became critical to monitor Michael's progress throughout the intervention period. With the assistance of the IAT, Michael's teacher conducted biweekly checks of Michael's acquisition of new words, his retention of learned words, his oral reading fluency, and his comprehension or understanding of the material. This information was fed back to Michael who maintained a chart of his gains. Michael's teacher found that having Michael keep track of his progress was highly motivating to him. He seemed to take pride in his gradual achievement of higher level of performance. As Michael displayed progress, his teacher set increasingly higher goals for him to achieve.

Home Support

The IAT worked closely with Michael's parents throughout the duration of the intervention so that strategies implemented in school could be reinforced at home. Michael's teacher and other team members advised his parents on how to structure Michael's homework time, and taught them the drill sandwich technique to help Michael practice his newly learned words. Particular emphasis was given to avoiding teaching new

Figure 1. The collaborative intervention planning process

1. A teacher or teachers describe their concern(s), differentiating between actual and desired student performance.	*Teacher(s) Describe Concern(s)*
2. Team members or the education professional share information with the teacher(s) about Instructional Environment Components, discussing how instruction will be planned, managed, delivered, and evaluated for the individual student.	*Share Information About Instructional Environment Components*
3. Team members arrive at a consensus about the student's instructional needs.	*Consensus About Needs*
4. Team members describe Home-Support-for-Learning Components	*Home-Support-for-Learning Components*
5. Team members identify ways to involve the student's parent(s) or guardian and invite parents' assistance.	*Invite Parent(s) Assistance*
6. Team members brainstorm ideas/options for interventions.	*Brainstorm Ideas/Options*
7. An intervention (or interventions) is (are) selected.	*Intervention(s) Selected*
8. Team members share resources, discussing ways they can work together to implement the selected intervention(s).	*Share Resources*
9. Teacher/parent questions not directly relevant to intervention are then discussed.	*Teacher/Parent Questions Discussed*

Note: Adapted from *The Instructional Environment System-II* by J. Ysseldyke and S. L. Christenson, 1993, Longmont, CO: Sopris West. Copyright 1993. Reprinted by permission.

tive instructional program for a student at risk of school failure. If the IAT members had limited their focus to variables related to student characteristics (e.g., his ability or background), they would not have designed an intervention that precisely met Michael's needs in this particular classroom. They may also have missed an opportunity to help Michael reach his optimal performance level.

It is worth noting that assessing the instructional environment facilitates a close match between the student's needs and the characteristics of the teacher and the classroom. The interventions developed through this approach will, therefore, be different for different students and different classrooms. In approaching each classroom setting, a careful assessment of the environment as well as the student's skills is needed. This increases the likelihood that an intervention appropriate for that classroom teacher as well as for that student will be developed. The use of this approach focuses on enabling the teacher and parents to be better facilitators of student engagement and outcomes.

concepts or reteaching old ones at home, which typically led to frustration for both Michael and his parents. The IAT also guided the family in the selection of easy reading material so that at home Michael could begin learning to read for pleasure.

Resolution

As the intervention proceeded, Michael began to make slow, but steady gains in his reading skills. As he progressed through more difficult material, he began to perceive himself as a competent reader. Providing tasks appropriate to his instructional level in both reading

and language arts led to a corresponding decrease in inattention and off-task behavior. His teacher indicated that the gap between actual and desired performance decreased. Michael's parents continued their close coordination of school and homework with the classroom teacher and were very gratified by Michael's progress.

Conclusion

This example of a common school situation highlights the usefulness of assessing the instructional environment when developing and implementing an effec-

References

Algozzine, B., & Ysseldyke, J. (1992). *Strategies and tactics for effective instruction.* Longmont, CO: Sopris West.

Gickling, E. E., & Thompson, V. P. (1985). A personal view of curriculum-based assessment. *Exceptional Children, 52,* 205-218.

Huck, R., Myers, R., & Wilson, J. (1989). *ADAPT: A developmental activity program for teachers* (2nd ed.). Pittsburgh: Allegheny Intermediate Unit.

Shapiro, E. S. (1992). Use of Gickling's model of curriculum-based assessment to improve reading in elementary age students. *School Psychology Review, 21,* 168-176.

Shinn, M. R. (1989). *Curriculum-based measurement: Assessing special children.* New York: Guilford.

Ysseldyke, J., & Christenson, S. L. (1987). *The instructional environment scale.* Austin, TX: Pro-Ed.

Ysseldyke J., & Christenson, S. L. (1993). *The instructional environment system-II (TIES-II).* Longmont, CO: Sopris West.

Adapting Textbooks for Children with Learning Disabilities in Mainstreamed Classrooms

Ruth Lyn Meese

Ruth Lyn Meese *(CEC Chapter #955) is an Assistant Professor of Special Education, Department of Education, Special Education, and Social Work, Longwood College, Farmville, Virginia.*

Cooperative efforts between special education and regular education teachers are vital if students with learning disabilities are to be successful in mainstreamed classes in which the textbook is the primary means for disseminating information.

Adapting textbooks to meet the needs of these students can be a complex task. For example, some children with learning disabilities have attentional deficits affecting their ability to differentiate what information they should attend to (Hallahan & Kauffman, 1988). The cluttered appearance of many textbooks complicates the decision as to what does or does not warrant attention. Other children are reading at a level far below that of the textbook. Their reading problems are compounded by the complex sentence and organizational structures, difficult vocabulary, and concept density typically found in expository text material (Carnine, Silbert, & Kameenui, 1990). Still other students may lack efficient strategies to comprehend and remember textbook reading assignments (Seidenberg, 1989).

Special education teachers do not have the time to rewrite textbooks. They can, however, provide adaptations based on the needs of the individual student, the demands of the textbook, and the needs of the regular classroom teacher (Margolis & McGettigan, 1988; Martens, Peterson, Witt, & Cirone, 1986).

A student listens to tape-recorded text in which the teacher has stopped periodically to summarize important information.

This article describes ways in which special educators can help students get the most from content area textbooks.

Modifying the Textbook

Modification usually involves highlighting information in the textbook, tape recording the textbook, or providing the student with a high-interest/low-vocab- ulary alternative—all of which can be both time consuming and costly. Since little research exists to document the effectiveness of highlighting, the focus here is on the other two alternatives.

Tape Recording the Text

Teachers can ask student or adult volunteer groups to prepare tape-recorded versions of textbooks (Smith &

Smith, 1985). Recorded text segments should be kept clear and short. On the tape, a teacher may also provide an overview of the selection before reading begins (Bos & Vaughn, 1988); give clear signals to the reader for page location; and stop periodically in order to summarize important information or ask the student to respond to questions (Salend, 1990). Tapes of textbooks commonly used in content classes are available free of charge, or for a small fee, from organizations such as Recordings for the Blind, 214 East 58th, New York, NY 10022.

Using High-Interest/Low-Vocabulary Materials

Special educators occasionally must provide students who have extremely poor reading skills with high-interest/low-vocabulary alternatives to their assigned reading selections. Care must be taken to discuss possible alternatives with the regular classroom teacher so that proper content coverage and mastery can be ensured. Excellent lists of commercially available materials can be found in Mercer and Mercer (1989) and Wood (1989).

Altering Instructional Procedures

Many students with learning disabilities can be helped to comprehend textbook materials by relatively minor changes in the teacher's instructional procedures. Usually, these alterations increase the level of teacher-directed instruction and/or the level of active student involvement with the text.

Teaching Textbook Structure

Students must use expository text and organizational structure to find and recall information from their textbooks (Seidenberg, 1989). Unfortunately, this is often problematic for a student with learning disabilities. Therefore, the special educator must directly teach these structures (e.g., "cues" for important information such as headings, subheadings, differing print, or introductory and summary paragraphs), particularly when the information is complex and the textbooks or concepts are new (Carnine et al., 1990). The teacher can focus attention on important features of the text by beginning each reading assignment with a systematic overview of the material. Archer and Gleason (1989) have suggested the following teacher-directed chapter warm-up procedure:

1. Read the chapter title and introduction.
2. Read the headings and subheadings.
3. Read the chapter summary.
4. Read any questions at the end of the chapter.
5. Tell what the chapter will talk about.

Previewing

To preview a reading selection before independent study, the teacher or a peer simply reads aloud the assigned passages (Salend & Nowak, 1988). Previewing is a simple procedure that can readily be combined with other techniques to increase active student involvement during reading. Examples of such techniques are guided questioning by the teacher after short textbook segments are read aloud and reciprocal teaching, in which students take turns assuming the role of teacher (see Palincsar & Brown, 1986).

Providing Advance Organizers

Advance organizers alert students to important information in the reading assignment (Darch & Gersten, 1986). For example, *graphic organizers* are diagrams depicting superordinate and subordinate relationships from the text and can provide students with a visual overview of the reading material before actual reading begins (Horton, Lovitt, & Bergerud, 1990). Similarly, teachers may provide students with a sequential partial outline of critical information, to be completed during the reading process (Bos & Vaughn, 1988). Pairing question numbers from a study guide or from blanks on a partial outline with page numbers on which the information can be found may also help students locate essential information (Wood, 1989).

In order to demonstrate the relationship between textbook questions and the structure of the text, students may be taught to rephrase headings, subheadings, or vocabulary words as questions to be answered during reading. For example, from the heading "The Greek Peninsula," numerous "What," "Where," "How," and "Why" questions might be generated (e.g., "What did the Greek Peninsula look like?"). After students generate their questions, the teacher asks them to state what types of information the answers will contain (e.g., name, date, location, event, cause, etc.). Archer and Gleason (1989) provided a similar technique for helping students understand the relationship between textbook questions and answers:

1. Read each question carefully.
2. Change the question into a part of the answer (e.g., "How did the location of the Greek Peninsula affect the daily lives of its citizens?" becomes "The Greek Peninsula affected the daily lives of its citizens by...").
3. Find the part of the chapter that talks about the topic.
4. Read the section to find the answer.
5. Complete the answer to the question.

Having students generate questions to be answered during reading improves their comprehension of the material (Swicegood & Parsons, 1989; Wong, 1985). Providing them with a structured overview in combination with self-generated questions is even more effective in facilitating comprehension (Billingsley & Wildman, 1988).

Preteaching Critical Vocabulary

Some teachers set up rotating committees of students to seek out and define words that are likely to be troublesome to classmates. Others suggest the use of mnemonic devices to aid students in recalling important vocabulary and concepts (Mastropieri & Scruggs, 1987).

Teaching Textbook Reading Strategies

The following strategies can help students with learning disabilities become active participants in the learning process (Schumaker, Deshler, & Ellis, 1986). Instead of passively reading textbooks, students are taught ways to ask questions, formulate answers, verbally rehearse important information, and monitor their comprehension.

Self-Questioning

Wong, Perry, and Sawatsky (1986, pp. 25–40) described a self-questioning strategy used in social studies by students with learning disabilities. In this strategy, students are taught to ask themselves the following questions:

1. In this paragraph, is there anything I don't understand?
2. In this paragraph, what's the main idea sentence? Let me underline it.
3. Let me summarize the paragraph. To summarize I rewrite the main idea sentence and add important details.
4. Does my summary statement link up with the subheading?
5. When I have summary statements for a whole subsection (paragraphs under a subheading):
   a. Let me review my summary statements for the whole subsection.
   b. Do my summary statements link up with one another?
   c. Do they all link up with the subheading?
6. At the end of a reading assignment, can I see all the themes here? If yes, let me predict the teacher's test question. If no, go back to step 4 (Wong et al., 1986).

Active Reading

Archer and Gleason (1989) have presented a simple strategy, called *active reading*, to involve students in verbally rehearsing and monitoring their comprehension of textbook passages. During active reading, the student proceeds paragraph by paragraph using the following steps:

1. Read a paragraph. Think about the topic and about the important details.
2. Cover the material.
3. Recite. Tell yourself what you have read. Say the topic and the important details in your own words.
4. Check yourself. If you forgot something important, start again.

Study Cards

Students can place each important new vocabulary word on one side of an index card, with the definition and page number on the reverse (Wood, 1989). The cards are filed by chapter for continuing review and study.

Rooney (1988) detailed an excellent system for producing study cards. Students are asked to:

1. Read the subtitle and the paragraphs under the subtitle. Write on separate index cards all names of people or places, and important numbers or terms.
2. Go back to the subtitle and turn it into a test question. Write the question on one side of an index card and the answer on the other side.
3. Repeat this procedure to produce a set of study cards containing all the main ideas and important details from the reading.
4. Look at each card. Ask yourself, "How are the details related to the material?" Try to answer the main idea questions from memory.

Conclusion

Adapting a textbook does not mean rewriting the text. Altering instructional procedures and/or teaching students strategies to help themselves become more involved participants in the reading process are effective ways to help them use content area textbooks. The following common-sense guidelines can be useful to special educators collaborating with regular classroom teachers in this endeavor:

1. Examine the textbook for vocabulary and concept density and difficulty and for clear organizational structures.
2. Talk to the student regarding his or her perceived difficulties and needs. Ask the student to locate parts of the textbook, to read aloud from the text, and to answer questions about the passage.
3. Talk with the regular classroom teacher regarding his or her perceived needs. Discuss critical knowledge and skills to be mastered.
4. Choose the simplest adaptation that is most likely to meet the needs of both the student and the teacher.
5. Monitor carefully and make changes as necessary.

References

Archer, A., & Gleason, M. (1989). *Skills for school success.* Boston: Curriculum Associates.

Billingsley, B. S., & Wildman, T. M. (1988). The effects of prereading activities on the comprehension monitoring of learning disabled adolescents. *Learning Disabilities Research, 4,* 36-44.

Bos, C. S., & Vaughn, S. (1988). *Strategies for teaching students with learning and behavior problems.* Boston: Allyn and Bacon.

Carnine, D., Silbert, J., & Kameenui, E. J. (1990). *Direct instruction reading* (2nd ed.). Columbus, OH: Merrill.

Darch, C., & Gersten, R. (1986). Direction setting activities in reading comprehension: A comparison of two approaches. *Learning Disability Quarterly, 9,* 235-243.

Hallahan, D. P., & Kauffman, J. M. (1988). *Exceptional children.* Englewood Cliffs, NJ: Prentice-Hall.

Horton, S. V., Lovitt, T. C., & Bergerud, D. (1990). The effectiveness of graphic organizers for three classifications of secondary students in content area classes. *Journal of Learning Disabilities, 23,* 12-22.

Margolis, H., & McGettigan, J. (1988). Managing resistance to instructional modifications in mainstreamed environments. *Remedial and Special Education, 9,* 15-21.

Martens, B. K., Peterson, R. L., Witt, J. C., & Cirone, S. (1986). Teacher perceptions of school-based interventions. *Exceptional Children, 53,* 213-223.

Mastropieri, M. A., & Scruggs, T. E. (1987). *Effective instruction for special education.* Boston: College-Hill.

Mercer, C. D., & Mercer, A. R. (1989). *Teaching students with learning problems* (3rd ed.). Columbus, OH: Merrill.

Palincsar, A., & Brown, A. (1986). Interactive teaching to promote independent learning from text. *The Reading Teacher, 39,* 771-777.

Rooney, K. (1988). *Independent strategies for efficient study.* Richmond, VA: J. R. Enterprises.

Salend, S. J. (1990). *Effective mainstreaming.* New York: Macmillan.

Salend, S. J., & Nowak, M. R. (1988). Effects of peer previewing on LD students oral reading skills. *Learning Disability Quarterly, 11,* 47-54.

Schumaker, J. B., Deshler, D. D., & Ellis, E. S. (1986). Intervention issues related to the education of LD adolescents. In B. K. Wong & J. Torgeson (Eds.), *Psychological and educational perspectives in learning disabilities.* New York: Academic Press.

Seidenberg, P. L. (1989). Relating text-processing research to reading and writing instruction for learning disabled students. *Learning Disabilities Focus, 5,* 4-12.

Smith, G., & Smith, D. (1985). A mainstreaming program that really works. *Journal of Learning Disabilities, 18,* 369-372.

Swicegood, P. R., & Parsons, J. L. (1989). Better questions and answers equal success. *TEACHING Exceptional Children, 21*(3), 4-8.

Wong, B. Y. L. (1985). Self-questioning instructional research: A review. *Review of Educational Research, 55,* 227-268.

Wong, B. Y. L., Wong, R., Perry, N., & Sawatsky, D. (1986). The efficacy of a self-questioning summarization strategy for use by underachievers and learning disabled adolescents in social studies. *Learning Disabilities Focus, 2,* 20-35.

Wood, J. W. (1989). *Mainstreaming: A practical approach for teachers.* Columbus, OH: Merrill.

MASTERY LEARNING

IN THE REGULAR CLASSROOM : HELP FOR AT-RISK STUDENTS WITH LEARNING DISABILITIES

THOMAS R. GUSKEY · PERRY D. PASSARO · WAYNE WHEELER

One of the major goals of educational intervention programs for students with mild disabilities and those who are at risk is to offer a least restrictive learning environment (Roddy, 1984). Although this has been interpreted in a variety of ways, often it means mainstreaming, or the placement of such students in a regular classroom (Brickel & Brickel, 1986; National Longitudinal Transition Study (NLTS), 1990; U.S. Department of Education, 1990). In some cases students are mainstreamed for the entire school day. More often, however, they spend only part of the school day in regular classes and the rest of the time in a special education class (NLTS, 1990).

During the time students are in the special education setting, they typically receive individualized instruction provided by a special educator. This individualized attention allows them to learn at their own pace, provides them with immediate feedback on their learning progress, and offers specific help in correcting learning errors. Many educators now realize that it is possible to provide students at all grade levels with similar individualized assistance within regular education classes. The vehicle used to accomplish this is a process known as *mastery learning*.

Mastery Learning Theory

In the middle 1960s, Benjamin S. Bloom began a series of investigations on how the most powerful aspects of individualized instruction might be adapted to improve student learning in group-based classrooms. He noted that while different students learn at different rates, *all* can learn well if provided with the necessary time and proper learning conditions. Bloom (1968) believed that under these more appropriate learning conditions, 80% or more of students could reach the same high level of achievement typically attained by only the top 20% of students under more traditional forms of instruction.

To provide these more appropriate learning conditions, Bloom (1971) recommended that the material to be learned be divided first into instructional units, similar to the way the chapters are organized in a course textbook. Following a teacher's initial instruction in each unit, a *formative* evaluation or quiz is administered, not as part of the grading process, but to provide feedback to both the students and the teacher about what material was learned well and what was not. Special *corrective* activities are then offered to students who require additional time and practice to learn the material. For those who have learned the material well, special *enrichment* activities are planned to give them opportunities to strengthen and extend their learning. Following the corrective work, a second formative evaluation is administered to verify student success. Figure 1 illustrates this mastery learning process.

Typically, corrective activities are made specific to each item or part of the test so that each student needs to work on only those concepts or skills that he or she has not yet mastered. Thus, the results from the formative assessment provide the student with a specific prescription for what more needs to be done to master the unit's learning objectives. The activities are designed to present the material differently and involve the student in alternative approaches to learning the material. The corrections may be worked on with the teacher, with peers in cooperative learning teams, or by the student independently.

The formative assessment process, combined with systematic correction of individual learning difficulties, provides each student with a more appropriate quality of instruction than is possible under more traditional approaches to classroom teach-

From *Teaching Exceptional Children*, Vol. 27, No. 2, Winter 1995, pp. 15-18. © 1995 by The Council for Exceptional Children. Reprinted by permission.

"THIS IS SO MUCH BETTER FOR THE STUDENT AND ME."

Figure 1. The process of instruction under mastery learning.

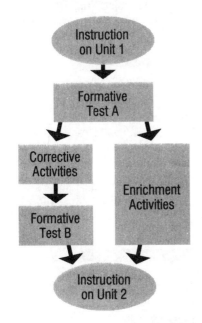

ing. Using this approach, according to Bloom (1976), virtually all students could master the subject material.

Practical Implications

Programs incorporating mastery learning strategies have been initiated in school systems across the United States, resulting in impressive gains in student learning. Research syntheses of mastery learning studies using meta-analysis (a statistical technique that describes the results of tests of similar hypotheses across many studies) report effects of nearly one standard deviation at some grade levels (Guskey & Pigott, 1988; Kulik, Kulik, & Bangert-Downs, 1990). This means that the average student in a mastery learning class achieves at a level attained by only the top 15% of students in classes taught by more traditional methods.

Improvements in student learning resulting from the implementation of mastery learning approaches have not been restricted to regular education settings. Significant improvement has also been noted in the achievement of students with learning disabilities or behavior disorders (Kulik, & Kulik, 1986; Kulik, Kulik, & Bangert-Downs, 1990; Walberg, 1990; Ward, 1987). This research evidence demonstrates that students with disabilities often experience greater achievement gains in mastery learning classes than do their more able counterparts in traditionally taught classrooms.

One highly successful mastery learning program that is meeting the individual needs of students with disabilities in regular classrooms is at the Thorpe-Gordon Elementary School in Jefferson City, Missouri. Beginning in 1987, the staff of the Thorpe-Gordon School voluntarily committed to implementing the ideas and techniques of mastery learning. In this effort they were assisted by staff members from the Missouri State Department of Education. The goal of the program was not only to ensure each student's mastery of the learner outcomes presented in the regular classroom, but also to help students in (a) self-concept, (b) attitude toward learning experiences, (c) peer relationships, (d) on-task behaviors, (e) learning strategies, and (f) independence in their own learning experiences (Ciolli, Allen, & Wheeler, n.d.).

As part of Thorpe-Gordon's improvement effort, 40 4th-,5th-, and 6th-grade students who had mild disabilities or were considered at risk for disabilities were mainstreamed into regular classrooms for the entire school day. As is typical in most states, students in Missouri who are suspected of having a learning disability undergo a comprehensive evaluation to determine their eligibility for special education services. This evaluation includes administration of a variety of standardized developmental, intellectual, academic, and psychomotor tests. All students identified as at risk for or having mild to moderate learning disabilities are considered for this program. In the case of students eligible for special education services, however, the final placement determination is based on the recommendation of the student's individualized education program (IEP) committee.

Thorpe-Gordon students recommended for this program were placed into regular classes where mastery learning was the primary instructional method for the entire school day. Within these classes, the regular classroom teacher provided initial instruction and then administered the first formative assessment. For those students who did not attain mastery on the first formative assessment (usually 80%–90% correct), a learning disabilities teacher provided corrective instruction within the regular classroom. Students who reached mastery on the first formative assessment worked with the regular classroom teacher on special enrichment activities. This team teaching model provides individualized assistance for students who need additional time and support. It also provides regular classroom teachers with a model for specific methods of correcting learning difficulties.

Program Results

Evidence from a variety of sources has been used to evaluate the effectiveness of the mastery learning program at the Thorpe-Gordon school. One source is students' performance on annual statewide achievement tests known as the Missouri Mastery Achievement Test (MMAT). The first year the MMAT were administered, students' scores were grouped into quintiles. That is, the range of test scores were divided into five intervals, each containing approximately 20% of the scores.

Results in subsequent years were then compared to these original score interval quintiles as a means of documenting progress.

Students with mild disabilities or those identified as being at risk typically score in the lower quintiles of the MMAT. If the mastery learning program at Thorpe-Gordon School was working well then the number of students scoring in these lower quintiles should have decreased as these students achieved greater learning success.

This is precisely what has happened. The effect of the mastery learning program on students who had been low performers is substantial. When the program began in 1987, 40% of Thorpe-Gordon students were in the bottom two quintiles, which is comparable to the statewide totals. By 1989, however, only 10% of the students scored in the bottom quintiles. Furthermore, 70% to 90% of the Thorpe-Gordon students scored in the top two quintiles, with 50% to 75% scoring in the highest quintile, depending upon subject area. A comparison of students with learning disabilities in the Thorpe-Gordon program to their peers in traditional pullout programs on the MMAT reveals that from 1988 to 1989 Thorpe-Gordon students' MMAT scores increased by 13.64% (more than a one-standard-deviation increase), while students with disabilities placed in traditional resource programs gained only 3.89%.

Another source of data used to evaluate the program has been student grades. Here again the results are impressive. Each year since 1987, 75% of the students using mastery learning in inclusive classes attained a grade of C or better in all academic areas within the regular education curriculum.

The comments offered by teachers involved in the program have also been overwhelmingly positive. One of the regular classroom teachers at Thorpe-Gordon who taught a class including several students with disabilities and students who were at risk summarized her feelings about the program by saying, "This is so much better for the students and me. It has been really helpful in meeting particular students' needs within the class. It is wonderful!"

School administrators at Thorpe-Gor-

don have reported positive impressions as well. Several mentioned that the mastery learning process enabled their regular class teachers to gain information on learning styles and strategies, while their special educators learned more about the school curriculum and regular classroom procedures. As a result, both groups were more effective as teachers.

Parents have also been highly supportive. One parent expressed her perceptions as follows:

> I think this program has helped my son's attitude about the stigma of being in special education. His self-confidence has improved and he now comments about the fact that mastery learning feels like having another teacher, yet not a "special" teacher, and this is acceptable… This program works: Take a look at his grades—there's the proof.

Perhaps most important, the students themselves have expressed positive feelings about the change and the subsequent improvements in their academic performance. Of the students mainstreamed in this program, 80% stated that they prefer the mastery learning/mainstreaming model to the resource room programs in which they had participated previously.

Conclusion

With the inclusive schools movement calling for better cooperation between regular and special education (Will, 1986), many teachers are struggling to provide more effective instruction for all of the students they teach. Most would like to spend a greater portion of their time offering individualized instruction to students who are performing poorly, but the demands of large-group-based classrooms make it impossible or impractical to do so. These teachers would also like to help more of their students be successful in learning and gain the many benefits of that success.

Mastery learning offers a means by which these goals can be accomplished. Teachers can generally implement mastery learning with relatively minor changes in their teaching procedures. Although it does not make teaching any easier for them, it offers them a valuable tool to help many more of their students

"I THINK THIS PROGRAM HAS HELPED MY SON'S ATTITUDE ABOUT THE STIGMA OF BEING IN SPECIAL EDUCATION."

Mastery Learning Program percent of students in lower quintiles

1987 Before Mastery Learning

40%

0   100

1989 After Mastery Learning

10%

0   100

Increase in MMAT test scores of students with disabilities, 1988-1989

Mastery Learning program students

13.64%

Traditional resource program students

3.89%

learn well (Guskey, 1985). In addition, teachers who adopt mastery learning generally find that their students become more involved in the learning process, attendance rates increase, behavior problems are reduced, and students feel better about learning and about themselves as learners. As success fosters success, this increased confidence is likely to be carried over to future learning situations.

Teachers also report that the use of mastery learning helps decrease unhealthy competition among students. School becomes a place where *all* students, regardless of disabilities, work together with the teacher and all can master the material. In addition, teachers who use mastery learning often describe how it renews their enthusiasm for teaching, provides an effective way to deal with difficult educational problems, and serves to increase their professional pride (Guskey, 1985).

Thus, mastery learning instructional strategies provide a useful and purposeful technique for accomplishing an inclusive environment, as well as providing special education services in the least restrictive environment. By using the correction and enrichment process in mastery learning, teachers can provide more students with an individualized approach to instruction while dealing with real-world classroom constraints.

References

Baker, O., King, R., & Wulf, K. M. (April, 1989). *The Missouri comprehensive statewide project for improving student achievement.* Paper presented at the annual meeting of the American Educational Research Association, Boston, MA.

Bloom, B. S. (1968). Learning for mastery. *Evaluation Comment* (UCLA-CSIEP), *1*(2), 1–12.

Bloom, B. S. (1971). Mastery learning. In J. H. Block (Ed.), *Mastery learning: Theory and practice.* New York: Holt, Rinehart and Winston.

Bloom, B. S. (1976). *Human characteristics and school learning.* New York: McGraw-Hill.

Brickel, W. E., & Brickel, D. D. (1986). Effective schools, classrooms, and instruction: Implications for special education. *Exceptional Children, 52,* 489–500.

Ciolli, J., Allen, A., & Wheeler, W. (n.d.) *Rationale for class within a class.* Unpublished manuscript. Jefferson City, MO: Jefferson City Schools.

Guskey, T. R. (1985). *Implementing mastery learning.* Belmont, CA: Wadsworth.

Guskey, T. R., & Pigott, T. D. (1988). Research on group based mastery learning programs: A meta-analysis. *Journal of Educational Research, 81*(4), 197–216.

Guskey, T. R., Passaro, P. D., & Wheeler, W. (1990). *Missouri's Thorpe-Gordon School: A model for school improvement.* Manuscript in progress.

Kulik, C. L., Kulik, J. A., & Bangert-Downs, R. L. (1990). The effectiveness of mastery learning programs: A meta-analysis. *Review of Educational Research, 60*(2), 265–299.

Kulik, J. A., & Kulik, C. L. (1986). Mastery testing and student learning. *Journal of Educational Technology Systems, 15,* 325–345.

National Longitudinal Transition Study (NLTS). (1990). *The school programs and school performance of secondary students classified as learning disabled: Findings from the National Longitudinal Transition Study of special education students.* Menlo Park, CA: SRI International.

Roddy, E. A. (1984). When are the resource rooms going to share in the declining enrollment trend? *Journal of Learning Disabilities, 17*(5), 279–281.

U.S. Department of Education. (1990). *Twelfth annual report to Congress on the implementation of the Education of the Handicapped Act.* Washington, DC: U.S. Department of Education.

Walberg, H. J. (1990). Productive teaching and instruction: Assessing the knowledge base. *Phi Delta Kappan,* 470–478.

Ward, J. (1987). *Educating children with special needs in regular classrooms: An Australian perspective.* Sydney, Australia: Macqarie University, Special Education Centre.

Thomas R. Guskey, *Professor of Education, University of Kentucky, Lexington.* **Perry D. Passaro,** *Assistant Professor of Curriculum and Instruction, College of Education, Black Hills State University, Spearfish, South Dakota.* **Wayne Wheeler,** *Director, Curriculum and Staff Development, Jefferson City Public Schools, Missouri.*

A detailed description of the Missouri Statewide improvement program can be found in Baker, King, and Wulf (1989). For a detailed description of the Thorpe-Gordon school and how it brought about its educational innovations, see Guskey, Passaro, and Wheeler (1990).

The Missouri Mastery Achievement Test (MMAT) is a criterion-referenced test developed by the Missouri State Department of Education to assess core competencies and key skills identified by over 300 elementary, secondary, and tertiary teachers; subject area specialists; and school administrators from across the state. See Baker, King, and Wulf (1989) for a detailed description of this instrument and its development.

Children with Mental Retardation

The U.S. Individuals with Disabilities Education Act (IDEA) mandates free and appropriate public school education for every child, regardless of mental ability. While the U.S. legal windows on education are from ages 6 to 16, individuals with disabilities are entitled to a free and appropriate education from age of assessment (birth, early childhood) to age 21. This encompasses parent-child education programs and preschool programs early in life and transitional services into the community and world of work after the public school education is completed.

Children with mental retardation (MR) were once classified as "educable," "trainable," or "custodial" for purposes of placement. These terms are strongly discouraged today. Even severely retarded children are educable and can benefit from some schooling. The preferred categorical terms today for children who are mentally challenged are "intermittent," "limited," "extensive," and "pervasive." These terms refer to how much support they need to function as capably as possible.

A child with MR who is in the classification "intermittent" needs support at school, at times when special needs arise, and at times of life transitions. This terminology is generally used for children whose MR does not create an obvious and continual problem. These children have slower mentation but also have many abilities. The level of support classified "limited" is usually used for children whose MR creates daily limitations on their abilities, but who can achieve a degree of self-sufficiency after an appropriate education. Limited refers to the period of time from diagnosis (infancy, early children) until adulthood (age 21). The "extensive" support classification extends the support throughout the lifespan for individuals whose MR prohibits them from living independently. The "pervasive" support classification is used infrequently. It is only for those individuals whose MR prevents them from most activities of self-help. Pervasive support is intensive and life-sustaining in nature.

The majority of children with MR can be placed in the intermittent support classification. To casual observers, they often do not appear to have any disabilities. How-

ever, their ability to process, store, and retrieve information, is limited. In the past, this group of children was given IQ measurements between two and three standard deviations below the mean (usually an IQ below 70 but above 55). Intelligence testing is an inexact science with problems of both validity and reliability. The current definition of MR endorsed by the American Association on Mental Deficiency (AAMD) does not include any IQ scoring results other than to use the phrase "subaverage intellectual functioning." It emphasizes the problems individuals with MR have with adaptive skills such as communication, self-care, home living, social skills, community use, self-direction, health and safety, functional academics, leisure, and work.

The causes of mental retardation are unclear. About one-half of all individuals with MR are suspected to have sustained some brain damage prenatally, neonatally, or in childhood. (Brain damage after age 18 that results in impaired mentation is not referred to as MR.) Several hundred factors have been identified that can singly or in combination alter brain functioning or destroy neurons. Most of these factors are silent killers. We lack the technology to even detect small areas of brain damage, much less to determine what caused it. Among the better-known factors that damage brain tissue are anoxia, malnutrition, drugs, viruses, radiation, trauma, and tumors.

The first article in this unit on MR provides an excellent overview of the dangers encountered by the developing brain of the embryo/fetus when a pregnant woman uses drugs. Drug abuse occurs at every socioeconomic, ethnic, and maternal age category. Legal as well as illegal drugs can impair the developing infant's chance of ever having normal intelligence. The myth that intelligence is inherited has persisted despite years of evidence to the contrary. Starting a unit on MR by discussing prenatal factors influencing a child's intelligence helps to dispel the notion that only genes matter.

The second article in this unit addresses the problem of providing appropriate support for children with mental retardation who are enrolled in inclusive education classes

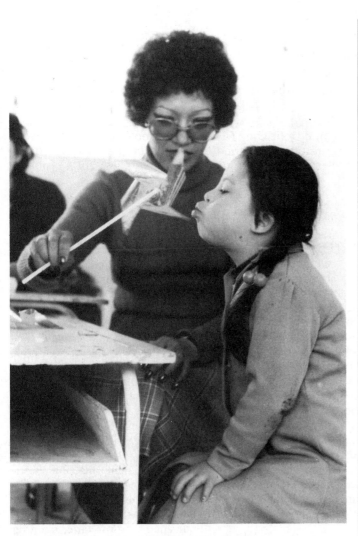

termittent," "limited," or "extensive" support, as prescribed in the individualized education program (IEP) of each child with a disability, is mandated by law. Everyone involved in the process needs to work toward solving the problem of making the education appropriate to the needs of each child.

The third unit article is a heartwarming personal account of one family's experience with all the roadblocks to inclusive education for children with MR. Jeanne and Carlos Oberti knew that their son, who was born with Down Syndrome, was entitled to a free and appropriate public school education in the least restrictive environment possible. They wanted him to attend their neighborhood school. The struggles of this family will stimulate a great deal of discussion. It is difficult to read this article without becoming intellectually involved with the pros and cons of the case. The struggles and compromises described extend beyond the Oberti case to general problems faced by all families and schools complying with current educational laws.

The last article in this section describes a much-needed addition to the education of every child with a disability: leisure. The AAMD's new MR definition specifies leisure as an area in which individuals have difficulty. Mary Ann Demchak appeals to everyone involved with education of exceptional children to include recreational activities in their educational programs.

Looking Ahead: Challenge Questions

How does prenatal drug exposure put a fetus at risk for mental retardation?

How can students with MR be successfully integrated into, and supported in, regular education classes?

How willing are courts to uphold the IDEA mandate for appropriate education of children with MR in the least restrictive environment?

How do recreational activities fit into the appropriate education of children with MR?

in their schools. Inclusive education does not mean regular education. It means supported education for every child with a disability in the regular classroom. The authors provide teachers, future teachers, and child-care workers with much helpful advice. The provision of "in-

Prenatal Drug Exposure: An Overview of Associated Problems And Intervention Strategies

Prenatal drug exposure places a child at "high risk" for long-term difficulties. But, as Dr. Tyler makes clear, poor outcomes can be avoided or ameliorated by intervention.
....

RACHELLE TYLER

RACHELLE TYLER, M.D., is a pediatrician in the Los Angeles area who works with high-risk children in hospitals, outpatient clinics, and schools.

PRENATAL exposure to drugs has been occurring for centuries. In the Bible (Judg. 13:14), Samson's mother was warned against drinking wine or beer during her pregnancy. However, it was not until the latter part of the 20th century that fetal alcohol syndrome was described in this country.

In the 1960s the medical profession began to address the medical complications associated with prenatal drug exposure. These were mainly found to be vomiting, diarrhea, irritability, and poor feeding. These problems caused poor weight gain and fluid loss or imbalance, sometimes leading to shock or even to death.

In the 1960s and 1970s, research projects began to evaluate both the medical and the developmental problems of children with prenatal drug exposure. Most of the research followed up on prenatal exposure to heroin and methadone. The major reasons for this focus were that heroin abusers were presenting themselves for prenatal care in order to receive methadone treatment and thus were the most visible substance abusers. In addition, these infants had higher morbidity and mortality rates than infants who had not been exposed to drugs, and their problems had to be addressed.

Initially, the feeling was that the children would have no long-term problems after their acute medical conditions had been treated. Further study showed that there could be some long-term developmental problems associated with prenatal drug exposure. However, the culprit was felt to be the chaotic postnatal environment: living with parents who continued to use drugs or being placed in a number of different homes. More recent investigations have found some evidence that these children continue to be at risk for developmental or learning problems despite the stabilization of the home environment.

PATTERNS OF DRUG USE

When looking at the problem of prenatal drug exposure, we must include not only illicit drugs, but also alcohol, nicotine, and prescription medicines. The majority of drugs or medications taken by a pregnant woman can cross the placenta and show up in the bloodstream of the fetus. Because the potentially adverse effects of using drugs during pregnancy have been widely trumpeted in the media, a woman who continues to use illicit drugs or alcohol or to abuse prescription drugs during pregnancy almost certainly has a problem with addiction.

When an infant has been exposed to drugs during gestation, there is usually polydrug exposure, because most drug abusers use more than one drug. Although a user may have a drug of choice, when that drug is unavailable a substitute is often found. In other instances, users combine drugs to achieve a particular effect, such as prolonging the "high" or diminishing the "low" after the drug of choice has run its course. Furthermore, illicit drugs are rarely pure; they are usually diluted with other substances to some degree. Since there are no legal restrictions on the manufacture of illicit drugs, most addicts know neither the ac-

From *Phi Delta Kappan*, May 1992, pp. 705-708. © 1992 by Phi Delta Kappa, Inc. Reprinted by permission.

> # Prenatal drug exposure places the fetus at risk for a number of medical problems.

tual dosage they are taking nor the elements used to dilute each dose. Thus the drug history given by the mother may not be particularly revealing. Moreover, a mother may not recall all the substances she took during the course of her pregnancy.

Drug abuse knows no socioeconomic, ethnic, racial, or age limits. The wealthy and the poor, the highly educated and the minimally educated, and all racial and ethnic groups are affected by drug abuse. The problem of drug abuse can begin early and can last a lifetime. Often, drug abuse begins in the preadolescent years with what are called "gateway drugs": alcohol, marijuana, and tobacco. As time goes on, a user may move on to the abuse of other drugs, such as heroin, cocaine, or amphetamines. Children may be introduced to drugs by their peer group or, as is frequently the case, by a family member, either directly or by example. There is strong evidence for an intergenerational component to drug abuse, and this is often a major obstacle in drug treatment.

IDENTIFYING PRENATALLY EXPOSED CHILDREN

A conservative estimate of the incidence of prenatal exposure to illicit substances in the U.S. is 11% of live births. However, this estimate is based on random sampling. Not all infants and mothers are screened at the time of birth and delivery. Before a drug screening occurs for a particular mother/infant pair, there must be some indications of maternal

drug use. These indications include aspects of maternal history, maternal signs and symptoms, or infant signs and symptoms. Only if such indications exist are the mother and baby tested. In addition, maternal histories are often incomplete, and the evaluating health professional must be sensitive to the signs and symptoms of drug exposure.

Urine or blood toxicology screens are used to detect the presence of drugs in the infant's or the mother's system. These tests are not always reliable in revealing the substances to which an infant has been exposed. If there has been no exposure within 72 hours of testing, the screen may be negative despite a history of repeated and prolonged drug use. For this reason, toxicology screens must be combined with a good medical and social history as well as with neurobehavioral evaluation of the infant.

Because not all mothers are screened for drug use during pregnancy, a number of children may escape detection in the newborn period and will not have the opportunity to participate in an early intervention program. These children may show up in school at age 5 or 6 without having had any evaluation since birth. At that point, the most important issue is not to determine whether or not the children have had prenatal drug exposure but rather to assess their functional level, follow their progress, and offer help in the appropriate areas. Drug exposure may be an issue if there is a possibility of postnatal exposure in the home or in the caretaking environment.

MEDICAL COMPLICATIONS

Prenatal drug exposure places the developing fetus at risk for a number of medical problems. Some children may display minimal or undetectable effects, whereas others may exhibit major problems. But exposure to alcohol or illicit drugs during any trimester of pregnancy is detrimental to the developing fetus to some degree. In the first trimester, the developing fetus is most susceptible to malformations of major organs that may be apparent upon inspection or assessment of function.

In the second and third trimesters, the problems brought on by drug exposure can be more subtle and less readily apparent. Fetal growth is often poor, lead-

ing to smaller infants or possibly to miscarriage or premature birth. Premature infants are more likely to have chronic respiratory problems that will require medication during infancy and childhood. They are more likely to suffer from intracranial hemorrhages that place them at risk for cerebral palsy or to have more subtle motor and cognitive problems. They are also at risk for visual and auditory impairments that can affect their functioning in a school setting.

Because of congenital malformations due to early fetal insult or problems related to prematurity, a child may have ongoing medical problems. If these medical problems are significant, recurrent illnesses can lead to frequent school absences. Such problems include recurrent ear infections or a recurrent stuffy nose, particularly if the child has continued to be exposed to drugs in the postnatal environment. And this may be the case if a parent continues to smoke cigarettes or illicit drugs in the presence of the child. Recurrent ear infections interfere with a child's hearing and can have an adverse effect on learning even if the damage is not severe or permanent.

DEVELOPMENTAL COMPLICATIONS

Infants and children with a history of prenatal drug exposure exhibit a variety of signs or symptoms that range from minimal to severe. Major effects can be quite debilitating, whereas minimal effects may have no major impact on the child's school performance or social functioning. In infancy, the baby exposed to drugs may be quite fussy and difficult to soothe, or it may be lethargic for extended periods of time. As the child grows, these behaviors may translate into difficulty with self-regulation. Problems with self-regulation frequently show up as difficulty in sustaining attention or adjusting to transitions during the school day, such as changing from one subject to the next or quieting oneself appropriately after recess.

Infants with prenatal drug exposure often have tremors of their arms and legs. As they progress through childhood, this often translates into motor difficulty of varying degrees, depending on the child and the extent of the exposure. Some children with continued motor difficulty have tremors on a periodic basis, whereas others have problems performing tasks that require motor dexterity, including writing or speaking. It is important to remember that speaking clearly requires a certain amount of motor control. Problems in this area can lead to difficulty in producing understandable speech. If this is combined with intermittent hearing loss caused by recurrent ear infections, then the child is at double the risk for developing speech difficulty. Speech is our primary means of communicating with one another. Major problems in this area make communication difficult and quite frustrating for the child. This frustration may in turn lead to problems with self-esteem and to "acting out" both at home and in the school setting.

As I noted above, infants and children with prenatal drug exposure may spend much of their early life either lethargic or irritable for extended periods of time. They may have few moments of quiet alertness when they are available for social interaction. As they progress through childhood, they acquire, in varying degrees, the ability to quiet themselves and make themselves available for social interaction. Some drug-exposed children can learn to quiet themselves as well as any child who was not exposed to drugs in the womb. Others may continue to have only brief periods of availability, and this must be taken into consideration when the child enters school. The teacher must remember that, through no fault of his or her own, the child may be intermittently unavailable for social interaction or academic work.

Other areas of concern relate to the processing of visual and auditory information and to problems with short-term memory. A drug-exposed child can have difficulty understanding incoming auditory and/or visual information and may require frequent repetitions on the part of the teacher or caretaker. If there are problems with recalling lessons from day to day, the teacher must be patient.

ENVIRONMENTAL INFLUENCES

In addition to the medical and developmental risk factors associated with prenatal drug exposure, environmental issues affect the child as well. The chaotic lifestyle of a drug abuser is not conducive to the healthy development of a child. In such a home, children are rarely exposed

to consistently nurturing caretaking, and there is also a possibility of reexposure to drugs. In such cases developmental setbacks can occur that inhibit a child's school performance.

> **The drug-exposed child may be intermittently unavailable for social interaction or academic work.**

Another environmental problem results from the fact that a child who is in the foster care system rarely remains in one placement from birth to adulthood. Although some children experience few changes, most have multiple placements or are forced to live in group homes. Across the country there is a growing shortage of family-style foster homes, and group homes are growing more common. Even if there has been no history of prenatal drug exposure, children who experience multiple foster placements or who reside in group homes are at risk for learning or school problems. The situation is only made worse when the risks associated with prenatal exposure to drugs are added to the equation.

Children who have had only a few foster placements can still be at risk when the court system is fervently working to reunite them with their biological parents. The well-meaning legal system may be placing a child back into a high-risk home with parents who have had but minimal rehabilitation. Even in cases in which parents have received a great deal of help in dealing with their drug abuse, these family reconstructions must be handled carefully. In such cases, the child should have gradually increasing contact with the parents over time, while still remaining legally in foster placement.

For some children, however, the transition from foster placement to parental care is abrupt. In such situations there is minimal time for the child to adjust to a significant change in life, leaving him or her vulnerable to regression both emotionally and academically. Even if the transition is gradual, younger children can become confused and can sometimes be fearful of encounters with parents with whom they are not familiar. Older children may experience feelings of ambivalence toward or fear of their parents. Such uncertainties can lead to "acting out" behaviors, difficulty in attending to work in school, and learning problems.

Still another environmental problem is that caretakers may not always have a working understanding of normal child development, much less know how to deal with the special problems of children who are at high risk. While this is frequently true of the biological parents, it may also be true in well-meaning foster homes.

INTERVENTION

Prenatal drug exposure places a child in what is termed a "high-risk" category. This essentially means that the child is more likely to have long-term difficulties than a child who did not experience such adverse conditions. However, poor outcomes can be avoided or ameliorated by intervention.

Effective intervention entails prevention on all levels, combined with a comprehensive approach. School personnel can be instrumental in prevention on the primary, secondary, and tertiary levels. Primary prevention consists of prevention of the drug abuse altogether. Secondary prevention entails cessation of the drug abuse or drug exposure after it has begun. Tertiary prevention involves intervening after the effects of the drug exposure have been realized.

Primary prevention can take the form of education regarding the risks of drug use, combined with classroom experiences that help build the child's self-esteem. Education regarding the adverse effects of drug abuse is important on one level; however, success in the school setting is also beneficial in helping a child to develop a positive sense of self-esteem. In working toward this end, an individualized approach that takes each child's learning style into account is recommended.

Secondary prevention can take the form of referral to social services that can direct the family toward treatment or family counseling in the event of ongoing drug use in the family or by the child. Tertiary prevention consists of helping the child to work around any possible deficits in order to optimize his or her learning and school performance.

Effective intervention must be comprehensive and interdisciplinary. The major aim must be to stabilize the environment and to provide positive interactions whenever possible. All service providers from all disciplines should be urged to work together to deal with those children who are at high risk. Those involved in the interdisciplinary approach should include teachers, administrators, social workers, physicians, nurses, physical education teachers, psychologists, speech and language specialists, representatives of community resource agencies, and parents or caretakers. It is important that the team work to develop the home/school partnership whenever possible. Sometimes, when parents are not available, there may be family members or community resources in place that can aid in networking to provide services or needed interventions. Each child's social environment must be assessed to determine the major influences in that child's life. For example, those who would intervene on behalf of a child who resides in a home with biological parents and members of an extended family need to determine who has the primary responsibility for decisions involving the child. Without including that individual, all attempts at forming an effective home/school partnership may be in vain.

At times, effective intervention will require the reporting of suspected child abuse or neglect to the appropriate legal authorities. Children may also speak of ongoing drug abuse in the home. And some changes in behavior or school performance may be indications of abuse or neglect. In such cases the teacher is often the first to suspect that there are problems in the home. It is important that each school have a team of staff members who are available to come together in the assessment and reporting of these cases.

A health assessment is important for all children. Poor health can interfere with learning and school performance. Chronic illnesses, such as asthma or skin conditions, should be adequately addressed. Children should have vision and hearing screens every one to two years, and any problems that are discovered should be treated. In order to maintain optimum health, there should also be well-child visits to a physician at the intervals recommended by the American Academy of Pediatrics.

Pharmacological treatment for a child with prenatal drug exposure must be recommended with caution and monitored closely. Before medications are prescribed, there should be a thorough investigation of the child's health, learning difficulties, psychological condition, and social circumstances. After a trial of medication has been conducted, the child must be followed and reevaluated regarding the benefits versus the risks of ongoing pharmacological treatment. Medication alone will not fully address any biochemical or anatomical changes that may have taken place in the central nervous system as a result of prenatal drug exposure. Furthermore, medications are not without problems or side effects themselves and must be taken in appropriately prescribed doses. If a child's home is chaotic, the child may not receive his or her medication regularly or may be overdosed. Teachers and parents must also understand that, although the medication may prolong the child's attention span, learning disorders or retardation must be addressed from a behavioral standpoint.

Classroom strategies must be tailored to the child or children served, whether or not there has been prenatal drug exposure. Ideally, a class should be small, containing 15 students at most, with one teacher and an aide. This allows for more individualized attention with less rigidity in the schedule and makes a second adult available to attend to any child who may be having difficulty during the school day.

In reality, most school districts have large classes of 30 or more children with one teacher and no aide. In such cases schools are forced to work within the constraints of minimal resources. In an effort to provide regularity or consistency in the school experience, the school should make sure that the child has the same teacher throughout the school year. In the case of combined grades in a single classroom, the child should be allowed to remain with the same teacher for a second year. If a child is retained in a grade, every effort should be made to allow that child to remain with the same teacher for a second year if the child/teacher match is reasonably good.

Some schools with large classes do have teacher aides available. And it is important that an aide remain in the same classroom with the same children and teacher in order to minimize environmental changes. Sometimes the aide can be a volunteer who is approved by the school district to act as teacher aide. Retired teachers can be approached and encouraged to become involved, or students' grandparents who have a history of teaching experience may be considered.

It is important that teachers, administrators, social workers, and all others involved in working with children have a basic knowledge of child development as well as of the special problems associated with high-risk children. This knowledge is best acquired through a combination of instruction and experience. Such knowledge increases understanding, and along with understanding come tolerance and patience in dealing with difficult cases.

When working with children who have been exposed to drugs before birth, one must guard against preconceptions regarding outcomes. Drug exposure places children at high risk, but environmental influences play a crucial role in determining long-term outcomes — outcomes that range along a continuum from minimal to severe. Although drug exposure places students at risk, chaotic environmental influences alone can lead to poor outcomes in children's development. Because of the important contribution of environmental influences, the provision of a stable and nurturing environment in all aspects of the child's life is imperative.

When referring to children with prenatal drug exposure, we must remember that each child is an individual first. Terms such as *drug baby* and *crack baby* emphasize the drug exposure first and the child second. They also imply that the child is somehow at fault for his or her adverse prenatal conditions. Deleting such terms from our discussions of children who are at risk is a major first step in early intervention.

INTEGRATING
Elementary Students with Multiple Disabilities into Supported Regular Classes
Challenges and Solutions

Susan Hamre-Nietupski
Jennifer McDonald
John Nietupski

Susan Hamre-Nietupski *(CEC Chapter #88) is an Associate Professor, Division of Curriculum and Instruction/Special Education, The University of Iowa, Iowa City.* **Jennifer McDonald** *is a Special Educator, Adams Elementary School, Des Moines, Iowa.* **John Nietupski** *(CEC Chapter #88) is an Adjunct Associate Professor, Division of Developmental Disabilities and Division of Curriculum and Instruction, The University of Iowa, Iowa City.*

Integrated placement of students with multiple disabilities in regular classes (Strully & Strully, 1989) is being advocated by professionals and parents alike. With this model, assistance is provided in the areas of curriculum modification, participation, and social integration by special education/support teachers, paraprofessionals, integration facilitators (Ruttiman & Forest, 1987), and/or nondisabled peers (Forest & Lusthaus, 1990). Students with disabilities are offered increased opportunities for interactions with nondisabled peers as well as meaningful curricular content (Ford & Davern, 1989; Sailor et al., 1989; York, Vandercook, Caughey, & Heise-Neff, 1990).

The professional literature has described strategies for preparing regular educators and students for positive integration experiences (Certo, Haring, & York, 1984; Gaylord-Ross, 1989; Stainback & Stainback, 1985) and for teaming special educators with regular educators to promote regular class integration (Vandercook, York, & Forest, 1989; York & Vandercook, 1991). One practical concern for teachers is how they can promote both skill gains and social acceptance while involving students in regular class activities.

This article describes four potential challenges to supported education along with solutions that have been effective in meeting those challenges in an elementary school setting. Our observations are based on 4 years of experience in integrating students with multiple disabilities, including students with moderate and severe mental disabilities or autism with accompanying physical, visual, and/or behavior challenges. Our efforts focused on integrating elementary-age students into kindergarten through sixth-grade classes.

Background

The case of Stephanie, a first-grader, illustrates points in each challenge and solution. Stephanie was a student with multiple disabilities, including mental retardation in the moderate to severe range with accompanying physical disabilities and a vision impairment. She attended a 350-student elementary school in a midwestern community of 35,000 people. When Stephanie was kindergarten age, she spent half her day in a regular kindergarten class. The following year, she spent the entire school day in a regular first-grade class.

Challenges and Solutions

Challenge 1: Providing Functional Curriculum in a Regular Class

Instruction on the functional skills necessary to live, work, and participate in recreation activities in integrated community environments is a critical component of an appropriate education for students with multiple disabilities (Falvey, 1989). Since functional skills such as grooming and dressing rarely are taught in regular education, a challenge to supported education is how to teach these skills in the primarily academic environment of a regular class.

Five possible solutions might be considered to address this challenge. First, partial assistance might be provided by a peer in the context of class activities. For example, when Stephanie arrived at school in the winter, she could remove

From *Teaching Exceptional Children*, Vol. 24, No. 3, Spring 1992, pp. 6-9. © 1992 by The Council for Exceptional Children. Reprinted by permission.

her boots easily. However, putting on her shoes was time-consuming, and she often missed out on much of the opening routine. One solution was to have Stephanie remove her boots upon arrival and take her shoes to the opening-group area. There she was taught to ask a nondisabled peer for assistance in putting on and tying her shoes. The peer was shown how to assist Stephanie with the difficult steps while encouraging her independence on the easier steps. This solution resulted in positive interactions between Stephanie and her peers, enabled her to take part in the opening routine, and allowed her to progress in this self-care skill.

A second strategy is to identify the "down times" during the school day in which functional skill instruction could be provided without disrupting the class routine. For example, Stephanie often had a runny nose and had not yet learned to blow her nose independently. The support teacher took her aside at such times as arrival, between academic activities, and prior to and after recess and lunch for brief, unobtrusive instruction. As a result, she missed very little regular class activity and she showed increased independence by the end of the school year.

A third potential solution is to provide parallel instruction on functional skills in the regular classroom while peers participate in their academic work. For example, when the nondisabled students were working on place value in mathematics, part or all of that period could be spent teaching Stephanie functional mathematics skills such as matching coins or other skills. One regular teacher reduced the possible stigma associated with parallel programming by identifying nondisabled students who needed similar instruction and rotating them through the self-care lessons with Stephanie. Since the teacher referred to this as a "health" or "hygiene" unit and involved nondisabled students, Stephanie was not singled out as different from her peers. Nondisabled children can benefit from this functional life skills instruction as well as their peers who have disabilities.

When none of the previously mentioned strategies seems feasible, brief removal of the student from the regular class for specialized instruction might be considered. For example, when nondisabled students receive instruction on academic activities clearly beyond the student's present skill level, instruction on functional skills such as bathroom use, snack preparation, and street-crossing outside the classroom may be more appropriate.

Finally, to guarantee that instructional time is not sacrificed, districts should ensure that individualized education program (IEP) goals are drawn from an approved curriculum guide (e.g., Falvey, 1989; Ford et al., 1989). Such a guide can provide assurances that important instructional goals will not be overlooked.

Challenge 2: Providing Community-Based Instruction

Another challenge to regular class integration is including community-based instruction within the educational program. Community-based instruction is needed because of the generalization difficulties experienced by students with multiple disabilities. However, little opportunity for such instruction currently is provided to students in regular elementary education.

In addition to following an approved curriculum guide that includes community-based instruction, two strategies might be employed to address this challenge. The first is to bring the community into the classroom. An example of this strategy was implemented in conjunction with a creative writing unit in which students were required to write about turtles. In order to make this unit more meaningful to Stephanie, who had limited exposure to turtles, arrangements were made to borrow a turtle from a local pet store. After the morning visit by the turtle, Stephanie, three of her nondisabled peers, and the support teacher returned the turtle to the pet store. All four students were able to see, touch, and learn about a variety of exotic birds and animals. As Stephanie and two other students looked at the animals, another wrote down the group's favorite pets and their cost. Upon returning to school, the four wrote and shared a story about their trip and sent a thank-you note to the pet store. Thus, all four students had a community experience that was integrally related to the creative writing unit and allowed the nondisabled students to apply their skills to a meaningful situation. While use of community resources may be difficult to achieve on all units, careful consideration of such opportunities can both enhance the regular curriculum and provide opportunities for community-based instruction.

Another possible strategy involves providing community-based instruction to the student with disabilities in an integrated manner (Ford & Davern, 1989). Small groups of nondisabled students could accompany a peer with disabilities on a rotating basis. The community experiences would allow all students to apply skills being taught in the classroom to real-world settings. For example, integrated instruction in a supermarket could be structured so that a student with multiple disabilities locates various grocery items while peers practice adding costs and comparing prices.

Challenge 3: Scheduling Staff Coverage

Special education staff can support integrated students in many ways, including (a) making adaptations when needed; (b) assisting the classroom teacher in working with a student; (c) coaching nondisabled peers; (d) providing direct instruction; and (e) facilitating positive interactions among students. The scheduling challenge lies in providing this support when it is needed for the student to participate in classroom activities.

One solution in Stephanie's situation was for the regular education and support teachers to determine cooperatively when support was most needed. The support teacher developed a flexible schedule so she could assist Stephanie during activities that were the most challenging for her and/or were most difficult to individualize.

While scheduling support during critical periods is helpful, teachers occasionally need to support several students in several classes simultaneously. In those situations, university students or parent volunteers might provide additional support. With training, these volunteers could assist in regular classrooms when the support teacher is unable to do so.

Another strategy is to empower regular teachers to assume greater instructional responsibility for students with multiple disabilities. Our experience has been that regular teachers can be as effective as special education teachers in meeting the needs of students with disabilities. Encouraging them to do so, involving them in solving instructional problems, demonstrating particular techniques, and reinforcing accomplishments are all strategies for increasing the competence and confidence of regular class teachers.

Another strategy for dealing with the coverage challenge is to work closely with the classroom teacher to identify when and how nondisabled peers might serve in a support role. For example, activities might be designed on the basis of cooperative learning (Johnson & Johnson, 1989), whereby students become responsible for working together and assisting each other.

One additional solution to providing adequate staff coverage is to reduce class size when integrating a student with multiple disabilities. Sailor and colleagues (1989) suggested that this strategy can make support from the regular classroom teacher a more realistic option.

Challenge 4: Promoting Social Integration

The final challenge addressed here is that of promoting social integration and friendships between students with and without disabilities. Strully and Strully (1989) argued that supported education is important because it facilitates the formation of friendships and long-lasting, supportive, personal relationships. Research by Guralnick (1980) has suggested that these relationships do not occur simply through integrated physical placement but must be facilitated.

Administrator Support. Administrators can facilitate friendships in several ways. First, students with multiple disabilities can be assigned to the regular school they would attend if they were not disabled, along with children from their neighborhood, making participation in after-school activities such as parties and school functions more feasible (Brown et al., 1989; Sailor et al., 1989).

Second, administrators can set the tone for integration in a school. In Stephanie's school, the principal strongly believed that all children belonged in regular classes and that promoting positive, cooperative social interactions was an important goal in each classroom. Thus, teachers had a heightened awareness of the social aspects of education and focused on promoting positive relationships among students.

Third, administrators can arrange for after-school social opportunities.

Stephanie's principal was instrumental in developing monthly recreational drop-in programs and summer recreation offerings that allowed all students to socialize.

Teacher Support. Regular class teachers, too, can address the challenge of promoting social interactions and friendships. One well-documented strategy is cooperative learning (Johnson & Johnson, 1989), in which rewards and evaluations are based on the quality of the work and student collaboration.

Regular class teachers also can promote a positive social atmosphere by treating students with multiple disabilities as normally as possible. Stephanie's teacher, for example, placed Stephanie's name on the class roster and assigned her a desk, coathook, and materials space amidst those of the other students. She expected, encouraged, and reinforced adherence to classroom rules for all students, including Stephanie. These actions communicated to all students that Stephanie was as much a member of the class as anyone else.

Finally, regular class teachers can actively promote social relationships (Stainback & Stainback, 1987). Stephanie's teacher did so by pairing children for many activities, modeling and encouraging social interactions, and reinforcing students when positive interactions occurred.

Special educators, support teachers, and integration facilitators can address the challenges of promoting social interaction in several ways. They can model and encourage social interactions. Early in the school year, nondisabled students often would ask the support teacher whether or not Stephanie would like to play and whether or not she enjoyed certain activities. The support teacher would encourage the children to ask Stephanie themselves or show them how to do so. By the end of the year, nondisabled students initiated conversation directly with Stephanie, not through her support teacher.

A second strategy is to develop sensitization sessions that focus on recognizing similarities and differences and getting along with people who are different in some way (Hamre-Nietupski & Nietupski, 1985). In Stephanie's class, her support teacher and the guidance counselor developed a six-session unit on how children are similar and different, how to be friends with those around you, and how to communicate

in different ways. Activities included having all children identify their strengths and weaknesses and likes and dislikes, generate specific ways to be friends with people in the class, and learn how to initiate and respond to social interactions. These activities were carried out in a large group that included Stephanie but did not single her out.

Support teachers can develop circles of friends to promote social interactions (Forest & Lusthaus, 1990). In Stephanie's school, a student with autism was integrated into a regular fifth-grade class. The support teacher, concerned about the lack of social integration, organized a circle of friends with nondisabled volunteer companions. This group identified in- and out-of-school interaction opportunities such as going to the library together and attending the drop-in recreation program, and they socialized with her.

Finally, support teachers can keep parents informed about interaction opportunities and encourage parental support. Stephanie's support teacher regularly kept Stephanie's parents informed about the students she interacted with and upcoming after-school events. On occasion, she even made transportation arrangements so Stephanie could participate with her peers.

Parental Support. Parental support is also necessary to promote social relationships and friendships. Parents can become active in the parent-teacher organization and in school-wide activities. They might encourage their child's participation in extracurricular activities such as Cub Scouts, Brownies, and 4-H or help in initiating play opportunities by having their child invite a nondisabled friend to spend the night or hosting or having their child attend birthday parties. Such activities are extremely important in making and maintaining friendships.

Parents also can promote social relationships through sensitivity to clothing selection and hairstyle. Nondisabled students, even in elementary schools, are keenly aware of "in" clothing. Since this a sensitive and value-laden issue, interventions may need to be quite subtle. For example, when asked, teachers might suggest holiday or birthday gift ideas for students (e.g., "I've noticed that Stephanie really likes Tracy's [name brand] sweatshirts") as a way to assist parents in facilitating social acceptance.

Conclusion

While we are encouraged by the outcomes of the strategies described here, two limitations should be noted. First, the strategies were developed for elementary-age students. Additional research and demonstration are needed to guide teachers serving older students. Second, questions have been raised about how and the degree to which students with profound, multiple disabilities might be integrated into regular classes. At this point, perhaps those questions should remain open—with practitioners and researchers encouraged to examine them through empirical demonstration activities.

Supported regular education for students with multiple disabilities is not without challenges, but potential solutions are beginning to emerge. It is our hope that, through examples such as these, increasing numbers of school systems will be encouraged to integrate elementary-age students with multiple disabilities more fully into regular education classes.

References

Brown, L., Long, E., Udarvi-Solner, A., Davis, L., VanDeventer, P., Algren, C., Johnson, F.,

Gruenewald, L., & Jorgensen, J. (1989). The home school: Why students with severe intellectual disabilities must attend the schools of their brothers, sisters, friends, and neighbors. *Journal of the Association for Persons with Severe Handicaps, 14,* 1-7.

Certo, N., Haring, N., & York, R. (1984). *Public school integration of severely handicapped students.* Baltimore: Paul H. Brookes.

Falvey, M. (1989). *Community-based curriculum: Instructional strategies for students with severe handicaps.* Baltimore: Paul H. Brookes.

Ford, A., & Davern, L. (1989). Moving forward with school integration: Strategies for involving students with severe handicaps in the life of the school. In R. Gaylord-Ross (Ed.), *Integration strategies for students with severe handicaps* (pp. 11-32). Baltimore: Paul H. Brookes.

Ford, A., Schnorr, R., Meyer, L., Davern, L., Black, J., & Dempsey, P. (1989). *The Syracuse community-referenced curriculum guide for students with moderate and severe disabilities.* Baltimore: Paul H. Brookes.

Forest, M., & Lusthaus, E. (1990). Everyone belongs with the MAPS Action Planning System. *TEACHING Exceptional Children, 22,* 32-35.

Gaylord-Ross, R. (Ed.). (1989). *Integration strategies for students with severe handicaps.* Baltimore: Paul H. Brookes.

Guralnick, M. (1980). Social interactions among preschool children. *Exceptional Children, 46,* 248-253.

Hamre-Nietupski, S., & Nietupski, J. (1985). Taking full advantage of interaction opportunities. In S. Stainback & W. Stainback (Eds.), *Integration of students with severe handicaps into regular schools* (pp. 98-112). Reston, VA: The Council for Exceptional Children.

Johnson, D., & Johnson, R. (1989). Cooperative learning and mainstreaming. In R. Gaylord-Ross (Ed.), *Integration strategies for students with handicaps* (pp. 233-248). Baltimore: Paul H. Brookes.

Ruttiman, A., & Forest, M. (1987). With a little help from my friends: The integration facilitator at work. In M. Forest (Ed.), *More education/integration* (pp. 131-142). Downsview, Ontario: Roeher Institute.

Sailor, W., Anderson, J., Halvorsen, A., Doering, K., Filler, J., & Goetz, L. (1989). *The comprehensive local school: Regular education for all students with disabilities.* Baltimore: Paul H. Brookes.

Stainback, S., & Stainback, W. (Eds.). (1985). *Integration of students with severe handicaps into regular schools.* Reston, VA: The Council for Exceptional Children.

Stainback, W., & Stainback, S. (1987). Facilitating friendships. *Education and Training in Mental Retardation, 22,* 10-25.

Strully, J., & Strully, C. (1989). Friendships as an educational goal. In S. Stainback, W. Stainback, & M. Forest (Eds.), *Educating all students in the mainstream of regular education* (pp. 59-68). Baltimore: Paul H. Brookes.

Vandercook, T., York, J., & Forest, M. (1989). The McGill Action Planning System (MAPS): A strategy for building the vision. *Journal of The Association for Persons with Severe Handicaps, 14,* 205-215.

York, J., & Vandercook, T. (1991). Designing an integrated program for learners with severe disabilities. *TEACHING Exceptional Children, 23*(1), 22-28.

York, J., Vandercook, T., Caughey, E., & Heise-Neff, C. (1990, May). Regular class integration: Beyond socialization. *The Association for Persons with Severe Handicaps Newsletter, 16,* p. 3.

What's Right for Rafael?

The Clement, N.J., public schools wanted to place Rafael Oberti, a child with Down syndrome, in a special education classroom with other severely disabled students. But the boy's parents wanted their son educated in a regular classroom in their neighborhood school.

Lynn Schnaiberg

Jeanne Oberti speeds her family's white minivan past a Gloucester Township school bus and then navigates a turn off the twisting two-lane road at a stand selling Jersey tomatoes. Eventually, she pulls up in front of Ambassador Christian Academy, a stucco building with three white crosses rising from the manicured grass, and there she unloads her four children. Her eldest, 11-year-old Rafael, heaves a backpack over his shoulder and walks down the hallway to Arlene Burnett's 4th grade classroom. Rafael spends this Monday morning tracing his name in cursive and then slowly printing the numbers and letters that tell where he lives. A classroom aide reminds him to cross his t's and dot his i's.

Rafael has Down syndrome. When he started 1st grade here in 1992, he spent the first two weeks sitting in a chair, jacket on, clutching his backpack. The staff let him sit like that until he was ready. Now Rafael is doing pretty well in school, as his work this morning seems to indicate. Still, it's not what Rafael's parents had envisioned for their son. They had hoped he would attend the local public schools. But more than that, they wanted him enrolled in a regular classroom in the local public schools.

Jeanne and Carlos Oberti felt so strongly about this that they took the Clementon, N.J., public schools to court, hoping to force resistant district officials to comply with their wishes. In their suit, they asked a state administrative-law judge to order the district to educate Rafael in a regular classroom in their neighborhood school rather than in a special education classroom. That judge ruled against the Obertis, but then—to the astonishment of many—a U.S. District Court took their side. And a year later, the U.S. Court of Appeals for the 3rd Circuit concurred. "Inclusion is a right, not a privilege for a select few," the District Court judge wrote. Those words—perhaps the

strongest ever written by a judge in support of educating disabled children in regular classrooms—thrust the Obertis and the Clementon public schools into the national spotlight. The news media descended on the small town and its 500-student elementary school district. And advocates of inclusion adopted the judge's words for their cause.

Throughout the legal battle, the school district argued that Rafael was too disabled and too disruptive to be taught in a regular classroom. The Obertis said the district never provided their son with the services and support he needed; Rafael's classroom behavior—which the couple maintains the district grossly exaggerated—resulted from deficiencies in the educational program, they said, not from their son. The federal courts agreed. They ordered the district to develop a more inclusive plan for Rafael, but they did not explain exactly what that meant. By the time the family and district officials sat down to talk about what it might mean, the Obertis decided there was too much bad blood to negotiate and opted, instead, to keep Rafael at the Christian academy he'd been attending in the meantime.

Rafael's story is emblematic of a larger national conflict between the staunch advocates of including children with severe disabilities in regular classrooms and those who question the wisdom and fairness of such a policy. The Oberti case unfolded as the disability-rights movement was gaining steam and as our national thinking about what children—and adults—with disabilities can and should be expected to do was beginning to evolve. It raises important questions about control and balance. Whose expectations should govern a child's education? Do the rights of the many—in this case, an entire class of children—weigh more than the rights of one?

Reprinted with permission from *Teacher* magazine, March 1996, pp. 32-37. © 1996 by Editorial Projects in Education, Inc., Washington, DC.

"For Sale" signs poke out of the front

lawn of the Obertis' two-story home, which sits on one of the biggest lots on the block. A wooden fence encircles the backyard, which, over the nine years the family has lived in the house, Carlos Oberti has filled with a mini-basketball court, above-ground swimming pool, and car park.

Since the Obertis began sending their children—Rafael; Christopher, age 9; Stephanie, 7; and Gabrielle, 6—to Ambassador Christian Academy a half-hour away in Glassboro, the family has retreated from life in Clementon. Not that they ever felt too comfortable there to begin with. "We live in Clementon, but we're not of Clementon," explains Jeanne, who is finishing a college degree in music education. Carlos, a native of Ecuador, markets licorice extract abroad for a company in nearby Camden. He describes Clementon, a working-class community of 5,600 residents, as "a small, nothing town."

The Obertis are hoping to move to Glassboro to be closer to the children's school. There isn't much keeping them in Clementon. The children used to play organized sports in the community. But when the family received a notice suggesting that Rafael join a T-ball league for children with disabilities, instead of the one he was already playing in, they decided to drop out altogether. Family is the center of their lives. It's where everything starts and finishes, Carlos says.

Rafael used to have his own bedroom in the Oberti house, but since Carlos' parents came to live with them from Ecuador, he's had to share a room with Christopher. They take turns sleeping on the top bunk. Among other things, Rafael is responsible for dressing himself, making his bed, helping set and clear the table, and checking little Gabrielle's math homework with a calculator after doing his own. All the Oberti children are expected to look out for each other, particularly for Rafael. Which is why the Obertis are willing to pay roughly $8,000 a year for the four children to attend the same private school.

When Rafael smears cream cheese from his bagel on his face during breakfast, Christopher tells him: "Rafael, wipe your mouth off and eat right. Don't tear off the food. Do it like this." He bites gingerly into his bagel. Stephanie laces Rafael's hiking boots for a trip to the corner convenience store. On the way back, Christopher and Stephanie race home. Rafael takes off behind them. When he wanders into the street, Stephanie tells him to move back. He does. Later, when the children come in from playing a game of touch football, Carlos asks Christopher if Rafael had his jacket on. Christopher admits that he doesn't know. Carlos admonishes: "It's your job to know; he's your brother."

Carlos had called the children in from the football game. He doesn't much like them playing with the neighborhood kids. They have, on occasion, teased Rafael. Too many of their families, he says, don't have "good values." So, until the Obertis move, much of the children's free time is spent inside the house or within the wooden fence in the backyard.

Jeanne describes her husband as tenacious. When he needs something, he refuses to take no for an answer. His standards are high. Before the children leave for school, he dabs their sweaters with tape to remove lint, smooths their hair, and wipes their hands and faces until they glow. When Rafael's mouth falls slightly open, as it does from time to time, Carlos taps his son's face lightly, and his jaw clamps shut. When Rafael sings in the junior choir at church, Carlos cues him from the pew, motioning for him to sing louder or pay attention to the director. Later, sitting next to his son on a pew, Carlos softly touches Rafael's hands, a signal that he should clasp them in prayer.

Even though Rafael does not attend Clementon Elementary, the Obertis believe things have worked out for the best. They won the case, they say, for families following in their footsteps. "We did feel we were supporting 'the cause,'" Jeanne says. "There was some peer pressure from other parents of kids with disabilities to put Rafael back in Clementon. We wanted to finish what we'd started, but we came up against the realization that we had to put our child first. It's a compromise. We're not heroes."

In one of the family's many photo albums, sandwiched between shots of the children at the beach and Rafael reclining on a chaise lounge on a business trip to Latin America with his father, is a picture that takes up almost a page by itself. It shows the four smiling children in front of a large hand-lettered sign hanging from their front porch: "U.S. 3rd Circuit Court. Rafael Oberti vs. Clementon Elementary. We won...AGAIN."

The Obertis are self-described idealists and risk-takers. From the time Rafael was born, when they were told they should put him up for adoption and try again, Carlos and Jeanne have been wary of outside opinions. Jeanne recalls a time, years ago, when a speech therapist suggested that Rafael learn to use a speech board, a device that allows nonverbal children to communicate by pressing letter keys. "I said, 'Wait a minute. You're supposed to work on articulation, not say my child won't ever speak,'" Jeanne says. "It really put us on our toes. Low expectations are a very, very dangerous thing." Later, they were told Rafael probably would never read, but he now does, albeit at the kindergarten-1st grade level.

Carlos tells "the bicycle story." Rafael and his younger brother Christopher had training wheels on their bikes. When the time came, Carlos took Christopher's training wheels off, and he rode away. But Carlos didn't take the training wheels off Rafael's bike. Then one day, months later, Rafael picked up his brother's bike and took off. "I was worried that he wouldn't do it," Carlos says. "Then I realized, of course he'll do it, just a little more slowly."

None of this has been easy for the Obertis. When Rafael was born, Carlos struggled for three months to accept his son's condition. "I couldn't deal with it at all," he says. "But I finally accepted it. And I made a promise to myself; I promised to help Rafael succeed at anything he decided to do."

Court documents show that in 1989,

when Rafael was 5 years old, he had limited speech skills and an IQ of about 59. As far as New Jersey was concerned, that made him EMR—"educable mentally retarded." He had been in a variety of special education programs since infancy, but when the time came to enroll him in kindergarten, the

Obertis asked the Clementon district to place him in a regular classroom.

The Obertis knew traditional special education was not going to take their son where they wanted him to go. They had seen other children like Rafael wind up in sheltered workshops or group homes. And they didn't want any part of that. "I didn't know at that point that inclusion was so new to the district," Jeanne says. "I didn't know the ramifications of what we were proposing. All I knew was that was the atmosphere I wanted my child in."

The Obertis don't put much stock in IQ or other standardized tests; they believe that special educators rely too heavily on such measures when it comes to placing children like Rafael in school. The federal Individuals with Disabilities Education Act, they point out, requires the development of individualized-education plans for each disabled student. Labels like "multiply handicapped," they argue, simply allow educators to "ship children off to the nearest [multiply handicapped] program."

At first, Clementon school officials complied with the Obertis' wishes. Rafael was assigned to Melinda Reardon's morning developmental kindergarten class, which was designed to help children lacking in skills prepare for standard kindergarten. Reardon and an aide taught Rafael and 11 other students in a classroom divided by a set of bookshelves from a regular kindergarten class. Rafael spent his afternoons in a special education class in a neighboring district. Reardon, who had been at the school 14 years, later testified in court that Rafael demanded too much of her time and that the other children suffered as a result. Rafael, she said, would throw pencils and crayons, crawl under desks, spit, scream, and cry. On the playground one day, the teacher said, Rafael choked another student.

Speech therapist Karen Lightman testified that Rafael slapped her and was often disruptive during their sessions. In her opinion, Rafael needed to be in a special education class where he could receive more extensive speech therapy than Clementon could offer. "He had difficulty following directions and expressing his wants and needs, and that was my big concern," Lightman testified.

To complicate matters, Rafael was not fully toilet trained. On the first day of school, Reardon said she received a note from the Obertis asking her to take him to the bathroom every 15 minutes. "The parents [also] requested that I send home a page of every single assignment that I did, so they could reinforce it, which was not a reasonable request." Reardon eventually got another aide to work with Rafael, but it didn't seem to help much.

Peggy McDevit, Clementon's special education coordinator and a school psychologist, testified that she didn't oppose including disabled children in the regular classroom, but she felt that Rafael wasn't prepared. "I feel strongly that at some point in time it might be a beneficial experience for him, but at this time it would not be," she stated. McDevit thought Rafael was frustrated in Reardon's class, even with the aide. "The frustration came because I think that the expectations of Mr. and Mrs. Oberti were clearly that he would be exposed to everything in the kindergarten program," McDevit testified. "The frustration that I saw in Rafael was, perhaps, in his own perception that he was not able to do many of the things that were going on in the classroom."

The Obertis blame the conflict on what they describe as the "mediocrity" of the Clementon schools. For their part, they were thrilled with Rafael's progress in the class. He learned to recognize 16 letters of the alphabet. "Of course, the other kids knew all 26, but I said, 'Look at the progress,' where the school said, 'Oh, we failed, so he's not in the right place,'" Jeanne says. "They kept saying he's not ready. In their minds, I don't think Rafael would ever be 'ready.'"

Based on Rafael's year in Reardon's

class, Clementon proposed that he be placed in a special education kindergarten class for the 1990-91 school year. At the time, Clementon didn't have a program geared for children classified as EMR. So district officials wanted to bus Rafael to such a program in another district. The Obertis rejected that idea because it was a separate special education classroom where most students stayed for four years.

In August 1990, the parents and district agreed that Rafael would be sent to a new program for children classified as multiply handicapped just starting up in the Winslow Township school district, 45 minutes away from the Obertis' home. The agreement stipulated that Rafael would be mainstreamed with nondisabled students in some of his Winslow classes, including music. But the promised mainstreaming never materialized. Rafael sat in the cafeteria with students from regular classes, but he wasn't allowed to leave his special education class's table.

Winslow's speech therapist later testified that Rafael had progressed from using just a few words at the beginning of the year to using three- and four-word sentences. But the Obertis said Rafael had started wetting his bed again and, for the first time, was saying he didn't want to go to school. The experience sent the Obertis to lawyers Frank Laski and Penelope Boyd of the Public Interest Law Center in Philadelphia. By February of 1991, the couple and Clementon district officials were facing off before a state administrative-law judge in what would prove to be the first in a long series of courtroom battles.

Clementon won round one. "This is not to say that the time may not come when mainstreaming in Winslow Township and/or Clementon will not be called for," Judge Joseph Lavery wrote in his March 1991 ruling. "The present record only discloses that now is not such a time." That same day, the Obertis decided to take their case to the federal courts. It was at this point, Clementon superintendent Bill Sherman says, that he and the Obertis stopped talking, and the lawyers took over.

As the lawyers began to put together their arguments, the Obertis enrolled Rafael in Clementon's summer program, open to all the town's K-6 students. Karen Albanese taught a 38-student class with two aides. Albanese later testified in court that Rafael crawled under tables, kicked an aide, poked children with pencils, and lay in the middle of the classroom and cried. On a field trip to the Campbell Soup Museum in Camden, Albanese said, Rafael refused to stay with the group and she had to restrain him. "At one point, he literally pulled me across the room," Albanese testified. "At that point, he broke away from me and then started to run around that section of the museum.... And I'm holding him and trying to describe the tureens to the children. After a point, I couldn't hold him anymore....I was sitting with Rafael in the chair, and he was kicking his legs and flailing his arms. I was trying to hold him and say, 'Rafael I need you to calm down now.'"

After the museum trip, Albanese insisted that Jeanne Oberti accompany the class on outings.

In the fall of 1991, Clementon offi-

cials again recommended the program in Winslow for Rafael. Instead, the Obertis enrolled their son at a Catholic school in Stratford, N.J. Rafael spent roughly two months in Patricia Caponi's class of nine learning-disabled students, also attending a few classes with nondisabled students. Caponi later testified in court that when he was frustrated, Rafael hit other students, yelled, and tried to run out of the school. By the end of October, the school had asked Rafael to leave. Jeanne Oberti spent the remainder of 1991 homeschooling her son.

By the time the Obertis' lawyers were ready to argue their case in federal district court, they had enough depositions, evaluations, videotapes, and expert testimony to fill four drawers of a file cabinet in the law center's office. For three days in May 1992, every detail of Rafael's school life was scrutinized in a Camden courtroom. The Obertis' lawyers flew in a nationally known inclusion expert from Wisconsin and called to the stand two other special educators—one from New Jersey, the other from Pennsylvania. The district's lawyer, Thomas Murphy, offered up a special education professor from nearby Glassboro State College. Rafael, almost 8 years old then, spent most of his time during the trial quietly coloring in the courtroom's front row.

On Aug. 17, Chief Judge John Gerry of the District Court ruled for the Obertis. The next day, superintendent Sherman's phone started ringing off the hook. Overnight, the case had become national news. "It all got interpreted as some kind of mandate, pro or con inclusion," Sherman says. "To me, it was never that. It was one child. It just took on a life of its own."

Sherman believes that Clementon was singled out "to make a point," in part because of its small size and relatively limited resources. (The district has a $2.9 million annual budget.) "I knew the judge couldn't imagine our little school district of 500 kids," the superintendent says, shaking his head. "I know they didn't understand that."

Sherman says the Obertis had "very high expectations" for Rafael and for the changes Clementon should have made to accommodate him. "I felt like they were asking for changes that were ahead of the game," he says. And advocates for inclusion do not necessarily disagree. "All of this was really just beginning in New Jersey," says Joanne McKeown, mother of a child with Down syndrome and an inclusion advocate who testified for the Obertis. "I think Clementon had the bad luck to choose the wrong family [to take on]."

On May 28, 1993, the federal appeals court affirmed the lower court's ruling. The Oberti case showed up on the *Today* show. Rafael was featured in a *U.S. News & World Report* cover story on inclusion, titled "Separate and Unequal."

Although the appellate ruling in *Oberti* vs. *Board of Education of the Borough of Clementon School District* did not create any new legal standard by which inclusion cases should be judged, legal experts say it did clarify some issues.

Paramount among them is that school districts generally carry the burden to prove why a student should not be included in the regular classroom. The Individuals with Disabilities Education Act of 1975 requires school districts that accept federal money to provide a "free, appropriate public education" to children with disabilities in the "least restrictive environment." The law also requires schools to educate children with disabilities to the "maximum extent appropriate" alongside their nondisabled peers.

As Perry Zirkel, professor of education law at Lehigh University in Bethlehem, Pa., describes it, the law presents "a steep and slippery slope" for school districts. "The words of the law are tilted heavily toward placing students in the regular classroom for a major portion of the day, but it's slippery because the language—'maximum extent possible'—is imprecise."

Thomas Murphy, Clementon's lawyer, wanted to appeal the ruling to the U.S. Supreme Court. Sherman did not; the district had already spent some $214,000 on the case, and the superintendent had had enough. Today, Murphy accuses Sherman of selling out on his principles and giving in to "political correctness." But Sherman says he realized the appellate ruling was a sound one, and, besides, he wanted the matter to end.

The summer after the final ruling, the Obertis briefly sat down with Clementon officials but found no common ground. The district wanted to reevaluate Rafael and offered to have a team outside Clementon do it. But ultimately, the Obertis decided that the long case had created too much hostility between the district and the family. Rafael was progressing at the Christian school he was then attending, so they decided to leave him there. They simply walked away from the district and haven't returned since.

Ambassador Christian Academy deci-

ded to take a chance with Rafael. He is one of nine students in Arlene Burnett's class there. An aide, Jeanie Cook, works primarily with Rafael and another disabled student. Depending on the subject, Rafael either sits at a desk with the other students—albeit in the back row—or at a small table pushed against the wall. A few times a week, he receives speech therapy and help in mathematics and reading from the Gloucester County Special School District, which provides itinerant teachers to serve students with disabilities in the county's nonpublic schools.

On this particular day, while the other students practice spelling words like "successful" and "bargain" for an upcoming quiz, Rafael works on one of three functional words his teacher hopes he will learn this quarter. He will spend the next three or four weeks on today's word, "exit."

"What does that word mean? Show me the exit," Burnett asks Rafael, while Cook floats among the other students. Rafael points to the classroom door. "What do we do when we exit? Show me," the teacher says. Rafael walks out the door, then, at Burnett's request, points to exit signs at either end of the hallway. "What do the signs say?" she asks. "Sign," the boy says. "No," Burnett says. "Exit." "Oh yeah," Rafael says. "Exit." He grins. Rafael returns to the table to trace the word exit and print his own sentence: "Exit means to go out." He quietly draws a picture of himself and an exit.

Things don't always go so smoothly. During a math lesson, while other students stand at the chalkboard dividing 97 by 60 and 74 by 20, Rafael uses a calculator to add two-digit figures. At one point, he gets frustrated and lays his head on Cook's shoulder. "It's hard," he complains. "Come on, Rafael, you can do it," she says. He puts his head on the table. Burnett comes over. "Come on, Rafael. Easy as cake, right?" Rafael starts to cry. Cook brings over a box of tissues. After Rafael spends a few minutes playing with a tissue, Cook gets him to refocus on his math. After he does a problem correctly, he exclaims, "All right" and makes the thumbs-up sign. Rafael is a master of slang.

Some of the children in Rafael's class have been with him now since 1st grade. Most are unfazed when he starts to hum in class or cry or play with his pens and pencils. A few, however, still find it hard to ignore. For now, Rafael's language skills make it difficult for him to converse freely with his classmates. But during lunch break, several make room for him as they practice a dance step. Rafael follows, a half beat behind. Later, at recess in the tree-lined meadow behind the school, he hangs off to one side with a few other boys, while the girls commandeer a soccer ball.

With only 78 children in its pre-K through 6th grade program, the academy prides itself on its family environment and strong parental involvement. While there are other students in the school with learning problems, Rafael is the most severely disabled student the school has ever enrolled. "This wasn't a crusade or a policy issue for us," principal Wellington Watts says. "It was just, here's a family with a need who came looking for help." Watts says the academy accepted Rafael because he and others at the school knew the Obertis "would bend over backward to make this work." The family has organized in-service training for Rafael's teachers and put them in touch with a special education consultant who helps develop Rafael's curriculum. For its part, the academy has given teachers release time to attend inclusion conferences and hired an aide. In addition, faculty members meet with the Obertis at least once a month to discuss Rafael's program.

But even at Ambassador, some parents have expressed concern over Rafael's behavior. One family pulled their daughter from the school because, as Watts puts it, "they didn't feel Rafael had developed the social graces they wanted their child exposed to." Another couple approached the principal because they were worried their son was not receiving enough attention in class. That worry, Watts says, has since diminished. He has had to call Rafael's father twice. Once because Rafael refused to cooperate with the teacher. And again, recently, because he put his jacket on and threatened to leave the school. Carlos arrived, spanked Rafael, and that was the end of the problem.

Without exception, the teachers Rafael has had say he is a challenge in the classroom but a rewarding one. They tell how they've spent hours drawing up lesson plans just for him and how, at times, they have disagreed with the Obertis about what's best for Rafael. "Sometimes, I just had to say to them flat out, 'This isn't going to work,'" says Sue Sawyer, who was Rafael's 2nd grade teacher. "They started to trust me. So they let me take over."

Still, the question remains: Is Rafael in the right place? Or would he be getting and learning more in a special education

setting? "I don't know if his skills would be higher," Burnett, Rafael's current teacher, says. "Some would say yes." (Two of Burnett's own children attend special education classes in public schools.) Sancha Hughes, a Gloucester County speech therapist who works with Rafael, wonders if the Obertis aren't in some ways denying reality. "I know in their hearts they believe this is best for Rafael," she says, "but I'm not sure that it is."

For Watts, who used to teach in the public schools, the question about whether to place children like Rafael in a regular class environment all comes down to attitude. "Anytime something is mandated, people do it because they have to," he says. "But for inclusion to work, it has to be because you want it, and you can't mandate attitude."

Most people in Clementon seem to

have forgotten about the Oberti case, if they ever knew about it in the first place. On a blustery day this past fall, a group of parents gathered with their children outside the fire station for a Halloween parade. One mother said she'd heard of the case and thought that the family had won. Others had heard that the family had moved away some time ago.

But there are some locals who need no reminding. One such person is Barbara Cremean, mother of two girls, one of whom was in Rafael's class at Clementon Elementary five years ago. "I just remember thinking, why is he here? He isn't ready for this school," she says. "And Clementon wasn't ready for him, either."

A number of area residents who are familiar with the case simply don't want to talk about it. The local PTA president, the teachers' union representative, and Rafael's public school teachers all declined to be interviewed for this story, as did several school board members, past and present. Superintendent Sherman believes their reluctance to discuss the matter has more to do with a desire to put it behind them than anything else.

Murphy, the lawyer who argued the case for the district, is now out of the school-law business altogether. But he still argues that inclusion turns regular classrooms into special education classes for all the students. "I wouldn't want my child in that class," he says. "This is the guts of the whole issue, and judges don't want to hear that. They want to see it as civil rights. Parents don't want their children stigmatized, and they don't want that stigma for themselves."

For his part, Sherman insists that he never opposed inclusion outright. He says he believed then as he does now that the question of including disabled students in regular classrooms should be addressed on a case-by-case basis. "My fear is that some districts have implemented inclusionary programs out of a fear of litigation, and possibly those programs are not best for the child," he says, smoothing the wrinkled and heavily highlighted copy of the appellate court ruling that he keeps at his desk. "Personally, I've never spent so much time on one student, one situation in my life. I don't even know what winning means in this case anymore."

To Stephen Leibrand, who left the Clementon school board last year after serving for nearly a decade, the case was about setting limits. "I saw this whole thing as maybe setting precedent for going too far," he says. "School districts are afraid to say no. And we weren't."

It's difficult to gauge what practical impact the Oberti case has had on the Clementon schools. A look at placement data from 1989 to 1995 shows that the special education students who have been educated within the walls of Clementon's regular classrooms are overwhelmingly those with mild learning disabilities; students with more severe problems are still being placed in special classrooms outside of the district.

Though New Jersey ranks 48th in the nation when it comes to including disabled children in the regular classroom, some changes are afoot, sparked in part by the Oberti case. Last spring, the state board of education revamped its rules on inclusion to incorporate the ruling. And a state task force currently is looking to rebuild the state's school-funding system, which gives districts fiscal incentives to ship students out rather than keep them in regular classes in their neighborhood schools.

Not all parents of disabled children are pleased by these developments. And some, like Terry Bair, whose 11-year-old daughter Elizabeth has Down syndrome, even feel threatened. Bair's number-one fear is that special classes and schools for the disabled will eventually be shut down as pressure mounts to mainstream such children. For three years, Elizabeth has attended Kingsway Learning Center, a private school in Haddonfield, N.J. Her local public school district pays her $21,000-a-year tuition. Bair believes the special attention and instruction Elizabeth received at the center is just what she needs. She says her daughter would feel overwhelmed in a regular classroom in her neighborhood school.

Bair says she does not oppose inclusion; she just wants to make sure parents have choices. "I think most teachers are overwhelmed with the children they already have in their classrooms without special-needs children being added,"

she says. "The bottom line to me is, are they going to be resentful that they are being asked to teach 'these kids'?"

For now, Rafael is where his parents

want him to be. Legally, if they decided tomorrow to send him back to the Clementon public schools, the district would be obligated to serve him in a regular classroom in their neighborhood school. But it won't likely come to that.

Still, the Obertis will have to decide where they want Rafael to attend school once he reaches the 8th grade, the highest grade level at Ambassador Christian Academy. "I don't know where the future will be for Rafael," says Watts, the principal. "We've been constants in his life. I don't know if there's another school that would attempt what we've done. It's going to be a big bridge to cross."

The Obertis' long-term vision for Rafael is that he be surrounded by a supportive circle of family and friends, not people merely paid to care for him. They would like to see him develop as an individual, maybe one day living on his own and starting a family. Or maybe he will live with his brother. It's hard to say at this point. But there is one thing the Obertis are adamant about: They aren't going to place any limits on Rafael. "Life can hold something much bigger than my hopes for him," Carlos says.

Seated with his family at the Laurel Hill Bible Church, Rafael runs his hand across his father's freshly shaved face, tracing the lines of his jaw and throat. He eventually lets it fall onto his father's leg. Carlos grasps his son's hand in his own, and with the other, he points out the words in the hymn book from which the congregation is singing. Rafael gently nudges his father's hand aside and points to the words himself, his own voice, softly, half a beat behind, joining the others.

Helping individuals with severe disabilities find leisure activities

MaryAnn Demchak

Leisure and recreational activities are important for all individuals, but they may be especially important for individuals with severe disabilities. Many of these individuals have an abundance of free time, which is, unfortunately, often used inappropriately. For example, they may engage in stereotypic behaviors such as body rocking or hand flapping or may use materials inappropriately (e.g., mouthing toys).

Learning to participate appropriately in recreational activities may decrease these problem behaviors (Carr, Robinson, Taylor, & Carlson, 1990). Moon and Bunker (1987) summarized research supporting the importance of recreational activities and concluded that (a) appropriate use of free time may prevent institutionalization and (b) there is a positive relationship between instruction in recreational activities and improvements in other skills.

Guidelines for Selecting Leisure Activities

Integration

Integration with students who do not have disabilities is an important element of an effective program for students with severe disabilities (Meyer, Eichinger, & Park-Lee, 1987). The program philosophy should reflect a goal of maximum participation in integrated community environments (Meyer et al., 1987). The practitioner should visit the site of the proposed recreational activity to determine whether or not nondisabled peers are present in the setting and for the specific recreational activity. However, the mere presence of nondisabled peers does not guarantee that they will interact with a student with disabilities. Therefore, the practitioner must also evaluate the activity and setting in terms of the likelihood that individuals with and without disabilities will interact with one another. The activities in which students with severe disabilities may become involved include school-based activities such as social clubs, dances, and sporting events and community-based activities such as video arcades, shopping, swimming, and bowling.

Because the presence of specialized personnel such as the special education teacher may result in unnecessary stigmatization for a person with a disability, the practitioner should determine what degree of involvement is required. For example, the practitioner could lessen his or her involvement by having a nondisabled peer accompany and interact with the student with disabilities. The practitioner would be present, but would be involved only in an observational or supervisory capacity.

The practitioner should also evaluate the instructional methodologies used in integrated settings. Because intrusive prompting systems or reinforcement procedures may contribute to stigmatization, practitioners should use the least intrusive and most natural types of prompting and contingencies in integrated settings. For example, in a sporting event, if the typical reinforcer is for team members and coaches to provide verbal praise and

From *Teaching Exceptional Children*, Vol. 27, No. 1, Fall 1994, pp. 48-53. © 1994 by The Council for Exceptional Children. Reprinted by permission.

a pat on the back, that same contingency would be recommended for the individual with disabilities. Less intrusive prompts such as natural verbal instructions or gestures are preferable to full physical guidance.

Age Appropriateness

A second consideration is the chronological age appropriateness of the setting, materials, and activity. Participation in activities or use of materials that are inappropriate for a given chronological age may perpetuate stereotypes pertaining to individuals with severe disabilities. In contrast, individuals who use materials and participate in activities that are chronologically age appropriate may be viewed more positively (Bates, Morrow, Pancsofar, & Sedlack, 1984). Moreover, nondisabled peers may be more likely to interact with students with severe dis-

abilities when these students engage in functional, age-appropriate activities (Albin, Horrocks, Ferguson, & Wilcox, 1990).

A questionnaire such as that validated by York, Vandercook, and Stave (1990) can be used to determine what activities nondisabled peers engage in and to validate the activities being targeted for instruction or participation. This questionnaire focuses on what activities individuals engage in alone, with friends, with family, in school, at home, and in the community. Other questions focus on types of magazines, music, board games, and hobbies enjoyed. The authors provide suggestions for using the questionnaire with elementary through high school age students.

Choice/Preference

Perhaps the most important considera-

tion in selecting recreational activities is that of choice. Typically, nondisabled individuals choose their own leisure activities. Unfortunately, opportunities to express preferences are frequently omitted from programs for individuals with disabilities (Guess, Benson, & Siegel-Causey, 1985). It is imperative to recognize that individuals with severe disabilities have preferences, even though they may be unable to display those preferences through conventional means. Moon and Bunker (1987) suggested conducting observations over a period of several days using latency and duration recording as two methods of ascertaining individual preference. For example, the practitioner might provide a person with several choices and observe how quickly the person selects one activity (i.e., latency) and then how long he or she participates in it (i.e., dura-

Individuals can be taught to participate in a variety of activities to some degree, or activities can be adapted to allow participation.

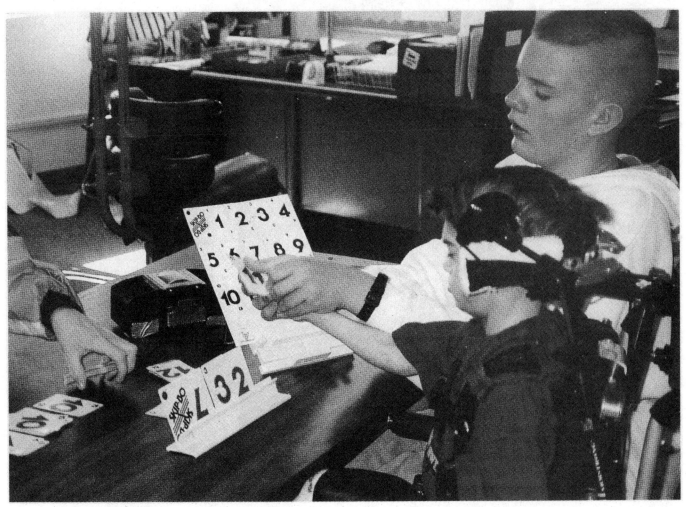

tion). Activities involving shorter latencies and longer durations may indicate preferred activities. Moon and Bunker also stressed the importance of examining the type of interactions. For example, does the person use the materials in an appropriate manner? Wuerch and Voeltz (1982) provided an excellent form for evaluating interest in leisure activities for individuals with limited communication skills. It should be noted that all of these methods of attempting to ascertain preference rely on repeated observations, as opposed to a single observation or subjective judgment.

It is important to rotate activities to maintain interest. For example, when presenting choices to a student, the teacher can make an effort to rotate the activities that are provided as options. The teacher can devise a choice board or menu that includes words, pictures, photos, or actual objects to depict various options. As satiation occurs and new preferences are observed, activities can be deleted from the choice board and new ones added.

In addition to the preferences of individuals with disabilities, it is important to examine the preferences of their families or caregivers. If they are not inter-

ested in having these individuals participate in a particular recreational activity, it is unlikely that they will provide access to the activity after school.

Adaptations and Partial Participation

It is not always necessary for an individual to participate in a recreational activity to the same degree as nondisabled peers for that activity to be enjoyed. For example, a person playing *Yahtzee* may not be able to add numbers independently when it is his or her turn. However, that person can still enjoy the game and the fun of being with peers. Partial participation is a valid goal as long as meaningful participation is encouraged. The principle of partial participation states that, regardless of severity of disability, individuals can be taught to participate in a variety of activities to some degree, or activities can be adapted to allow participation (Baumgart et al., 1982). Thus, it is important to ask whether or not the recreational activities being considered can be adapted, if necessary, by (a) changing the rules, (b) using prosthetics, (c) modifying the materials, and/or (d) using personal assistance strategies.

One example of changing the rules in a game is to eliminate reversing play in the game *Uno*. A student who has difficulty following when it is his or her turn could find it extremely confusing to have the order of turns reversed frequently. Making this simple change in the rules still allows the game to be enjoyed by all. A few examples of prosthetics include card holders for someone who cannot hold cards; calculators to add numbers displayed on the dice in a game such as *Yahtzee*; and adaptive switches to allow activation of items such as radios, remote-control vehicles, battery-operated toys, or televisions. An example of a simple modification that can be made is placing colored tape on the play button of a cassette player to help the individual discriminate among several buttons that look the same.

Personal assistance strategies might be employed for various games by having a person with a disability and a nondisabled peer work as a team. The peer com-

There is a correlation between instruction in recreational activities and improvements in other skills.

This student uses a calculator to add numbers on the dice while playing Yahtzee.

pletes aspects of the game that cannot be performed by the person with the disability. Personal assistance strategies allow the individual with a disability to participate in the activity to the maximum extent appropriate. Additional examples of adaptations for leisure activities can be found in Moon and Bunker (1987).

Feasibility Issues

A final area of consideration is the feasibility of the activity. For example, one consideration is whether or not the individual is able to pay any costs associated with the activity. If the family has difficulty providing the money, fee waivers or sliding fee scales may be available. If the activity is targeted as part of an individualized education program, the teacher

may be able to use money from the school's petty cash fund or from the community-based education fund. If specific materials, equipment, or clothing are needed, it is necessary to determine whether or not the individual is able to borrow, rent, or purchase these items.

Another consideration is whether the person will be able to get to and from the activity using public or private transportation. If not, it is unlikely that he or she will participate in the activity on an ongoing basis. The practitioner should also visit the site to make sure it is accessible to individuals who use wheelchairs or need other assistance.

Finally, it is necessary to consider whether the person will have a use for the activity in future settings and whether

it could be easily adapted for other settings. Other factors being equal, recreational activities that have long-term usefulness should be taught before those that are not likely to be used in future environments.

Evaluation of Potential Recreational Activities

The form shown in Figure 1 provides a systematic way for practitioners to evaluate potential recreational activities for individuals with severe disabilities of any age or grade. It permits practitioners to rate several activities simultaneously. The activities that receive the highest ratings on the form are those that meet most of the considerations discussed. Thus, these are the ones that are targeted for instruc-

Figure 1. Form for Evaluating Potential Recreational Activities.

Name: _____ Date: _____

Completed by: _____

Directions: List each recreational activity and the setting in which each activity will occur. Score a 1 for each "yes" answer and a 0 for each "no" answer. Total your answers for each activity.

Activity and Setting:				
1. Are nondisabled peers present in the setting?				
2. Do nondisabled peers participate in the activity?				
3. Is it likely that nondisabled peers will interact with the student in the activity?				
4. Can the person participate in the activity with a minimum of assistance or supervision by specialized personnel (e.g., special education teacher)?				
5. Can the least intrusive, natural prompts and contingencies be used, if needed, to help the person to participate in the activity?				
6. Is the setting appropriate for the chronological age of the student?				
7. Are the materials appropriate for the chronological age of the student?				
8. Is the activity appropriate for the chronological age of the student?				
9. Have repeated observations verified that this is a preferred activity for the individual?				
10. Is the individual presented with a choice at the onset of the activity?				
11. Can the individual self-initiate this activity or be taught to do so?				
12. Is it a preference of the family or caregiver that the individual participate in this activity?				
13. If needed, can the rules be adapted to allow participation?				
14. If needed, can the materials be adapted or prosthetics be used to allow participation?				
15. If needed, can personal assistance strategies be used to allow participation?				
16. Can the person partially (or independently) participate in the activity?				
17. Is the person able to meet any financial costs associated with the activity?				
18. Is the person able to obtain the necessary materials, equipment, and clothing to enable participation?				
19. Is transportation to and from the activity available?				
20. Is the setting accessible?				
21. Are the setting and activity safe for the person?				
22. Is the activity one that is useful in current and future environments?				
Totals				
Activity				
Setting				

Personal assistance strategies might be employed for various games by having a person with a disability and a nondisabled peer work as a team.

tion or participation. However, low scores do not necessarily eliminate certain activities. Instead, the practitioner can review each "no" or "0" rating to determine how the activity or setting could be modified to allow for a "yes" or "1" rating.

For example, in one instance use of a remote control car in the classroom resulted in a lower score than some other activities because nondisabled peers were not present in the setting. However, when the setting was changed from the classroom to the playground at recess time, when nondisabled peers were present, this activity received a higher rating because it provided the student with a meaningful way to interact with his peers. Finally, the form can be used to obtain a balance between activities that are done alone and those that are done with others.

Teachers who have used the form have rated it as an efficient means for prioritizing activities to target for instruction or participation and as an excellent way of helping them focus on current best practices in recreation.

Conclusion

By increasing involvement in recreational activities that meet the considerations discussed in this article, practitioners can have a tremendous long-term impact on the lives of individuals with severe disabilities. By learning to self-initiate appropriate recreational activities, these individuals may gain the opportunity to be active participants in their leisure-time planning. Through participation in appropriate recreational activities, individuals with severe disabilities are given the opportunity to engage in more appropri-

ate behaviors and have a better chance for success in community environments.

References

Albin, R. W., Horrocks, C. R., Ferguson, D. L., & Wilcox, B. (1990, December). *Effects of functional vs. nonfunctional curriculum activities on perceived expectations and intentions to affiliate of typical junior high school students.* Paper presented at the annual conference of The Association for Persons with Severe Handicaps, Chicago.

Bates, P., Morrow, S. A., Pancsofar, E., & Sedlack, R. (1984). The effect of functional vs. nonfunctional activities on attitudes/expectations of non-handicapped college students: What they see is what we get. *Journal of The Association for Persons with Severe Handicaps, 9,* 73-78.

Baumgart, D., Brown, L., Pumpian, I., Nisbet, J., Ford, A., Sweet, M., Messina, R., & Schroeder, J. (1982). Principle of partial participation and individualized adaptations in educational programs for severely handicapped students. *Journal of The Association for the Severely Handicapped, 7*(2), 17-27.

Carr, E. G., Robinson, S., Taylor, J. C., & Carlson, J. I. (1990). *Positive approaches to the treatment of severe behavior problems in persons with developmental disabilities: A review and analysis of reinforcement and stimulus-based procedures.* Seattle: The Association for Persons with Severe Handicaps.

Guess, D., Benson, H. A., & Siegel-Causey, E. (1985). Concepts and issues related to choice-making and autonomy among persons with severe disabilities. *Journal of The Association for Persons with Severe Handicaps, 10,* 79-86.

Meyer, L. H., Eichinger, J., & Park-Lee, S. (1987). A validation of program quality indicators in educational services for students with severe disabilities. *Journal of The Association for Persons with Severe Disabilities, 12,* 251-263.

Moon, M. S., & Bunker, L. (1987). Recreation and motor skills programming. In M. E. Snell (Ed.), *Systematic instruction of persons with severe handicaps* (3rd ed., pp. 214-244). Columbus, OH: Merrill.

Wuerch, B. B., & Voeltz, L. M. (1982). *Longitudinal leisure skills for severely handicapped learners: The Ho'onanea curriculum component.* Baltimore: Paul H. Brookes.

York, J., Vandercook, T., & Stave, K. (1990). Recreation and leisure activities: Determining the favorites for middle school students. *TEACHING Exceptional Children, 22*(4), 10-13.

MaryAnn Demchak *(Nevada Federation), Associate Professor, Department of Curriculum and Instruction, University of Nevada, Reno.*

Children with Behavioral Disorders and Autism

The 1994 revision of the *Diagnostic and Statistical Manual of Mental Disorders* (4th edition) of the American Psychiatric Association (DSM-IV) placed autistic disorder in a category of developmental disorders quite separate from mental retardation (MR), learning disabled (LD), and cognitive disorders. While intuitively one might want autism classified as a form of MR (most children with autism have MR), one could also argue that autism should be classified as a form of communication disorder (most children with autism have communication disabilities). Autism truly belongs in a category by itself. It is a pervasive developmental disorder characterized by disruptive behaviors, cognitive disorders, communication disabilities, and a loss of contact with and interest in the outside world. Children with autism prefer aloneness. They may insist on sameness and show perseverative behaviors (uncontrollable repetition of a particular word or gesture). A few children with autism show savant abilities (extraordinary knowledge in a few small areas such as music, art, or mathematics). This is paradoxical in light of their seeming mental retardation in other areas of learning.

The category *behavioral disorders*, as defined by the DSM-IV, is subsumed under the category of disorders usually first diagnosed in infancy, childhood, or adolescence. Among the DSM-IV disorders of childhood not reviewed elsewhere are disruptive behaviors, eating disorders, tic disorders, elimination disorders, separation anxiety disorders, and reactive attachment disorders.

For educational purposes, children with behavior disorders are usually divided into two main behavioral classifications: (1) withdrawn, shy, or anxious behaviors; and (2) aggressive, acting-out behaviors. The debate about what constitutes a behavior disorder, or an emotional disturbance, has not been fully resolved. In 1990, the U.S. Department of Education elected to remove autism from its list of emotionally disturbed behaviors and gave it a separate classification under the Individuals with Disabilities Education Act (IDEA). An alliance of educators and psychologists then proposed that IDEA simply remove the term "serious emotional disturbances" and instead focus on behaviors that adversely affect educational performance. Conduct usually considered a sign of emotional disturbance, such as anxiety, depression, or failure of

attachment, can be seen as behaviorally disordered if it interfered with academic, social, vocational, and personal accomplishment. So, also, can conduct disorders, eating disorders, tic disorders, elimination disorders, and any other responses outside the range of "acceptable" for school or other settings. Such a focus on behavior could link individualized educational program (IEP) curriculum activities to children's behavioral response styles.

Should children with chronic and severe behavior disorders, especially those which interfere with the education processes in the regular classroom, be allowed to enroll in inclusive education programs? IDEA ruled yes, both in its original form and in amendments written more recently. Although teachers, other pupils, and school staff may be greatly inconvenienced by the presence of one or more behaviorally disordered students in every classroom, the law is clear. The school must "show cause" if a child with disruptive behavior is to be moved from the regular classroom to a more restrictive environment.

Inclusive education does not translate into acceptance of disordered behaviors in the regular education classroom. Two rules of thumb for the behavior of all children, however abled or disabled, are that they conform to minimum standards of acceptable conduct and that disruptive behaviors be subject to fair and consistent disciplinary action, rather than condoned.

The first article in this unit deals with children whose behaviors range to an extreme of withdrawal, shyness, or anxiety. These behaviors interfere with education and cannot be explained by intellectual, sensory, or health factors. These children can learn, but they do not. Jerome Bruns has become well known for his book, *They Can but They Don't: Helping Students Overcome Work Inhibition.* In this manuscript, he summarizes his more important principles for working with inhibited children. Bruns speaks with a voice of experience and in a language that will capture and hold each reader's attention.

The second unit article, also retained from the previous edition, addresses the question of how to provide fair, consistent disciplinary action for unacceptable disruptive behaviors in the classroom. First, it speaks to the question "What is unacceptable?" Thomas McIntyre cautions every adult working with children to consider culturally socialized behaviors before deciding if they are appropriate or inappropriate. Fair discipline must be sensitive to culturally different behaviors. If a behavior is suited to the demands of the educational environment, it should not be modified just to suit the preferences of a teacher. Discipline, per se, should be positive rather than negative or confrontational.

The next essay addresses the problem of working with children whose behaviors range to an extreme of aggressiveness and acting out. They may be expelled. However, a school cannot refuse to readmit them when the terms of the expulsion have expired without "due cause" proven in a court of law. Just like all other children with exceptional conditions, children with serious behavioral disturbances are entitled to a free and appropriate education in the least restrictive environment. This article reports research data on the variables that affect the reintegration of students who have behavioral disorders.

The last article in this unit is an exposition on autism—its onset, symptoms, diagnosis, possible etiology, and prognosis. The unusual behaviors present in children with autism are described, along with suggestions on how to make life a little easier both for children with the disorder and adults and peers interacting with them.

Looking Ahead: Challenge Questions

Why are some students withdrawn and unmotivated in learning situations? How can teachers empower inhibited children and help them get an appropriate education?

How can teachers provide fair, consistent, and culturally sensitive discipline for students with behavioral disorders who happen to be from ethnically diverse backgrounds?

Discuss whether behaviorally disordered students can be successfully reintegrated into regular education classrooms. What variables affect beneficial reunification?

What is autism? Why is it included in a unit about children with behavioral disorders? How can life be made more hospitable for children with autism?

They Can But They Don't

Helping Students Overcome Work Inhibition

Jerome H. Bruns

Jerome H. Bruns has more than twenty years of experience as a teacher, counselor, and school psychologist. For a more in-depth treatment of the problem of work-inhibited students, with chapters devoted to what teachers, parents, and counselors can do to help, see his recent book, on which this article is based: They Can But They Don't—Helping Students Overcome Work Inhibition, *published by Viking Penguin.*

A S MANY as 20 percent of American public school students may be work inhibited—that is, they can but they don't do the work of school. They may have the intellectual capability necessary to understand the concepts their teachers present, they may have well-educated parents who want them to do well, and they may have no learning disabilities. Something, however, is blocking them from succeeding. They do not stay on task, do not complete class assignments, do not finish their homework on their own.

Over a period of eight years, in my work as a school psychologist, I conducted a broad series of experimental and empirical studies concerning work inhibition. The impetus for this work came from a series of failed attempts to help teachers and parents by using traditional approaches to make work-inhibited students comply with the demands of school. I observed that the teachers and parents of these students felt defeat and frustration and that it was not unusual for them to go to war with each other over who was responsible for the child's failures.

The term "work inhibition" was coined because the problem is unrelated to abilities, knowledge, or skills. Certain students have no trouble learning; they just have extreme difficulty engaging in the work of school. This condition stirs a range of feelings—from puzzlement to rage—among teachers and parents over generally articulate and able children who do not sustain independent effort to complete school tasks.

Even outstanding teachers have difficulty getting these students to engage in the work of school. One such teacher described her experiences with Jason, a third-grade pupil:

> Jason is never a problem in class or at recess. During oral reading, he enjoys being called on and reads fluently and with meaning. He usually has an appropriate answer or question, and he loves just about any game. His major problem—or maybe it's my problem—is completing assignments.
>
> I always make sure he understands what is required. For example, during math I go to his desk and ask if he understands the directions. If he says, "Yes," I ask him to do the first problem. While I'm kneeling beside him, he invariably completes the problem correctly. I give him an encouraging pat and tell him to continue working. I then go about the room seeing to the other students.
>
> After a period of time, I come back to Jason to see how he is progressing. He usually hasn't completed anything beyond the one problem we began with. I ask him why, and he usually just shrugs or says something like, "I don't know."

When teachers talk about students like Jason, they rarely share tales of success. Rather, they speak of their frustrations getting these children to complete almost any assignment on time or as directed. Since these students are always forgetting, teachers ascribe the behavior to disorganization and memory problems.

"I don't know what else to do. I've tried everything." This teacher spoke of how she kept students in from recess when they hadn't completed their work. She went so far as to make special transportation arrangements for some students to stay after school to finish their assignments. But when 5:00 P.M. arrived and one student had not yet begun to work, it was time to throw in the towel. "I gave up," she said. "There was no way I could make him do the work."

The defeat and frustration teachers often feel is minor compared to what many parents experience. Most parents want their children to be successful, and when they receive negative reports from the school, they usually take it upon themselves to see that their child improves. When efforts fail, their frustration grows and they begin

From *American Educator,* Winter 1992, pp. 38-44. Reprinted by permission of *American Educator,* the quarterly journal of the American Federation of Teachers.

to blame the child and the teachers. Teachers, in turn, frequently believe it is the parents who hold the key, and they expect them to do more to help.

WHO IS WORK INHIBITED?

When I began my studies in 1985, the focus was to discover how many students were work inhibited and if they shared any common traits. Were these children of below-average intelligence? Did they tend to be the students who caused discipline problems in the classroom?

The subjects of the studies resided in Falls Church, Virginia, a small (population 9,500) suburb of Washington, D.C. In general, residents of this city are white middle-class, well-educated professionals.

The community's school system is considered by many to be excellent. A favorable ratio of teachers to pupils enables classes to be small, average scores on national standardized tests are high (in the 70th and 80th percentiles), almost all students are on grade level for reading skills, and less than 1 percent of all students drop out of school.

The first step in my study was to undertake an extensive survey identifying students suffering from work inhibition. To this end, teachers and counselors reviewed the work history of their charges and prepared lists of students in grades three through twelve who routinely submitted significantly less work than typical students. To be considered work inhibited, a student had to have a history of not completing school assignments in all subjects for at least two years. The student's whole record—report cards, notes from parent conferences, plus additional interviews with teachers and parents—was used to analyze the work patterns.

Once identified, further information was sought through student records to determine any distinguishing factors that could explain their work inhibitedness.

The findings surprised parents and teachers alike.

■ Nearly 20 percent of the school population met the definition for work inhibited.

■ Three of every four work-inhibited students were boys.

■ Work inhibition appeared across the continuum of students' abilities and skills (including gifted and learning-disabled). Most of the work-inhibited students not only had good cognitive abilities but had above-average to superior thinking skills, as measured by tests of intellectual ability.

■ Work inhibition did not appear to be a function of socioeconomic class.

■ Work inhibition is not related to birth order.

■ In spite of a history of work inhibition, these students frequently had good academic knowledge and skills. Even for students who hadn't done much work for years, they continued to obtain above-average standardized achievement test scores. The skills most likely to suffer were math computation, spelling, and written composition.

■ The overwhelming majority of work-inhibited students were not disruptive in the classroom. Discipline records revealed that work-inhibited students were sent out of the classroom because of disruptive behavior nearly as often as the general student population.

Demographic studies revealed that the advantages of high socioeconomic status, good solid intellectual abilities, and excellent educational opportunities do not insulate students from becoming work inhibited.

PERSONALITY CHARACTERISTICS

In an effort to develop a descriptive profile, parents and teachers were invited to provide descriptions of work-inhibited students. Other methodologies included case studies, two experimental studies, a correlation study, and clinical interviews.

Dependency

Work-inhibited students will do their work if their teacher is standing or sitting right next to them. Under these circumstances, even chronically work-inhibited students will do their academic assignments.

Teacher after teacher recounted similar experiences at all grade levels. One fourth-grade teacher gave up her daily break to supervise one of her students during recess. Although Philip liked playing with the other students and clearly enjoyed recess, he was kept in almost daily because he failed to complete his morning class assignments.

The teacher was repeatedly amazed, however, at how well Philip worked when they were alone and next to each other; Philip finished each assignment with minimal effort. But on occasions when his teacher was not able to remain in the classroom with him during recess, Philip did not complete his work. He only finished his assignments when his teacher was right next to him.

Self-Esteem

Parents and educators invariably note poor self-esteem as a central characteristic of work-inhibited students. The behaviors associated with dependency are also frequently associated with poor self-esteem.

Work-inhibited students express their poor self-esteem in many ways. Some are obviously self-conscious. They hold back not only in the completion of assignments, but also in opportunities to lead games and discussions. These students are often constricted; they find it difficult to express their feelings and opinions and seem to want to evaporate or disappear from the classroom. When they do interact, they are often silly and immature. Their classmates may laugh at them. Shy, fragile, and preoccupied with feelings of self-doubt, these students often prefer the company of younger children.

Other work-inhibited students express a bravado. They declare that much of their schoolwork is beneath them: "Why bother with this drivel my teacher asks us to do? Who needs it?" "I can do it when I want to. I just have more important things to do!"

In contrast, students who do their work not only share a strong desire to succeed, they also have confidence in their abilities to persevere, solve problems, and complete their work. They have an openness that contrasts with the work-inhibited students' bravado. While these successful students may not all be outgoing, they usually don't appear fragile. They are willing to take risks, do not fear failure, and are confident.

The studies of self-esteem were conducted in a community in which parents placed a high value on education. Failing at endeavors that are most valued by one's parents exacts a great emotional toll. It is possible that parents contribute to a lowered sense of self-worth by reminding their work-inhibited children of their frequent failures to do well. Many of these children feel they are not successful in their relationships with their parents; they report significantly less approval from their family than do students who are successful at school.

Passive Aggression

Another characteristic of many work-inhibited students—and one that is often misunderstood—is the dimension of passive aggression. Passive-aggressive behaviors are subtle, indirect expressions of anger. Passive-aggressive people cannot openly express anger because it frightens them to do so. They may feel it is better to deny the feelings than to allow them to surface.

The paradox is that the passive-aggressive person *does* express anger, but not openly. Passive-aggressive children are not likely to say no or to openly refuse to follow the directions of teachers or parents. Instead, the passive-aggressive student is more likely to smile, say yes, and then "forget."

Passive-aggressive behaviors take many forms; being forgetful is just one of the most common. Some kids play verbal lawyer. They argue any point—often just for the sake of doing so. These children are very good at picking out the exception to almost any rule. Once a teacher spends considerable time explaining complex directions, this verbal lawyer will introduce some highly unlikely, but plausible, exception. After hearing the student's exceptions, the teacher then has to redirect the class before continuing the lesson.

Another powerful weapon in passive-aggressives' battles is withholding. Such children *will* do what is asked, but they take forever doing so. One father called his son "Dilly Dally" since the boy always took so much time to get ready or to do any chore.

Sooner or later the persistent tactics of the passive-aggressive child will result in temper tantrums. But it is not the child who has the tantrum—it's the parent or teacher. When this happens, the child is bewildered and does not really understand why the parent or teacher is so angry. The child is also frightened, because it's scary to see an important adult out of control. Furthermore, the angry response confirms for the passive-aggressive child that feelings of anger are dangerous and should be denied or kept under control.

Some children are maddeningly passive-aggressive; in others the problem may be less severe. It may seem paradoxical that these passive-aggressive children are often likable and engaging, yet these negative behaviors are not to be denied. The passive-aggressive child wants to please, but angry feelings push up to the surface in maladaptive ways. The child is often unaware of the depth of these angry feelings and doesn't understand their cause.

In Perspective

Most parents and teachers believe that most work-inhibited students are not severely emotionally disturbed. Rather, they have emotional conflicts. In spite of their burdens, endearing qualities are often evident. For example, they clearly want to do better. Just ask work-inhibited children or teenagers what they would like to change about their lives. "I'd get better grades. The problem is I don't do the work. I could if I wanted to. It's like I get up and tell myself that I'm going to do it today! And then, I don't know. I put it off and then it's too late."

One parent told of how happy her son was when he did finish a lesson. Others have noted that work-inhibited students relished their occasional good performances. These students want to be successful—just as successful as their parents' dreams for them.

A personality questionnaire given to both work-inhibited and achieving students showed that most personality traits common to work-inhibited students are no different from those of achieving students, with some important exceptions.

As a group, work-inhibited students lack persistence and drive; instead, they are expedient, self-indulgent, and have difficulty in delaying gratification. These students are very insecure. They feel guilty and troubled about their inability to take care of themselves, to do their work, and to live up to their own expectations and those of others. Work-inhibited students are not tough or resilient. In general, they lack the emotional fitness to stay the course when faced with difficult tasks and are unable to assert themselves. They need far more help than most students—not only in doing their work, but also in developing a sense of adequacy.

ETIOLOGY OF WORK INHIBITION

"Why is it so difficult for my son to spend just a few hours a week doing homework? I know he isn't stupid!"

It is clear that the cause of work inhibition is not related to intelligence or to a specific weakness in reading or mathematics. Nor is it due to parental neglect. Most work-inhibited students come from homes where academic success is stressed as an important pursuit, and parents are actively involved in "helping."

Case histories reveal that the beginnings of this problem occur early in children's development. Although the manifestations of work inhibition are not always apparent until the third or fourth grade (the time when the demand for independent academic work becomes substantial), the origins begin during infancy.

Some children come to school secure and ready to be on their own. Others do not. Why do some children have the socially and emotionally adaptive skills to engage in independent schoolwork while these skills are lacking in others?

At the earliest stages of human development, babies are highly dependent upon adults for food, warmth, attention, and affection. Yet very early, infants display an amazing interest in their world and derive satisfaction from exploring their environment.

One of life's major struggles is the quest for independence. Growth toward autonomy becomes particularly evident in the second year of a child's life. The child is motivated to explore, understand, and control its world. The two-year-old's desire to do things in his or her own way is easily remembered by parents: This period is often referred to as the "terrible twos."

The success a young child experiences in becoming psychologically separate from his or her parents is very important to the child's future. A person who has been successful in separating psychologically from parents is equipped to function independently in both play and work.

With work-inhibited students, a breakdown in the independence process appears evident. Something has gone awry to keep these children from developing the social and emotional skills necessary to function well apart from their parents or other significant adults. Perhaps there is something in a child's unique makeup that makes it difficult for him or her to be independent. Perhaps some children receive tacit messages from Mom and Dad that separation from them is not safe—that they won't do well on their own.

Work-inhibited students have not developed the *emotional* skills necessary to do independent schoolwork, which often requires children to be on their own, apart from others, doing a task that is neither easy nor pleasurable. Over time, children who are not autonomous do not develop a healthy sense of self-esteem. The problem evolves into a vicious cycle. As they experience failure to initiate independence successfully, children do not receive the positive reinforcement of a job well done that will, in turn, provide them with the encouragement and good emotional feedback to continue going forth with new tasks.

While standard educational practices are not in themselves the root causes for work inhibition, these practices typically exacerbate the problem. Vulnerable, sensitive, weakly assertive children have difficulty in environments that stress competition rather than cooperation, that are more negative than positive, that reject rather than embrace, that fail rather than encourage, and that blame rather than understand.

As educators begin to understand the dynamics of work inhibition, they will have the opportunity to work in concert with parents to solve this bewildering problem. It certainly would be a relief to parents if positive programs of early intervention existed, so that parents and teachers could join together to help children before undue harm occurred.

HELP FOR WORK-INHIBITED STUDENTS

IDENTIFICATION

Work inhibition is rarely diagnosed as the reason for children's inability to do work; its symptoms are often confused with other educational disabilities. Parents can certainly recognize when their children have difficulty settling down and doing their work, but they rarely know what causes the problem. Even teachers who observe these children daily are often perplexed. At times both parents and teachers suspect that a child's failure to do work is caused by a subtle learning disability, attention-deficit disorder, or perhaps a fine-motor coordination weakness that impairs the ability to write and complete assignments. These questions must be answered if a child is to be helped.

A successful system for evaluating work-inhibited students must accomplish two major objectives. First, educators must identify those students who do not engage in the work of school. Second, educators, working with parents and mental health professionals, must devise and implement a plan to ensure that each of these students is individually understood.

WHAT TEACHERS CAN DO

For work-inhibited students, sitting down and doing schoolwork is painful. It simply is the worst part of their life. They hate it. For many, this problem is of long standing and simple quick fixes are not in the cards. Teachers can, however, make a difference.

Work-inhibited students may be helped in a number of general ways. They benefit from positive relationships with their teachers; they achieve more with supportive help to complete tasks; they benefit when they are actively helped to become independent; and they benefit from opportunities to develop their individual strengths.

Build Nurturing Relationships

In order to grow toward independence, work-inhibited students need friendly, positive, and optimistic relationships with important adults, including teachers. It is reassuring and important to them to feel that their teacher is in their corner.

Most people tend to do better work, or at least enjoy it more, when they work with someone who likes them. Providing work-inhibited students with friendly hellos, greeting them each day with a smile, finding a way to extend unconditional positive regard nurtures a student's sense of well-being.

A teacher's friendliness may be positively disarming to these students. They usually have long histories of negative self-perceptions and do not expect their teachers to be truly interested in them. In response to their teachers' friendly "hello"—away from the classroom, where teachers are not obligated to take notice of them—the students feel a bit better about their teachers and about themselves. Such friendly, inviting greetings in themselves can improve attitudes toward school and pave the way for further positive dialogue.

There is probably no better way to convey interest and nurturance than through listening. Most teacher-student social exchanges are momentary—just a few words and a smile. But sometimes the opportunity presents itself to be with a student in a situation that has nothing to do with schoolwork. Exploit such opportunities to be attentive to remarks about the student's interests. The act of really listening is a tremendous compliment and a powerful tool in building a relationship.

Help Students Develop Stick-to-it-tiveness

Work-inhibited students need help in learning persistence—to stay on task, to withstand failure, and to forge ahead. They need to learn the skills of stick-to-it-tiveness more than academic skills.

Teachers may choose among a variety of strategies to

assist the work-inhibited student to move slowly, incrementally, toward competence. Sometimes an entire class may have the same assignment—which a work-inhibited student may well be able to complete if it is broken down into small incremental steps. As the student completes each part, the teacher gives a pat on the back, a bit of encouragement—an emotional "pick-me-up"—to proceed on to the next step. The teacher tries to extend the student just a little bit.

This method is much like training to run faster. Runners set intervals during which they run hard and fast for a brief period, and then recover. Then they repeat the pattern. The goal is to run faster for short distances and then gradually extend the distance.

Varying the approach helps. Students like novelty. Surprise the child by insisting that only three questions be completed. Set up a challenge to work quickly. Use a timer and ask the student to beat the clock. Highlight or underline certain items and ask the student to finish only those that are so marked.

Maintain a careful record of assignments completed and graph the results. Student and teacher alike may be surprised and positively reinforced by viewing a graph that shows progress.

Do not let the work pile up. At the end of each period, go on to the next activity. If possible, collect any work, both complete and incomplete, and go on. Work-inhibited students easily feel overwhelmed and are unlikely to tackle a tableful of incomplete assignments. They do need to learn to tackle longer and longer assignments, but it is foolish to encourage work-inhibited students to climb a mountain when they are still unable to scale a hill.

Working incrementally means always taking it one day at a time. It means the teacher is pleased to see a work-inhibited student increase effort 100 percent when going from two minutes to four minutes, while most of the other students are able to work independently for half an hour. Bit by bit, focusing on successes, breaking assignments into smaller units, giving assignments that may be completed—this is the direction in which success lies.

Offer Helping Hands

Through positive regard and problem-solving conferences, a work-inhibited student's readiness for accepting help may improve. But a teacher with twenty-five students in a classroom can spend only a fraction of the day being next to and assisting any one individual. Therefore, it may be useful to recruit helpers to assist work-inhibited students. The classmates of work-inhibited students may be a rich resource. Pair classmates and encourage them to assist each other. Older work-inhibited students often welcome the opportunity to tutor younger children with similar weaknesses. It not only adds variety to their day but tutoring also helps them feel important. In high school, members of the National Honor Society, Key Club, or other service organizations may be ready and willing to give tutorial assistance. Each school is filled with helping hands.

Providing positive, effective feedback to students is a powerful tool but not necessarily easy to use. For praise to be effective, certain rules should be remembered.

Reward the action or product, not the person, with positive attention. Comment specifically about what it is the student has accomplished. Comments should not be exaggerated or insincere, but rather true and to the point. "Nineteen out of twenty correct! You really understand!" "Your use of shading in this painting gives the scene perspective and a sense of distance." "Your paragraph included three funny examples of what can happen on the first day of school." "Joe, your speech kept everyone's attention."

Sometimes positive reinforcement does not require words. Just a smile or a pat on the back may keep a student working. What is important is to notice what the student is doing or has accomplished.

Teachers are not the only ones who may give positive reinforcement. Everyone in the class might do it! Encourage classmates to support each other by modeling positive communication. The goal is to create a climate of encouragement.

Empower the Child

Work-inhibited students need all the help they can get in order to bolster their weak egos. These students benefit from opportunities to develop their individual strengths—to feel empowered. Encourage work-inhibited students to participate in extracurricular activities and provide them with opportunities for leadership (safety patrols, office helper).

Another important facet of feeling empowered relates to decision making. In high school, students have opportunities to make important decisions as to what courses they will take and what career paths they may embark on. At all levels, it is important to empower students to make decisions regarding daily activities, including how to accomplish tasks and what is to be studied. Being asked "What do you think?" or "What do you want to do first?" imparts a sense of importance to students and fuels feelings of control and independence. The goal is to promote autonomy so that students may stand on their own and feel a sense of adequacy.

Practices To Avoid

Our schools should not be reluctant to change those practices that are not in the best interests of students. If students are able to demonstrate their acquisition of knowledge and skills without certain homework assignments—give up those assignments. Requiring a child to repeat a grade for failure to complete assignments, punishing children by keeping them in for recess or by denying them access to extracurricular activities are not likely to promote the growth of their interests or their sense of well-being in their school.

In communicating to parents, provide clear descriptions of the student's strengths and weaknesses. Parents need to know that their children have allies in the school. Don't blame. Rather, be objective about the instructional setting and the requirements for success. Parents need to know that school work is not their responsibility. Parents can set the stage by providing a place and establishing a schedule for homework; but they should tell their children that the contract for doing school work is between students and teachers; and then nurture, love, and encourage.

The Culturally Sensitive Disciplinarian

Thomas McIntyre

Thomas McIntyre, Professor, Department of Special Education, Hunter College of City University of New York, 695 Park Avenue, New York, New York 10021

ABSTRACT

Given the increasing cultural diversity of the schoolage population, teachers must become more aware of cultural differences in behavior. This article addresses some of these differences and recommends behavior management modifications.

Since their inception, our schools have changed from predominantly white institutions to multicultural environments. While the 25 largest school systems have a student population comprised mostly of minority students (National Information Center for Children and Youth with Handicaps, 1988), nonurban areas are also seeing such developments (Alston, cited in Armstrong, 1991). By the year 2000, one-third (Grossman, 1990) to one-half (Wilson, 1988) of America's school students will be from a minority group.

At present, 92% of the teaching force is from the white majority culture. This figure will increase to 95% by the turn of the century (Henry, 1990). The contrast in cultural background between teachers and students applies to an even greater extent in special education where minority youth are overrepresented in various programs for the disabled including those for pupils with emotional or behavioral disorders (Chinn & Hughes, 1987; Viadero, 1992). Much of this phenomenon may be attributable to the mismatch between the expectations present in the students' homes and those of the school environments (Almanza & Moseley, 1980; Grossman, 1990).

Behavioral patterns and actions considered to be abnormal vary by culture (Light & Martin, 1985; Toth, 1990). When educators and their charges come from different backgrounds, it can be expected that each will often display behaviors different from those in the other's culture. Given that most individuals truly understand only their own culture and find it difficult to appreciate behavior culturally different from their own (Garcia, 1978; Grossman, 1990; McIntyre, 1992), there is a strong chance that teachers will misinterpret their pupils' culturally-based behavior as requiring a referral for special education or at least disciplinary action (Foster, 1986; Grossman, 1990; Hanna, 1988). Indeed, children who display culturally diverse behaviors, especially recent immigrants (Sugai, 1988), are particularly susceptible to diagnosis for behavioral disorders (Hanna, 1988; Sugai & Maheady, 1988).

CULTURAL DIFFERENCES IN BEHAVIOR

A lack of appreciation and tolerance for cultural differences is often found among educators. These teachers expect their students to adopt majority culture behaviors overnight, denying the validity of centuries of cultural practice. "The teacher's expectation is that the student should be compliant, docile, and responsive to authority. The student is expected to conform to a standard of behavior that the teacher is familiar with, the compliant child standard that was indicative of the teacher's upbringing" (Dent, 1976, p. 178). These teachers are at risk for reacting to culturally determined behavior in ways that are insensitive, inappropriate, counterproductive, or offensive to students and their culture.

As an example of culturally disrespectful intervention, consider that in the majority American culture a child is expected to look at the authority figure when being disciplined. Lowered eyes are associated with deceit or inattention (Armstrong, 1991; Grossman, 1990). To gain eye contact, the instructor may lift the student's chin and say, "Look at me when I'm talking to you." The educator may not realize that in many Asian, African-American, and Hispanic homes, children are taught to lower their eyes when being disciplined as a sign of respect and submission (Armstrong, 1991; Grossman, 1990; Nine-Curt, 1976). *Assertive Discipline* (Canter & Canter, 1976) and other behavior management systems that recommend gaining eye contact while disciplining unknowingly fail to respect the behavior promoted in the student's home environment. Additionally, the teacher probably fails to realize that direct eye contact by these students during disciplinary situations typically indicates defiance rather than respect (Grossman, 1990; Hanna, 1988). The educator may also not realize that many culturally diverse children smile during disciplinary situations, not to express defiance, but rather, due to anxiety, appeasement attempts or confusion as to why the instructor is confronting them (Henkin & Nguyen, 1981; Nine-Curt, 1976).

Minority students are often penalized by teaching methods which contrast with their culturally based preferred style of learning (Blackorby & Edgar, 1990). Consider, for example, the individualistic and competitive environment of the typical classroom which works against the more cooperative learning style com-

From the *Severe Behavior Disorders Monograph*, Vol. 15, Summer 1992, pp. 107-115. © 1992 by The Council for Exceptional Children. Reprinted by permission.

mon among Hispanics, African-Americans, and Native Americans (Brendtro, Brokenleg, & Van Bockern, 1991; "CASSP national workshop," 1988; Grossman, 1990). While displaying their culture's helpfulness, brotherhood, or generosity, students may assist their peers or allow them to copy their answers, not considering this to be "cheating" (Grossman, 1984). If criticized for doing this in front of their peers or made to compete against their will, these pupils may rebel against such treatment or withdraw from further attempts to succeed in school or relate to their teachers (Grossman, 1990). Majority culture educators may then use their own culturally based disciplinary behavior: removing affection (Grossman, 1984). However, this reaction is less commonly found in the students' culture and may not gain the desired results (Grossman, 1984).

Other traditional methods of promoting positive classroom behavior such as checks, gold stars, sweets, and prizes may also be less effective with Hispanic and other learners. The reason, explains Grossman (1984, pp. 37 and 40), is that "Hispanics tend to be more interested in and dependent on the approval of others than Anglos who are more likely to be receptive to more impersonal and materialistic forms of recognition." Instead, teachers should use praise, hugs, pats on the back, and other personal contact. They should also stress that Hispanic students' families will be proud of them and share the honor of their accomplishments. This particular strategy might also be useful in motivating Arab and Asian students who wish to bring pride to their families (Nydel, 1987; Wei, 1984).

While touch is often recommended as a reinforcement procedure, especially for cultural groups that use a great deal of bodily contact, it may be contra-indicated for some Asian students. Those whose heritage was influenced by Confucianism view the body as being more sacred as one approaches the area of the head where the soul is believed to reside (Kaczor, 1988). Given this wide body spacing and the lack of touch between Asian individuals (Yao, 1980), teachers should avoid certain actions that are used to motivate and reinforce Hispanic, Arabian, and African-American students (e.g., hair mussing, placing hands on the shoulder, back slapping).

While the majority culture places great emphasis on promptness and work-ing diligently on task (Althen, 1988), most other groups have a more flexible view of time (Nine-Curt, 1976; Sung, 1987). As a result, minority students may be late to school or might not complete classroom work as quickly as their majority culture peers. They may be viewed as being "off task" and tersely told to "get to work." When rushed, or told to stop working before completion of that assignment in order to begin the next task with their peers, the students may resist, appearing to misbehave (Grossman, 1984).

Other groups may also be negatively affected by the demands of the traditional school setting. A teacher's expectations for quiet, nonactive student behavior would be in opposition to the more active and emotionally outspoken contributory styles of Arabian students (Nydel, 1987). This can result in the students' behavior being viewed as inappropriate. A similar learning style is frequently evident among African-American pupils who show attention and cognitive involvement with vocal responses, exuberance, and physical movement (Gay, 1975; Ogbu, 1988). Teachers oftentimes consider these students to be inattentive, restless, disruptive, or hostile (Gay, 1975), and evidencing "an attitude" (Gilmore, 1985). They may impose disciplinary procedures rather than incorporating spontaneity, performance, and audience reaction into their lessons.

Another common misunderstanding involves a teacher who explains a task to an Asian student and then asks if the directions are understood. Although the student says "yes", upon later review the teacher finds that the instructions were not comprehended. He or she is perplexed by the apparent dishonesty of the student, unaware that the pupil may have been attempting to "save face" (Woo, 1985). Among the Asian cultures there is a commonly held belief that one should avoid conflict or public embarrassment which would shame not only the individuals involved, but by extension, their families (Henkin & Nguyen, 1981; Leung, 1988; Wei, 1984). The student in the testing situation may have been trying to prevent the dishonor or humiliation of admitting that he or she was incapable of understanding the directions (Woo, 1985), or perhaps the pupil was trying to avoid humiliating the teacher for not having done a good job of explaining the task (Wei, 1984). These students may also fail to volunteer answers during class discussions for fear of giving an incorrect response (Henkin & Nguyen, 1981; Woo, 1985).

The same applies to the "pow-wow" (Hobbs, 1966) in which a student's report on whether he or she has achieved preselected goals is followed by peer commentary as to whether they agree. This could be quite uncomfortable for Asian students as they might publicly "lose face" if goals have not been attained.

Therefore, teachers should not assume that the less direct and more subdued behavior common in the Asian cultures is indicative of "sneakiness" or noncompliance. While penalizing the student for this behavior is inappropriate, any shame and embarrassment is compounded when public reprimands such as those in the warning system recommended in *Assertive Discipline* (Canter & Canter, 1976) are used (Jones, 1991). Listing the student's name, followed by checkmarks indicating recurring misbehavior, may cause Asian students (and many Arabian students whose families also place great emphasis on family honor) to "lose face." A private rather than public critique of behavior is the intervention of choice.

Contrary to the facesaving behavior promoted by certain cultures, other groups provide an upbringing which may increase the likelihood of teacher-student conflict. For example, in the Hispanic culture which tends to be male dominant (Arredondo, 1991; Devore & Schlesinger, 1987), adolescent boys may resist complying with commands from female educators (Grossman, 1984). With these students, cooperation is best gained through nonauthoritative methods which request rather than demand compliance (Grossman, 1984).

Defiance may also be demonstrated to a great extent by low income urban African-American youth whose parents often teach them to fight to avoid being victimized in their tough neighborhoods (Hanna, 1988; McIntyre, 1991, in press). Growing up in these areas is more likely to produce traits that impede success in school (e.g., a more physical style of action, a greater approval of the use of violence, less disguised aggression, lack of subtlety in verbiage, and ridiculing of others; Hanna, 1988; McIntyre, 1991, in press). These behaviors and the previously mentioned learning style differences may explain why African-American youth receive one-third of the corporal punishments (Quality Education for Minorities,

1990), are twice as likely as whites to be suspended (Gibbs, 1988), and are suspended for longer periods than whites (Gibbs, 1988).

Few teachers realize that African-American, Mexican-American, Native Hawaiian, and Native American youth are often under great pressure from their peers *not* to achieve in school (Gollnick & Chinn, 1990; Hanna, 1988; Ogbu, 1990). Individual success in schooling or professions is viewed as inappropriate if the group does not also advance (Fordham, 1988; Ogbu, 1990). For many students merely attending school is viewed as evidence of rejection of their culture (Fordham, 1988; Ogbu, 1990). For others, misbehavior is a strategy of resistance to being pressured to think and act "white" in the schools (Fordham, 1988; Gibson, 1988; Ogbu, 1988, 1990; Quality Education for Minorities, 1990). Because of the peer pressure, those who strive for academic excellence may feel the need to camouflage their academic efforts (Fordham, 1988).

This rejection of schooling may result in disciplinary action or referral for behavior disorders services. Teachers can best assist and support these students by using private disciplinary action (and even allowing usually compliant students to misbehave at times), modifying instruction to better match their culturally determined learning styles, allowing them to downplay accomplishments, and avoiding public recognition unless approved by them (McIntyre, in press). Teachers can expect that these students might not respond well to public praise and rewards for actions which may be perceived as "acting white."

Even devoid of racial influences, defiant and aggressive behaviors occur more often in the lower socioeconomic stratum (McIntyre, in press; Strom, 1965). As a result of harsh and inconsistent home discipline (Hanna, 1988; Horton & Hunt, 1976), low income urban pupils may have developed an escape and avoidance reaction style to discipline, or come to view physical punishment as a sign of caring (Rosenfeld, 1971; Silverstein & Krate, 1975). They may be confused by the subtle and supportive behavior management practices of middle-class teachers (Hanna, 1988; Harrison-Ross & Wyden, 1973).

While some educators support corporal punishment in the belief that these students are best disciplined by a style to which they are accustomed (Bauer, Du-banoski, Yamauchi, & Honbo, 1990), most middle-class oriented educators believe in permissiveness and an appeal to reason. The first group's methods are ineffective because schools cannot offer aversive consequences as severe as those at home. The second group fails to realize that lower-class youth have a different frame of reference regarding discipline that involves physicalness and toughness (Foster, 1986; McIntyre, in press). These youth "test" teachers to see if they can "make" the youth behave (Foster, 1986) and come to view whites and middle-class minorities as passive and weak if they cannot do so (Hanna, 1988). Implementing a structured behavior management approach in which predetermined penalties are consistently administered for violations of clearly stated rules gives one "clout" and influence. However, this should still be blended with reinforcement for appropriate behavior in order to promote a positive classroom climate.

The emphasis on positiveness also applies to working with Native American students. The imposition of authority in a demanding or demeaning manner typically results in passive resistance and withdrawal on the part of these pupils (Hurlburt, Gade, & McLaughlin, 1990; Kleinfeld, 1972). An appeal to their good nature and the use of appropriate reinforcement is more productive than coercive or confrontational strategies (Brendtro et al., 1991).

The same principle applies for Arabian-American students. As in the Hispanic and Native American cultures, frank criticism may be perceived as a personal insult (Nine-Curt, 1976). Best practice includes indirect criticism mixed with encouragement and praise regarding any positive points or expectations that were met (Nydel, 1987).

RECOMMENDATIONS

It is imperative that educators practice respect for culturally different behavior. Instead of viewing behavior as *right* or *wrong,* it is best judged by how well it is suited to the demands of the educational environment (although schools must also assess how well they are meeting the needs of their culturally diverse populations). To better serve their charges, educational personnel need to develop an awareness of how cultural background affects the way one behaves, and con-versely, how one perceives and judges the behaviors of those not like oneself.

As Light and Martin (1985, p. 43) point out, "An understanding of cultural expectations and roles can contribute to the development of child management techniques specifically designed to eliminate value differences between a child's family, the school system, and the larger society." By working *with* rather than *against* a culture, any student resentment about having to behave differently in school can be managed (Grossman, 1990). One recommendation regarding discipline which pertains to all groups is to be positive rather than negative or confrontational. A skilled, culturally sensitive behavior manager entices rather than coerces students into proper behavior (Bauer et al., 1990).

For students from African-American, Hispanic, Native American, and Arabian cultures which place greater emphasis on socializing and bodily contact than the white and Asian cultures (Kleinfeld, 1972; Nine-Curt, 1976; Nydel, 1987), teachers can increase their effectiveness by displaying more "warmth" (Kleinfeld, 1972). This involves reinforcing students via the use of touch, hugs, smiles, and closer body spacing. When discipline is necessary, because of their desire to socialize with peers, timeout may be especially effective with these pupils (Hanna, 1988).

In order for our schools to become more culturally sensitive in their disciplinary practice, changes will need to be implemented at each educational stratum (McIntyre, 1992). Teacher training institutions must assume the larger share of the burden of imparting cultural information. At this level, it can be assured that future teachers will study this information and be guided in its use in practicum settings. Generally, however, university programs in education are not presenting this information (Garcia, 1978; Yates, 1988). Before teacher trainers can impart information regarding cultural characteristics, instructional modifications, and culturally sensitive behavior management practices, they must first educate themselves in this area.

Schools can promote cultural understanding in a number of ways ranging from conducting inservice sessions with national level consultants or local civic leaders of particular cultures to hiring individuals from minority groups who are able to communicate information across cultures (Armstrong, 1991). Additionally, schools might provide services to culturally diverse students to assist them in becoming *cultural chameleons* capable of displaying *school behavior* if their culturally-based actions interfere with educational achievement or interaction with others. This is not an easy decision for educators and the community at large who must wrestle with the issue of whether to promote and/or teach majority culture behaviors to the student population. Caught in the horns of a cultural dilemma, they must decide whether to chance making one culture look preferable to another or hazard impairing students' future employability by failing to expose them to the expectations of the typical workplace.

If it is deemed necessary to teach white behavior, this can be accomplished via specially designed lessons perhaps utilizing activities from published social skills curricula. Students would then role-play common situations. Career education lessons that focus on the benefits of being able to display office behavior might also be planned.

Paramount at the classroom level, however, is the creation of an atmosphere of cultural tolerance and acceptance. Students of all ethnic cultures need to feel valued, respected, and psychologically and physically safe. This is accomplished by proactively adapting one's classroom management study to the students' culturally-based characteristics (Grossman, 1990).

Finally, it is imperative that professional organizations concerned with cultural diversity and behavioral disorders focus more on culturally-based differences in behavior and culturally sensitive behavior management practices in their publications and conference planning.

CONCLUSIONS

Teachers oftentimes create much of the misbehavior about which they complain. Via modification of traditional behavior management procedures one can create a productive classroom environment that values the culture of one's students (Jones, 1991). When educators are knowledgeable of and able to critically examine differences in culturally-based behavior, they can be more confident that all students are being treated fairly and respectfully.

REFERENCES

Althen, G. (1988). *American ways.* Yarmouth, ME: Intercultural Press.

Almanza, H., & Moseley, W. (1980). Curriculum adaptions and modification for culturally diverse handicapped children. *Exceptional Children, 46,* 608–614.

Armstrong, L. (1991, March 20). Census confirms remarkable shifts in ethnic makeup. *Education Week,* pp. 1, 16.

Arredondo, P. (1991). Counseling Latinas. In C. Lee & B. Richardson (Eds.), *Multicultural issues in counseling: New approaches to diversity* (pp. 143–156). Alexandria, VA: American Association for Counseling and Development.

Bauer, G. B., Dubanoski, R., Yamauchi, L. A., & Honbo, K. M. (1990). Corporal punishment and the schools. *Education and Urban Society, 22,* 285–299.

Blackorby, J., & Edgar, E. (1990). A third of our youth? A look at the problem of high school dropout among mildly handicapped students. *Journal of Special Education, 24,* 508–510.

Brendtro, L. K., Brokenleg, M., & Van Bockern, S. (1991). The circle of courage. *Beyond Behavior, 2*(1), 5–12.

CASSP national workshop identifies culturally specific needs of minority children with emotional handicaps. *Focal Point, 3*(1), 5–6.

Canter, L., & Canter, M. (1976). *Assertive discipline: A take-charge approach for today's educator.* Los Angeles: Canter & Assoc.

Chinn, P., & Hughes, S. (1987). Representation of minority students in special education classes. *Remedial and Special Education, 8*(4), 41–46.

Dent, H. L. (1976). Assessing Black children for mainstream placement. In R. L. Jones (Ed.), *Mainstreaming and the minority child* (pp. 77–91). Reston, VA: The Council for Exceptional Children.

Devore, W., & Schlesinger, E. G. (1987). *Ethnic-sensitive social work practice* (2nd ed.). Columbus, OH: Merrill.

Fordham, S. (1988). Racelessness as a factor in Black students' school success: Pragmatic strategy or pyrrhic victory? *Harvard Educational Review, 58*(1), 54–84.

Foster, H. (1986). *Ribbin', jivin', and playin' the dozens.* New York: Ballantine.

Garcia, R. (1978). *Fostering a pluralistic society through multi-ethnic education.* Bloomington, IN: Phi Delta Kappa.

Gay, G. (1975, October). Cultural differences important in the education of Black children. *Momentum,* pp. 30–33.

Gibbs, J. B. (Ed.). (1988). *Young, Black, and male in America: An endangered species.* New York: Auburn House.

Gibson, M. (1988). *Accommodation without assimilation: Sikh immigrants in an American high school.* Ithaca, NY: Cornell University Press.

Gilmore, P. (1985). Gimme room: School resistance, attitude, and access to literacy. *Journal of Education, 167,* 111–128.

Gollnick, D., & Chinn, P. (1990). *Multicultural education in a pluralistic society.* Columbus, OH: Merrill.

Grossman, H. (1984). *Educating Hispanic students: Cultural implications for instruction, classroom management, counseling, and assessment.* Springfield, IL: C. C. Thomas.

Grossman, H. (1990). *Trouble-free teaching: Solutions to behavior problems in the classroom.* Mountain View, CA: Mayfield.

Hanna, J. (1988). *Disruptive school behavior: Class, race, and culture.* New York: Holmes & Meier.

Harrison-Ross, P., & Wyden, B. (1973). *The Black child.* Berkeley, CA: Medallion.

Henkin, A., & Nguyen, L. (1981). *Between two cultures: The Vietnamese in America.* Saratoga, CA: Rand.

Henry, W. (1990, April 9). Beyond the melting pot. *Time,* p. 28.

Hobbs, N. (1966). Helping disturbed children: Psychological and ecological strategies. *American Psychologist, 21,* 1105–1115.

Horton, P., & Hunt, C. (1976). *Sociology* (2nd ed.). New York: McGraw-Hill.

Hurlburt, G., Gade, E., & McLaughlin, J. (1990, May). Teaching attitudes and study attitudes of Indian education students. *Journal of American Indian Education,* pp. 12–18.

Jones, V. (1991). Responding to students' behavior problems. *Beyond Behavior, 2*(1), 13–16.

Kaczor, B. (1988, December 20). Military course helps avoid cross-cultural clashes, gaffs. *Saint Petersburg Times,* p. 6B.

Kleinfeld, J. (1972). *Effective teachers of Indian and Eskimo high school students.* Anchorage: University of Alaska, Institute of Social, Economic, and Government Research.

Leung, E. (1988). Cultural and acculturational commonalities and diversities among Asian Americans: Identification and programming considerations. In A. Ortiz & B. Ramirez (Eds.), *Schools and culturally diverse exceptional students* (pp. 86–95). Reston, VA: The Council for Exceptional Children.

Light, H., & Martin, R. (1985). Guidance of American Indian children. *Journal of American Indian Education, 25*(1), 42–46.

McIntyre, T. (1991). Understanding and defusing the streetcorner behavior of urban Black socially maladjusted youth. In R. B. Rutherford, Jr., S. A. DiGangi, & S. R. Mathur (Eds.), *Severe behavior disorders of children and youth* (Vol. 14, pp. 85–97). Reston, VA: Council for Children with Behavioral Disorders.

McIntyre, T. (1992). A primer on cultural diversity for educators. *Multicultural Forum, 1,* 6, 13.

McIntyre, T. (in press). Teaching urban behavior disordered youth. In R. Peterson & S. Ishii-Jordan (Eds.), *Behavior disorders in the context of culture and community.* Boston, MA: Brookline.

National Information Center for Children and Youth with Handicaps. (1988). *Minority issues in special education: A portrait of the future.* Washington, DC: Author.

Nine-Curt, C. (1976). *Nonverbal communication in Puerto Rico.* Cambridge, MA: National Assessment and Dissemination Center for Bilingual/Bicultural Education.

Nydel, M. (1987). *Understanding Arabs.* Yarmouth, ME: Intercultural Press.

Ogbu, J. (1988). Class stratification, racial stratification, and schooling. In L. Weiss (Ed.), *Class, race, and gender in American education* (pp. 163–180). Albany, NY: State University of New York Press.

Ogbu, J. (1990). Minority education in comparative perspective. *Journal of Negro Education, 1*, 45–57.

Quality Education for Minorities. (1990). *Education that works: An action plan for the education of minorities.* Cambridge, MA: Massachusetts Institute of Technology.

Rosenfeld, G. (1971). *Shut those thick lips! A study of slum school failure.* New York: Holt.

Silverstein, B., & Krate, R. (1975). *Children of the dark ghetto: A developmental psychology.* New York: Praeger.

Strom, R. (1965). *Teaching in the slum school.* Columbus, OH: Merrill.

Sugai, G. (1988). Educational assessment of culturally diverse and behavior disordered students: An examination of critical effect. In A. Ortiz & B. Ramirez (Eds.), *Schools and culturally diverse exceptional students* (pp. 63–75). Reston, VA: The Council for Exceptional Children.

Sugai, G., & Maheady, L. (1988, Fall). Cultural diversity and individual assessment for behavior disorders. *Teaching Exceptional Children,* pp. 27–31.

Sung, B. (1987). *The adjustment experience of Chinese immigrant children in New York City.* Staten Island, NY: Center for Migration Studies.

Toth, M. K. (1990). *Understanding and treating conduct disorders.* Austin, TX: Pro-Ed.

Viadero, D. (1992, April 29). New definition of 'emotionally disturbed' sought. *Education Week,* p. 24.

Wei, T. (1984). *Vietnamese refugee students: A handbook for school personnel.* Cambridge, MA: Lesley College (EDAC).

Wilson, R. (1988, May 4). Bennett notes improvement of schools in past 5 years but paints bleak portrait of U.S. education in report. *Chronicle of Higher Education,* p. A29.

Woo, J. (1985). *The Chinese-speaking student: A composite profile.* New York: Hunter College, Bilingual Education Multifunctional Support Center.

Yao, E. (1980). Implications of biculturalism for the learning process of middle-class Asian children in the United States. *Journal of Education, 61*(4), 61–72.

Yates, J. (1988). Demography as it affects special education. In A. Ortiz & B. Ramirez (Eds.), *Schools and culturally diverse exceptional students* (pp. 1–5). Reston, VA: The Council for Exceptional Children.

Variables Affecting the Reintegration Rate of Students with Serious Emotional Disturbance

ELANA ESTERSON ROCK
MICHAEL S. ROSENBERG
DEBORAH T. CARRAN
Johns Hopkins University

ABSTRACT: *This study examined educational program and teacher variables to identify factors that predict the reintegration of students with serious emotional disturbance (SED) into less restrictive placements. Data on program demographics, reintegration orientation, teacher reintegration training, and teacher attitudes toward reintegration were collected from 162 special education teachers and 31 administrators in restrictive placements for K-12 students with SED. This information was compared to the reintegration rates of students in those schools through the use of a hierarchical set regression analysis. Results indicated that reintegration orientation, demographic characteristics of restrictive SED programs, and particular experiences/training of special educators predict the reintegration of students with SED into less restrictive programs.*

Although the goal of special education programs is to help students function in the least restrictive environment, the complex behavioral, social, emotional, and academic problems of students with serious emotional disturbance often make the process of reintegration difficult (e.g., Braaten, Kauffman, Braaten, Polsgrove, & Nelson, 1988; Downing, Simpson, & Myles, 1990; Gable, Laycock, Maroney, & Smith, 1991; Gresham, Elliott, & Black, 1987). Fewer than one half of the children identified with serious emotional disturbance have been reintegrated for all or part of their education (Downing et al.,1990; Peterson, Smith, White, & Zabel, 1980). Moreover, some experts (e.g., McNutt, 1986; Reynolds, Wang, & Walberg, 1987; Will, 1986) believe that the integration of students with serious emotional disturbance will continue to be limited in the future.

The U.S. Department of Education (USDOE) *Annual Reports to Congress* (USDOE, 1987,

1990, 1992) have revealed that the majority of students identified with serious emotional disturbance continue to be educated in segregated programs: separate classes, separate schools, residential facilities, and home/hospital programs. For example, it was reported that in the 1984-85 school year, 46% of students with serious emotional disturbance were served in regular and resource classes, with the remaining 54% in separate classes, separate programs, and other segregated settings (USDOE, 1987). During the 1987-88 school year (USDOE, 1990), 45% of the students were served in regular and resource classes; and only 43% were served in these placements in the 1989-90 school year (USDOE, 1992). It appears that increasingly fewer students are being included in regular programs despite numerous least-restrictive-environment and "inclusion" initiatives, as well as the increasing body of literature on effective inclusion and reintegration practices (e.g.,

From *Exceptional Children*, December/January 1995, pp. 254-268. © 1995 by The Council for Exceptional Children. Reprinted by permission.

Goodlad & Lovitt, 1993; Stainback & Stainback, 1991).

FOCUS OF PREVIOUS STUDIES

One possible cause for the failure of many programs serving youth with serious emotional disturbance to promote increased integration may be that little research has been undertaken to isolate specific variables that promote integration or increase the likelihood that children with serious emotional disturbance will be reintegrated (Schneider & Byrne, 1984). Of the studies investigating the decision to mainstream children with serious emotional disturbance, the focus has typically been on (a) the behavior or academic achievement of the student or (b) the characteristics of the regular education (mainstream) teacher.

Although the behavior of the child with serious emotional disturbance might logically be considered a major determinant in placement decisions, there is evidence to indicate that behavioral, social, interpersonal, and task-oriented skills are not being considered when reintegration decisions are made (Downing et al., 1990; Hundert, 1982; Walker & Rankin, 1983). Further, neither behavioral improvement nor academic achievement has been shown to differentiate students who were reintegrated from those who were not (Downing et al., 1990; Foley, Cullinan, & Epstein, 1990; Rosenbaum, 1981; Schneider & Byrne, 1984; West, 1981).

The importance of the selection of the regular education teacher to the actual reintegration decision is equally limited. Although the flexibility and attitudes of the regular education teacher are related to the success of reintegration once it has been undertaken (Grosenick, 1971; Simek, 1979; White, 1980), planning teams often do not select or identify the receiving teacher before planning reintegration or even before actually placing the students (Peterson et al., 1980), especially when students have been served in segregated facilities. The special educators may have no input into, or knowledge of, the specific school, class, or teacher who will receive a reintegrated student. Thus, information on the receiving teacher may often be unavailable for use in the decision to reintegrate a child with serious emotional disturbance.

Another problem in the identification of an appropriate "receiving teacher" is that regular educators are particularly resistant to the integration of students with serious emotional disturbance into their classes (Gersten, Walker, & Darch, 1988; Safran & Safran, 1987). This resistance to reintegration has not diminished significantly over the past 10 years (Gable, Hendrickson, Algozzine, & Scully, 1989). Because few regular educators receive training in dealing effectively with these students (Baker & Zigmond, 1990; Brown, Gable, Hendrickson, & Algozzine, 1991; Laycock & Tonelson, 1985), they often feel unprepared to accept these students. Because of this limited pool of "willing and able" regular educators, it seems unlikely that teacher characteristics play a major role in reintegration decision making.

In summary, past studies investigating characteristics of students and receiving teachers may contribute to our understanding of the variables related to the *success* of integration, but they have not been demonstrated to relate to the likelihood or *prediction* of integration. Identifying and understanding the factors that influence the decision to integrate a child into a less restrictive placement is the first step in increasing the likelihood of integration. Stated another way, if a child's chances of reintegration are seriously limited or denied by unidentified factors, the knowledge of how to make reintegration more successful is irrelevant. Therefore, the focus of this study is on other, heretofore unidentified, variables related to the preliminary decision-making process, which may significantly affect the likelihood of reintegration for children with serious emotional disturbance. Once these factors are identified and used to increase integration opportunities, awareness and programming for success will be of even greater value.

ALTERNATIVE FACTORS IN REINTEGRATION DECISION MAKING

In attempting to isolate factors that may affect the decision to reintegrate, we have focused on two major variables: (a) the special education teacher and (b) the special education program from which the reintegration is to occur.

Few researchers have studied the role of the special teacher in influencing the reintegration process. This lack of attention is surprising because the special educator typically is responsible for (a) the initial determination of reintegration readiness, (b) the initiation of the reintegration process, (c) referral to the Admission, Review, Dismissal (ARD) team, (d) reintegration planning, (e) student preparation, (f) follow-through, and (g) subsequent follow-up (Burrows & O'Meara, 1988; Carroll, Katz, Waters, & Zaremba, 1978; Peterson et al., 1980; Smith, White, & Peterson, 1979; White, 1979). Although we have found no studies that demonstrate the significance of the special teacher's role in initiating reintegration of students with serious emotional disturbance, many authors continue to identify teacher responsibilities and competencies as crucial for successful planning and reintegration for these students (e.g., Maroney & Smith, 1991). In addition, researchers continue to urge training in reintegration procedures for inservice and preservice training programs (Meier, 1992; Smith et al., 1979; White, 1979, 1980).

Looking beyond the competencies of individual teachers, researchers have found that a school's orientation toward reintegration may be an even more important determinant of reintegration. Individual school administrations may or may not promote, facilitate, support, and train for reintegration. Elements of program orientation toward reintegration may include reintegration expectations, schoolwide reintegration goals, placement options, clarity of reintegration procedures, and reintegration training. Schools that have not developed plans to foster reintegration are unlikely to integrate students with serious emotional disturbance into regular education activities. There is evidence that few schools have established reintegration procedures and criteria. For example, Salend, Brooks, and Salend (1987) found that 18 of 21 school districts surveyed had no criteria for reintegration, and only 7 specifically prepared students for reintegration. Rizzo and Zabel (1988) found that only 50% of school districts surveyed had written policies governing reintegration. Although significant variability exists across states, far too many programs do not have established procedures for reintegration. Moreover, though many researchers have called for schoolwide procedures and planning regarding reintegration (e.g., Gable et al., 1991; Maroney & Smith, 1991), we have found no studies that assess the contribution of school reintegration procedures to actual reintegration practices.

Another programmatic problem that is likely to affect the reintegration of students with serious emotional disturbance is the need for cooperative planning for integration. The current literature on "best practices" in the reintegration of students with serious emotional disturbance urges collaborative planning and detailed program design (Gable et al., 1991; Grosenick, George, & George, 1987; Maroney & Smith, 1991; Muscott & Bond, 1986; White, 1980; Zabel, Peterson, Smith, & White, 1982). Yet few schools establish procedures for this programming to occur, and even fewer allocate teachers the necessary time for planning and preparation (Zabel, 1988). Further, because a large portion of students with serious emotional disturbance are educated in segregated facilities, collaborative programming may be a logistical improbability.

To evaluate the effects of both program and special teacher variables on the reintegration rate of children with serious emotional disturbance to less restrictive educational environments, we identified and assessed four sets of variables: (a) program reintegration orientation, (b) program demographics, (c) the experience and training of teachers of children with serious emotional disturbance, and (d) these teachers'

attitudes and opinions related to reintegration. Each of these sets was then examined for its contribution to the reintegration rate of students with serious emotional disturbance in each school.

METHOD

Participants

We invited all teachers from 6 nonpublic programs and 25 public schools serving students with serious emotional disturbance (SED) to participate in this study. A total of 162 teachers serving four major Maryland counties returned their questionnaires (73% of sample). The participants in this study represented a majority of all teachers of students with SED in restrictive placements in the state of Maryland. Thirty-three percent of the participating teachers worked at elementary schools, 25% at middle schools, and 42% at high schools. Teachers with all levels of training and experience took part in the study. In addition to teachers, 31 administrators or public school liaisons (100% of sample) provided program information regarding school practices and reintegration options.

Settings

The 31 schools involved in this study were Maryland State Department of Education-approved, Level V programs for children with SED. Before October 1991, Maryland used a level system to designate the amount of special education services required. A Level V program was defined as "a comprehensive special education setting for [the] entire school day in a special wing, or day school" that provides intensive therapeutic and academic interventions for students with severe disabilities (COMAR 13A.05.01.06E; Code of Maryland Regulations, 1978).

Four Maryland counties with a total of 25 Level V programs, as well as 6 nonpublic Level V facilities, participated in the study. The county systems included schools that were located in both urban and suburban locations, serving students of all races and socioeconomic-status (SES) levels. Most of the nonpublic schools, primarily supported by federal or state funds, served children from all races, SES levels, and locales. Seventy-five percent of the responding teachers were from public settings, and 25% were from nonpublic schools. Participation from the four counties ranged from 12% to 39% of the total sample, with the participation directly related to the number of Level V programs and teachers within each system.

Experimental Variables

Independent variables. We identified, validated,

assessed, and compared four sets of program and teacher variables with SED student reintegration rates. The variable sets evaluated were (a) special program reintegration orientation, (b) special program demographic information, (c) SED teacher experience and training, and (d) SED factors related to teacher attitudes and opinions. We used survey questionnaires to compile information from SED teachers and program administrators. Table 1 shows the specific variables composing each independent variable set.

Dependent variable. The dependent variable was rate of reintegration, defined as the percentage of students from each responding teacher's class who were integrated into a less restrictive class for one or more periods during the previous school year. Such placements included transitional programs, trial/furlough placements, or movement to a less restrictive programs. Students did not have to be placed in regular education classes to be considered reintegrated; instead, any movement on the continuum of services involving less restriction was considered reintegration. We collected these data from school administrators, using existing archival pupil records. This procedure was intended to ensure that teachers would not respond inaccurately or randomly by relying on memory or personal records. The rate of reintegration was calculated as a percentage using the following formula for each teacher's class:

$$\text{Rate of Reintegration} = \frac{\text{\# Reintegrated}}{\text{\# Reintegrated} + \text{\# Not Reintegrated}} \times 100$$

TABLE 1
Independent Variable Sets

Set	Descriptor
Set 1. Special Program Reintegration Orientation	
a. RE OPTIONS	Number of reintegration placement options
b. RE EXPECTATIONS	Teacher familiarity with reintegration class expectations
c. CLASS SELECTION	Reintegration class selection opportunity
d. RE GOALS	Schoolwide reintegration goals
e. RE PROCEDURES	Clarity and documentation of reintegration procedures
f. RE TRAINING	In-school reintegration training
Set 2. Special Program Demographic Information	
a. LOCATION	Program location—wing/separate building
b. RE PROXIMITY	Distance to reintegration site
c. RE SITES	Number of reintegration sites
d. SPECIFIC PROGRAM	Program type—public/nonpublic and specific Maryland county
e. GRADE LEVEL	Grade level of students—elementary/middle/high
f. CLASS SIZE	Average class size
g. CLASS ORGAN	Class organization—self-contained/departmentalized/rotating
Set 3. SED Teacher Experience and Training	
a. PAST RE TRAINING	Prior reintegration training
b. RE EXPERIENCE	Past reintegration experience
c. SED EXPERIENCE	Experience with children with SED
d. CERTIF STATUS	Certification status with Maryland State Department of Education (None, Provisional, Standard, Advanced)
e. CERTIF SPEC EDUC	Certification in special education
f. TEACHER EDUCATION	Overall education level/degree
g. MAJOR	Major in Special Education
Set 4. SED Teacher Attitudes and Opinions (Original construct variables prior to factor analysis)	
a. Comfort with reintegration procedures	
b. Flexibility in, and support of, the reintegration process	
c. Role responsibility/locus of control in reintegration	
d. Expectations and attributions regarding reintegration	

Note: RE = reintegration; SED = serious emotional disturbance; CERTIF = certification; SPEC EDUC = special education

Because the rate of reintegration counted numbers of students (not numbers of integration placements), multiple furloughs, trials, or successive placements of individual children did not affect the ratio.

Design and Analysis

The research design and analysis for this survey study occurred in two parts: (a) construction and validation of the survey questionnaire designed for data collection and (b) analysis of data gathered from the completed surveys. Validation of the survey is discussed in this section. The statistical analysis of the survey results, a set hierarchical regression model, is presented in the results section.

The survey was designed with four sections. We hypothesized that four main variable sets would predict the rate of reintegration and that individual subvariables composing each set would demonstrate a unique significant relationship to the rate. We determined that the four sets and the items contained therein (see Table 1) were representative of the theoretical and applied research topics relevant to reintegrating students. Three of the sets were validated using professional advisors; and the fourth set, SED teacher attitudes and opinions, was factor analyzed to determine factor scores for the set items.

We used a set regression analysis to assess contributions to the total variance in rate of reintegration by each set of independent variables. Hierarchical analysis creates a strict ordering of sets, based on theoretical conceptualizations, prior to data analysis. The creation, ordering, and testing of whole sets prior to examination of individual variables greatly reduces the chances of finding spuriously significant results and aids in interpretation. This model is considered "an effective strategy of inference" (Cohen & Cohen, 1983, p. 171) that prevents variables of lower priority from reducing power of the tests on higher priority variables. In this study, we used professional literature and ratings by panels of experts to order the variable sets prior to analysis. For example, because Set 1, Program Reintegration Orientation, was ranked "essential to reintegration" by the panel of experts in the fields of reintegration and SED and was corroborated by the literature as extremely important in planning and decision making for reintegration, we entered it first into the regression analysis.

Instrumentation

We constructed a 66-item survey instrument (available on request from the first author), presented in 4 sections, to assess four independent variable sets. Variable Sets 2 and 3 required teachers to select from several possible answer choices or to provide short answers to questions relating to program demographics and SED teacher experience and training, respectively. These two sections, containing 11 and 12 items, respectively, were numerically coded for entry into the regression analysis. Sets 1 and 4, assessing program integration orientation and SED teachers' attitudes/opinions, required teachers to respond to statements on a 5-point, Likert-type scale. These two sections included 16 and 27 items, respectively, and were also coded numerically for analysis. The use of both quantitative and qualitative forms of information collected in this survey is supported and accommodated in multiple-regression analyses (Cohen & Cohen, 1975; 1983; Pedhazur, 1982).

Survey Validation. We undertook survey development and validation in several steps. First, we culled items addressing (a) best practices in facilitating reintegration and (b) teacher preparation for reintegration from the professional literature in the fields of emotional disturbance, reintegration, behavioral change, teacher training, special education, and general education. Next, we compiled these items into a preliminary survey draft. Third, we sent the preliminary draft to a panel of 25 experts chosen for their knowledge of, or experience in, the fields of reintegration; education of children with SED; and other related educational, behavioral, and administrative areas. The panel rated each survey item for its face validity, as well as its ability to assess a construct area defined by the literature. Further, panel members provided information on the range, depth, and importance of the main constructs surveyed. Members also generated additional items for inclusion in the final survey.

Analysis of the panel's recommendations assisted in the development of the final survey instrument. Each of the 66 items on the final survey received a mean rating by experts of 4.5 or better on a 5-point scale. Thus each item included in the final survey was deemed "important" or "extremely important" in assessing program and teacher variables related to best practices in reintegration students with SED.

Reliability. We obtained measures of reliability for the Likert-type scales of the survey instrument through computer reliability analyses. The first variable scale, Set 1 (which assessed Program Reintegration Orientation), was found to have a Chronbach's alpha coefficient (133 cases) of .90. The fourth variable scale (Set 4) assessing Teacher Attitudes and Opinions regarding reintegration was also analyzed for reliability. Chronbach's alpha coefficient for this scale (140 cases) was .86.

Factor Analysis: Validity of Set 4. The use of factor scores in regression analyses is purported

TABLE 2
Teacher Opinion and Attitude Factors Identified Through Factor Analysis of Set 4

Factor	Descriptor
A. Factor TKM. Familiarity with Reintegration Procedures	Self-reported (a) understanding of one's role in the reintegration process and (b) knowledge of specific procedures necessary for reintegration
B. Factor CIM. Comfort with the Practical Implementation of Reintegration	Teachers' comfort with the frequent inconveniences associated with reintegration
C. Factor LTX. Long-Term (Theoretical) Expectations Related to Reintegration	Teachers' expectations and attributions regarding the eventual reintegration of their students
D. Factor STX. Short-Term (Practical) Expectations Related to Reintegration	Teachers' expectations for students' behavioral and academic improvement, as well as the consideration of reintegration as a realistic goal for the present and the near future
E. Factor IMP. Individualization of Reintegration Preparation	Teachers' comfort and willingness to personalize reintegration preparation for each student in the class
F. Factor PRM. Personal Risk in Reintegration	Teachers' willingness to face uncertainty and take personal initiative in the reintegration process
G. Factor KBS. Knowledge of Behavioral Strategies	Teachers' knowledge of specific strategies that help students to change, maintain, and generalize their behavior

to represent a construct with greater reliability and validity, to aid in the interpretation of results, and to reduce the likelihood of error (Cohen & Cohen, 1983; Kerlinger & Pedhazur, 1973; Pedhazur, 1982). To identify factors and create subvariables from the 27 opinion items comprising Set 4 (Teacher Attitudes and Opinions Regarding Reintegration), we entered response ratings into a factor analysis involving principal-components solutions and varimax rotations (Harman, 1967). Because 20 out of 27 items had correlations of .40 or better, sphericity was calculated at $p < .001$, and the Kaiser-Meyer-Olkin measure was .748, the use of factor analysis was supported.

Principal-components analysis identified eight factors with Eigenvalues greater than 1.0 that explained a cumulative 62.6% of the variance. Seven of the eight factors were identified as "true" through the use of the Scree test (Cattell, 1952). Using the factor loadings on the varimax rotation matrix, we interpreted and named the factors. Table 2 lists and describes the seven distinct factors of Set 4 that reflect teachers' opinions and attitudes regarding reintegration.

We obtained factor scores for each of the seven factors by summing the values of the corresponding variables. Due to skew, factor scores were transformed with an arcsine transformation to normalize the distribution curve. The seven resulting transformed factor scores were then entered as Set 4 into the set regression analysis.

Specific Procedures

After we designed and validated the survey instruments, we invited school systems and non-public schools to participate. First, school administrators completed a brief (one-page) information sheet reporting the total number of students who had been enrolled and the number of children reintegrated from their restrictive programs during the previous school year, indexed by each classroom teacher or case manager. Administrators also provided information on programmatic elements related to reintegration, such as reintegration procedures and options. Next, the classroom teachers of students with SED in each of the 31 schools completed a four-page survey on personal background, program information, school reintegration practices, and opinions regarding reintegration. Data were coded and analyzed using SPSSx statistical software (SPSS, 1988).

RESULTS

A forced-order, hierarchical, set multiple-regression analysis (Cohen & Cohen, 1975, 1983) was performed on the four variable sets to provide predictive information about each of the following predictor variable sets on the criterion variable Rate of Reintegration: (a) Program Reintegration Orientation, (b) Program Demographics, (c) Teacher Experience and Training, and (d) Teacher Opinion Factors (as identified by factor analysis). Each variable set contained six or seven functionally related independent components. Using related literature and colleague review, the sets were constructed and ordered based on their theorized significance of contribution toward Rate of Reintegration.

A set regression analysis allowed the unexplained variance of the variable sets to be partialled out from the variance of the other sets, while maintaining a low "investigation-wise" Type I error. The independent variable components in the resulting significant sets were then evaluated for significance compared to that of the total set through the use of protected t procedures. F-ratios for testing significant differences of the R, R^2, R^2 change, and the standardized beta (B) regression coefficient were set at the .05 level of significance.

Zero-order correlations between the independent variables ranged from .01 to .42. Sixty-seven percent of the predictor variables were significant at the .05 level, 48% at the .01 level, and 22% at the .001 level (correlation matrix available on request from the first author). Table 3 lists the beta weights of the independent variables and the results of the set regression analysis.

Set 1. Program Reintegration Orientation was entered as step one of the regression equation. The F test of the R^2 was significant, $p < .001$. The explained variance of this set was 25%, or 20% adjusted for the number of variables (see Table 3). Because the explained variance of this set was found to be significant, examination of the individual variables within the set was appropriate. Individual t-tests were performed on each component variable to identify those that contributed to the overall significance of the set. All variables within this set were found to be correlated significantly, $p < .05$, with rate of reintegration at the zero-order level, indicating a positive relationship between these factors and likelihood of reintegration. Of these, beta weights indicated that only one variable, Reintegration Class Selection, contributed uniquely to the *prediction* of the criterion variable, $p < .01$, as indicated by the beta weight (see Table 3).

Set 2. Program Demographic Information was entered second into the regression equation. The F test of the R^2 change was significant, $p < .001$. The variance explained by this set beyond what was explained by Set 1 was 22%. The total R^2 for the equation with two sets entered was 46%, or 39% adjusted. In this set, five of the seven variables were associated with the criterion variable at the zero-order level, $p < .05$. Examination of the beta weights indicated

that three component variables contributed uniquely to the prediction of the criterion variable: Program Location was significant at the $p < .01$ level, Reintegration Proximity at the $p < .05$ level, and Specific Program at the $p < .05$ level.

Set 3. SED Teacher Experience and Training was entered next into the regression equation. The F test of the R^2 change was significant, $p < .05$. The variance explained by this set beyond what was explained by Sets 1 and 2 was 9%. The total R^2 change for the equation was 55%, or 45% adjusted. Five of the seven variables were correlated with the criterion variable at the zero-order level, $p < .05$. Of these, beta weights indicated that one variable, Reintegration Experience, contributed uniquely to the *prediction* of Rate of Reintegration, at $p < .01$.

Set 4. Finally, the Teacher Opinion Factor Set was entered into the equation. The F test of the R^2 change was not significant at the .05 level. There was no significant variance explained by this set beyond what was explained by Sets 1, 2, and 3. Though these variables did not significantly *predict* Rate of Reintegration, four of seven variables were strongly associated with Rate of Reintegration, $p < .01$.

Total variance explained by the three significant sets, then, was a total of 55%, or 45% adjusted for the number of variables. Table 4 shows the relative contributions of each variable set to the prediction of reintegration of students with SED.

DISCUSSION

The purpose of this study was to identify program and teacher variables that would predict the reintegration of children with SED. Of the four sets of variables presented, three were demonstrated to account for a significant and relatively large proportion of the variance in the reintegration rate.

Set 1

The significance of Set 1 indicates that programs with a more positive reintegration orientation have significantly higher rates of reintegration than programs with less developed or less emphasized reintegration orientation. When combined, the following program components can be considered to describe a "positive" reintegration orientation, and consequently, to predict higher rates of reintegration:

a. Multiple reintegration options, such as part-day, trial, and transitional reintegration.
b. Opportunity for special teachers to become familiar with reintegration class expectations.

c. Ability of the special teacher to select the reintegration placement for a particular student.

d. Programwide reintegration goals, including goal-setting for all students, goal-setting at time of admission to the program, and reintegration planning at the annual IEP review of each student.

e. Written, documented, and easy-to-implement reintegration procedures.

f. Reintegration training provided to special teachers including annual training in procedures and methods; regular, formal meetings to provide reintegration information; and informal reintegration education sessions

given by administrators to individuals or groups.

Each of these variables was related positively to increased rates of reintegration and, in combination, explained a significant amount of the variance in rate of reintegration. It was noted, also, that "positive" reintegration orientation did not appear to be dependent on severity of emotional disturbance in the special school population. For example, several schools serving the most extremely disturbed students in separate public and nonpublic facilities had a "more positive" reintegration orientation and, consequently, higher rates of reintegration than did other

TABLE 3
Results of Regression Analysis of Four Variable Sets on Reintegration Rate

Predictor Variable Set	Zero Order R	Beta	Set R²	Total R²	Adjusted R²
1. Program Reintegration Orientation			.246***	.246***	.203***
1a. RE OPTIONS	.182*	−.069			
1b. RE EXPECTATIONS	.208**	.120			
1c. CLASS SELECTION	.172*	.339**			
1d. RE GOALS	.223**	.221			
1e. RE PROCEDURES	.213**	.024			
1f. RE TRAINING	.163*	−.063			
2. Program Demograpic Information			.217***	.462***	.392***
2a. LOCATION	−.396***	−.240**			
2b. RE PROXIMITY	−.234**	−.220*			
2c. RE SITES	.163*	.023			
2d. SPECIFIC PROGRAM	.309***	.234*			
2e. GRADE LEVEL	.088	.142			
2f. CLASS SIZE	−.238**	.062			
2g. CLASS ORGANIZATION	.059	−.025			
3. SED Teachers' Experience and Training			.087*	.550***	.452***
3a. PAST RE TRAINING	.128*	.034			
3b. RE EXPERIENCE	.416***	.310**			
3c. SED EXPERIENCE	.211**	−.017			
3d. CERTIF STATUS	.013	.014			
3e. CERTIF SPEC EDUC	.160*	.047			
3f. TEACHER EDUCATION	.163*	.047			
3g. MAJOR	−.080	.042			
4. SED Teachers' Opinion Factors			.042	.591***	.462***
4a. FACTOR TKM	.226**	.044			
4b. FACTOR CIM	.084	.076			
4c. FACTOR LTX	.360***	.161			
4d. FACTOR STX	.236**	.022			
4e. FACTOR IMP	.093	.021			
4f. FACTOR PRM	.290***	.190			
4g. FACTOR KBS	.124	.019			

Note: RE = reintegration; SED = serious emotional disturbance; CERTIF = certification; SPEC EDUC = special education. Intercorrelation matrix available upon request from Elana Esterson Rock, Johns Hopkins University, Baltimore, Maryland.
* = $p < .05$. ** = $p < .01$. *** = $< .001$. $R^2 = .452$.
Std. Error of Estimate = 22.204   Mean Reintegration Rate = 21.65   Std. Dev. Reintegration Rate = 29.99

TABLE 4
Variance in Rate of Reintegration Explained by Experimental Variable Sets

Variable Set	Explained Variance (%)	Cumulative Explained Variance Adjusted for Variables (%)
1. Program Reintegration Orientation	25**	20**
2. Program Demographic Information	22**	39**
3. SED Teacher Experience and Training	9*	45**
4. SED Teacher Opinion Factors	4	46**
Total Variance Explained	59**	46**

Note: SED = serious emotional disturbance.
*p < .05. **p < .001.

public Level V programs located in comprehensive schools.

Examination of the individual variables composing Reintegration Orientation revealed that the best single predictor of reintegration was the ability of special education teachers to select the particular class for reintegration of a student. Students in classes and programs that had this option had a significantly greater chance of being reintegrated than did students in classes where teachers had no such opportunity. Reintegration class selection is considered a program variable because the reintegration organization of each school determines which options exist for selection of reintegration sites, as well as the degree to which teachers are involved in the reintegration process.

Although some programs are designed to allow teachers to select or give input into students' specific reintegration experiences, other programs provided no opportunities for selection of reintegration placements. Peterson et al. (1980) found that one fourth of the special class teachers of students with SED had no opportunity to select the specific class into which to reintegrate a particular student. The results in this study were even more discouraging, with 26% of the teachers able, 39% sometimes able, and 33% not able to select a reintegration class placement for any of their students. In explanation, the special program administrators reported that often the reintegration placements are predetermined (such as a return to the home school) or are decided by other individuals (such as administrators in the less restrictive programs). In these cases, interagency planning was nonexistent. Because it was found that students were significantly less likely to be reintegrated when served in programs without opportunities for specific class selection, collaborative or interagency reintegration programming for students with SED is supported.

Set 2

The significance of Set 2, Program Demographic Information, indicates that the programs with specific demographic characteristics had higher reintegration rates than did those without such characteristics. Although not all component variables in this set were correlated at the zero-order level with the criterion, interpretation of set regression analysis results requires the presentation and examination of the complete set of variables. When combined, the following demographic variables were found to predict higher rates of reintegration:
a. SED program was located in a wing of a comprehensive school building, as opposed to a separate building.
b. Program was zero to 1 mile from the most likely reintegration site.
c. Program had multiple reintegration sites, including less restrictive classes in the same building, in nearby public schools, in students' home school or prior school, or in another setting (such as a vocational center).
d. Program was public rather than nonpublic, and within certain counties as opposed to others (some counties have significantly higher rates of reintegration than others).
e. Program served older rather than younger students.
f. Program had smaller class sizes.
g. Classes were departmentalized/rotating, rather than self-contained.

Clearly, some of these characteristics are interrelated. In addition, many demographic characteristics are not modifiable—and others may be irrelevant. Closer examination of the zero-order correlations and beta weights of the individual variables is necessary to draw conclusions and identify implications.

Five of the seven variables in this set were associated with the rate of reintegration. These included location in wing, proximity, available sites, specific program, and smaller class sizes.

Grade level of students and class organization did not appear to be related to the rate of reintegration.

Of the five related variables, three, (a) program location in comprehensive school wing as compared to special facility, (d) specific counties/public programs, and (b) proximity to reintegration site were found to be uniquely responsible for the significance of the set, and therefore are to be considered the best demographic predictors for reintegration.

It was demonstrated in this study that programs located in wings of public schools reintegrated students with SED at a higher rate than did programs in separate buildings. However, it must be considered that there may be other underlying factors that affect both program placement and rate of reintegration. For example, the student population within the two locations may not be truly comparable. It may be that students with more severe emotional disturbance are not served within their local public schools, but are placed in public and nonpublic programs in separate buildings. Then, either due to the degree of severity of their disability or their distance from less restrictive placement, they are less frequently reintegrated. Similarly, the fact that placement in public programs was associated with higher rates of reintegration than was placement in nonpublic programs may reflect differences in severity of emotional disturbance.

On the other hand, there were school systems and individual programs included in this study that served students with extremely severe disabilities in public programs in both wings and separate buildings rather than in separate, nonpublic facilities. The reintegration success of these schools supports the finding that public school placements and, especially, wing-program placements are the important factors in predicting likelihood of reintegration, rather than the severity of the emotional disturbance. Further research into the degree to which program placement affects reintegration is indicated.

In addition to differential rates in reintegration between public and nonpublic schools, there were significant differences in rates of reintegration across the four public schools systems surveyed. These findings confirm the data that indicate a significant variation in the prevalence of reintegration of children with SED (Peterson et al., 1980; Smith et al., 1979; Smith & McGinnis, 1982). As computed in this study, rates of reintegration of these children varies widely—from a low of zero annually to a high of 100%. The mean reintegration rate was 18%, with nearly one half of the responding teachers reporting reintegration of 0%. The median

teacher reintegration rate was 10%, and 7% had a 100% reintegration rate.

Some of the interschool variation may be the result of underlying factors that affect numbers of special education students and service delivery, such as a county's relative wealth, percentage of students with disabilities, size of the local education agency (LEA), systemwide special educational services (e.g., centralized versus decentralized services), quality of pupil personnel and ARD team services, and continuum of special education services offered by LEAs. For example, systems with a continuum-of-service option do not have to attempt "all or nothing" reintegration to a regular classroom; instead, they may use several less-restrictive placements for students who have demonstrated a slight or significant improvement in behavioral, academic, or social functioning. In this study, the typical continuum of services and options for placement were found to be fairly restricted and not very "flexible."

Proximity to the Reintegration Site was the third determinant of rate of reintegration, indicating that programs located closer to reintegration sites had higher rates of reintegration than those farther away. In addition, Proximity to Reintegration Site was not significantly correlated with public/nonpublic placement or wing/building placement, indicating that it provides nonredundant information. This means that the closer children with SED are placed to the reintegration site, the more likely they are to be reintegrated. This is logistically understandable; if students can move easily to a reintegration site for one or more classes, they are more likely to be given options to "prove themselves"; and the arranging of trial or temporary placements may be facilitated.

Because distance to reintegration site predicts reintegration regardless of other factors (e.g., wing/building, public/nonpublic placement), it is suggested that program planners and boards of education seriously consider the physical locations of new and existing programs intended to serve youth with SED in order to facilitate students' subsequent reintegration.

Set 3

SED Teacher Experience and Training was also a significant predictor of reintegration. Although not all of the variables in the set were significantly related, the following combination of teachers' experiences and characteristics was found to predict higher rates of reintegration:

a. Greater number of places a teacher has received reintegration training, including undergraduate school, graduate school, in-school training, inservice courses, professional literature, and other sites.

b. Higher number of students who have been reintegrated from a teacher's class, plus the number of students for whom the teacher has had primary (case manager) or secondary (team member) reintegration planning responsibilities.

c. More years worked with children with SED either in a teaching or nonteaching capacity.

d. An "Advanced Professional" certification status with Maryland State Department of Education (as compared to Standard, Temporary/Provisional, or none).

e. MSDE certification in special education.

f. A higher level of overall teacher education (e.g., Master's as compared to Bachelor's degrees).

g. Teacher's educational specialization (major) in special education.

It is clear from the data that teachers with more experience and training in reintegration and serving youth with SED reintegrate more students than teachers with less experience. However, only five of the seven variables were positively related to increased rates of reintegration. These variables were reintegration training, reintegration experience, experience with emotional disturbance, MSDE certification in special education, and overall education. This means that the existence of higher levels of these characteristics was associated with increased rates of reintegration.

Although these five variables were all significantly correlated with rate of reintegration, the unique contribution of these variables to the prediction of reintegration has likely been decreased by communality, intercorrelations among variables, or unidentified underlying factors relating these variables to the variables in the first two sets.

Of the five variables correlated significantly with Rate of Reintegration, only reintegration experience was found to be the best single predictor of reintegration, contributing uniquely to the explained variance of the set. This indicates that teachers who, in the past, have reintegrated more students and who have had more primary and secondary reintegration planning responsibility have higher rates of current and future reintegration than do teachers with less reintegration experience. It is likely that underlying factors affect reintegration experience, specific program, and location variables. This would be logical because programs that encourage and expect high levels of reintegration are likely to have teachers with high rates of reintegration. This relationship is further borne out by the high intercorrelations between these variables.

Set 4

The set describing SED Teacher Attitudes and Opinions was not found to add significantly to the explained variance in Rate of Reintegration beyond the contributions of the first three sets. However, four of the seven zero-order correlations were significant, indicating that although these variables are associated with higher rates of reintegration, they are also related to or caused by other variables in the previous sets that have already contributed to the explained variance. For example, Factor TKM (teachers self-reported technical knowledge of reintegration) was significantly related to increased frequency of reintegration. However, it was not found to be predictive of reintegration. In this case, factor TKM was found to be correlated significantly with five of six variables in Set 1, as well as four other variables from Sets 2 and 3. This is logical because teachers' perceived roles in, and knowledge of, specific procedures in the reintegration process are closely related to (and possibly determined by) specific program procedures, options, and expectations, as well as past experience. It is likely, then, that the relationship between the teacher opinions and actual reintegration has already been accounted for in other variables in Sets 1-3.

Since results indicate that program and teacher variable sets account for a large portion of the unexplained variance rate of reintegration, the results of this study provide both policy and practical implications. In regard to policy, questions are raised as to (a) whether all students are being given equal access to opportunities for integration into least-restrictive activities, (b) whether current reintegration practices reflect "best practices" as described in the literature, and (c) how the reintegration prediction model can be further refined. Further research is warranted into the newly identified roles of special programs and special educators in the integration process.

On a practical level, results suggest applications for program planners in the following areas: (a) program placement, (b) reintegration options, and (c) interagency cooperation. Programs housed physically closer to regular education programs provide multiple options for reintegration and foster cooperation between regular and special educators; and administrators will have a higher likelihood of integrating students with SED into mainstream activities and classes.

Program administrators may want to ensure that: (a) reintegration procedures are clearly defined and in writing, (b) schoolwide reintegration goals and expectations exist for all students, and (c) inservice teacher training is implemented as described previously.

Special educators should (a) be involved in the selection of reintegration classes and (b) be familiar with reintegration expectations and procedures. Once programming, collaboration, and training are used to promote equity in integration *opportunity*, existing and future research findings must be used to improve the *success* of reintegration efforts.

REFERENCES

Baker, J. M., & Zigmond, N. (1990). Are regular classroom teachers equipped to accommodate students with learning disabilities? *Exceptional Children, 56,* 515-526.

Braaten, S., Kauffman, J. M., Braaten, B., Polsgrove, L., & Nelson, C. M. (1988). The regular education initiative: Patent medicine for behavioral disorders. *Exceptional Children, 55,* 21-27.

Brown, J., Gable, R. A., Hendrickson, J. M., & Algozzine, B. (1991). Prereferral practices of regular teachers: Implications for regular and special teacher preparation. *Teacher Education and Special Education, 14*(3), 192-197.

Burrows, A., & O'Meara, L. (1988). Reintegration plan: General concepts. In McGinnis, Sodak, Smith, & Wood (Eds.), *Iowa program standards in behavioral disorders.* Manual published by Iowa State Department of Education, Office of Special Education: Des Moines. (ERIC Document Reproduction Service No. 308 689)

Carroll, J., Katz, S. G., Waters, C., & Zaremba, S. (1978, May). *An effective model for mainstreaming emotionally impaired students.* Paper presented at the 56th Annual International Convention, The Council for Exceptional Children, Kansas City. (ERIC Document Reproduction Service No. ED 153 406)

Cattell, R. (1952). *Factor analysis.* New York: Harper.

Code of Maryland Regulations (COMAR). (1978). *Programs for the handicapped* (13A.05.01). Annapolis: Maryland State Board of Education.

Cohen, J., & Cohen, P. (1975). *Applied multiple regression/correlation analysis for the behavioral sciences.* New York: Halsted Press.

Cohen, J., & Cohen, P. (1983). *Applied multiple regression/correlation analysis for the behavioral sciences.* (2nd ed.). New York: Halsted Press.

Downing, J. A., Simpson, R. L., and Myles, B. S. (1990). Regular and special educator perceptions of nonacademic skills needed by mainstreamed students with behavioral disorders and learning disabilities. *Behavioral Disorders, 15*(4), 217-226.

Foley, R. M., Cullinan, D., & Epstein, M. H. (1990). Academic and related functioning of mainstreamed and nonmainstreamed seriously emotionally disturbed students. *Severe Behavior Disorders Monograph, 13,* 80-89.

Gable, R. A., Hendrickson, J. M., Algozzine, B., & Scully, V. (1989). Reintegration of behaviorally disordered students through behavioral consultation. In R. B. Rutherford, Jr., & S. DiGangi (Eds.), *Severe behavior disorders of children and youth. Monograph in Behavioral Disorders., 12,* 118-131. Reston, VA:The Council for Children with Behavior Disorders.

Gable, R. A., Laycock, V. K., Maroney, S. A., & Smith, C. R. (Eds.). (1991). *Preparing to integrate students with behavioral disorders. Working with behavioral disorders: CEC mini-library.* Reston,VA: Council for Exceptional Children.

(ERIC Document Reproduction Service No. ED 333658)

Gersten, R., Walker, H., & Darch, C. (1988). Relationship between teachers' effectiveness and their tolerance for handicapped students. *Exceptional Children, 54,* 433-438.

Goodlad, J. I., & Lovitt, T. (1993). *Integrating general and special education.* New York: Merrill/Macmillan.

Gresham, F. M., Elliott, S. N., & Black, F. L. (1987). Teacher-rated social skills of mainstreamed mildly handicapped and nonhandicapped children. *School Psychology Review, 16,* 78-88.

Grosenick, J. K., (1971). Integration of exceptional children into regular classes. *Teaching Exceptional Children, 2,* 113-119.

Grosenick, J. K., George, M. P., & George, N. L. (1987). A profile of school programs for the behaviorally disordered: Twenty years after Morse, Cutler, and Fink. *Behavioral Disorders, 12*(3), 159-168.

Harman, H. H. (1967). *Modern factor analysis.* Chicago: University of Chicago Press.

Hundert, J. (1982). Some considerations of planning the integration of handicapped children into the mainstream. *Journal of Learning Disabilities, 15,* 73-81.

Kerlinger, F. N., & Pedhazur, E. J. (1973). *Multiple regression in behavioral research.* New York: Holt, Rinehart, & Winston.

Laycock, V. K., & Tonelson, S. V. (1985). Preparing emotionally disturbed adolescents for the mainstream: An analysis of current practices. In S. Braaten, R. B. Rutherford, Jr., & W. Evans (Eds.), *Programming for adolescents with behavioral disorders.* (Vol. 2, pp. 63-73). Reston, VA: Council for Children with Behavioral Disorders. (ERIC Document Reproduction Service No. ED 267-531)

Maroney, S. A., & Smith, C. R. (1991). Teacher responsibilities in providing high-quality instruction for students with behavioral disorders. In R. A. Gable, V. K. Laycock, S. A. Maroney, & C. R. Smith, (Eds.), *Preparing to integrate students with behavioral disorders* (pp. 15-34). Reston, VA: The Council for Exceptional Children. (ERIC Document Reproduction Service No. ED 333 658)

McNutt, G. (1986). The status of learning disabilities in the states: Consensus or controversy? *Journal of Learning Disabilities, 1,* 12-16.

Meier, F. E. (1992). *Competency-based instruction for teachers of students with special learning needs.* Boston: Allyn & Bacon.

Muscott, H. M., & Bond, R. (1986). A transitional education model for reintegrating behaviorally disordered students from residential treatment centers to public school programs. *Teaching Behaviorally Disordered Youth, 2,* 33-43.

Pedhazur, E. J. (1982). *Multiple regression in behavioral research: Explanation and prediction.* New York: Holt, Rinehart, & Winston.

Peterson, R. L., Smith, C. R., White, M. A., & Zabel, R. (1980). *Practices used in the reintegration of behavior disordered children in three midwestern states.* Paper presented at the National Topical Conference on Seriously Emotionally Disturbed, The Council for Exceptional Children, Minneapolis. (ERIC Document Reproduction Service No. ED 201 122)

Reynolds, M. C., Wang, M. C., Walberg, H. J. (1987). The necessary restructuring of special and regular education. *Exceptional Children, 53,* 391-398.

Rizzo, J. V., & Zabel, H. (1988). *Educating children and adolescents with behavioral disorders: An integrative approach.* Boston: Allyn & Bacon.

Rosenbaum, J. D. (1981). Differential behavioral and academic characteristics as re-entry criteria for mainstreaming. *Dissertation Abstracts International, 42/03A,* 1101. (University Microfilms No. AAC8119786)

Safran, J. S., & Safran, S. P. (1987). Teachers' judgments of problem behaviors. *Exceptional Children, 54,* 240-244.

Salend, S. J., Brooks, L., & Salend, S. (1987). Identifying school districts' policies for implementing mainstreaming. *The Pointer, 32,* 34-37.

Schneider, B., & Byrne, B. M. (1984). Predictors of successful transition from self-contained special education to regular class settings. *Psychology in the Schools, 21,* 375-380.

Simek, R. (1979, April). *An investigation of the relationship between specific organizational variables and integration of emotionally disturbed and neurologically impaired students.* Paper presented at the 57th Annual International Convention, The Council for Exceptional Children, Dallas. (ERIC Document Reproduction Service No. ED 170 999)

Smith, C., & McGinnis, E. (1982). *Professional and ethical issues related to teaching behaviorally impaired students.* Lincoln: Barkley Memorial Center, University of Nebraska-Lincoln. (ERIC Document Reproduction Services No. ED 243 255)

Smith, C., White, M., & Peterson, R. (1979). *Reintegration of emotionally disabled pupils. Iowa study: Preliminary report.* Iowa Department of public instruction, Division of Special Education. (ERIC Document Reproduction Service No. ED 176 439)

SPSS, Inc. (1988). *SPSSX* (Version 3.1). Chicago: Author.

Stainback, S., & Stainback, W. (1991). *Curriculum consideration for inclusive classrooms.* Baltimore: Paul H. Brookes.

U.S. Department of Education. (1987). *Ninth annual report to Congress on the implementation of the Education of All Handicapped Children Act.* Washington, DC: U.S. Government Printing Office. (ERIC Document Reproduction Service No. ED 346-631)

U.S. Department of Education. (1990). *Twelfth annual report to Congress on the implementation of the Education of All Handicapped Children Act.* Washington, DC: U.S. Government Printing Office. (ERIC Document Reproduction Service No. 321-513)

U.S. Department of Education. (1992). *Fourteenth annual report to Congress on the implementation of the Individuals with Disabilities Education Act.* Washington, DC: U.S. Government Printing Office. (ERIC Document Reproduction Sercvice No. ED 347-779)

Walker, H., & Rankin, R. (1983). Assessing the behavioral expectations and demands of least restrictive settings. *School Psychology Review, 12,* 274-284.

West, N. A. (1981). Mainstreaming and behavior disordered children (Doctoral dissertation, University of Michigan, 1980). *Dissertation Abstracts International, 41/8A.* (University Microfilms No. 80-25, 802)

White, M. A. (1979, April). *Considerations in the integration of behaviorally disordered students into the regular classroom: Teacher concerns and considerations.* Paper presented at the 57th Annual International Convention, The Council for Exceptional Children, Dallas. (ERIC Document Reproduction Service No. ED 171 082)

White, M. A. (1980). Strategies for planning and facilitating the reintegration of students with behavioral disorders. *(Iowa Monographs). Iowa State Department of Public Instruction, Division of Special Education.* (ERIC Document Reproduction Service No. ED 201 120)

Will, M. (1986). Educating children with learning problems: A shared responsibility. *Exceptional Children, 52,* 411-415.

Zabel, R. H. (1988). Use of time by teachers of behaviorally disordered students: A replication. *Behavioral Disorders, 13*(2), 89-97.

Zabel, R. H., Peterson, R. L., Smith, C. R., & White, M. A. (1982). Availability and usefulness of assessment information for emotionally disturbed students. *School Psychology Review, 11,* 433-437.

ABOUT THE AUTHORS

ELANA ESTERSON ROCK (CEC #2), Assistant Professor, MICHAEL S. ROSENBERG (CEC #2), Professor and Chair, and DEBORAH T. CARRAN, Assistant Professor, Department of Special Education, Johns Hopkins University, Baltimore, Maryland.

Address correspondence to Dr. Elana Rock, Department of Special Education, 100 Whitehead Hall, John Hopkins University, 3400 Charles Street, Baltimore, Maryland 21218.

Manuscript received March 1993; revision accepted February 1994.

Autism

*Autistic individuals suffer from a biological defect.
Although they cannot be cured, much can be done
to make life more hospitable for them*

Uta Frith

UTA FRITH is a senior scientist in the Cognitive Development Unit of the Medical Research Council in London. Born in Germany, she took a degree in psychology in 1964 at the University of the Saarland in Saarbrücken, where she also studied the history of art. Four years later she obtained her Ph.D. in psychology at the University of London. Besides autism, her interests include reading development and dyslexia. She has edited a book in the field of reading development, *Cognitive Processes in Spelling*, and is the author of *Autism: Explaining the Enigma*.

CHARACTERISTIC ALONENESS of autistic children has evoked the image of a child in a glass shell

Rodica Prato

The image often invoked to describe autism is that of a beautiful child imprisoned in a glass shell. For decades, many parents have clung to this view, hoping that one day a means might be found to break the invisible barrier. Cures have been proclaimed, but not one of them has been backed by evidence. The shell remains intact. Perhaps the time has come for the whole image to be shattered. Then at last we might be able to catch a glimpse of what the minds of autistic individuals are truly like.

Psychological and physiological research has shown that autistic people are not living in rich inner worlds but instead are victims of a biological defect that makes their minds very different from those of normal individuals. Happily, however, autistic people are not beyond the reach of emotional contact.

Thus, we can make the world more hospitable for autistic individuals just as we can, say, for the blind. To do so, we need to understand what autism is like—a most challenging task. We can imagine being blind, but autism seems unfathomable. For centuries, we have

known that blindness is often a peripheral defect at the sensory-motor level of the nervous system, but only recently has autism been appreciated as a central defect at the highest level of cognitive processing. Autism, like blindness, persists throughout life, and it responds to special efforts in compensatory education. It can give rise to triumphant feats of coping but can also lead to disastrous secondary consequences—anxiety, panic and depression. Much can be done to prevent problems. Understanding the nature of the handicap must be the first step in any such effort.

Autism existed long before it was described and named by Leo Kanner of the Johns Hopkins Children's Psychiatric Clinic. Kanner published his landmark paper in 1943 after he had observed 11 children who seemed to him to form a recognizable group. All had in common four traits: a preference for aloneness, an insistence on sameness, a liking for elaborate routines and some abilities that seemed

remarkable compared with the deficits.

Concurrently, though quite independently, Hans Asperger of the University Pediatric Clinic in Vienna prepared his doctoral thesis on the same type of child. He also used the term "autism" to refer to the core features of the disorder. Both men borrowed the label from adult psychiatry, where it had been used to refer to the progressive loss of contact with the outside world experienced by schizophrenics. Autistic children seemed to suffer such a lack of contact with the world around them from a very early age.

Kanner's first case, Donald, has long served as a prototype for diagnosis. It had been evident early in life that the boy was different from other children. At two years of age, he could hum and sing tunes accurately from memory. Soon he learned to count to 100 and to recite both the alphabet and the 25 questions and answers of the Presbyterian catechism. Yet he had a mania for making toys and other objects spin. Instead of playing like other toddlers, he arranged beads and other things in groups of different colors or threw them on the floor, delighting in the sounds they made. Words for him had a literal, inflexible meaning.

Donald was first seen by Kanner at age five. Kanner observed that the boy paid no attention to people around him. When someone interfered with his solitary activities, he was never angry with the interfering person but impatiently removed the hand that was in his way. His mother was the only person with whom he had any significant contact, and that seemed attributable mainly to the great effort she made to share activities with him. By the time Donald was about eight years old, his conversation consisted largely of repetitive questions. His relation to people remained limited to his immediate wants and needs, and his attempts at contact stopped as soon as he was told or given what he had asked for.

Reprinted with permission from *Scientific American*, June 1993, pp. 108-114. © 1993 by Scientific American, Inc. All rights reserved.

Autistic Behavior

The traits most characteristic of autistic people are aloneness, an insistence on sameness and a liking for elaborate routines. At the same time, some autistic individuals can perform complicated tasks, provided that the activity does not require them to judge what some other person might be thinking. These traits lead to characteristic forms of behavior, a number of which are portrayed here.

Displays indifference

Indicates needs by using an adult's hand

Are you going? *Are you going?*

Parrots words

Laughs and giggles inappropriately

Joins in only if an adult insists and assists

Does not play with other children

Does not make eye contact

Does not pretend in playing

Familiar route *Different route*

Prefers sameness

Is one-sided in interactions

Talks incessantly about one topic

Behaves in bizarre ways

Handles or spins objects

Yet some do certain things well if the task does not involve social understanding.

Rodica Prato

Some of the other children Kanner described were mute, and he found that even those who spoke did not really communicate but used language in a very odd way. For example, Paul, who was five, would parrot speech verbatim. He would say "You want candy" when he meant "I want candy." He was in the habit of repeating, almost every day, "Don't throw the dog off the balcony," an utterance his mother traced to an earlier incident with a toy dog.

Twenty years after he had first seen them, Kanner reassessed the members of his original group of children. Some of them seemed to have adapted socially much better than others, although their failure to communicate and to form relationships remained, as did their pedantry and single-mindedness. Two prerequisites for better adjustment, though no guarantees of it, were the presence of speech before age five and relatively high intellectual ability.

The brightest autistic individuals had, in their teens, become uneasily aware of their peculiarities and had made conscious efforts to conform. Nevertheless, even the best adapted were rarely able to be self-reliant or to form friendships. The one circumstance that seemed to be helpful in all the cases was an extremely structured environment.

As soon as the work of the pioneers became known, every major clinic began to identify autistic children. It was found that such children, in addition to their social impairments, have substantial intellectual handicaps. Although many of them perform relatively well on certain tests, such as copying mosaic patterns with blocks, even the most able tend to do badly on test questions that can be answered only by the application of common sense.

Autism is rare. According to the strict criteria applied by Kanner, it appears in four of every 10,000 births. With the somewhat wider criteria used in current diagnostic practice, the incidence is much higher: one or two in 1,000 births, about the same as Down's syndrome. Two to four times as many boys as girls are affected.

For many years, autism was thought to be a purely psychological disorder without an organic basis. At first, no obvious neurological problems were found. The autistic children did not necessarily have low intellectual ability, and they often looked physically normal. For these reasons, psychogenic theories were proposed and taken seriously for many years. They focused on the idea that a child could become autistic because of some existentially threatening experience. A lack of maternal bonding or a disastrous experience of rejection, so the theory went, might drive an infant to withdraw into an inner world of fantasy that the outside world never penetrates.

These theories are unsupported by any empirical evidence. They are unlikely to be supported because there are many instances of extreme rejection and deprivation in childhood, none of which have resulted in autism. Unfortunately, therapies vaguely based on such notions are still putting pressure on parents to accept a burden of guilt for the supposedly avoidable and reversible breakdown of interpersonal interactions. In contrast, well-structured behavior modification programs have often helped families in the management of autistic children, especially children with severe behavior problems. Such programs do not claim to reinstate normal development.

The insupportability of the psychogenic explanation of autism led a number of workers to search for a biological cause. Their efforts implicate a defective structure in the brain, but that structure has not yet been identified. The defect is believed to affect the thinking of autistic people, making them unable to evaluate their own thoughts or to perceive clearly what might be going on in someone else's mind.

Autism appears to be closely asso-

ciated with several other clinical and medical conditions. They include maternal rubella and chromosomal abnormality, as well as early injury to the brain and infantile seizures. Most impressive, perhaps, are studies showing that autism can have a genetic basis. Both identical twins are much more likely to be autistic than are both fraternal twins. Moreover, the likelihood that autism will occur twice in the same family is 50 to 100 times greater than would be expected by chance alone.

Structural abnormalities in the brains of autistic individuals have turned up

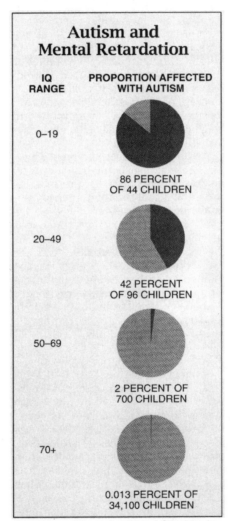

Autism and Mental Retardation

IQ RANGE	PROPORTION AFFECTED WITH AUTISM
0–19	86 PERCENT OF 44 CHILDREN
20–49	42 PERCENT OF 96 CHILDREN
50–69	2 PERCENT OF 700 CHILDREN
70+	0.013 PERCENT OF 34,100 CHILDREN

SOURCE: Lorna Wing, Medical Research Council, London

CLOSE LINK between autism and mental retardation is reflected in this chart. The percentage of children showing the social impairments typical of autism is highest at low levels of intelligence as measured by tests in which an intelligence quotient (IQ) below 70 is subnormal. For example, 86 percent of 44 children in the lowest IQ range showed the social impairments of autism. The data are drawn from a population of about 35,000 children aged under 15 years.

in anatomic studies and brain-imaging procedures. Both epidemiological and neuropsychological studies have demonstrated that autism is strongly correlated with mental retardation, which is itself clearly linked to physiological abnormality. This fact fits well with the idea that autism results from a distinct brain abnormality that is often part of more extensive damage. If the abnormality is pervasive, the mental retardation will be more severe, and the likelihood of damage to the critical brain system will increase. Conversely, it is possible for the critical system alone to be damaged. In such cases, autism is not accompanied by mental retardation.

Neuropsychological testing has also contributed evidence for the existence of a fairly circumscribed brain abnormality. Autistic individuals who are otherwise able show specific and extensive deficits on certain tests that involve planning, initiative and spontaneous generation of new ideas. The same deficits appear in patients who have frontal lobe lesions. Therefore, it seems plausible that whatever the defective brain structure is, the frontal lobes are implicated.

Population studies carried out by Lorna Wing and her colleagues at the Medical Research Council's Social Psychiatry Unit in London reveal that the different symptoms of autism do not occur together simply by coincidence. Three core features in particular—impairments in communication, imagination and socialization—form a distinct triad. The impairment in communication includes such diverse phenomena as muteness and delay in learning to talk, as well as problems in comprehending or using nonverbal body language. Other autistic individuals speak fluently but are overliteral in their understanding of language. The impairment in imagination appears in young autistic children as repetitive play with objects and in some autistic adults as an obsessive interest in facts. The impairment in socialization includes ineptness and inappropriate behavior in a wide range of reciprocal social interactions, such as the ability to make and keep friends. Nevertheless, many autistic individuals prefer to have company and are eager to please.

The question is why these impairments, and only these, occur together. The challenge to psychological theorists was clear: to search for a single cognitive component that would explain the deficits yet still allow for the abilities that autistic people display in certain aspects of interpersonal interactions. My colleagues at the Medical Research Council's Cognitive Development Unit in London and I think we have identified just such a component. It is a cognitive mechanism of a highly complex and abstract nature that could be described in computational terms. As a shorthand, one can refer to this component by one of its main functions, namely the ability to think about thoughts or to imagine another individual's state of mind. We propose that this component is damaged in autism. Furthermore, we suggest that this mental component is innate and has a unique brain substrate. If it were possible to pinpoint that substrate—whether it is an anatomic structure, a physiological system or a chemical pathway—one might be able to identify the biological origin of autism.

The power of this component in normal development becomes obvious very early. From the end of the first year onward, infants begin to participate in what has been called shared attention. For example, a normal child will point to something for no reason other than to share his interest in it with someone else. Autistic children do not show shared attention. Indeed, the absence of this behavior may well be one of the earliest signs of autism. When an autistic child points at an object, it is only because he wants it.

In the second year of life, a particularly dramatic manifestation of the critical component can be seen in normal children: the emergence of pretense, or the ability to engage in fantasy and pretend play. Autistic children cannot understand pretense and do not pretend when they are playing. The difference can be seen in such a typical nursery game as "feeding" a teddy bear or a doll with an empty spoon. The normal child goes through the appropriate motions of feeding and accompanies the action with appropriate slurping noises. The autistic child merely twiddles or flicks the spoon repetitively. It is precisely the absence of early and simple communicative behaviors, such as shared attention and make-believe play, that often creates the first nagging doubts in the minds of the parents about the development of their child. They rightly feel that they cannot engage the child in the emotional to-and-fro of ordinary life.

My colleague Alan M. Leslie devised a theoretical model of the cognitive mechanisms underlying the key abilities of shared attention and pretense. He postulates an innate mechanism whose function

is to form and use what we might call second-order representations. The world around us consists not only of visible bodies and events, captured by first-order representations, but also of invisible minds and mental events, which require second-order representation. Both types of representation have to be kept in mind and kept separate from each other.

Second-order representations serve to make sense of otherwise contradictory or incongruous information. Suppose a normal child, Beth, sees her mother holding a banana in such a way as to be pretending that it is a telephone. Beth has in mind facts about bananas and facts about telephones—first-order representations. Nevertheless, Beth is not the least bit confused and will not start eating telephones or talking to bananas. Confusion is avoided because Beth computes from the concept of pretending (a second-order representation) that her mother is engaging simultaneously in an imaginary activity and a real one.

As Leslie describes the mental process, pretending should be understood as computing a three-term relation between an actual situation, an imaginary situation and an agent who does the pretending. The imaginary situation is then not treated as the real situation. Believing can be understood in the same way as pretending. This insight enabled us to predict that autistic children, despite an adequate mental age (above four years or so), would not be able to understand that someone can have a mistaken belief about the world.

Together with our colleague Simon Baron-Cohen, we tested this prediction by adapting an experiment originally devised by two Austrian developmental psychologists, Heinz Wimmer and Josef Perner. The test has become known as the Sally-Anne task. Sally and Anne are playing together. Sally has a marble that she puts in a basket before leaving the room. While she is out, Anne moves the marble to a box. When Sally returns, wanting to retrieve the marble, she of course looks in the basket. If this scenario is presented as, say, a puppet show to normal children who are four years of age or more, they understand that Sally will look in the basket even though they know the marble is not there. In other words, they can represent Sally's erroneous belief as well as the true state of things. Yet in our test, 16 of 20 autistic children with a mean mental age of nine failed the task—answering that Sally would look in the box—in spite of be-

ing able to answer correctly a variety of other questions relating to the facts of the episode. They could not conceptualize the possibility that Sally believed something that was not true.

Many comparable experiments have been carried out in other laboratories, which have largely confirmed our prediction: autistic children are specifically impaired in their understanding of mental states. They appear to lack the innate component underlying this ability. This component, when it works normally, has the most far-reaching consequences for higher-order conscious processes. It underpins the special feature of the human mind, the ability to reflect on itself. Thus, the triad of impairments in autism—in communication, imagination and socialization—is explained by the failure of a single cognitive mechanism. In everyday life, even very able autistic individuals find it hard to keep in mind simultaneously a reality and the fact that someone else may hold a misconception of that reality.

The automatic ability of normal people to judge mental states enables us to be, in a sense, mind readers. With sufficient experience we can form and use a theory of mind that allows us to speculate about psychological motives for our behavior and to manipulate other people's opinions, beliefs and attitudes. Autistic individuals lack the automatic ability to represent beliefs, and therefore they also lack a theory of mind. They cannot understand how behavior is caused by mental states or how beliefs and attitudes can be manipulated. Hence, they find it difficult to understand deception. The psychological undercurrents of real life as well as of literature—in short, all that gives spice to social relations—for them remain a closed book. "People talk to each other with their eyes," said one observant autistic youth. "What is it that they are saying?"

Lacking a mechanism for a theory of mind, autistic children develop quite differently from normal ones. Most children acquire more and more sophisticated social and communicative skills as they develop other cognitive abilities. For example, children learn to be aware that there are faked and genuine expressions of feeling. Similarly, they become adept at that essential aspect of human communication, reading between the lines. They learn how to produce and understand humor and irony. In sum, our ability to engage in imaginative ideas, to interpret feelings and to understand intentions beyond the literal content of speech are all accomplishments that depend ultimately on an innate cognitive mechanism. Autistic children find it difficult or impossible to achieve any of these things. We believe this is because the mechanism is faulty.

This cognitive explanation of autism is specific. As a result, it enables us to distinguish the types of situations in which the autistic person will and will not have problems. It does not preclude the existence of special assets and abilities that are independent of the innate mechanism my colleagues and I see as defective. Thus it is that autistic individuals can achieve social skills that do not involve an exchange between two minds. They can learn many useful social routines, even to the extent of sometimes camouflaging their problems. The cognitive deficit we hypothesize is also specific enough not to preclude high achievement by autistic people in such diverse activities as musical performance, artistic drawing, mathematics and memorization of facts.

It remains to be seen how best to explain the coexistence of excellent and abysmal performance by autistic people on abilities that are normally expected to go together. It is still uncertain whether there may be additional damage in emotions that prevents some autistic children from being interested in social stimuli. We have as yet little idea what to make of the single-minded, often obsessive, pursuit of certain activities. With the autistic person, it is as if a powerful integrating force—the effort to seek meaning—were missing.

The old image of the child in the glass shell is misleading in more ways than one. It is incorrect to think that inside the glass shell is a normal individual waiting to emerge, nor is it true that autism is a disorder of childhood only. The motion picture *Rain Man* came at the right time to suggest a new image to a receptive public. Here we see Raymond, a middle-aged man who is unworldly, egocentric in the extreme and all too amenable to manipulation by others. He is incapable of understanding his brother's double-dealing pursuits, transparently obvious though they are to the cinema audience. Through various experiences it becomes possible for the brother to learn from Raymond and to forge an emotional bond with him. This is not a farfetched story. We can learn a great deal about ourselves through the phenomenon of autism.

Yet the illness should not be romanticized. We must see autism as a devastating handicap without a cure. The autistic child has a mind that is unlikely to develop self-consciousness. But we can now begin to identify the particular types of social behavior and emotional responsiveness of which autistic individuals are capable. Autistic people can learn to express their needs and to anticipate the behavior of others when it is regulated by external, observable factors rather than by mental states. They can form emotional attachments to others. They often strive to please and earnestly wish to be instructed in the rules of person-to-person contact. There is no doubt that within the stark limitations a degree of satisfying sociability can be achieved.

Autistic aloneness does not have to mean loneliness. The chilling aloofness experienced by many parents is not a permanent feature of their growing autistic child. In fact, it often gives way to a preference for company. Just as it is possible to engineer the environment toward a blind person's needs or toward people with other special needs, so the environment can be adapted to an autistic person's needs.

On the other hand, one must be realistic about the degree of adaptation that can be made by the limited person. We can hope for some measure of compensation and a modest ability to cope with adversity. We cannot expect autistic individuals to grow out of the unreflecting mind they did not choose to be born with. Autistic people in turn can look for us to be more sympathetic to their plight as we better understand how their minds are different from our own.

FURTHER READING

AUTISM: EXPLAINING THE ENIGMA. Uta Frith. Blackwell Publishers, 1989.

THE COGNITIVE BASIS OF A BIOLOGICAL DISORDER: AUTISM. Uta Frith, John Morton and Alan M. Leslie in *Trends in Neurosciences,* Vol. 14, No. 10, pages 433-438; October 1991.

AUTISM AND ASPERGER SYNDROME. Edited by Uta Frith. Cambridge University Press, 1992.

UNDERSTANDING OTHER MINDS: PERSPECTIVES FROM AUTISM. Edited by Simon Baron-Cohen, Helen Tager-Flusberg and Donald J. Cohen. Oxford University Press, 1993.

Children with Communication Disorders

The terms *communication, language,* and *speech* are not synonymous. Communication refers to an exchange of information between sender and receiver. It may be through language. However, the exchange may be a movement, a nonlanguage vocal noise, or a symbolized marking in a nonlanguage medium (e.g., art, scent, sculpture). Both human and nonhuman species can communicate without language. Language refers to the use of voice sounds (or writing that represents these voice sounds) in combinations and patterns that follow rules that are accepted by the users of the language. Speech refers simply to the vocal utterances of language. The three terms are subsumed in descending order. Communication includes language and speech. Language includes speech. The opposite is not accurate. Communication is not under the general principle of language. Language is not subordinate to speech. Communication

disorders, as they affect children with disabilities, are usually separated into the subcategories of language and speech.

Language problems refer to the use of voice sounds in combinations and patterns that follow the arbitrary rules for that language, or to a delay in the use of voice sounds relative to normal development in other areas (physical, cognitive, social). Language delays can also be diagnosed in conjunction with other developmental delays (health, sensory, motoric, mental, personal, social). Delays in language are fairly common and can usually be resolved with proper treatment.

Disordered language is usually more difficult to remediate than delayed language. Disordered language may be due to a receptive problem (difficulty understanding voice sounds) or an expressive problem (difficulty producing the voice sounds that follow the arbitrary rules for that language) or both. Language disorders include aphasia (no language) and dysphasia (difficulty producing language). Many language disorders are the result of difficulty in understanding the rules and structural principles of the language (form) or in perceiving the semantic meanings of the words of the language (content). Other language disorders are due to difficulty in using the language pragmatically, in a practical context (function). Physical disorders such as damaged vocal cords, lips, palate, teeth, or tongue, and/or brain injuries can contribute to disordered language in form, content, or function.

Speech, the vocal utterance of language, is considered disordered in three underlying ways: voice, articulation, and fluency. Voice involves coordinated efforts by the lungs, larynx, vocal cords, and nasal passages to produce recognizable sounds. Voice can be considered disordered if it is incorrectly phonated through the lungs, larynx, and vocal cords (breathy, strained, husky, hoarse) or if it is incorrectly resonated through the nose (hypernasality, hyponasality). Articulation involves the use of the tongue, lips, teeth, and mouth to produce recognizable sounds. Articulation can be considered disordered if sounds are added, omitted, substituted, or distorted. Fluency involves appropriate pauses and hesitations to keep speech sounds recognizable. Fluency can be considered disordered if sounds are very rapid with extra sounds (cluttered) or if sounds are blocked and/or repeated, especially at the beginning of words (stuttered).

All children with language and/or speech disorders are entitled to assessment as early in life as the problem is realized and to remediation under the auspices of the Individuals with Disabilities Education Act (IDEA) and its amendments. In addition, they are entitled to a free and appropriate education in the least restrictive environment possible and to transitional help into the world of work, if needed, after their education is completed.

The first article in this unit is a research-based treatise on how to prevent language delays in infancy and early childhood, especially in children who, historically, have been at risk for language disorders. William Fowler presents data from a series of research projects. He articulates the principles of language development as currently known. Fowler also presents several methods that he and his colleagues have devised to increase language stimulation in infant day care and preschool settings. These techniques are illustrated with representative case studies to show how successfully they have been used.

The second article stimulates discussion about the sticky problems associated with assessing and diagnosing language disorders. Language differences are not language disorders. The American Speech-Language-Hearing Association (ASLHA) has clearly articulated the view that regional, social, or ethnic variations in symbol systems (dialects) should not be considered disorders of language or speech. However, while a dialect is just a difference, disorders existing within a dialectally different language must not be overlooked. A child may have limited English proficiency, but a delay or disorder in the mother tongue or in learning English must not be ignored. The author discusses the diagnostic pie in a conceptual framework that will help educators determine what is what.

The third article builds on the information presented in the preceding article. Once a diagnosis of a communication disorder has been made, what programs and services are necessary? What methods work best with students who have dialectally different languages or limited English proficiency? This article has been retained from a previous edition because of rave reviews by readers. It gives articulate answers to the questions of what to include in individualized education programs and how to select materials, enhance the learning environment in the classroom, and implement multicultural education.

The last article in this unit alerts readers to all the ways in which children communicate in the classroom without speech. Nonverbal language is body language. It is frequently used by children to communicate the thoughts and emotions that they cannot put into vocal utterances. Understanding this language is an important adjunct to working successfully with all children.

Looking Ahead: Challenge Questions

What kinds of verbal interactions are most helpful to young children learning language?

How can a culturally sensitive educator decide if language used by a child is dialectally different speech or a language-speech disorder?

What kinds of practical suggestions will work in an inclusionary classroom with children with limited English proficiency, dialect differences, and communication disorders?

How can teachers learn to comprehend the nonverbal communication practices of children?

Language interaction techniques for stimulating the development of at risk children in infant and preschool day care

WILLIAM FOWLER

Center for Early Learning and Child Care, Inc., 29 Buckingham St., Cambridge, MA 02138, USA

It is often assumed that children's language will develop normally in the average, "good" day care and home environments. In fact teachers and parents from all social backgrounds vary widely in the quality of language interaction they furnish to children in the early years. These variations, moreover, are highly correlated with how well children develop language and other skills. Over a series of research projects in both day care and the home, principles and methods have been devised that have been shown to enable both normal and at risk young children to develop high and long-lasting competencies in language and other cognitive and social skills. The approach centers on engaging the whole child to interact with language informally in play and the ordinary routines of child care, both individually and in small groups, and emphasizing both the social, communicative and cognitive functions of language. A variety of specific techniques for use in day care are described and illustrated with several successful cases with at risk children.

Key words: Language, delay, enrichment

When a child of two or three comes into day care saying nothing at all or at best only a few words we say her language is delayed. We are then likely to ask why and begin to think about what to do to help her learn to talk. Yet in a "normal" day care program we almost expect children will learn to talk as a matter of course. Many people assume that a good, average environment furnishes all the language experiences young children need to foster speech development.

Actually, it turns out that both teachers in day care and parents in the home vary enormously in the quality of language they provide for young children. And these large differences have important effects on how children develop, not only in their verbal skills, but also in their overall cognitive development. McCartney (1984), for example, found that the varying quality of language day care teachers used in different day care centers in Bermuda in infants from 19 months on made highly significant differences in the children's language and intellectual development between 3 and 5 ½ years. Carew (1980) reported that the cognitive experiences guided by language interaction with adults, in both day care and the home, in children between 18 and 34 months, were the chief factors relating to language and cognitive development at age 3. Of special interest is the fact that the children's own experimentation in play activities during infancy showed no effect on later development.

It is important to note that in these and other studies, these differences were true in families and day care centers of all social backgrounds, from the lowest to the highest socioeconomic and educational levels. Huttenlocher and her associates (1991) in a longitudinal study measured the actual range of difference in the amount of parent verbalization and vocabulary development in children in two-parent, well-educated families. The most talkative mothers used vocabularies of 33 more words than the least talkative, which resulted in vocabulary differences between the extremes of 131 words at 20 months and 295 words at 24 months.

It seems clear that the traditional view that what are often considered "good" homes and "good" day care centers typically produce well skilled, verbal children is far from universally true, as these and other studies show (see Fowler, *et al.*, 1992). Given the variation, many programs must be falling short in the quality of attention to language needed to ensure children develop their full potential. Our concerns

From *Early Childhood Development and Care*, Volume 3, 1995, pp. 35-48. © 1995 by Gordon and Breach Science Publishers, Inc. Reprinted by permission.

here are with day care, of course, though effective teachers are likely to express concerns to parents when they feel the child may not be getting enough attention at home.

The Dilemma

But if many ordinary children are not experiencing the kind of interactions they need to foster good verbal skills, how can busy teachers also manage to tend to the special needs of the delayed or at risk child? Is there a way out of this dilemma? If we are going to have millions of the nation's children enrolled in group care from an early age, and to mainstream delayed children as well, can teachers be expected to pay more attention to the language needs of the average child and still take care of the child with special needs? It is one thing to ask parents and child care providers in the home to devote more attention to talking activities with one or two children. It is quite another for teachers in day care to furnish the same high quality to groups of infants, toddlers and preschoolers who often vary widely in skills they bring to group care.

SOME ANSWERS FROM RESEARCH

Some years ago I undertook a series of research projects with infants and preschoolers in group day care and in homes with parents. While two major longitudinal projects in day care (Fowler, 1972; Fowler, 1978) embraced a broad curriculum designed to foster high quality language, cognitive and social development, curriculum goals in the home centered for the most part on guiding parents to enrich the child's language experiences. In all studies, however, the quality of language was a major focus in all daily activities. The day care children came from a wide spectrum of social, ethnic and educational backgrounds, many of them single parent families and all with working mothers, compared to home-reared control families of two parents with non-working mothers. One day care center included a group of high risk infants from largely single-parent families on welfare with less than a high school education. Another included a large number of children from immigrant families with less than a complete high school education. Children entered with widely different levels of developmental competence, including children with various forms of risk and delay and some with bilingual/non-English-speaking backgrounds. It proved possible, nevertheless, to resolve the apparent dilemma of tending to the needs of both the "average" and the "special" child.

Out of that original research has come an approach (since applied in all later projects) to infant and child care or enriching language through play and the informal routines of basic care. The approach is really a whole child, developmental strategy in which language communication is embedded in the activities of daily care. These methods have recently been discussed at length in a recent book and illustrated in a companion videotape, both entitled, *Talking from Infancy: How to Nurture and Cultivate Early Language Development*, (Fowler, 1990a and 1990b). The book includes a chapter on working with language-delayed children.

In these and successive projects children have typically progressed in speech development easily months ahead of norms and no child has failed to develop well in social and general cognitive skills. Both in the projects with infants reared at home (Fowler, 1983; Fowler and Swenson, 1979; Ogston, 1983; Roberts, 1983; Swenson, 1983) and in the day care studies (Fowler, 1972, 1978), children have developed as well and sometimes better than randomized controls (home studies) or comparison groups (day care studies).

In follow-up studies of day care children at ages 4 and 5 (Fowler and Khan, 1974), and as late as age 9 in a study in progress, the day care children scored above average or higher in IQ, language and social skills, as high or higher than children in the home reared comparison group, despite the higher proportion of single parents and the working-mother status of the day care families.

In follow-up studies through high school of infants enriched through guiding parents in the home, most children have developed high competence in multiple skills, including verbal, math and science, are well balanced socially, active in sports and independently motivated intellectually (Fowler, Ogston, Roberts-Fiati and Swenson, 1992, 1993a, b, and c). Over half are creative writers. Throughout our collected studies, ensuring mastery of verbal skills in the early years appears to be central to promoting children's development in cognitive and social skills and later school learning. Further follow-up studies are now in process on the long-term development of these subjects, now approaching early adulthood.

METHODS OF LANGUAGE AND CARE ENRICHMENT

Principles for Stimulating Language Learning

The methods themselves embraced certain core principles and a variety of supporting ones that can easily be applied in virtually any kind of language activity with children. Language is in fact such a convenient educational tool that it requires only the human voice to implement. No external aids are needed, leaving the hands and eyes free to conduct other tasks freely, including the care of the child. Among the most important principles are to:

1. Interact with the child, taking turns in any activity: respond to the child as much as taking initiative.
2. Use language as a tool of social communication, engaging the child in the give and take about personal wants, feelings and interests.
3. Use language to guide the child in understanding how words represent meanings—the world and our ideas about it.
4. Engage the child in a warm and friendly manner, encouraging and personalizing according to the child's style.

Of all these principles, interacting with the child in a balanced way, seems to have an especially critical role. Yet it is apparently the one easiest to overlook. Thus, in the follow-up studies of our original early home intervention studies, turn-taking in language play during infancy proved to be the most powerful predictor of the later language competencies during both early and later development (Fowler, Ogston, Roberts-Fiati, and Swenson, 1993b). How well parents took turns in the language play with their infants turned out to correlate with the children's later SAT scores in high school, significantly with TSWE (Test of Standard Written English) and Reading Comprehension scores.

No doubt many teachers (and parents) use language games with young children to some degree in this way without thinking about it. But in fact adults vary widely in how well they apply them, as the research cited above on teacher differences and how children develop shows. Moreover, the fact that parents furnished with special guidance in our early language intervention research could still vary significantly in the quality of their interacting, underscores the need for special focus on this principle.

Care and consistency in using them becomes of special importance, of course, in the case of children who already have or are moving out of infancy with fewer communication or other cognitive skills than the average child. The complete set of principles is outlined in my book, *Talking from Infancy*.

Applying the Principles in Practice

Principles may sound impressive, and may have worked with parents in the home and with specially structured research programs in day care, but how will they work in the practice of the ordinary day care center? Actually, the research in both the day care and home settings included a substantial number of at risk children, and in any case, these principles have been applied successfully in other group programs and home settings.

Let us consider a variety of situations, drawing on experience in various projects and paying special attention to situations involving a language delayed child in some way. Keep in mind that the focus is on infants at risk or preschoolers with mild to moderate problems of delay or difficulties in verbal communication. Children with severe communication disorders or delays will usually require referral to specialized therapy of some kind. (See especially, Harris, 1990). Marked hearing loss, organic involvement or severe emotional difficulties are often implicated in such cases.

The delayed or slow-learning child alone

Let us suppose a teacher has some free time to work with a delayed child for a few minutes in some secluded corner of the play room, while the rest of a group of two year olds are otherwise engaged. What to do?

The first thing to keep in mind is to identify the stage of language development, in very general terms, the child has attained. Table 1 outlines four main stages and some important steps in language development, comparing the development of the average child with the development of language enriched children in our projects.

To a large extent, use language according to how well the child can talk, regardless of the child's age. With many delayed children, a few words and perhaps a phrase or two that functions as a holophrase (a phrase serving as a unit, such as "go bye-bye", in which the individual component words have no separate meaning for the child), is all that some delayed children use. This means that, whereas the average child is well on the way to building a good vocabulary by 20 months and the enriched child as early as about 10 months, the slow child may hardly have gotten any start with words at all by age two, as shown in Table 2 with a moderately delayed child. In any case, even if the child is as old as three or more, the focus in language play needs to be on using single words.

Here are some things to do:

1. *Prepare a set of toys in advance*, choosing items likely to appeal to the child's interests

and small objects with frequently used common names (e.g., block, doll, car, truck, ball, clock, spoon). Keep objects in a box or other container, ready to bring them out from time to time to involve the child in repeated sessions. Substitute new toys when the child tires of the toys or new items are needed to expand the child's vocabulary.

2. Engage the child in *play with the toys,* introducing one or two at time and letting the child explore and use them in play spontaneously.

3. *Label each toy as the child handles it.* Be sure to time your naming of the item to the child's attention to the object.

4. *Keep the language simple:* start with the names of small, interesting toys and common objects—nouns, and concrete actions like run, walk, jump, kiss, hug—verbs. Prepositions (up, down, in and out) also function as action terms in the early stages.

5. Keep the play interesting by *introducing variations* of an activity. Engage the child in *sociodramatic play* by pretending that any of the objects are "live" and have them do different social activities (e.g., walk, run, jump, eat, drink, etc.). Social play can often be combined with construction activities with blocks and other building toys.

6. Try to fit in *a series of mini sessions* of 2 or 3 minutes or so several times a day or even only once or twice a day. Such a pattern will quickly start to yield real progress in the delayed child's mastery of verbal skills. Brief time slots of this kind have some realistic chance of being fitted into busy teaching schedules. Should schedules occasionally permit, longer spans of as much as 15 minutes are also productive, as long as the child remains interested.

Avoid Withholding and Correcting Errors

Some teachers withhold opportunities for a child to play with some toy, until the child says a word or phrase. Although sometimes recommended by behaviorist philosophies, in our studies we have found that such withholding strategies are likely to arouse a child's resentment and resistance. Although withholding techniques can be effective in the hands of skilled therapists, too often they lead to subtle or not-so-subtle battles of negative social interaction. The delayed child, especially, often has underlying feelings of failure that lead to the passive resistance of not talking, which is only reinforced by adult withholding. *Warmth, support and encouragement of effort are the most important ingredients to foster learning.*

A better strategy is simply to engage children, including the passive resisters, in the play, letting them start to say words and progress at their own speed in their own way. By the same token, avoid correcting errors (saying the wrong word or choosing a "block" when the teacher has asked the child to put a "ball" in a container). It is particularly important to spare children who have already felt a sense of failure in learning to talk, from meeting another failure experience. A better method is for the teacher simply to label the missed object correctly by making another demonstration in a play task, without referring to the child's "error", and the teacher should continue to do so over a series of play sessions, along with labeling various other objects. In this manner even the slow learning children will gradually understand and eventually say more and more words as they develop confidence.

Avoid Correcting Pronunciation and Grammar

There is also little need to stress correct pronunciation, following some model of standard English or even some dialect. Adequate pronunciation and adequate mastery of grammatical forms (e.g., pronouns, plurals, tenses, and sentence structures) will gradually be shaped as teachers demonstrate the correct or useful forms while interacting with the child. The same is true when the child uses the wrong label, mispronounces a word, uses "you" when "I" is meant, or uses present tense when past tense is called for. All these errors will be most easily corrected sooner or later by the children themselves as they come to grasp the relevant concept.

Teachers need only to label objects and actions correctly themselves, to use correct pronominal designations, and to employ tenses properly for the child gradually to understand and correct his or her own errors. Giving multiple, varied and accurate examples in the course of play furnishes all the material a child needs to make cognitive inferences of various rules for correct usage. At the same time, modeling in the course of play keeps the activity lots of fun for the child, without the burden of being labeled "wrong". The advantage of this focused language activity, anchored in manipulating objects directly, over the ordinary adult speech of everyday life, which is too often much of what children have to make inferences from, is that the language is simplified, relevant and more accessible in helping the child make useful inferences.

5. CHILDREN WITH COMMUNICATION DISORDERS

OTHER DEVICES AND SITUATIONS

Many programs and teaching situations may not allow much room for scheduled play time alone with any child on a regular basis. But even if they do, what about the rest of the day, the 6 to 7 or more hours of the day spent in working with groups of children? Actually, the routines of child care for children under two, and often up to 2 ½ or more, typically require individualized care for a number of activities, especially, changing diapers and beginning toileting routines, dressing and undressing on departure and arrival or even movement to and from the playground in inclement weather, feeding and eating routines, and washing and bathing activities. If nothing else, such activities represent large blocks of otherwise lost learning time and they are in fact ideal settings for engaging the child in language learning. Indeed, some infant-toddler enrichment projects have been based on embedding cognitive and language interactions in just such routines (Lally, Mangione and Honig, 1986).

Basic care routines

Think about the routines of getting dressed or washing hands. Activities repeated several times a day become demanding tasks to be gotten through with each child in turn, hopefully with sensitivity and warmth—but in any case executed with despatch to get on to the main "business" of care, activities of some kind in the play room or on the playground. But what if such routines involved a teaching goal, in which one could see progress in the child's development, almost day to day, from one's efforts?

Language interaction is just such an activity. A few well-timed words said during each routine, repeated every time, will in a matter of days bring about noticeable progress. Use vocabulary of the names of clothes—shirt, sock, diaper, pants, and the concrete actions performed each time—sit, stand, lie, up, down. These terms are used so often that the prespeech infant is soon showing evidence of understanding, then imitating here and there and finally saying them. In the same way, the delayed child will begin to make up for time lost.

The same flexible, informal style, *timing* the saying of each key word to your or the child's action, will engage the child's interest in language, in the same way individual play sessions do. Equally important, the tasks become rewarding to the teacher and the child is also involved in gradually learning about the steps to master her or his own self-care.

Small group activities

But can caregivers use language effectively in the same focused manner with groups of infants and preschoolers? Two-to-five year olds in most centers are of course regularly assembled into groups of different sizes around a table for eating or on the floor for singing, story time, and circle activities, or to observe plants, frogs or other phenomena for "science" learning. Much of the time, however, the flow of words may not relate closely to the item talked about. If the pace is not too fast, and some children are not left on the periphery in an oversized group, language and understanding will be far enough along in the average child for them to learn something about the activity. For infants under two, however, and even many two-year-olds, and especially the child with very little language, little understanding may get through—certainly not in understanding words, parts of speech and syntax. Keep in mind that the so-called "average" child is a mathematical myth. In any group of children of the same age, language skills often vary widely. For example, the skills of a group of two-year-olds may range from the child who spouts sentences to the one who only occasionally stumbles through two or three words. What to do?

How about breaking up main groups of 8 two-year-olds or 12 three-year-olds into more manageable groups of 3 and 4 each? But how can this be done when there is only a single teacher for each set of 8 or 12 children? One way to accomplish this is to find a relatively quiet corner to engage 3 or 4 children at a time in a separate language activity for a few minutes while the rest of the children are engaged in free play. If there is no such corner, set up one. Arrange an area with a small table and chairs. Just a throw rug will do sometimes. Give the activity additional focus and shield the group from intrusions from other children by placing two toy shelves to form an angle. Leave only a small entry way, blocked by a small chair that can quickly be removed for teacher exit in an emergency.

Groups of 3 or 4 little ones in a close circle are small enough so that every child can see every block, truck, or nose on a doll, at the exact moment the toy is labeled by the teacher. The teacher can also easily go from child to child, asking each one in turn to "put a block in a box" or "make the doll walk", without a long waiting period in between. Small groups thus combine the advantage of children learning in groups with highly focused individual attention. Extended discussions of engaging small groups of children in interactive play in language and concept learning activities may be found in my text, *Infant and Child Care* (Fowler, 1980).

(Photo credit: United Nations/L. Solmssen)

The quality of language interaction varies greatly in the environment of the young child. In the early development of the whole child, it is important for them to communicate informally in groups and in the ordinary routines of early education.

It is also easy to keep track of each child's individual needs in small circle groups. Tailor your comments and requests according to the child's level. For example, with one child it may be important to stick to the simplest nouns—ball, car and bell. With another, use verbs—roll, walk and jump; and with still another a few more abstract terms like adjectives—round, big and little, can be woven in. When there are wide gaps between levels, then hesitant and slower children sometimes become intimidated and the fast and confident ones become bored. Some of these problems can be handled by involving the fast learners in leadership roles. It is vital to ensure that even the slowest child gets turns in performing tasks. Another alternative is to organize groups on the basis of skill levels instead of age. On this basis a group might consist of 4 children, all of whom are only beginning to say their first few words, yet range in age from 12 to 20 months or even more.

By rotating the small subgroups, every child gets a turn with this relatively individualized form of language play with toys. It is often useful to make up different combinations of children from time to time to vary the kind of stimulation and play interests children provide for one another. But little ones sometimes feel more secure if they can count on a familiar friend in their group.

Parent and other teacher assistants

Teacher assistants can add a great deal to a program, but too often they are not used for much more than setting out and putting away toys and art materials and moving groups of children from activity to activity. When aides are assigned to watch over children in free play, at least for short periods, the teacher can be free to engage a small group in language play, or even occasionally an individual child with special learning needs. Taking time to guide an assistant (or parent assistant) in techniques of handling and guiding children multiplies the amount of individual teacher attention for children. Many assistants can readily learn to work effectively in the language interactions activities, certainly individually in toy play and the child care routines, if not so easily in groups.

KEEPING TRACK OF EACH CHILD'S PROGRESS

Perhaps the most pleasant reward for a teacher is observing children's progress in development. Language growth is one of the easiest areas in which to chart a child's progress. Such charting takes more time and the changes are often difficult to perceive in the development of such concepts as number or size. But language development follows a highly visible course from sounds, to words, phrases, sentences, and sequential telling about things in a string of phrases and sentences. It is true that the first understandings of words are sometimes tricky to verify, and documenting progress in the different parts of speech and forming sentences (syntax) can be more technical. But even here, rather simple day-to-day (or perhaps every other day or so) records will shed light on a child's learning in these areas, at least enough to ascertain that a child is actually progressing. Especially, for the delayed or slow learner, written records will supply information to reassure teachers of progress that casual memory may overlook.

The child's first understanding of words is easily verified by asking a child to give you the [toy] dog or cow, when three or four toys to choose from are placed in front of him or her. In this way, if children can repeatedly pick the right one, you can judge they understand a given word. They show *word recognition.* Varying the setting broadens the child's experience and gives evidence of how generalized the child's understanding is. But don't press the child with repeated requests and usually avoid asking, "What is this?" This task requires the child to *recall* a word, a much more abstract task, which will come spontaneously with practice in play.

Written records or charts need consist only of a single page in a notebook or chart posted on the wall, one page for each child, with two columns, one for the date and a second for the sound, word or phrase a child is heard to use that day. A third column could also describe the circumstances when the child said something, such as "imitating the teacher" or "in response looking at a picture of a duck." This additional information, while furnishing more insights on how the child is learning, may not be necessary except for a child with special difficulties.

Perhaps the *most important value of recording progress in language is to guide teachers on what to do next with a child,* especially with the slower children or those with special difficulties in pronunciation, use of adjectives, or forms of syntax. Checking over a child's record for the past week or two, for example, will reveal not only whether a certain child is learning much slower than others of a similar age, but that this child is learning no verbs, only the simplest nouns, or forms no phrases except occasional rote imitations (e.g., "big truck" or "go out") without ever applying them alone to new situations. A teacher can then zero in on desirable steps—using more examples with simple verbs or applying the same simple phrase to slightly varying situations, such as "more cars," "more blocks," etc.

Because time demands are of the essence of all teaching, jotting down any new term when a teacher has an odd moment free or at the end of the day, will probably serve very well. Don't give up if some term is missed or two or three days go by with no notations. Even spotty records can furnish valuable information on how well a child's language is progressing. This is particularly true in the early stages for infants up to 18 months or age two, and above all for the delayed and slow learning child.

Early records are the easiest to keep, because new sounds for the typical 6 months old, new words for the typical 12 months old and new phrases for the typical 20 months old start out slowly—one or two for the first week or two or even for several weeks. Gradually, the rates for most children accelerate at each stage, however. At some point in each successive stage, children grasp the concept of how to make new sounds, then that words have meaning—that they stand for things, and then that words can be put together (in phrases, later sentences) to describe actions and events of and about things. It is when these shifts occur that children learn new terms more and more rapidly and it becomes both increasingly difficult and relatively unimportant to keep track of the new terms. Just move on to recording progress for the next stage, from the now rapidly expanding vocabulary to the first halting, occasional phrases, or the rapid production of two word phrases to the beginning of constructing 3 or more word sentences.

SOME EXAMPLES

John[1]

John came from a well-off, college-educated family. When he entered our program at one year, it was almost immediately evident to everyone that he had a strange way of relating to people, and that there were none of the usual signs that he responded in any way to what a teacher said. Although lack of words is hardly surprising at one year, lack of any response to the human voice through smiling or gesture is. John usually totally ignored the speaker or looked very blank, and quite often looked right past the speaker, though tests given before entering day care had established that he had no hearing loss. In fact, John never made any rapport at all with adults or other children. It was quite evident that communication of any kind, gestural, vocal, or verbal, was out of the question with John. Yet, curiously, when the psychologist (myself) attempted to engage him in play with toys to diagnose his patterns, he did interact in manipulating the toys, though maintaining his usual stance of avoiding vocal communication and all except furtive eye contact. There was a distinct paranoid quality of complete mistrust and emotional blockage of relations with others. Later it was revealed that the mother could not stand infants, John included.

Because the center had a training program for students, we were able to assign an interested student, who soon formed a close attachment to John, as his main caregiver. With staff guidance she engaged John daily in toy play and frequently cared for him in basic routines. Gradually, she added more and more language into her play with him and involved him with the other children and teachers, with whom he was initially quite distant. Over the course of the 18 months he attended the program, John formed a close attachment to this student and gradually expanded relations to other caregivers and the children in play. By the time he was 2 ½, at graduation, he was speaking well in sentences and he was admitted to another preschool program, where he adapted well, despite being the youngest child attending by several months. Especially interesting were changes in the mother's perceptions of John as an interesting, verbal little boy she came to accept and love, no longer the dependent infant she initially could not abide.

Terry and Mary

Two infants from a poor, inner city English Canadian single parent family on welfare, Terry was only 13 months older than his younger sister, Mary. The mother had only an 8th grade education and a much below average IQ. Terry's developmental test scores were also extremely low when he entered day care at 3 ½ months. Over the course of 14 months in the program his language skills blossomed and his test scores rose to very high average levels, which were maintained through the last follow-up with him at age 4 ½.

By the time his sister entered day care at 4 months, the mother had been engaged in a year of parent education and Mary had enjoyed the daily undivided attention of her mother during her early months while Terry attended day care. Mary's test scores were about average at entry. Her language and other test scores also rose to very high average like Terry's while she was in the program, but were found to have receded to average levels over the course of her final follow up at just over age 3. Given her circumstances, the mother could apparently sustain the care and stimulation of one child, the older boy, but not two, once the children no longer attended day care.

Ed

The language focus of our day care program was particularly important for Ed. Despite his college-educated family background, when he enrolled at 14 months Ed could neither imitate nor say any words, though he had good perceptual-motor skills. By the time he left the program 16 months later, his language and other skills were all at the superior level and remained this high when last followed up at age 4 ½. Had he been in a program where nothing but free play prevailed without much teacher-child interaction and attention to language, his mild language delay might have expanded to become serious, since he was also getting little attention to his language at home. The mother was working at two jobs and the father was chronically ill.

CONCLUSION

Children having a wide range of language and other skills, including children from high risk backgrounds, can be accommodated in day care for infants and preschoolers, just as children with a wide range of other learning problems and emotional styles are regularly fit into the ordinary environment. The "average" or "ordinary" child is in fact an extraordinarily varying individual, who because of different backgrounds, varies in both the pace of development and the variety of courses followed. Within the average environment, a teacher strategy of bringing language into special focus, and anchoring it in the child's "natural" world of play to enhance accessibility, will enable the fast, the moderate, the slow and the different child all to progress in their own ways to acquire language and related cognitive skills at minimal acceptable levels of competence.

---

[1] All names of children are pseudonyms to preserve privacy.

References

Bzoch, K. R. and League, R. (1971) *Receptive Expressive Emergent Language Scale.* Tallahassee, FL: Tree of Life Press.

Carew, J. V. (1980) Experience and the development of intelligence in young children at home and in day care. *Monographs of the Society for Research in Child Development,* **45,** Serial no. 187.

Fowler, W. (1972) A developmental learning approach to infant care in a group setting. *Merrill-Palmer Quarterly,* **18,** 145–175.

Fowler, W. (1978) *Day Care and Its Effects on Early Development: A Study of Group and Home Care in Multi-Ethnic Working Class Families.* Toronto: Ontario Institute for Studies in Education.

Fowler, W. (1980) *Infant and Child Care: A Guide to Education in Group Settings.* Boston: Allyn and Bacon.

Fowler, W. (1983) *Potentials of Childhood.* Vol. 2: *Studies in Early Developmental Learning.* Lexington, MA: Lexington Books.

Fowler, W. (1990a) *Talking from Infancy: How to Nurture and Cultivate Early Language Development.* Cambridge, MA: Brookline Books.

Fowler, W. (1990b) (same title) Cambridge, MA: Center for Early Learning and Child Care.

Fowler, W. and Khan, N. (1974) *The Later Effects of Enfant Group Care: A Follow-up Study.* Toronto: Ontario Institute for Studies in Education.

Fowler, W. and Swenson, A. (1979) The influence of early language stimulation on development. *Genetic Psychology Monographs,* **100,** 73–109.

Fowler, W., Ogston, K., Roberts-Fiati, G. and Swenson, A. (1992) *The influence of early language term development of abilities: Identfying exceptional abilities through educational intervention.* Paper presented at the 1992 Esther Katz Rosen Symposium on the Psychological Development of Gifted Children: Developmental Approaches to Identifying Exceptional Ability. (To be published in Proceedings by the American Psychological Association).

Fowler, W., Ogston, K., Roberts-Fiati, G. and Swenson, A. (1993a) Accelerating Language Acquisition. In K. Ackrill (ed.) *The Origins and Development of High Ability.* Chichester, UK: Wiley.

Fowler, W., Ogston, K., Roberts-Fiati, G. and Swenson, A. (1993b) Increasing societal talent pools through early enrichment. Paper presented at A Gifted Globe: Tenth World Congress on Gifted and Talented Education. Toronto, Ontario, Canada, August 8 to 18, 1993. Submitted for publication in Proceedings.

Fowler, W., Ogston, K., Roberts-Fiati, G. and Swenson, A. (1993c) *The longterm development of giftedness and high competencies in children enriched in language during infancy.* Paper presented at the 1993 Esther Katz Rosen Symposium on the Psychosocial Development of Gifted Children: Relating Life Span Research to the Development of Gifted Children (To be published in Proceedings by the American Psychological Association).

Griffiths, R. (1970) *The Abilities of Young Children.* London: Child Development Research Centre.

Harris, J. (1990) *Early Language Development: Implications for Clinical and Educational Practice.* London: Routledge.

Huttenlocher, J., Height, W., Bryk, A., Seltzer, M. and Lyons, T. (1991) Early vocabulary growth: Relation to language input and gender. *Developmental Psychology,* **27,** 236–248.

Lally, J. R., Mangione, P. L. and Honig, A. S. (1986) Syracuse University Family Development Research Project: Long-Range Impact of Early Intervention on Low Income Children and Their Families. In D. R. Powell (Ed). *Parent Education as Early Childhood Intervention: Emerging Directions in Theory Research, and Practise* (pp. 79–104), Norwood, NJ: Ablex.

McCartney, K. (1984) Effect of quality day care environment on children's language development. *Developmental Psychology,* **20,** 244–260.

Menyuk, P. (1977) *Language and Maturation.* Cambridge, MA: MIT Press.

Ogston, K. (1983) The effects of gross motor and language stimulation on infant development. In W. Fowler (ed.) *Potentials of Childhood.* Vol. 2. Lexington, MA: Lexington Books.

Roberts, G. (1983) The effects of a program of stimulation in language and problem solving on the development of infants from lower-income, black Caribbean immigrant families. In W. Fowler (ed.) *Potentials of Childhood.* Vol. 2. Lexington, MA: Lexington Books.

Swenson, A. (1983) Toward an ecological approach to theory and research in child language acquisition. In W. Fowler (ed.) *Potentials of Childhood.* Vol. 2. Lexington, MA: Lexington Books.

Distinguishing Language Differences

from

Language Disorders

in

Linguistically and Culturally Diverse Students

Celeste Roseberry-McKibbin

Celeste Roseberry-McKibbin is an associate professor in the Department of Communicative Sciences and Disorders, California State University, Fresno.

Introduction

Many educators today view bilingualism as a great linguistic and social advantage (Cummins, 1994; Wong Fillmore, 1993). However, sometimes educators are confronted with linguistically and culturally diverse (LCD) students who appear to be struggling in school. When this happens, one of the first questions usually asked is: "Does this LCD student have a language difference or a language disorder?" In other words, can the problems be traced to cultural differences and/or the student's lack of facility with English, or is there an underlying disability that requires special education intervention? The question of distinguishing a language difference from a language disorder is a very challenging one. (The terms "language disorder" and "language-learning disability" are used interchangeably in this article.)

The "diagnostic pie" is a simple conceptual framework that can help educators begin to distinguish language differences from language disorders. The diagnostic pie paradigm assumes that LCD students speak their primary language and are in the process of learning English as a second language. Bloom and Lahey's (1978) definition of language is central here:

> Language is a system of symbols used to represent concepts that are formed through exposure and experience.

There are practical ramifications of this definition. I am assuming that exposure and experience refer to exposure to good language models, to a variety of "mainstream" experiences (that are consistent with schools' expectations), to literacy, and to environmental and linguistic stimulation. For example, when students come to kindergarten, some educators assume that the children have looked at books; that they have been read to; that they know how to listen in groups; that they have used scissors, crayons, and pencils before. The educators may further assume that

children have been taken to stores, zoos, libraries, and other places in the community; that the children have had literacy experiences which prepare them to learn the alphabet, print their names, etc.

Some LCD students come from backgrounds where they have had all these experiences. Some LCD students, especially older ones, may even have a broader experience base than many monolingual English-speaking students who are born and raised in the United States. These LCD students may be bilingual or even trilingual, have traveled in different countries, and be bicultural. These students have a great deal to offer to mainstream American students. Mainstream American students can be enriched and learn many things from these sophisticated LCD students.

Other LCD students come from non-literate backgrounds. They and their families may be non-literate for one or more reasons. Perhaps family members have not had educational opportunities; these opportunities are extremely limited in some countries, especially if the family is of refugee status. Others come from backgrounds where the language is oral only and has not been put in written form. Van Deusen-Scholl (1992) gives the example of a number of Morrocan children in the Netherlands who come from isolated rural areas where no formal education is available; they struggle in the Netherlands' school system. Some of these children speak Berber languages which do not have a tradition of print literacy. Other linguistic groups, such as some Native Americans and speakers of Haitian Creole, have predominantly oral traditions and no written language.

Some educators do not stop to ask themselves whether or not students have had some or any of the usual mainstream experiences that are inherently assumed, like exposure to literacy. And this is often where deficits in students are created: when students' exposure and experiences are different than those expected in the mainstream school environment, then educators may assume that there are deficits inherent in the students themselves.

A centrally important idea in this article is that before educators even begin to ask whether or not a student manifests a language disorder, they must stop and remind themselves of what language really is: a system of symbols that represents concepts formed through **exposure** and **experience**. If a student's background experiences and exposure to life situations and linguistic models are different than those expected by schools, then it follows that their language will represent *their unique backgrounds*, which are not necessarily consistent with those expected by the school.

This difference in students' backgrounds and schools' expectations can lead to misdiagnosis of students and consequent inappropriate placement into special education. Many experts point out that historically in United States schools, disproportionate numbers of LCD children have been placed in to special education unnecessarily (Ruiz & Figueroa, 1993). The "diagnostic pie" (see page 112) can help educators begin to conceptualize students' backgrounds and current status, and see that there are various alternatives to special education.

Diagnostic Pie Quadrant 1

Students who fall into this quadrant of the pie are those LCD students who have normal underlying ability to learn language. They come from backgrounds that may be rich in stimulation and general experiences, but the backgrounds have not been consistent with expectations in mainstream United States schools. Some older immigrant students are good examples of this: they had schooling in their country of

origin, and generally have a good enough conceptual foundation to succeed academically. If these students are dominant in their primary language and thus are having some difficulty in all-English classrooms, their needs can usually be served best through placement into good bilingual classrooms where both English and the primary language can be developed. If bilingual education is not available, then these students can benefit from Sheltered English or, barring this, English as a second language teaching. Again, if these students are given time, attention, and help, they will generally succeed in school.

Diagnostic Pie Quadrant 2

These students have normal underlying ability to learn language. However, they come from backgrounds where they may have experienced some limitations or differences in environmental stimulation and linguistic exposure. These students may come from backgrounds where society has placed them and their families at profound economic disadvantage. I have worked with many children like this: they have good ability to learn, but life circumstances have curtailed their opportunities to learn and be exposed to various experiences before they come to school. These students often perform poorly on standardized tests, many of which are based on mainstream, White middle-class expectations. If these students have not been exposed to certain experiences and thus developed the conceptual background assumed by these tests, they will often appear "language disordered" simply because the tests do not adequately tap into their unique and individual backgrounds.

Several years ago, I had the experience of taking the WAIS (Wechsler Adult Intelligence Scale) and being penalized for lack of knowledge of items on the "General Knowledge" subtest. Because I grew up in the Philippines (ages 6-17 years), I had not had the exposure to facts that the WAIS assumed everyone had—and my overall IQ score was lowered because of it! Although I was taking the WAIS mostly out of personal interest, I was poignantly reminded of how often our standardized tests penalize LCD students for not having life experiences consistent with test writers' expectations.

Students in Quadrant 2 will usually show good gains in school if they can receive adequate quantities of input, exposure, and stimulation that may have been unavailable in their homes. These students will benefit from good bilingual education, ESL, and/or Sheltered English programs that enhance both the primary language and English. These students often also need extra stimulation which

can be provided through tutoring and participation in school enrichment programs. Unfortunately, these students often are placed into special education programs. Special education is usually unnecessary for students whose underlying language-learning ability is intact. If extra programs outside of special education are provided and the student can attend school consistently enough to benefit from them, usually good academic gains can be made without special education assistance.

Diagnostic Pie Quadrant 3

Quadrant 3 students come from backgrounds where they have had adequate exposure and language stimulation. Their life experiences are often consistent with those assumed by mainstream schools. Often, their parents have given them as much help as possible in the home, and the students still do not succeed in school. Many of them have a history of academic failure. Often, school personnel have given these students opportunities such as extra tutoring and participation in school programs designed to foster academic growth. Despite these measures, however, the students still do not learn and make adequate academic gains. These students have underlying language-learning disabilities that prevent them from learning and using any language adequately despite backgrounds that have attempted to provide environmental and linguistic stimulation.

These students need to be placed into special education so that their unique disabilities can be appropriately addressed. No matter how hard schools and parents try to use traditional methods to assist these students, the students will still struggle because they have underlying language-learning disabilities. As one speech-language pathologist puts it, "These students have a glitch in the computer." Students with these needs will benefit from (ideally) bilingual special education where the primary language is used. Because this ideal option is often not available, these students may be served by special education in English with as much primary language support as possible. Students with disabilities still benefit greatly from being taught concepts initially in their primary language.

Diagnostic Pie Quadrant 4

Students in Quadrant 4 come from backgrounds where there are differences and/or limitations of environmental experience and exposure. These students are very similar to those described in Quadrant 2, except that the students in Quadrant 4 also have underlying language-learning disabilities. These students are very difficult to assess because educators can never be sure whether the students' low test scores are due to background/environment, an underlying disability, or both.

Most educators wrestle with the issue of whether to place these students into Quadrant 2 or Quadrant 4. On the one hand, educators do not want to place into special education a Quadrant 2 student who would be adequately be served through additional school enrichment programs such as ESL. On the other hand, educators do not want to deprive Quadrant 4 students of the opportunity to receive special education help because that is what they need. According to Ortiz (1994), we are so afraid of mislabeling LCD students unnecessarily that the pendulum has swung in the other direction: some LCD students who genuinely need special education assistance are not receiving it, and are failing in school year after year.

Quadrant 4 students ideally need bilingual special education with additional enrichment experiences to compensate for limitations/differences of linguistic and environmental experience and stimulation. Barring the provision of these ideal services, Quadrant 4 students may be served by English special education with as much primary language support as possible. They can also benefit from participating in whatever additional enrichment experiences are available.

What to Look For

Comparing LCD students to monolingual English-speaking peers is very biased and provides a poor point of reference from which to make decisions. It is critical to analyze student behaviors in interactions in natural settings **with peers from similar cultural and linguistic backgrounds**. For example, I recently evaluated a 15-year old Russian immigrant ("Viktor") who was having learning difficulties. A major question I asked was: "How does Viktor perform/interact in comparison to other newcomer Russian students who have been in the United States the same length of time that he has?" When we compare students to their linguistic and cultural peers, our decisions will be much more fair and accurate.

I have found that interpreters who work regularly with LCD students are wonderful sources of information in this regard, because they have a great deal of experience with certain populations and thus can validly (albeit subjectively) compare the student in question with other students from the same cultural and linguistic background. I have also found that educators—especially general education classroom teachers—can serve as excellent resources for referral of LCD students who need special services.

Some teachers are fluent in the student's primary language, and can thus make judgments about delays or deviancies in the student's primary language assessment and comprehension. Other teachers, while not speaking a particular student's primary language, have many years of experience working with ESL students. These teachers may have worked, for example, with many Filipino students in the past and may have a number of Filipino students in their current classes. The teachers frequently have a frame of reference for what is "normal" behavior for Filipino learners of English as a second language, and can tell when a particular student is not performing as his/her peers are. While the teachers cannot make the judgment as to whether there is an actual language-learning disability, they can refer the student to personnel who have access to Filipino interpreters and who have the resources and background to make this type of diagnosis.

The classroom teacher, then, frequently serves as the "first layer" of the referral process. For example, an African American monolingual English-speaking teacher referred a Filipino kindergartener to me for language testing. In her opinion, his classroom performance was less than optimal and she was concerned that he might have a language-learning disability. This teacher had 15 years of teaching experience. When I asked her how the child compared to other ESL students in her experience, especially Filipino students, she replied "I have never seen a child like this one." She went on to describe some of the student's deviant academic and linguistic behaviors. When I and a Filipino interpreter (who also knew the family) tested the student, it turned out that he had a learning disability that was manifested even in his Filipino languages of Tagalog and Ilocano. In this case, the experienced teacher's insight turned out to be accurate.

Summary

Educators can provide appropriate services to LCD students who may show difficulties in the classroom. Using the "diagnostic pie" as a starting point can help

---

Student Behaviors to Observe when Distinguishing a Language Difference from a Language Disorder

Teachers can tell when an LCD student might need special education services for a language-learning disability when some of the following behaviors are manifested in comparison to similar peers:

1. Nonverbal aspects of language are culturally inappropriate.
2. Student does not express basic needs adequately.
3. Student rarely initiates verbal interaction with peers.
4. When peers initiate interaction, student responds sporadically/inappropriately.
5. Student replaces speech with gestures, communicates nonverbally when talking would be appropriate and expected.
6. Peers give indications that they have difficulty understanding the student.
7. Student often gives inappropriate responses.
8. Student has difficulty conveying thoughts in an organized, sequential manner that is understandable to listeners.
9. Student shows poor topic maintenance ('skips around').
10. Student has word-finding difficulties that go beyond normal second language acquisition patterns.
11. Student fails to provide significant information to the listener, leaving the listener confused.
12. Student has difficulty with conversational turn-taking skills (may be too passive, or may interrupt inappropriately).
13. Student perseverates (remains too long) on a topic even after the topic has changed.
14. Student fails to ask and answer questions appropriately.
15. Student needs to hear things repeated, even when they are stated simply and comprehensibly.
16. Student often echoes what she or he hears.

If an LCD student manifests a number of the above behaviors, even in comparison to similar peers, then there is a good chance that the student has an underlying language-learning disability and will need a referral to special education.

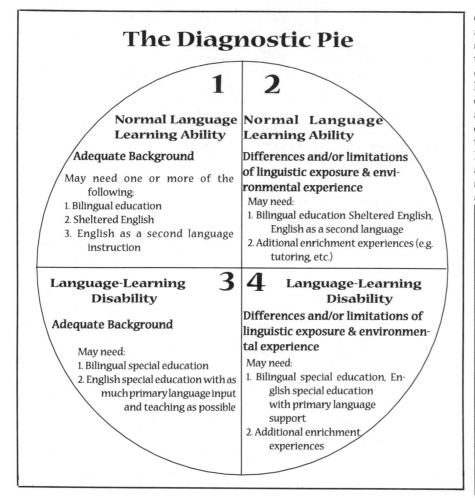

The Diagnostic Pie

1

Normal Language Learning Ability

Adequate Background

May need one or more of the following:
1. Bilingual education
2. Sheltered English
3. English as a second language instruction

2

Normal Language Learning Ability

Differences and/or limitations of linguistic exposure & environmental experience

May need:
1. Bilingual education Sheltered English, English as a second language
2. Aditional enrichment experiences (e.g. tutoring, etc.)

3

Language-Learning Disability

Adequate Background

May need:
1. Bilingual special education
2. English special education with as much primary language input and teaching as possible

4

Language-Learning Disability

Differences and/or limitations of linguistic exposure & environmental experience

May need:
1. Bilingual special education, English special education with primary language support
2. Additional enrichment experiences

educators to classify students appropriately and thus provide services commensurate with students' background and abilities. When educators suspect that a student may have an underlying language-learning disability that requires special education assistance, they can use the above list as a guideline to assist in differential diagnosis. It is imperative not only to avoid "false positives" in identifying LCD students with special needs, but to avoid "false negatives" that deprive these students of assistance which they need and deserve.

References

Bloom, L., & Lahey, M. (1978). *Language development and language disorders*. New York: John Wiley & Sons, Inc.

Cummins, J. (1994, March). Accelerating second language and literacy development. Paper presented at the California Elementary Education Association, Sacramento, CA.

Ortiz, A. (1994, June). Keynote address. Symposium on Second Language Learners in Regular and Special Education, Sacramento, CA.

Ruiz, N., & Figueroa, R. (1993). Why special education does not work for minority children. Paper presented at National Association for Multicultural Education, Los Angeles, CA.

Wong Fillmore, L. (1993). Educating citizens for a multicultural 21st century. *Multicultural Education Magazine, 1* (1), 10-37.

Toward Defining Programs and Services for Culturally and Linguistically Diverse Learners in Special Education

Shernaz B. García and Diana H. Malkin

Shernaz B. García *(CEC Chapter # 101), Lecturer and Associate Director, Bilingual Education Program and* **Diana H. Malkin** *(CEC Chapter # 101), recently completed a máster's degree, Department of Special Education, The University of Texas at Austin.*

Effective program design for services for students from culturally and linguistically diverse (CLD) backgrounds who also have disabilities is based on the same principles and purposes of multicultural education that create supportive learning environments in general education. In the absence of appropriate programs in regular and special education, these students are at higher risk of being misidentified as having disabilities, and their educational experiences may not take into account the reality that linguistic and cultural characteristics coexist and interact with disability-related factors. For example, a girl with a learning disability may also have limited English proficiency (LEP), be living in poverty, and come from a family of migrant farm workers. Special education programs for this student must address the interacting influence of these variables. How will bilingual education and English as a second language (ESL) in-struction be modified for this child? How do the family and larger community respond to her disability? How does the presence of an impairment influence the family's goals and expectations for their daughter? Would these differ if the child were male? How? Do her language characteristics—in the native language and in English—reflect linguistic differences, or do they, instead, result from socioeconomic factors? Failure to consider such issues may result in inadequate student progress or dropping out of school.

Special education services must be culturally and linguistically appropriate if they are to be truly inclusive. To meet the needs of CLD students with exceptionalities, special educators need knowledge and skills in four specific areas: (1) information about the language characteristics of learners with disabilities who are bilingual or have limited English proficiency that will assist in the development of a language use plan (Ortiz & García, 1990; Ortiz & Yates, 1989); (2) information about cultural factors that influence educational planning and services; (3) characteristics of instructional strategies and materials that are culturally and linguistically appropriate; and (4) characteristics of a learning environment that promotes success for all students.

Addressing Language Characteristics

Several aspects of the individualized education program (IEP) are influenced by students' language characteristics. Even when students are proficient in English, their cultural backgrounds may influence language use in academic settings. Dialectal differences, different patterns of language use and function among varied language communities, and nonverbal communication style differences among cultures can have a significant impact on student performance.

Gathering Essential Language Information

An accurate description of the language characteristics of students from language minority backgrounds, obtained from many sources, is necessary before decisions can be made regarding the language(s) of instruction as well as type(s) of language intervention to be provided in special education. For each language spoken by the student, several aspects of language proficiency and use should be considered, including information about the student's (a) language

From *Teaching Exceptional Children*, Vol. 26, No. 1, Fall 1993, pp. 52-58. © 1993 by The Council for Exceptional Children. Reprinted by permission.

dominance and proficiency; (b) acquisition of the surface structures (grammar, syntax, vocabulary, phonology, etc.), as well as functional language use (pragmatics); and, (c) receptive and expressive language skills. Language information should be current to ensure that educational planning is reponsive to language shifts that may have occurred since any previous testing. (Readers interested in a more detailed discussion of language profiling are referred to Ortiz & García, 1990.)

Developing the Language Use Plan

When educators assume that students with disabilities who have limited English proficiency will be confused by two languages, or that services for their disability-related difficulties should receive priority over services for their language needs, they are likely to remove students from language programs, or they may fail to realize the importance of coordinating services across bilingual and special education settings. However, students with LEP are entitled to bilingual and ESL instruction and should receive both to ensure that goals and strategies are pedagogically appropriate for their disability, as well as their language status. Foremost in the IEP should be a language use plan that specifies the language(s) of instruction for each goal and related objectives, the person(s) responsible for instruction in the targeted language(s), and the type of language intervention recommended (Ortiz & Yates, 1989).

In all instances except ESL instruction, ways of providing native language or bilingual instruction to these students should be explored, even if such services are not readily available. Alternatives may include the use of bilingual paraprofessionals, parent and community tutors in the native language(s), bilingual peer tutoring, collaboration with the student's bilingual/ESL teacher, and any other resources available in the district. Even when students do not qualify for bilingual education and ESL programs or have recently exited from these programs, some may

still need language support to succeed in academic tasks that demand greater English proficiency than they possess. Unless teachers understand that the English performance of students from language minority backgrounds may reflect language status rather than cognitive ability, instruction may be geared to the former rather than the latter. These students need instruction that accommodates their language level while teaching concepts that are at the appropriate cognitive level. The learning environment should support the language of instruction in a variety of contextualized, nonverbal, multisensory ways.

The Influence of Cultural Factors

In the most general sense, culture provides a world view that influences our ways of perceiving the world around us. It defines desirable attitudes, values, and behaviors, and influences how we evaluate our needs. As a result, the culture and subcultures of the school are likely to impact what and how children should be taught, as well as when and how successfully it is taught (Lynch, 1992). These culturally conditioned influences on educational programs and curriculum development are more difficult to perceive if educators do not have adequate cultural self-awareness and an understanding of other cultures. In order to truly understand how culture mediates school experiences, it is important to go beyond the "tourist" curriculum that focuses on external characteristics such as food, music, holidays, and dress (Derman-Sparks, 1989). An awareness of the internal (values, thoughts, cognitive orientations) and hidden (unspoken rules, norms) aspects of culture is also needed. For instance, it is helpful to understand the influence of culture on the size and structure of the family; standards for acceptable behavior (decorum and discipline); language and communication patterns (including rules for adult, adult-child, child-child communication); religious influences on roles, expectations and/or diet; and

traditions and history (e.g., reason for immigration, contact with homeland) (Saville-Troike, 1978).

Influences on Childrearing Practices

Enculturation is the part of the socialization process through which children acquire the language and characteristics of their culture (Gollnick & Chinn, 1986). For example, the community's values and orientation toward dependence-independence-interdependence will influence parents' goals for their son or daughter from infancy through adulthood. How the roles and status of children in the family and community are defined influences acceptance or rejection of specific behavior in a range of situations, including child-child, child-adult, family-school, and family-community interactions. In the case of students with disabilities, it is also helpful to know how parents' expectations and goals for their child have been influenced by cultural values, beliefs, and expectations for individuals with disabilities. Cultures vary in their definition of *family*; consequently, "the term…must be defined in a way that is relevant to the targeted cultural groups; otherwise, a very important resource for classroom learning and motivation may be overlooked" (Briscoe, 1991, p. 17). Failure to do this can lead to false assumptions about the role of parents in the care and education of their children and the extent to which parents or other primary caregivers should be involved in formal schooling activities, as well as the beliefs of school personnel that minority parents do not value education.

Finally, how children acquire strategies for learning and which patterns of thinking and learning are reinforced by the family have also been shown to vary across cultural contexts (Philips, 1983; Ramirez & Castaneda, 1974). When the culture of the classroom values behaviors such as independent seatwork, self-direction, and competition, or when success is defined primarily in academic terms, students whose families value interdependent behavior, or those for whom family well-being supersedes individual success, may have difficulty in school and are at risk of being mislabeled as "overly dependent," seeking "excessive" adult approval, or lacking the ability to become independent learners.

Influences on Communication Styles

Effective cross-cultural communication requires a knowledge of the cultural referents as well as individual and situational factors that influence how students use language in conversational and academic contexts. Examples include pragmatic variables such as turntaking behavior, greeting conventions, proximity, and rules of conversation—including unspoken rules (Cheng, 1987). In addition, cultural values and orientations are influential in defining the norms, rules, roles, and communication networks that govern interpersonal and intercultural communication. How students process information (their cognitive style); how they deal with conflict; and which strategies they prefer during negotiation, persuasion, or other types of communication may be influenced by the cultural context in which they are raised. Their self-concept and social identity (the influence of group membership on self-concept) are also affected by their membership in a particular cultural community (Gudykunst & Ting-Toomey, 1988). Given the "hidden" nature of many of these rules, norms, roles, and expectations, our awareness of their existence may develop only when they are violated and we attempt to identify the source of the misunderstanding.

Variations in communication styles also exist as a function of gender, socioeconomic status, and/or ethnicity (e.g., Heath, 1986; Hecht, Collier, & Ribeau, 1993), and they are present in any language, including native English-speaking communities. For example, African-American students, Appalachian children, or individuals from rural or low-income environments whose language does not reflect the language

and language uses valued at school may experience some of the same difficulties as speakers of other languages if they are not accustomed to the way language is used by teachers and in textbooks and other materials. In fact, class differences may negatively influence teacher responses, even when teachers and students are members of the same ethnic community. In such instances, teachers using an inclusive approach would

acknowledge and respect the language a child brings to school while focusing on building and broadening the child's repertoire of language varieties to include Standard English.

Instructional goals and strategies should be instrumental in helping students experience academic success, provide opportunities for them to try new learning situations, and increase the range of learning environments in

Table 1. Cultural and Linguistic Considerations Related to IEP Development

Selection of IEP Goals and Objectives

Considerations for IEP Development	Classroom Implications
IEP goals and objectives accommodate the student's current level of performance.	• At the student's instructional level • Instructional level based on student's cognitive level, not the language proficiency level • Focus on development of higher level cognitive skills as well as basic skills
Goals and objectives are responsive to cultural and linguistic variables.	• Accommodates goals and expectations of the family • Is sensitive to culturally based response to the disability • Includes a language use plan • Addresses language development and ESL needs

Selection of Instructional Strategies

Considerations for IEP Development	Classroom Implications
Interventions provide adequate exposure to curriculum.	• Instruction in student's dominant language • Responsiveness to learning and communication styles • Sufficient practice to achieve mastery
IEP provides for curricular/instructional accommodation of learning styles and locus of control.	• Accommodates perceptual style differences (e.g., visual vs. auditory) • Accommodates cognitive style differences (e.g., inductive vs. deductive) • Accommodates preferred style of participation (e.g., teacher- vs. student-directed, small vs. large group) • Reduces feelings of learned helplessness
Selected strategies are likely to be effective for language minority students.	• Native language and ESL instruction • Teacher as facilitator of learning (vs. transmission) • Genuine dialogue with students • Contextualized instruction • Collaborative learning • Self-regulated learning • Learning-to-learn strategies
English as a second language (ESL) strategies are used.	• Modifications to address the student's disability • Use of current ESL approaches • Focus on meaningful communication
Strategies for literacy are included.	• Holistic approaches to literacy development • Language teaching that is integrated across the curriculum • Thematic literature units • Language experience approach • Journals

which they can be successful. When parents' goals and expectations for their child are not consistent with the school's definition of success, attempts to "re-educate" the family should be avoided in favor of working collaboratively to determine mutually acceptable goals and helping parents in the decision-making process by sharing pertinent information.

Selection of Appropriate Instructional Strategies

Given the high frequency with which IEPs focus on instructional goals related to reading and language arts, this section addresses language and literacy development. However, many of the principles of effective literacy instruction are appropriate for use in other subject areas. In general, teaching/learning strategies and materials should be selected that facilitate high levels of academic content. Recent literature examining the instructional processes that foster literacy for students with disabilities (Cummins, 1984; Englert & Palincsar, 1991; García, Ortiz, & Bergman, 1990; Goldman & Rueda, 1988; Graves, 1985; Ruiz, 1989; Willig & Ortiz, 1991) emphasize the role of interactive learning environments. A critical assumption is that culture determines how literacy is defined, instructed, and evaluated. From this perspective, literacy is developed in environments that engage students and teachers in meaningful dialogue through activities that are authentic, holistic, and relevant (Cummins, 1984; Englert & Palincsar, 1991). Specifically:

1. Language and dialogue are essential to learning because they scaffold cognitive growth and mediate new learning for students.
2. Instructional goals should focus on student ownership of the literacy process to the extent that students can transform what they have learned into authentic writing activities.
3. Instruction cannot be transmitted or totally scripted by teachers, because learning occurs through student-

Table 2. Checklist for Selecting and Evaluating Materials

☐ Are the perspectives and contributions of people from diverse cultural and linguistic groups—both men and women, as well as people with disabilities—included in the curriculum?

☐ Are there activities in the curriculum that will assist students in analyzing the various forms of the mass media for ethnocentrism, sexism, "handicapism," and stereotyping?

☐ Are men and women, diverse cultural/racial groups, and people with varying abilities shown in both active and passive roles?

☐ Are men and women, diverse cultural/racial groups, and people with disabilities shown in positions of power (i.e., the materials do not rely on the mainstream culture's character to achieve goals)?

☐ Do the materials identify strengths possessed by so-called "underachieving" diverse populations? Do they diminish the attention given to deficits, to reinforce positive behaviors that are desired and valued?

☐ Are members of diverse racial/cultural groups, men and women, and people with disabilities shown engaged in a broad range of social and professional activities?

☐ Are members of a particular culture or group depicted as having a range of physical features (e.g., hair color, hair texture, variations in facial characteristics and body build)?

☐ Do the materials represent historical events from the perspectives of the various groups involved or solely from the male, middle-class, and/or Western European perspective?

☐ Are the materials free of ethnocentric or sexist language patterns that may make implications about persons or groups based solely on their culture, race, gender, or disability?

☐ Will students from different ethnic and cultural backgrounds find the materials personally meaningful to their life experiences?

☐ Are a wide variety of culturally different examples, situations, scenarios, and anecdotes used throughout the curriculum design to illustrate major intellectual concepts and principles?

☐ Are culturally diverse content, examples, and experiences comparable in kind, significance, magnitude, and function to those selected from mainstream culture?

teacher dialogue and classroom interactions that connect what students need to know to their current knowledge and experiences.
4. Teachers must view errors as a source of information regarding the emergence of new literacy skills rather than as student deficits or undesired behaviors.
5. Student difficulties should be interpreted as areas in which teachers need to provide greater mediation, rather than as problems that reside in the student.

Table 1 summarizes key variables to be considered when selecting instructional strategies for students with disabilities who are also culturally and/or linguistically different and suggests approaches that are more likely to be responsive to issues of student diversity.

Creating Supportive Learning Environments

Achievement of IEP goals and objectives depends on the context in which teaching and learning occur. A supportive classroom culture is part of the larger "psychological environment" of the school, and it can increase student motivation and attitudes toward learning (Maehr, 1990). Three ways in which the learning environment can be enhanced are by careful selection and evaluation of instructional materials, incorporation of students' language and culture, and involvement of parents and community.

Selecting and Evaluating Instructional Materials

Careful selection of instructional materials that promote high interest, motivation, and relevance to their sociocultural, linguistic, and experiential backgrounds increases the likelihood that students will respond to them positively. Materials published after the early 1970s are more likely to give attention to issues of diversity (Derman-Sparks, 1989). When using older instructional materials, teachers should develop and use relevant guidelines to determine whether they can be adapted and will be useful in increasing students' awareness of issues such as stereotyping, prejudice, and discrimination or it would be better to replace them. This is not meant to imply that classical literature that reflects gender or racial bias, for example, should be totally eliminated from the curriculum. Rather, in addition to appreciating the literary value of these materials, students can develop a better understanding of the historical contexts in which oppression occurs and can learn to identify ways in which discrimination against people, including individuals with disabilities, can be reduced or eliminated. Table 2 lists guidelines to assist special educators in developing their own criteria for evaluating materials they currently have available.

Incorporating Students' Language and Culture

Bilingual education programs are designed not only to provide native language instruction and ESL development, but also to enhance cognitive and affective development and provide cultural enrichment (Baca & Cervantes, 1989). Even in schools and communities where bilingual programs are not available and in situations where educators do not speak the students' language, it is possible to communicate a positive attitude toward students' backgrounds and heritage (Cummins, 1989). The following strategies are examples of ways in which classrooms and materials can reflect the diversity of backgrounds that is present in many schools and in the larger society (Cummins, 1989; Derman-Sparks, 1989).

1. Students are encouraged to use their first language around the school in various ways, even when they are not receiving native language instruction. For example, books are provided in several languages in each classroom and in the library for use by students and parents; bulletin boards, signs, and greetings employ various languages; and students are encouraged to use their native language to provide peer tutoring support.

2. Pictures and other visual displays show people from various backgrounds and communities, including individuals with varying abilities, elderly people, and men and women in blue-collar and white-collar roles. Images accurately depict people's contemporary daily lives—at work as well as in recreational activities.

3. Units developed for reading and language arts include literature from a variety of linguistic and cultural backgrounds and reflect the diversity in U.S. society across race, religion, language, class, gender, and ability. In addition to making children aware of a range of lifestyles, values, and characteristics of diverse groups, literature can reflect their struggles, achievements, and other experiences. Reflecting on such accounts, fictional as well as biographical, may also help some students understand and deal with their own struggles and difficulties.

4. Teachers and other school personnel understand that their interactions and behaviors, even if inadvertent and unintentional, may teach their students gender, racial, and other biases. This is reflected in educators' attention to their own verbal and nonverbal behaviors; avoidance of sexist or ethnocentric language; and parallel expectations for academic performance for girls, students with varying abilities, children from low-income environments, and so on.

5. The seating arrangement and organization of the classroom reflect consideration of learning style differences and encourage students to try new ways of interacting and learning.

Involving Parents and Families

As diversity in the student population increases, alternative models of parent involvement will have to be developed (Harry, 1992). Historically, many parents from language minority groups have had to overcome barriers to their effective participation in the regular and special education process, including educators' perceptions about these parents and their communities; their values regarding educational, linguistic, and cultural differences; and socioeconomic factors. Rather than being part of the problem, parents from culturally and linguistically diverse backgrounds can be effective advocates for their children. They represent a largely untapped resource to assist educators in responding effectively to multicultural issues (Briscoe, 1991).

Implementing Multicultural Special Education

Developing Intercultural Competence

Intercultural competence is an essential ingredient in teachers' ability to implement multicultural special education. Educators who possess such competence can feel comfortable and effective in their interactions with people from a variety of cultures, and they can help students and families feel comfortable as well. Finally, these skills are necessary to accomplish IEP goals. Acquisition of these skills is a gradual process, progressing through several stages. The following elements are helpful in this process (Lynch, 1992):

1. Developing an understanding and appreciation of one's own culture. This process of self-awareness and introspection allows us to examine our own assumptions and values, particularly those that may have been taken for granted because they are so much a part of our own family and community systems.

2. Gathering information about the other target cultures and analysis of this information with respect to individual students and families who reside within the community. Through our interactions with each family, we can determine the extent to which the family and its individual members share the cultural characteristics of their ethnic group. (Ethnic identity is determined by the individual and should not be assigned by others based on their observation of external traits.)

3. Discovering the parent's (or other primary caregiver's) orientation to childrearing issues, values, and orientations, including the family's goals and aspirations for their child with special needs.

4. Applying this knowledge to the development of cross-cultural skills. This results in interventions and interactions that are successful with students from diverse cultures.

Strategies for Enhancing Intercultural Understanding

The following questions may arise as special educators explore implications of multicultural education for their own programs.

While it sounds good, how can I, as one teacher, respond to so many diverse characteristics without being overwhelmed? How long will it take? Where do I start? Focusing on the cultures included at your school and within your community can be a good start, because this allows you to identify materials and strategies that are inclusive of the students you teach on a regular basis. It is a good idea to review your needs periodically—perhaps once at the beginning of each school year—to make sure that the information is updated. Which cultures are represented among your students? Does the information include any new families recently arrived in the community? Once a profile has been developed, you can reflect on your own knowledge of these cultural groups. How much do you know about each one? Which one is the most familiar? The least? This information will be useful as you evaluate what you feel comfortable about and identify areas in which you want to learn more.

How accurate is my current knowledge? What were my sources? Think about what you already know. How did you acquire this information? How extensive is your contact with the communities this knowledge presents? Is this information based on the students' country of origin, or does it encompass the experiences of the group in the United States (e.g., Mexican vs. Mexican American)? Is it based on traditional or contemporary life-styles? Pitfalls to avoid include information that is stereotypic; sources that fail to acknowledge within-group differences based on class, gender, language, religion, ethnicity, and geographic region; and information and experiences that are limited to a "tourist curriculum" (music, food, dress, holidays, etc.), which fail to highlight aspects of culture such as historical experiences related to the group's arrival in the United States, reasons for migration, accomplishments in various fields, values and belief systems, and communication patterns.

Where can I get more information? There are many ways of learning more about cultures, including formal study, reading, workshops, travel, and audiovisual materials. In addition, activities that allow students to share their experiences and the participation of parents and other community members in the school (e.g., speaking to the class about their language, culture, or religion) will make this information a part of the ongoing routine of school activities, and it will be acquired in a natural context. The following are some strategies to consider:

• As you prepare the demographic profile of your own classroom, school, or community, ask parents whether they would be willing to speak to the students about their cultural heritage, their own accomplishments, and any barriers they have overcome. Develop a resource directory that can support other curriculum development and planning efforts as well.

• Identify community organizations and groups that can provide access to audiovisual materials and other resources for personal study as well as instructional use.

• Identify print materials, journals, and other professional publications that highlight model programs, instructional strategies and curricula, and resources for multicultural education.

What if my classes do not reflect much cultural or linguistic diversity? Even in schools where students from diverse cultural and linguistic backgrounds are represented in very small numbers, or in predominantly middle-class communities, the larger culture is made up of subcultures from different religious, gender, and geographic backgrounds. White students also represent diverse ethnic backgrounds, and even when they may perceive their identity as "American," several cultures are represented in their ethnic heritage (Boutte & McCormick, 1992). Family histories and other activities can offer opportunities for them to explore and appreciate their unique characteristics. Finally, it is important to examine the influence of gender on teacher expectations, career counseling, and referral to special education.

A related, and equally important, issue for all students, regardless of color, gender, religion, or other differences, is the development of cross-cultural competence. As the diversity in U.S. society continues to increase, students must be prepared to become members of a workforce that is much more heterogeneous. Multicultural education can help *all* students increase their appreciation of diversity; develop positive self-concepts; respect individuals' civil and human rights; understand the historical context in which prejudice, oppression, and stereotyping occur; and ultimately fulfill their own potential while resisting and challenging stereotyping and barriers to success that exist in the society (Sleeter, 1992).

Conclusion

Efforts to implement multicultural special education services are more likely to succeed when teachers' individual efforts are supported by a school- or district-wide orientation toward improving academic achievement for all students from culturally and linguistically diverse backgrounds. Ensuring that all educators possess the necessary knowledge and skills is a long-term process. Ongoing staff development efforts must supplement preservice teacher preparation programs. In addition, effective instruction in multicultural special education requires greater collaboration between special educators and general educators, including bilingual educators, ESL specialists, migrant educators, Chapter I teachers, and other individuals who serve CLD students with disabilities. The school's multicultural resources can be considerably enhanced when collaborative efforts also involve parents and the community in meaningful ways. Effective services for a multicultural student population in general and special education requires a comprehensive, multidimensional approach that is capable of accommodating the diverse needs of students. We must develop a more effective interface with the programs that have traditionally served these children.

References

Baca, L. M., & Cervantes, H. T. (Eds.) (1989). *The bilingual special education interface* (2nd ed.). Columbus, OH: Merrill.

Briscoe, D. B. (1991). Designing for diversity in school success: Capitalizing on culture. *Preventing School Failure, 36*(1), 13-18.

Boutte, G. S., & McCormick, C. B. (1992). Avoiding pseudomulticulturalism: Authentic multicultural activities. *Childhood Education, 68*(3), 140-144.

Cheng, L. L. (1987). *Assessing Asian language performance: Guidelines for evaluating limited-English-proficient students.* Rockville, MD: Aspen.

Cummins, J. (1984). *Bilingualism and special education: Issues in assessment and pedagogy.* Clevedon, Avon, England: Multilingual Matters.

Cummins, J. (1989). A theoretical framework for bilingual special education. *Exceptional Children, 56,* 111-119.

Derman-Sparks, L. (1989). *Anti-bias curriculum: Tools for empowering young children.* Washington, DC: National Association for the Education of Young Children.

Englert, C. S., & Palincsar, A. S. (1991). Reconsidering instructional research in literacy from a sociocultural perspective. *Learning Disabilities Research and Practice, 6*(4), 225-229.

García, S. B., Ortiz, A. A., & Bergman, A. H. (1990, April). *A comparison of writing skills of Hispanic students by language proficiency and handicapping condition.* Paper presented at the annual conference of the American Educational Research Association, Boston, MA.

Goldman, S., & Rueda, R. (1988). Developing writing skills in bilingual exceptional children. *Exceptional Children, 54,* 543-551.

Gollnick, D. M., & Chinn, P. C. (1986). *Multicultural education in a pluralistic society* (2nd ed.). Columbus, OH: Merrill.

Graves, D. (1985). All children can write. *Learning Disability Focus, 1*(1), 36-43.

Gudykunst, W. B., & Ting-Toomey, S. (1988). *Cultural and interpersonal communication.* Newbury Park, CA: Sage.

Harry, B. (1992). Restructuring the participation of African-American parents in special education. *Exceptional Children, 59,* 123-131.

Heath, S. B. (1986). Sociocultural contexts of language development. In *Beyond language: Social and cultural factors in schooling language minority students* (pp. 143-186). Los Angeles: Evaluation, Dissemination and Assessment Center, California State University.

Hecht, M. L., Collier, M. J., & Ribeau, S. A. (1993). *African American communication: Ethnic identify and cultural interpretation.* Newbury Park, CA: Sage

Lynch, J. (1992). *Education for citizenship in a multicultural society.* New York: Cassell.

Maehr, M. (1990, April). *The psychological environment of the school: A focus for school leadership.* Paper presented at the annual meeting of the American Educational Research Association, Boston, MA.

Ortiz, A. A., & García, S. B. (1990). Using language assessment data for language and instructional planning for exceptional bilingual students. In A. L. Carrasquillo & R. E. Baecher (Eds.), *Teaching the bilingual special education student* (pp. 25-47). Norwood, NJ: Ablex.

Ortiz, A. A., & Yates, J. R. (1989). Staffing and the development of individualized educational programs for the bilingual exceptional student. In L. M. Baca & H. T. Cervantes (Eds.), *The bilingual special education interface* (pp. 183-203). Columbus, OH: Merrill.

Philips, S. U. (1983). *The invisible culture: Communication in classroom and community on the Warm Springs Indian reservation.* New York: Longman.

Ramírez, M. III, & Castañeda, A. (1974). *Cultural democracy: Bicognitive development and education.* New York: Academic Press.

Ruiz, N. (1989). An optimal learning environment for Rosemary. *Exceptional Children, 56,* 130-144.

Saville-Troike, M. (1978). *A guide to culture in the classroom.* Rosslyn, VA: National Clearinghouse for Bilingual Education.

Sleeter, C. (1992). *Keepers of the American dream: A study of staff development and multicultural education.* Bristol, PA: Palmer.

Willig, A. C., & Ortiz, A. A. (1991). The nonbiased individualized education program: Linking assessment to instruction. In E. V. Hamayan & J. S. Damico (Eds.), *Limiting bias in the assessment of bilingual students* (pp. 281-302). Austin, TX: Pro-Ed.

DO YOU SEE WHAT I MEAN?

BODY LANGUAGE IN CLASSROOM INTERACTIONS

Mary M. Banbury
Constance R. Hebert

Mary M. Banbury *(CEC Chapter #514) is Associate Professor, Department of Special Education and Habilitative Services, University of New Orleans, Louisiana.* **Constance R. Hebert** *is Psychiatric Social Worker, Orleans Parish School System, New Orleans.*

Photographs by Russ Thames.

The teacher uttering the mixed metaphor "Don't look at me in that tone of voice" to a student is intuitively aware of the impact of the student's nonverbal message. All teachers should be aware of nonverbal communication in the classroom in order to enhance their ability to (a) receive students' messages more accurately; (b) send congruent and positive signals to denote expectations, convey attitudes, regulate interactions, and reinforce learning; and (c) avoid incongruent and negative cues that confuse students and stifle learning (Miller, 1986; Woolfolk & Brooks, 1985). Nonverbal communication plays a significant role in all classroom interactions. According to Smith (1979), "Whether teachers are talking or not, they are always communicating" (p. 633). In fact, studies have revealed that 82% of teacher messages are nonverbal; only 18% are verbal (Grant & Hennings, 1971). Several studies have shown that the nonverbal component of classroom communication is more influential than the verbal component (Keith, Tornatzky, & Pettigrew, 1974; Woolfolk & Brooks, 1985).

In recent years investigators have examined commonly used nonverbal signals in educational settings. They have studied frequency and intensity of direct eye contact (Brooks, 1984), interpersonal distance (Brooks & Wilson, 1978), teacher-approval gestures (Nafpaktitis, Mayer, & Butterworth, 1985), and nonverbal criticisms (Simpson & Erickson, 1983). While teachers know about these nonverbal communication indexes, many are unaware of the influential role of nonverbal behaviors. They need to realize, for instance, that if there is incongruity or discrepancy between words and body language, the nonverbal message will dominate (Miller, 1986).

This article explains how teachers can analyze their own communication styles so that there is harmony between what they say and how they say it and they can learn to interpret selected nonverbal signals frequently used by students. In particular, it focuses on *proximics*, a person's use and perception of space, and *kinesics*, a person's facial and body cues. It should be noted that individual nonverbal behaviors do not have implicit meaning; they should be considered in context. As Bates, Johnson, and Blaker (1982) stated, "Nonverbal messages cannot be read with certainty. To suggest that they can is irresponsible, but to ignore them is equally irresponsible" (p. 129).

Physical Distance and Personal Space

The amount of space people maintain between themselves and others provides information about relationships, regulates interactions, and affects the impressions they develop about each other. According to Hall (1966), space tolerances range from the intimate zone,

From *Teaching Exceptional Children*, Vol. 24, No. 2, Winter 1992, pp. 34-38. © 1992 by The Council for Exceptional Children.
Reprinted by permission.

Scenario 1

Susan, a 16-year-old with mild learning and behavior problems, is sitting in the back of the room putting on makeup during her mainstreamed English class. Her teacher considers this to be unacceptable behavior and decides to correct her. He gives the assertive verbal message, "When you put makeup on during class discussion, I feel frustrated because my time is wasted while I wait for you to participate."

Don't

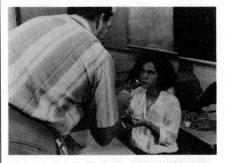

Figure 1. Hostile Body Language. *The teacher has clearly invaded the student's personal zone. His body positioning signals confrontation since his shoulders are squared with those of the student. He is using his height to dominate and possibly to intimidate. Finally, the pen pointing is not only a further intrusion into her space, but also a threatening and intimidating gesture. These aggressive nonverbal signals defeat the purpose of an assertive message.*

Figure 2. Passive Body Language. *Equally ineffective is the opposite approach pictured above. Here the teacher appears to be intimidated and fearful of confrontation. He approaches from the rear and does not enter the student's personal distance zone. His arms are drawn up over his chest in a protective manner. His chin is retracted inwardly and hidden behind his fists. His lips are taut, and there is no eye contact. With such submissive body language, it is unlikely that his message will be taken seriously.*

Do

Figure 3. Assertive Body Language. *The teacher gives himself a chance for a successful intervention by considering space, positioning, and body language. In this case he has approached the student from a nonthreatening lateral position, near enough to be effective but not invasive. His hands and arms are in a "open" position; his facial expression is relaxed, and his eyes are gazing at the student. Since his verbal message is congruent with his nonverbal one, he has increased the likelihood that the student will put away her makeup.*

with actual physical contact, to "personal distance," (approximately 1.5-3 feet), to "social or public distance" (more than 3 feet). Typically, people tend to get closer to those they like. They maintain more distance from those they dislike or fear; they also stand farther away from people who have disabilities or who are from different racial backgrounds (Miller, 1986).

By adjusting the distance at which they position themselves, teachers and students suggest desired levels of involvement and convey impressions about whether they are intimate, aloof, intrusive, or neutral. In certain situations a person may use close physical proximity to influence, intimidate, or warn another person. Generally, however, teachers and students use closeness to signal acceptance, concern, and approval (Richey & Richey, 1978). Conversely, they employ distance to indicate indifference, rejection, and disapproval (Brooks & Wilson, 1978).

The meaning of a given distance depends on the situation, the intentions of the individual, and the congruency between the verbal and nonverbal messages. For example, an assertive teacher sets limits by combining touch with a verbal message, eye contact, and the student's name (Canter & Canter, 1976). Likewise, a teacher who wants to increase positive communications and reinforce acceptable behaviors in the classroom says, "I like what you are doing," while making a conscious effort to move within the personal space zone of all the students, not only the favorite ones or high achievers (Miller, 1986).

Eye Contact and Facial Expressions

Eyes transmit the most expressive nonverbal messages (Marsh, 1988). They indicate mood, emotion, and feelings; they can also warn, challenge, or reassure. Although there are exceptions, most students associate wide open eyes, raised brows, and frequency of eye contact with approval, acceptance, and concern. Research demonstrates that direct and frequent teacher eye contact can improve attention, intensify participation, increase the amount of information students retain, and boost self-esteem (Woolfolk & Brooks, 1985).

Direct teacher eye contact can also express domination, disapproval, or dis-

like. Prolonged neutral eye contact with raised eyebrows serves as a powerful restraining or corrective measure. Students commonly refer to this as the "evil eye" or the "teacher look." Richey and Richey (1978) have warned teachers to keep their stares passive to avoid sending a message of dislike. Lowered eyebrows and eyes that squint or glare evoke feelings of antagonism, aggression, or denunciation.

Teachers can also use their eyes to guide discussions, promote or reward student participation, and regulate and monitor verbal exchanges. Open eyes and lifted brows signal the beginning of an activity or a request for an explanation; the brief glance serves as a conversational signal or a comprehension check. The actual amount of eye contact controls listening and speaking roles and signals information about personality, status, and culture (Marsh, 1988).

Other facial features combine with the eyes to communicate basic emotions. For example, smiles coupled with wrinkles around the eyes best predict happiness and transmit feelings of approval. (A smile is the teacher's most powerful social reinforcer; some refer to it as a "visual hug.") Lowered eyes and a downturned mouth reveal sadness or disappointment. Indicators of anger or disapproval include pursed or tightly closed lips, clenched teeth, and frowns or scowls (Hargrave, 1988).

Not all students are adept at discriminating facial affect or using social perceptual cues. In particular, students who have developmental delays, learning disabilities, or cultural differences or are inexperienced may have difficulty in describing affective states, judging nonverbal reactions, inferring information, and using body language (Wiig & Harris, 1974; Woolfolk & Brooks, 1985). Exacerbating this problem, some people may voluntarily control their facial expressions because of social dictates or cultural teachings. Therefore, the context in which they occur, as well as the accompanying verbal messages, play important roles in determining the meaning of nonverbal behaviors.

Gestures and Body Movements

Body motions or positions do not have specific meanings in and of themselves. The accompanying verbal message must be considered, as well as the individual's kinesic motions. Even then, there are times when the verbal message is not congruent with the nonverbal one. This occurs when an individual is purposely trying to mislead his or her audience or is actually unaware of the underlying emotion. For example, a young female may deny that she is angry while tightly clenching her teeth and rapidly tapping her foot; a teenage male with listless posture, overall passivity, and general drooping may refuse to acknowledge that he is depressed or, perhaps, suicidal; a teacher with fists clenched, arms crossed, and lips pursed may profess to be open to differences of opinions or other perspectives.

There are no universal clear-cut rules for interpreting body language. While it is relatively easy to read individual expressions, gestures, and movements, definitive conclusions should not be based on the observation of isolated kinetic movements. Since each element of body language can be controlled, simulated, amplified, or suppressed, it is important to observe the composite picture: the clusters of facial expressions and body movements and the congruency of verbal and nonverbal messages.

Table 1

Congruency of Verbal and Nonverbal Messages

	Approving/ Accepting	Disapproving/ Critical	Assertive/ Confident	Passive/ Indifferent
Verbal message	"I like what you are doing."	"I don't like what you are doing."	"I mean what I say."	"I don't care."
Physical distance	Sit or stand in close proximity to other person.	Distance self from other person; encroach uninvited into other's personal space.	Physically elevate self; move slowly into personal space of other person.	Distance self from other person.
Facial expressions	Engage in frequent eye contact; open eyes wide; raise brows; smile.	Engage in too much or too little eye contact; open eyes wide in fixed, frozen expression; squint or glare; turn corners of eyebrows down; purse or tightly close lips; frown; tighten jaw muscle.	Engage in prolonged, neutral eye contact; lift eyebrows; drop head and raise eyebrow.	Avert gaze; stare blankly; cast eyes down or let them wander; let eyes droop.
Body movements	Nod affirmatively; "open" posture; uncross arms/legs; place arms at side; show palms; lean forward; lean head and trunk to one side; orient body toward other person; grasp or pat shoulder or arm; place hand to chest.	Shake head slowly; "close" posture; fold arms across chest; lean away from person; hold head/trunk straight; square shoulders; thrust chin out; use gestures of negation, e.g., finger shaking, hand held up like a stop signal.	Place hands on hips; lean forward; touch shoulder; tap on desk; drop hand on desk; join fingers at tips and make a steeple.	Lean away from other person; place head in palm of hand; fold hands behind back or upward in front; drum fingers on table; tap with feet; swing crossed leg or foot; sit with leg over chair.

Table 1 is designed to assist teachers in interpreting and conveying congruent nonverbal messages; it depicts selected behavioral indexes and their verbal and nonverbal behavioral correlates. Classroom teachers who are able to recognize nonverbal signals can enhance their management techniques by curbing hostile or passive gestures and movements, matching verbal and nonverbal messages, and providing reliable and effective cues to their students.

Analysis of Nonverbal Behaviors

Teachers should examine the photographs shown here, analyze the nonverbal interactions of the teacher and the students, and match their interpretations with those of the authors. Since behavior is related to its context, there

may be more than one way to interpret the nonverbal behaviors. The purpose of this activity is to heighten teachers' awareness of nonverbal interactions during specific management and instructional activities. Scenario 1 shows how a teacher's body language can detract from or enhance his or her verbal language. Scenario 2 describes two students' nonverbal signals and suggests teacher responses.

Conclusion

The distance at which individuals position themselves, their eye focusing, facial expressions, gestures, and body movements all consciously or unconsciously complement, supplement, or supplant verbal communication. The individual significance of isolated nonverbal cues, however, is subject to as many

Scenario 2

John and Carol spend a portion of each day in a resource room for students with behavior disorders. They have been instructed to work on an in-class assignment.

Figure 4. *John is exhibiting a nonreceptive posture. His intense gaze suggests that he would like to engage in the "stare-down" game. His crossed arms and legs, indicative of a "closed" position, could be a sign of insecurity or defensiveness. This student, however, does not appear to be intimidated. His body position, in general, is one of reclining. A person interested in protecting himself generally does not recline. The shoulders are squared, not rounded, and he is turned away from his desk, not "hiding" behind it. In this case there may even be an unconscious attempt to hold back from physical aggression. This student is actually holding his left arm tightly into his chest rather than simply crossing his arms in resistance.*
A person who was aware of nonverbal signals would not openly confront this student. There should be no prolonged looks, sudden moves, aggressive gestures, or threatening comments. With arms at his or her side, a teacher would approach the student slowly from a lateral position, using nonthreatening comments to open a dialogue.

Figure 5. *At first glance, Carol, the student pictured above appears to be bored or uninterested. Upon closer examination, however, she is exhibiting several body signals for depression. Her shoulders are drooped and rounded; her torso is retracted; and her affect is flat. Her eyes are downcast; her jaw is slack and lowered; and her lower lip is in a pouting position. The twisting of the lock of hair, especially if it is done incessantly, could be a sign of anxiety. If her teacher observes a pattern or ongoing series of symptoms such as these, the student should be referred for further assessment.*

interpretations and intentions as there are people who receive or send messages. Therefore, observers of body language should concentrate on interpreting the total congruent picture, including context, verbal and nonverbal behaviors, and prior and subsequent events, before they reach conclusions based on observation and comprehension of isolated signals. Likewise, people who desire to use proximics and kinesics to enhance their communication style should verify that their body language is indeed communicating their intended messages and their nonverbal behaviors are congruent with their verbal ones.

To improve their communication styles, teachers could videotape their classroom performance, identify intended messages, and solicit structured feedback regarding the congruency of their verbal and nonverbal behaviors from students or colleagues by using a chart, checklist, or rating sheet. They could role play selected events or simulate interactions with peers to assure that they are sending congruent messages while responding to the expected defensiveness of certain students and parents. To develop and enhance their ability to interpret the nonverbal messages of other people, teachers could set aside 10 minutes a day to consciously

notice and interpret proximic and kinesic signals sent by students, friends, and family members. They could focus on academic or social interactions, using a videotape without the audio portion to read the body language and replaying the scene with sound to check their perceptions. Alternatively, they could examine photographs, especially family albums, paying particular attention to the body language and what it indicates about personal and interpersonal relationships, attitudes, and emotions. Taking the time to study ways of interpreting and conveying nonverbal messages can help teachers enhance the teaching and learning process.

References

Bates, M., Johnson, C., & Blaker, K. E. (1982). *Group leadership: A manual for group counseling leaders.* Denver: Love.

Brooks, D. M. (1984, April). *Communicating competence: Junior high teacher behavioral expression during the first day of school.* Paper presented at the annual meeting of the American Educational Research Association, New Orleans.

Brookes, D. M., & Wilson, B. J. (1978). Teacher verbal and nonverbal expression toward selected students. *Journal of Educational Psychology, 70,* 147-153.

Canter, L., & Canter, M. (1976). *Assertive discipline: A take charge approach for today's educator.* Los Angeles: Lee Canter.

Grant, B. W., & Hennings, D. G. (1971). *The teacher moves: An analysis of nonverbal activity.* New York: Teachers College Press.

Hall, E. T. (1966). *The hidden dimension.* Garden City, NY: Doubleday.

Hargrave, J. (1988, March). Actions speak louder than words. *OEA Communique,* pp. 28-31.

Keith, L. T., Tornatzky, L. G., & Pettigrew, L. E. (1974). An analysis of verbal and nonverbal classroom teaching behaviors. *Journal of Experimental Education, 42,* 30-38.

Marsh, P. (Ed.). (1988). *Eye to eye: How people interact.* Topsfield, MA: Salem House.

Miller, P. W. (1986). *Nonverbal communication* (2nd ed.). Washington, DC: National Education Association.

Nafpaktitis, M., Mayer, G. R., & Butterworth, T. (1985). Natural rates of teacher approval and disapproval and their relation to student behavior in intermediate school classrooms. *Journal of Educational Psychology, 77,* 362-367.

Richey, H. W., & Richey, M. H. (1978). Nonverbal behavior in the classroom. *Psychology in the Schools, 15,* 571-576.

Simpson, A. W., & Erickson, M. T. (1983). Nonverbal communication patterns as a function of teacher race, student gender, and student race. *American Educational Research Journal, 20,* 183-189.

Smith, H. (1979). Nonverbal communication in teaching. *Review of Educational Research, 49,* 631-672.

Wiig, E., & Harris, S. (1974). Perception and interpretation of nonverbally expressed emotions by adolescents with learning disabilities. *Perceptual and Motor Skills, 38,* 239-245.

Woolfolk, A. E., & Brooks, D. M. (1985). The influence of teachers' nonverbal behaviors on students' perceptions and performance. *The Elementary School Journal, 85,* 513-528.

Children with Hearing Impairments

Hearing disabilities are quite common. About 10 percent of school children have difficulty hearing at some time during their developmental period. However, hearing impairments are quite rare, and the extreme form, legal deafness, is rarer still. In order to be assessed as hard-of-hearing for purposes of receiving special educational services, a child needs some form of sound amplification to comprehend oral language. In order to be assessed as deaf for purposes of educational programming, a child cannot benefit just from amplification. A child with deafness is disabled to the extent that he or she cannot adequately hear even amplified speech through the ear. Children who are deaf are dependent on vision for language and communication.

Hearing impairments are classified in many ways beyond hard-of-hearing and deaf. When children are born with impaired auditory sensations, they are put into a classification of children with congenital (with birth) hearing impairments. Since these infants and children cannot hear sounds without amplification, or in the case of deafness even with amplification, their education is complicated and time-consuming. They should be assessed as early as possible and started in early childhood special educational programs for the hearing impaired. These programs are free and individualized to meet the needs of the hearing impaired child and his or her family. The amendments to the Individuals with Disabilities Education Act (IDEA) guarantee both early childhood programs and transitional services to hearing impaired children.

When children acquire problems with their auditory systems after birth, they are put into a classification of children with adventitious (added extrinsically) hearing impairments. If the adventitious loss of hearing occurs before the child has learned speech and language, it is called a prelinguistic hearing impairment. If the adventitious loss of hearing occurs after the child has learned language, it is called a postlinguistic hearing impairment. Prelingual hearing impairments are more debilitating and require more extensive special educational services than postlinguistic hearing impairments.

Children with hearing impairments are subsumed into etiological (causative) divisions of disability as well as being classified as hard-of-hearing or deaf and congenitally or adventitiously impaired. Children whose hearing losses involve the outer or middle ear structures are said to have conductive hearing losses. Conductive losses involve defects or impairments of the external auditory canal, the tympanic membrane (eardrum) or the ossicles (three tiny bones that vibrate to conduct sound). Children whose hearing losses involve the inner ear structures are said to have sensorineural hearing impairment. Sensorineural impairment involves defects of the cochlea, the semicircular canals, or the auditory nerve. They are difficult or impossible (depending on the problem) to correct with surgery, medicine, or sound amplification. Conductive losses are usually more amenable to treatment and/or correction.

IDEA mandates an appropriate education for children with hearing impairments in the least restrictive environment. To what extent is a regular education classroom more restrictive for a child with profound hearing loss or deafness? Many professionals working with individuals who are deaf feel that a community of other people who are deaf and use sign language is less restrictive than a community of people who hear and use oral speech. The unity of individuals who are deaf has many beneficial effects. The debate about inclusive education versus partial pullout for special education versus immersion in what has come to be known as the deaf culture has not been resolved.

The first article included in this unit deals with children with profound hearing impairments or deafness who are enrolled in inclusive educational programs. They are assigned educational interpreters to translate vocal language into signed language, which they can more readily comprehend. This special assistance enables them to "see" what the teacher is teaching. However, the educational interpreter can provide many other services to help ease the child's way through a world of people who hear. The interpreter can ask questions for the student if the teacher does not read sign language. The interpreter can help a student with a hearing impairment interact with peers, other teachers, coaches, and ancillary staff at school. The interpreter is often involved in interacting with parents as well. Most students with profound hearing losses spend only a portion of the day in the regular class and have pullout time for special education. The educational interpreter also has a role as an intermediary between special and regular education personnel.

The second article in this unit addresses two important concerns for children with hearing impairments. Today there are a host of new technological devices to assist individuals with hearing impairments, such as computers and telecommunication devices (TDDs). Part of the education of children with disabilities must include helping them help themselves with every possible assistive technology. In addition to learning how to use all aids available, children with hearing impairments benefit from learning how to help themselves without special assistance. John Luckner explains how to help children develop skills for independent learning (e.g., studying, managing time, taking notes) and skills for independent living (e.g., health care, leisure, personal-social skills). For students with hearing impairments to become independent and able to care for themselves, they need support, encouragement, and reinforcement when they exhibit responsible behaviors.

The third article included in this unit is a case study of Jaime, an elementary school student with multiple disabilities, including deafness. His parents elected to enroll him in a regular education school with predominantly pullout time for special education but some time in a regular classroom. The authors suggest that one of the most important things Jaime gained from his inclusion experience was friendship with children who were not hearing impaired. Three of his friends participated in his individualized education program (IEP) planning. This interaction was praised as extremely important for his language, cognitive, sexual, and academic development and his sense of self-esteem.

Looking Ahead: Challenge Questions

What roles do educational interpreters have beyond translating oral language to sign language? How should the educational interpreter interact with teachers, other students, parents, and other school personnel?

What skills should be taught to students with hearing impairments to help them become independent and responsible?

Why are friends without hearing losses important to children with hearing impairments?

THE ROLES OF THE EDUCATIONAL INTERPRETER IN MAINSTREAMING

Spencer J. Salend • Maureen Longo

Spencer J. Salend *(CEC Chapter #615), Professor, State University of New York at New Paltz.* **Maureen Longo,** *Educational Interpreter, Florida School for the Deaf and Blind, St. Augustine.*

As a result of Public Law 94-142, the Individuals with Disabilities Education Act (formerly known as the Education for All Handicapped Children Act of 1975), many students with hearing impairments are being educated in regular education settings with their hearing peers. Data from the *Fifteenth Annual Report to Congress on the Implementation of the Individuals with Disabilities Education Act* (U.S. Department of Education, 1993) indicate that approximately 47% of students with hearing impairments are taught in inclusive settings. These students need a variety of services to enhance their academic performance and social adjustment in such settings.

One essential service that many students with hearing impairments attending regular classes may need is an educational interpreter (Commission on

The authors would like to thank Ruth McLachlan for her valuable assistance in preparing this article.

the Education of the Deaf, 1988; Rittenhouse, Rahn, & Morreau, 1989). The National Task Force on Educational Interpreting (1989) has estimated that approximately 4,000 interpreters are needed to serve students with hearing impairments in school settings. An educational interpreter, sometimes referred to as an *educational transliterator,* facilitates the transmission of information between individuals who do not communicate with a common language or code (Massachusetts Commission for the Deaf and Hard of Hearing, 1988). Additionally, an educational interpreter can work with parents and professionals to guide the delivery of appropriate educational services to students with hearing impairments.

Since the preferred mode of communication of students with hearing impairments may vary, there is a variety of educational interpreting methods. A *signed system interpreter* translates spoken language directed toward a student

with a hearing impairment into a signed system such as American Sign Language (ASL), Conceptually Accurate Signed English (CASE), Manually Coded English (MCE), or Signs in English Word Order. An *oral interpreter* facilitates the hearing impaired student's understanding of verbal messages by silently mouthing the complete verbal message or its paraphrased equivalent (Castle, 1988). In either of these methods of interpreting, the interpreter employs voice interpretation if the student needs assistance in converting his or her responses into the preferred mode of understanding of the individual communicating with the student. Other students with hearing impairments may benefit from the services of a cued speech facilitator (Kipila & Williams-Scott, 1988).

Several states (e.g., Florida, Massachusetts, North Carolina, Virginia, and New York) and national groups (i.e., The Commission on the Education of

From *Teaching Exceptional Children,* Vol. 26, No. 4, Summer 1994, pp. 22-28. © 1994 by The Council for Exceptional Children. Reprinted by permission.

the Deaf, the National Task Force on Educational Interpreting) have begun to establish procedures to guide the development and delivery of educational services. In light of the uniqueness and newness of the use of interpreters in inclusive settings, their roles need to be clearly specified to avoid possible role confusion, facilitate collaborative interactions, and promote the independence of students with hearing impairments (National Task Force on Educational Interpreting, 1989).

This article offers guidelines and suggestions related to the interpreter's relationship with students with hearing impairments, teachers, the student's peers and parents, supportive service personnel, and administrators. Educators and interpreters should tailor the guidelines to the unique circumstances of their educational settings.

INTERACTING WITH STUDENTS WITH HEARING IMPAIRMENTS

The interpreter and the student should meet prior to the beginning of the school year to become acquainted and establish clear guidelines concerning their interactions. A sample agenda for the meeting is provided in Figure 1. The interpreter and student should discuss the roles the interpreter will perform to assist the student as well as instances when it would not be appropriate for the interpreter to intervene. While the language level used to convey information may vary depending on the age of the student, the interpreter and the student should discuss the following questions:

1. What method of communication should be used?
2. Will the interpreter be responsible for speaking for the student? (Some students may prefer to verbalize for themselves.)
3. What will be the interpreter's role with peers?
4. Will the interpreter be available to foster communication with teachers and peers after class?
5. At what times will the interpreter be available to translate for teachers and

students in tutoring sessions and when working on homework?
6. How will the interpreter maintain confidentiality and deal with personal information about the student?

In delineating roles, the student and the interpreter should examine each role with respect to its impact on the student's independence. Independence should follow a pattern of growth from dependence to independence, and the interpreter's role will vary depending on the student's level. For example, the interpreter and the student may agree to work toward an arrangement whereby (a) the student will direct all classroom communication to the teacher and peers; (b) the interpreter will not redirect the student's attention during class; and (c) the interpreter will only assist the student with peers outside the classroom when the student requests assistance.

At the end of the meeting, the interpreter and the student should exchange telephone numbers or determine an appropriate procedure for notifying each other when one will not be in school. Since perspectives change and new problems may arise, the interpreter and the student should meet periodi-

Figure 1. Sample Agenda for Interpreter/Student Conference

1. Introduce the interpreter and the student.
2. Review the purpose of the meeting.
3. Discuss the rationale for the use of an interpreter.
4. Discuss the roles of the interpreter from the interpreter's and the student's perspectives, including:
   Roles with teachers.
   Roles with students.
   Roles with parents.
   Roles with others.
5. Establish a consensus on roles.
6. Discuss time availability for out-of-class interactions.
7. Agree on policies regarding absences.
8. Summarize and review the results of the meeting.
9. Determine an appropriate date for the next meeting.

cally to evaluate their progress, identify their successes, and discuss and resolve their problems.

INTERACTING WITH TEACHERS

An educational interpreter can facilitate the academic performance of a student with a hearing impairment in the regular class setting by translating directions, content, and assignments presented orally by teachers and the comments of peers, as well as sharing the student's responses and questions with teachers and peers. However, interpreters can function most effectively as an instructional resource in the classroom only when they carefully coordinate their efforts with teachers.

Early in the school year, the teacher and the interpreter should agree upon the roles each will play in working with the student. They should come to a consensus concerning their responsibilities with respect to such issues as grading, contacting parents, working with other students, assigning and assisting with homework and other assignments, designing and administering tests, arranging for peer note takers, communicating with other professionals, using media, and disciplining students. Generally, roles should be defined so that the teacher has primary responsibility and the interpreter serves in a supportive role. For example, if a student is having difficulty with homework, the teacher, rather than the interpreter, should correct the homework and meet with the student to deliver remedial instruction. However, the interpreter should be present to facilitate the remedial process. To help schedule out-of-class activities, the teacher and the interpreter should exchange schedules and try to identify mutually convenient times.

Since the interpreter may not have prior exposure to the content and instructional strategies employed in the classroom, it would be helpful if the teacher provided him or her with an orientation to the curriculum. At the beginning of the school year or semester, the teacher could furnish the interpreter with curriculum guides, textbooks, and

The student may choose not to use an interpreter outside the classroom.

other relevant instructional materials and review them with the interpreter if necessary. A knowledge of class routines, projects, and long-term assignments can assist the interpreter in helping students with hearing impairments understand and prepare for these assignments. Additionally, the interpreter should be informed of the dates, times, and content of special assemblies and class trips (Florida State Education Department, 1986).

Throughout the school year, the teacher and the interpreter should meet to review curriculum and discuss their efforts to work collaboratively. When a unit of particularly difficult material is to be covered that includes new technical vocabulary and material that is hard to explain in alternative forms of communication, the teacher and the interpreter may want to meet on a more frequent basis. For example, when

teaching a unit about the geological history of the earth, the teacher might provide the interpreter with a list of key terms and a copy of lesson plans so that the interpreter can plan in advance how to translate and explain such terms as *Paleozoic era, Oligocene epoch,* and *the Jurassic period.*

An important factor for the teacher and the interpreter to examine is the location of the interpreter in the classroom. Whenever possible, the interpreter should be seated in a glare-free, well-lit location with a solid-colored background free of visual and auditory distractions (Hurwitz & Witter, 1979). Waldron, Diebold, and Rose (1985) have provided guidelines for interpreters to coordinate the visual and auditory messages associated with class presentations. They have suggested that the interpreter sit slightly in front of the student without blocking the view of the

chalkboard, overhead, or teacher; focus the student's attention by pointing with one hand to the visuals as the teacher refers to them; and use the other hand to communicate the dialogue of the teacher or the other students. Since many teachers move around when they present content to the class, they should understand that interpreters and students with hearing impairments may need to leave their seats to watch them.

The positioning of the interpreter also depends on the nature of the instructional activity (Florida State Department of Education, 1986). When the teacher is using a lecture format, it may be desirable for the interpreter to stand or sit to the side and slightly in front of the teacher, with the student's desk located 3 to 5 feet from the interpreter. In a one-to-one instruction setting, the interpreter should be placed next to the hearing individual and facing the student from a distance of about 4 to 6 feet. During group activities, the group should be seated in a circular fashion with the interpreter located across from the student. Additional guidelines are available for locating an interpreter who is interpreting for several students in a class or for oral students (Florida State Department of Education, 1986).

Procedures for maximizing the effectiveness of the interpreter and facilitating the process also should be discussed. The interpreter may need to sensitize the teacher to the processing time delays that are associated with interpreting (Hurwitz & Witter, 1979). The teacher should be told to talk to the student and not to the interpreter. The teacher should avoid directing comments or questions to the interpreter during class time and should discuss them after class (Frishberg, 1986). Similarly, the interpreter and the student should not engage in extended conversations in class. When communication problems arise during class that affect the translation process, such as the teacher talking too rapidly, or a peer speaking inaudibly, the interpreter should ask for clarification. For example, if an interpreter did not understand a peer's comment, he or she could say, "I'm sorry, I didn't understand that. Could you please repeat it?" If professionals notice recurrent behavior problems exhibited by students with hearing impairments—for example, two students talking to each other using sign language during a class lecture—they may want to signal each other or discuss their concerns at the next class break or after the class is completed.

Occasionally, the teacher may use media such as videocassettes and audiocassettes to convey information to students. These types of media can cause special problems for the interpreter and the student with a hearing impairment. When using such media, the teacher can reduce problems by providing the interpreter with a script, locating the interpreter near the screen, stopping periodically to paraphrase the content presented and check student comprehension, and asking the interpreter to bring an interpreter's lamp or a flashlight. Students with hearing impairments also may benefit from the opportunity to view media such as videocassettes privately with their interpreters so that they can review and discuss key points (R. C. McLachlan, personal communication, July 14, 1990).

INTERACTING WITH OTHER STUDENTS

The interpreter also may be called upon to interact with hearing students in the class. Since most hearing students will not have encountered an interpreter previously, the teacher should first introduce the student with a hearing impairment and the interpreter to the class. If the student feels comfortable, the student and the interpreter can discuss the student's needs and the role of the interpreter with the other class members. If the student uses a hearing aid, he or she can explain the parts and maintenance of the aid and allow other students to use it for a brief period of time. Similarly the teacher may ask the interpreter to introduce students to alternative communication systems by (a) teaching students the manual alphabet and having them practice their spelling words manually; (b) presenting math problems using hand signs for numbers; and (c) using basic signs to give directions (Salend, 1994).

The initial orientation also should provide hearing students with guidelines for interacting with the interpreter. Students should be informed that the interpreter is there to facilitate communication with the student with a hearing impairment and is not available to assist with assignments and tests or to tutor students. Similarly, students should be told not to ask the interpreter for permission to leave the room or assistance in resolving disputes. Students also should be cautioned that if the interpreter is asked by school personnel about inappropriate behaviors and negative comments, he or she may be required to report all observations.

Because they cannot read signs and write at the same time, students with hearing impairments may need a note taker. Therefore, the need for and role of a note taker also should be reviewed with the student's peers. Following this discussion, peer note takers should be solicited (Frishberg, 1986). Peer note takers should demonstrate mastery of the class content, skill in taking notes, sensitivity to students with disabilities, and an ability to work independently. Since peer note takers may be absent periodically, it also is necessary to identify backup note takers (R. C. McLachlan, personal communication, July 14, 1990). The note-taking process can be facilitated by offering training in note-taking skills to peers and providing the note takers with special carbonless paper (Wilson, 1981).

INTERACTING WITH PARENTS

The extent to which the interpreter will interact with the student's parents depends upon the hearing acuity of the parents. If the parents have hearing impairments, the interpreter may be asked to interpret in order to facilitate communication between them and school personnel. However, if the parents do not have hearing impairments, their interactions with the interpreter may be limited to meetings with professionals at which the student is present. While parents may look to the interpreter to serve as a liaison with teachers and school staff, they should be encouraged to interact directly with these professionals (Florida State Education Department, 1986). For example, rather than asking the interpreter about their child's progress in classes, parents should be asked to direct these questions to the appropriate school personnel. However, the educational interpreter may be a resource for parents concerning information about the efficacy of the communication methodology that the interpreter and student are using.

INTERACTING WITH SUPPORTIVE SERVICE PERSONNEL

In addition to teachers, the interpreter will interact with ancillary service personnel. Because the interpreter spends a large amount of time with students in a variety of instructional and social settings, he or she will have a unique perspective on the student's needs that can be helpful to the multidisciplinary planning team. Therefore, in evaluating and planning services for the student, the multidisciplinary team may want to solicit information from the interpreter. However, since confidentiality is an important aspect of the interpreter-student relationship, educational interpreters should follow the school district's policies and use discretion when sharing information that is essential to the student's safety, welfare, and educational program (National Task Force on Educational Interpreting, 1989). To facilitate the interpreter's ability to interact with others at multidisciplinary team meetings, many school districts are hiring another educational interpreter to interpret for the student during these meetings (R. C. McLachlan, personal communication, July 14, 1990).

The interpreter also may work closely with speech and language therapists. Speech and language therapists can provide information concerning the extent to which students with hearing impairments should verbalize. Although the interpreter can provide speech and language therapists with information regarding the student's communication skills, he or she is not trained to evaluate the student's speech skills and should not be asked to do so. However, while the multidisciplinary team will determine the modes of communication used by the student and the interpreter, the educational interpreter can provide useful information regarding the success of these communication methodologies in increasing the student's ability to acquire instructional content and interact with others (National Task Force on Educational Interpreting, 1989).

INTERACTING WITH SCHOOL ADMINISTRATORS

School administrators are usually responsible for coordinating the delivery of services to students with disabilities. When the need for an interpreter is identified, the school administrator, in consultation with others, should develop a job description that meets local needs and specifications (National Task Force on Educational Interpreting, 1989). The job description should identify the roles and responsibilities of the educational interpreter and include statements about the educational levels of the students and the mode(s) of communication to be used in interpreting. The job description also should specify (a) the job title, (b) the qualifications and skills required, (c) the supervisory arrangement, (d) nonclassroom interpreting activities, (e) professional development opportunities, and (f) salary and benefits (Florida State Education Department, 1986). To promote collaboration with others and an understanding of the roles of the educational interpreter, the job description should be shared with parents and professionals. Sample job descriptions are available (Massachusetts Commission for the Deaf and Hard of Hearing, 1988; National Task Force on Educational Interpreting, 1989).

When the multidisciplinary placement team determines that a student needs the services of an interpreter, the administrator should inform regular classroom teachers that the student will be included in their classes and will be receiving the services of an interpreter. Additionally, the administrator should introduce the interpreter to the teachers and review districtwide policies regarding the delivery of services by an interpreter. For example, the district may have a policy prohibiting the interpreter from being asked to watch or teach a class while the teacher cannot be in the room. Similarly, districtwide policies regarding communication modes should be reviewed. Administrators may be called upon to resolve disagreements between the interpreter and other school personnel, such as a teacher refusing to use the services of an interpreter. Administrators also should attempt to allay any fears that teachers may have about having another adult in the classroom and promote positive attitudes toward the student, the interpreter, and the process of inclusion.

If the interpreter is new to the school, a school administrator should provide an orientation including (a) a tour of the building; (b) an introduction of key school personnel; (c) an explanation of the need for and the rules relating to confidentiality; (d) a review of school dress codes and other standards of decorum; (e) an identification of out-of-class interpreting activities; and (f) a discussion of school schedules, calendars, and procedures relating to absences and emergencies.

The orientation also should include a discussion of the educational interpreter's schedule. This schedule should be carefully planned to promote the continued effectiveness of the interpreter. To facilitate collaborative interactions with teachers, parents, and other professionals, the schedule should provide time for the interpreter to meet with others and plan for interpreting activities. Additionally, to lessen the likelihood of fatigue or injuries associated with repetitive movements (e.g., carpal tunnel syndrome), the interpreter's schedule should include a break after each hour of continuous interpreting (National Task Force on Educational Interpreting, 1989).

Administrators also may be responsible for supervising the educational interpreter and coordinating the multidisciplinary team's evaluation of the services provided to the student. The interpreter's technical skills should be evaluated periodically. Since school administrators often are not trained as interpreters, qualified consultants can be hired to evaluate the interpreter's technical skills. For example, the Massachusetts Commission for the Deaf and Hard of Hearing offers the services of a staff member to perform evaluations of educational interpreters. The evaluation also should examine the effectiveness of and satisfaction with the services the interpreter provides from the perspectives of those who interact with the interpreter. Feedback from the interpreter also should be collected, including self-evaluation data. All involved individuals should be surveyed to identify potential solutions to problem areas as well as changes that need to be made in order to promote the independence of students with hearing impairments.

Sample evaluation questions may include the following:

1. Are teachers and the interpreter working cooperatively to deliver instruction to students?
2. In what ways is the present system assisting students to become independent?
3. What are the impacts of the interpreter on the student's peers and the social interactions between students with hearing impairments and their peers?
4. Has the interpreter aided professionals in communicating with parents who have hearing impairments?
5. Are administrative policies regarding the use of the interpreter appropriate?

Many states will hire only educational interpreters who have been certified by the Registry of Interpreters for the Deaf (RID). RID-certified interpreters must pass a test that includes both a written and a performance portion. The written portion assesses mastery of content related to the field of interpreting, including the history and ethics of the profession, sociological and cultural factors associated with hearing impairments, language development, and linguistics. The performance section examines the interpreter's skills in a variety of interpreting situations. While the RID has served as a national certifying agency for professional interpreters, it currently does not offer a specific certification for educational interpreters (Commission on Education of the Deaf, 1988). However, the RID is now working with the Council for the Education of the Deaf (CED) to develop standards and procedures to certify educational interpreters (R. C. McLachlan, personal communication, July 14, 1990). Additional guidelines regarding

certification for oral interpreters and cued speech facilitators are available from the Alexander Graham Bell Association for the Deaf and the National Cued Speech Association, respectively.

As with other professionals, the school administrator should assist educational interpreters in their professional development (National Task Force on Educational Interpreting, 1989). The school administrator or other professionals can work with individual interpreters to plan a series of appropriate professional development activities that address the interpreter's unique needs, interests, and job functions. For example, North Carolina has established a professional development model whereby trainers of interpreters work with interpreters to design inservice activities (R. C. McLachlan, personal communication, July 14, 1990). Professional development activities can include reading books and articles, viewing media, attending workshops and conferences, enrolling in courses, and visiting model programs. As part of the interpreter's professional development, it may be appropriate to offer inservice training sessions to teachers, ancillary support personnel, and parents to introduce them to the roles and responsibilities of the educational interpreter.

CONCLUSION

The primary goal of the educational interpreter is to facilitate communication between two parties who use different communication systems. To achieve this goal and to aid in the inclusion of students with hearing impairments, the interpreter must fulfill many roles that require interaction with a variety of individuals. These roles should be identified and discussed with the stu-

dent with a hearing impairment, school personnel, parents, and peers so that all are working to further the academic and social independence of students with hearing impairments.

REFERENCES

Castle, D. (1988). *Oral interpreting: Selections from papers by Kirsten Gonzalez.* Washington, DC: Alexander Graham Bell Association for the Deaf.

Commission on the Education of the Deaf. (1988). *Toward equality: Education of the deaf. A report to the President and the Congress of the United States.* Washington, DC: U.S. Government Printing Office.

Florida State Education Department. (1986). *Interpreting in the educational setting.* Tallahassee: Author.

Frishberg, N. (1986). *Interpreting: An introduction.* Rockville, MD: Registry of Interpreters for the Deaf.

Hurwitz, T. A., & Witter, A. B. (1979). Principles of interpreting in an educational environment. In M. E. Bishop (Ed.), *Mainstreaming: Practical ideas for educating hearing impaired students* (pp. 138–140). Washington, DC: Alexander Graham Bell Association for the Deaf.

Kipila, E., & Williams-Scott, B. (1988). Cued speech and speech reading. *Volta Review, 90,* 179–192.

Massachusetts Commission for the Deaf and Hard of Hearing. (1988). *An information guide related to standards for educational interpreting for deaf and severely hard of hearing students in elementary and secondary schools.* Boston: Author.

National Task Force on Educational Interpreting. (1989). *Educational interpreting for deaf students.* Rochester, NY: National Technical Institute for the Deaf, Rochester Institute of Technology.

Rittenhouse, R. K., Rahn, C. H., & Morreau, L. E. (1989). Educational interpreter services for hearing impaired students: Provider and consumer disagreements. *Journal of the American Deafness and Rehabilitation Association, 22,* 57–63.

Salend, S. J. (1994). *Effective mainstreaming: Creating inclusive classrooms (2nd ed.).* New York: Macmillan.

U. S. Department of Education. (1993). *Fifteenth annual report to Congress on the implementation of the Individuals with Disabilities Education Act.* Washington, DC: Author.

Waldron, M. B., Diebold, T. J., & Rose, S. (1985). Hearing-impaired students in regular classrooms: A cognitive model for educational services. *Exceptional Children, 52,* 39–43.

Wilson, J. J. (1981). Notetaking: A necessary support service for hearing-impaired students. *TEACHING Exceptional Children, 14,* 38–40.

DEVELOPING INDEPENDENT AND RESPONSIBLE BEHAVIORS

in Students Who Are Deaf or Hard of Hearing

John Luckner

John Luckner *(CEC Chapter #381), Associate Professor of Special Education, Division of Special Education, University of Northern Colorado, Greeley.*

For some students who are deaf or hard of hearing, the development of responsibility and the steps toward independence are relatively smooth. They receive support from family, school, and friends. They mature emotionally and socially so that they are able to manage adult financial and interpersonal responsibilities. However, many other deaf or hard-of-hearing individuals have difficulty moving out on their own. They get jobs and leave them after a few weeks or they go off to postsecondary programs only to return before the end of the semester (Commission on Education of the Deaf, 1988; Frisina, 1981; Rayson, 1987).

Prior to graduation, students who experience difficulty in making the transition from school to the "real" world have typically exhibited behaviors indicating that they might have a less than smooth path ahead. They have had problems getting work completed on time, maintaining a positive attitude while engaging in difficult tasks, accepting feedback, solving problems on their own, taking care of personal belongings, taking turns when working in a group, being able to work independently, controlling anger, showing respect for other individuals' property, and/or following school rules. As a result, many of the skills and behaviors necessary for success in the world of work or postsecondary education have not been developed or mastered during the students' elementary or secondary education program.

Responsibility means being able to distinguish between right and wrong, think and act rationally, and be accountable for one's behavior (*Webster's New World Dictionary*, 1987). Responsible self-direction does not "just happen"; therefore, it is important for students who are deaf or hard of hearing to have support and well-planned assistance in school and at home. Teachers of students who are deaf or hard of hearing cannot make them become responsible people. However, teachers can set up environments that promote the development of responsibility, and they can recognize and reinforce responsibility when it occurs. Simultaneously, they can learn to refrain from rewarding dependent behaviors. For example, teachers often help out when students forget books, homework, lunch money, or permission slips. The result is that students learn quickly that they can count on others rather than accept responsibility for their own actions. Teachers need to ask themselves, "Am I really helping? Is the assistance I am giving helping students to cope more effectively with the world that they will be living in after graduation? Or is it better to let them experience the real consequences of their behavior?"

In addition to monitoring the manner in which teachers interact with students, there are some specific interventions that can be implemented in order to help students develop responsibility. They include providing formal instruction in the area of decision making and responsibility, helping students understand and articulate their personal values, teaching goal setting, and working with students' families.

Instruction in Decision Making and Responsibility

Young people of today are asked to make many more decisions than were previous generations. Every day, people encounter life situations requiring thought, decision making, and action. Teachers can help students develop an awareness of how they make decisions and teach them the following six-step procedure for making and acting on decisions (Beyer, 1987):

1. Define the goal.
2. Identify the alternatives.
3. Analyze the alternatives.
4. Rank the alternatives.
5. Judge the highest-ranked alternatives.
6. Choose the best alternative.

Using these steps as a blueprint, teachers can model their own thought processes as they make decisions on a daily basis (e.g., "What will I eat for lunch?; what should I do when my car won't start?; what do I plan to do over the weekend?"). It is also helpful to give the class a true problem or a hypothetical situation and have the students generate responses to each of the steps in an effort to make a decision. Helping students learn to think ahead, make decisions, and be able to answer the question "What would you do if...?" is a valuable intervention. The following are some decision-making situations that can be used for discussion purposes:

1. You found another student's wallet or purse.

From *Teaching Exceptional Children*, Vol. 26, No. 2, Winter 1994, pp. 13-17. © 1994 by The Council for Exceptional Children.
Reprinted by permission.

2. You saw a small boy or girl being beaten up by some of your classmates.
3. Your friend asked you to smoke behind the school.
4. You want to buy a telecommunication device for the deaf (TDD).
5. Your friend told the teacher about something that you did and you got in trouble.
6. Someone was making fun of you because of your hearing aids and/or use of sign language.
7. You want to go to camp this summer with other kids who are deaf or hard of hearing.

To make things more personally relevant to the students you work with, have them develop their own list of problems or situations that occur at school or at home. As a group, they can analyze each situation for choices and consequences and discuss how and why they would make the decision they choose.

In addition to providing instruction and opportunities for discussion about decision making, you can teach a unit on responsibility. When teachers help students learn responsibility, they are focusing on three subgoals: teaching students to care about themselves, teaching them to care about others, and teaching them to care about the world around them (Pendergrass, 1982). Begin by helping the students understand what responsibility is and why it is something people hold in high regard. Provide clear examples of what is responsible behavior, as opposed to irresponsible behavior. Reinforce the students when they demonstrate responsible behaviors.

Figure 1 is an example of an activity sheet that has been adapted from Borba (1989) and Reasoner (1982). It can be used for discussion purposes and for having students evaluate themselves. It could also be used as a stimulus for goal setting, which is discussed later.

Develop a Sense of Purpose

A value is something that is desirable in and of itself. Without values, self-management becomes little more than choosing from an array of equally worthy or unworthy activities. Without values, it is easy to become motivated by objects and events that are immediate and easy, rather than those that are most meaningful. One of the ways to help students develop responsibility is to provide them with some different stimuli for thought and discussion to increase their awareness of the beliefs and behaviors that shape their decisions (see Figure 2, which has been adapted from Borba [1989] and Reasoner [1982]). After students have developed an awareness of their values, they can use this information to write personal goals.

Goal Setting

Responsible people set goals and establish steps to achieve the goals. Our goals lend direction to our lives. Without them we often flounder, uncertain of who we are and what we want to become. Teachers can help students develop an essential life skill by talking about goals and helping them learn to set and strive for achievable personal goals. These goals should (a) be concrete and specific; (b) be realistic; (c) be measurable in some quantitative and/or qualitative way; (d) include deadlines; (e) be anchored in personal values; and (f) be written. Figure 3 is an example of an activity sheet that can be used to help students establish and evaluate their goal-setting behavior.

While providing instruction in the area of goal setting, invite students to read stories or read stories to them about people who have set and achieved goals. *Great Deaf Americans* (Panara & Panara, n.d.), *I'm Deaf Too* (Bowe, 1973), *Hometown Heroes: Successful Deaf Youth in America* (Robinette, 1990), *Courageous Deaf Adults* (Toole, 1980), and *Successful Deaf Americans* (Toole, 1981) are excellent resources. You can also invite successful adults who are deaf or hard of hearing from the community to share their life experiences with your students.

Teach Skills for Independent Learning

Many students who are deaf or hard of hearing have difficulty acquiring the

"WHAT WOULD YOU DO IF...?"

You found another student's wallet or purse.

Your friend asked you to smoke behind the school.

You want to go to camp this summer with other kids who are deaf or hard of hearing.

skills to become active, independent learners (Schlesinger, 1988). Yet, lifelong learning is becoming a necessity for survival in an information-based society. Certain skills are essential for success in school and for continued learning after leaving formal education. Teachers can help students learn those skills by directly teaching them and establishing opportunities to use them. For example, managing time and materials, knowing how to study, and taking tests are critical to school success (Archer & Gleason, 1989). Students should learn to organize their time by learning to use an assignment calendar or notebook to keep track of work that needs to be completed. They can get prepared to complete homework by discussing where to work, the materials they will need, when to do the homework, and how to check their assignments before turning them in. Learning how to read and understand directions in workbooks is another skill necessary for school success. These skills should be introduced to students in the early grades and systematically reinforced throughout their educational careers. Additional skills that can be taught to help students become independent learners include the following:

- How to study.
- How to manage time.
- How to ask questions when you don't understand something.
- How to take notes.
- How to answer questions at the end of a textbook chapter.
- How to use a telecommunication device for the deaf (TDD) and relay services.
- How to proofread your work.
- How to take a multiple-choice, true-false, or essay test.
- How to use an interpreter.
- How to locate community support services.
- How to cope with stress.
- How to resolve conflicts.

Work with Students' Families

To help students become responsible and independent, teachers should work with students' families to establish carryover from what goes on in the school setting to what occurs at home. Inform parents that teaching independence and responsibility are essential educational goals. Share with them the desire to work together to reinforce the development of specific behaviors. Suggest to parents—during a conference or through a short letter—that you would like them to refrain from acting as rescuers for their children. Explain that when their children forget books, homework, hearing aids, permission slips, or lunch money they should experience the consequences of their behavior rather than having adults reinforce unwanted behaviors. Additional interventions to consider sharing with parents include asking them to:

- Give their child opportunities to make decisions for himself or herself.
- Invite their child to write future goals.
- Reinforce their child at home when he or she demonstrates responsible behavior.
- Discuss with their child how to establish plans in order to finish important work.
- Design a weekly schedule for recreation and TV viewing. Help their child learn to limit the amount of television and choose in advance the programs preferred.
- Teach their child different ways to write reminders about important materials, projects, or dates.
- Teach their child household organizational skills such as where to place important materials at night and in the morning so they will not be forgotten.
- Encourage their child to work independently on assignments.
- Demonstrate enthusiasm over high-quality completed work.
- Invite their child to be responsible by asking him or her to select

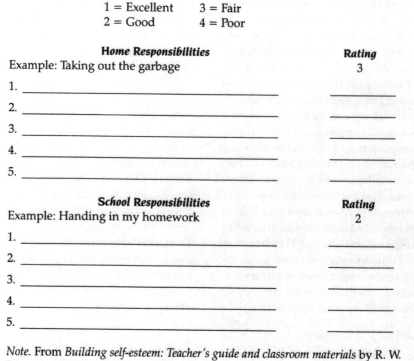

Figure 1. Personal Responsibilities

List five responsibilities that you have at home and five responsibilities that you have at school. Rate yourself on each responsibility to show how successful you are. Use the following numbers to rate yourself:

1 = Excellent   3 = Fair
2 = Good   4 = Poor

Home Responsibilities	**Rating**
Example: Taking out the garbage	3
1. _____	_____
2. _____	_____
3. _____	_____
4. _____	_____
5. _____	_____

School Responsibilities	**Rating**
Example: Handing in my homework	2
1. _____	_____
2. _____	_____
3. _____	_____
4. _____	_____
5. _____	_____

Note. From *Building self-esteem: Teacher's guide and classroom materials* by R. W. Reasoner, 1982, p. 87. Copyright 1982 by Consulting Psychologists Press. Adapted by permission.

chores to complete and budget money.

Conclusion

For students to become independent and responsible, they need environments that support their initiatives and allow them to make choices. Teachers cannot make students become responsible persons. They can, however, teach about responsibility and how to make decisions; assist them in developing an awareness of their values and how to develop and achieve personal goals; teach them the skills they need to continue to learn independently; work with their families; and reinforce them when they exhibit responsible behaviors.

References

Archer, A., & Gleason, M. (1989). *Skills for school success.* North Billerica, MA: Curriculum Associates.

Borba, M. (1989). *Esteem builders: A K-8 self-esteem curriculum for improving student achievement, behavior, and school climate.* Rolling Hills Estates, CA: Ialmar Press.

Bowe, F. (1973). *I'm deaf too.* Silver Spring, MD: National Association of the Deaf.

Commission on Education of the Deaf. (1988). *Toward equality: Education of the deaf.* Washington, DC: U.S. Government Printing Office.

Frisina, D. R. (1981). A perspective on the mental health of young deaf adults in modern society. In A. M. Mulholland (Ed.), *Oral education today and tomorrow* (pp. 485-494). Washington, DC: The Alexander Graham Bell Association for the Deaf.

Panara, R., & Panara, J. (n.d.). *Great deaf Americans.* Silver Spring, MD: T. J. Publishers.

Pendergrass, R. H. (1982). A "thinking" approach to teaching responsibility. *The Clearing House, 56* (2), 90-92.

Rayson, B. (1987). Emotional illness and deafness. In E. D. Mindel & M. Vernon (Eds.), *They grow in silence: Understanding deaf children and adults* (pp. 65-101). Boston: College-Hill.

Reasoner, R. W. (1982). *Building self-esteem: Teacher's guide and classroom materials.* Palo Alto, CA: Consulting Psychologists Press, Inc.

Robinette, D. (1990). *Hometown heroes: Successful deaf youth in America.* Washington, DC: Kendall Green Publications.

Schlesinger, H. (1988). Questions and answers in the development of deaf children. In M. Strong (Ed.), *Language learning and deafness* (pp. 261-291). Cambridge, England: Cambridge University Press.

Toole, D. (1980). *Courageous deaf adults.* Beaverton, OR: Dormac.

Toole, D. (1981). *Successful deaf Americans.* Beaverton, OR: Dormac.

Webster's new world dictionary of the American language. (1987). New York: World.

Figure 2. Personal Values

Read each statement. Decide how important it is to you and check the appropriate box.

Value	Very Important	Important	Not Important
Being healthy	☐	☐	☐
Getting good grades	☐	☐	☐
Playing well in games and sports	☐	☐	☐
Having a good friend	☐	☐	☐
Being with my family	☐	☐	☐
Having lots of friends	☐	☐	☐
Reading books and magazines	☐	☐	☐
Having money to spend	☐	☐	☐
Being good at making friends	☐	☐	☐
Being liked by teachers	☐	☐	☐
Watching television	☐	☐	☐
Being by myself	☐	☐	☐
Wearing nice clothes	☐	☐	☐
Eating good food	☐	☐	☐
Going to parties	☐	☐	☐
Going on vacations	☐	☐	☐

Note. From *Building self-esteem: Teacher's guide and classroom materials* by R. W. Reasoner, 1982, p. 227. Copyright 1982 by Consulting Psychologists Press. Adapted by permission.

Figure 3. Daily Goal Setting

Write a goal that you would like to accomplish each day. At the end of the day or the next morning, mark how well you feel you achieved your goal.

	Goal	Achieved	Partially Achieved
Monday:	_____	_____	_____
Tuesday:	_____	_____	_____
Wednesday:	_____	_____	_____
Thursday:	_____	_____	_____
Friday:	_____	_____	_____

Note. From *Building self-esteem: Teacher's guide and classroom materials* by R. W. Reasoner, 1982, p. 333. Copyright 1982 by Consulting Psychologists Press. Adapted by permission.

By June, Given Shared Experiences, Integrated Classes, and Equal Opportunities, Jaime Will Have a Friend

Kathryn Bishop
Kim Jubala

Kathryn Bishop *(CEC Chapter #95), Director of Special Education, School of Education, University of San Diego, San Diego, California.* **Kim Jubala** *(CEC Chapter #95), Teacher, San Diego Unified School District, California.*

Jaime's IEP looks different. Yes, the standard assessments have verified the fact that Jaime still has severe disabilities. He is 11 years old and has an IQ of 65. He is deaf and visually impaired, cannot count past 5, writes his first name accurately only 50% of the time, has mostly unintelligible speech, and does not initiate social interactions. However, this year's assessment also notes that Jaime likes chocolate ice cream, Bart Simpson, baseball, and, especially, other children. In the past, Jaime's IEP meetings focused on his physical and academic deficits. Goals were determined and objectives written in an attempt to improve the quality of his life by remediating those deficits. However, the quality of Jaime's life was not improving; it was time to change the focus.

Setting IEP Goals

This year's IEP meeting was led by Jaime and the people who knew him best: his mother and his special education teacher. Jaime, his mother, the special education teacher, and the 6th-grade teacher met at Jaime's home prior to the formal IEP meeting to discuss their ideas and make some preliminary plans. This in-home meeting helped determine goals for Jaime as part of his family and neighborhood, as well as addressing his school-based needs, with the use of tools such as parent interviews and discrepancy analyses (Falvey, 1989). The purpose of the IEP meeting was not only to formalize goals but also to generate strategies that would lead to a successful year. Also included in the formal meeting were the 6th-grade teacher, the speech therapist, the adaptive and regular P.E. teachers, the program specialist, and the principal. The team members agreed that Jaime should continue to work on increasing his academic skills. But for this year, the focus of his education was to be on developing social skills and, most important, developing friendships.

Jaime's mother was pleased that Jaime was learning new skills, but she was concerned that he was lonely and had no friends. Her concerns are supported in the literature, which suggests that children with severe disabilities have fewer nonpaid relationships and that friendships can play an important role in allowing children with disabilities to live, work, and play in the mainstream of their communities (Forest & Lusthaus, 1989; Haring, 1990; Taylor, Biklen, & Knoll, 1987). Without the opportunity to develop and maintain friendships, Jaime's educational and emotional well-being was at risk. Strain (1987) has suggested that while friendships are important for normally developing children, they may be even more important for children with disabilities in terms of language, cognitive, sexual, and academic development. In addition, friendships are considered an essential factor in the development of positive self-identity (Stainback, Stainback, East, and Sapon-Shevin, 1994). Because friendship was a stated goal for Jaime, it seemed logical to include it as such in his IEP.

The team hoped that Jaime would be able to count to 10 by the end of the school year, that he would write his first and last name with 80% accuracy, and that he would initiate interactions with a peer. But an important new goal was that by June, given shared experiences, integrated classes, and equal opportunities, Jaime would have one or more friends as measured by teacher observation and reports by Jaime and a nondisabled friend.

Creating Opportunities for Friendship

Jaime had previously been assigned to a special day class for students with multiple disabilities on a regular education

From *Teaching Exceptional Children*, Vol. 27, No. 1, Fall 1994, pp. 36-40. © 1994 by The Council for Exceptional Children. Reprinted by permission.

campus. This year it was agreed that his program would be implemented in a regular 6th-grade classroom with support from special education personnel. Although in the previous setting Jaime had opportunities to interact with his nondisabled peers during certain times of the day (art, music, lunch, and recess), it was determined that partial integration was not leading to the desired outcomes.

As Jaime began to attend the 6th-grade class, his special education teacher and regular education teacher met regularly to assess his needs and develop any necessary adaptations. The teachers examined the 6th-grade schedule and identified times when Jaime needed additional support or curricular modifications. Then, for each highlighted area, the teachers determined how the specific need could be met. For example, the special education aide spent 2 hours a week modifying the 6th-grade novel so Jaime could follow along with pictures. Also, instead of pulling him out of the classroom for speech therapy, the therapist adjusted her methods and provided services to Jaime within his small group during science. Most of the time Jaime required no additional support because of the cooperative learning structure of the classroom and the high levels of peer interaction.

Integration was not new to the children or the teachers. The major difference was including Jaime all day in the 6th-grade classroom. The students had seen Jaime around campus during lunch and recess, and some had worked in the special day class as peer tutors. Unlike many integration strategies, there was no disability awareness instruction for the students without disabilities. It was decided that a disability awareness lesson would put too much focus on Jaime's differences and interfere with his natural classroom inclusion. The special education teacher did, however, use the MAPS (Vandercook & York, 1989) and Circle of Friends (O'Brien, Forest, Snow, & Hasbury, 1989) strategies for peer-support and problem-solving activities as the need arose. For example, a meeting of Jaime's circle of friends was called when Jaime refused to wear his hearing aids for several days. His friends decided to bring their orthodontic retainers, eye-glasses, and soccer shinguards, to demonstrate how everyone has to wear special equipment. Jaime began wearing his aids, and he showed his friends how to put the batteries in.

Jaime's general education class did a great deal of its work in cooperative learning groups. These groups were formed frequently on the basis of nonacademic shared interests. For example, some groups were organized by favorite number between one and five, some by favorite sport, and some by what color shirt or dress was being worn that day. Thus, Jaime had the opportunity to be involved with small groups of his peers in a manner that promoted a sense of pride and belonging. The members of the "baseball group" thought that they were "totally more rad" than the "football group" regardless of their academic skills.

Achieving Goals and Objectives

Jaime's academic goals were incorporated into the general education classroom. For example, if other students were given individual seatwork tasks, Jaime worked at his seat on parallel tasks adapted by one or both of his teachers. To address his math goals, Jaime sometimes worked on different tasks such as taking attendance each day and counting the number of students present and absent. He also counted the number of correct answers on each weekly 30-item math test, assisted initially by the student in charge of recordkeeping that month. Soon Jaime was able to count the correct answers by himself, surpassing his objective of counting to 10. He worked on visual scanning by collecting finished papers from students who held them in the air from their desks. In addition to using adapted reading materials, Jaime increased his sight word reading by learning to read the names of all of the children in his class and the names of buildings and offices on campus during team games such as scavenger hunts and "whodunnit mysteries." Along with his peers, Jaime was assigned class and school jobs that rotated monthly to meet his vocational objectives. For community-based instruction, the special education teacher took Jaime and a few of his peers into the community during the week.

Jaime worked on purchasing and ordering, and his peers applied the concepts being worked on in the class (e.g., weighing produce in the market for math and interviewing the manager at McDonald's for language arts).

The easiest IEP objective for Jaime to meet was that of initiating conversations and interactions with his peers. Because of the cooperative learning groups, students relied on each other to complete projects. In art, for example, there would be one pair of scissors, one paintbrush, and one glue bottle per group and students had to share and negotiate to accomplish a task. As Jaime collected and returned papers from individual students, he interacted with them. He was relied upon as a team member with important pieces of information to share in every group to which he was assigned. Jaime learned to rely on his peers for help in completing tasks, as opposed to seeking the help of the adults in the room. He had plenty of opportunity to practice writing his name. As Jaime learned both good and bad practices from his newfound friends, he spent more than one recess washing his name off his desk along with them!

Forming Friendships

One of the main themes of the 6th-grade classroom was friendship, with an emphasis on treating every living thing with respect. Friendships are important to all sixth-graders, and his classmates' writing made it clear that Jaime had the potential to fit into their definition of friendship. Following are some excerpts from the sixth-graders' writings on the meaning of friendship:

I think friendship is having fun together and talking about our problems together. I also think friendship is sharing our special possessions and fun places we've been. Friendship is going places together. (Ryan)

Friendship means people who are there for you whenever you need them. There to cheer you up when you're down and to help you out when needed. (Anna)

Friendship to me means having a person who's considerate and caring. Someone who has both the same and different interests as you. (Jennifer)

Friendship means to be loyal and to feel sympathetic toward your friend. In order to be a true friend you have to build up a trusting lasting relationship and don't rush it. (Adam)

It is hanging out with each other at school or at home and just plain being nice to each other and once in awhile arguing but mostly being friends and helping each other when it's needed. (John)

In my opinion, in this world most people all need at least one friend to survive today. (Mario)

A friendship is the best thing out of all others that you could ever achieve in your whole entire lifetime. (Hong)

I want a friend. (Jaime)

Throughout the year, Jaime developed casual relationships with many students in the class, but in particular he developed close friendships with three boys: José, Zach, and Mark. These relationships were considered to be true friendships because the boys sought each other out at lunch and recess, traded possessions, lent money, stood up for each other when there was trouble, and talked to and about each other at home. Each of the boys was asked to write some answers to a few questions about his friendship with Jaime. The following is a list of the questions and the boys' responses:

1. How did you meet Jaime?

José: In P.E. one day and ever since we were friends. He is a funny guy and he makes me crack up. I sure won't forget the day we met.

Zach: I first met him in Speech on Tuesdays and Thursdays. Then he was chasing me around the playground shouting "eauovenapa!" The next day I was trying to understand my new friend.

Mark: Well, first we bumped into each other. Then I saw him and we became friends. We played at recess, I like playing with Jaime.

2. How has Jaime changed while being in 6th grade?

José: He can talk better, he can write better. He is polite and not mean in any shape or form. He has gotten popular.

Zach: He has changed a lot by being nice and a little bit calmer and he listens better. He has also become more popular. I can understand him now that he taught me some sign language.

Mark: I don't think Jaime has changed a lot. He's always been grown up about things and he's always kind and understanding and he's always been a terrific friend.

3. What have you learned from being friends with Jaime?

José: He makes me feel good when I am sad, and when I get mad, he slows me down. I helped Jaime run a 7:15 in the mile run, and I won't forget that ever.

Zach: I learned that he could fit in with everyone in the school and he wanted to be friends and he is my friend. Being friends with Jaime has its advantages. He is very nice, considerate, kind, polite, and my favorite, a cool kid.

Mark: I learned what a real friend would be like. He is truly a good friend. I learned that a friend has to be kind and I learned that from Jaime.

When Jaime was asked to talk about his friends, he replied, "I have three friends, Zach, José, and Mark, one, two, three. I like my friends. I like to tease and run and play."

Parents' and Teachers' Reactions

The mothers of the boys also shared their feelings on the friendship that their sons had developed with Jaime, a boy who had so many disabilities. The following are edited excerpts from their writings:

I feel José has made as much of a difference in Jaime's life as Jaime has made in José's life. José has learned a second language (sign language) and has become more sensitive to people's needs in general. José is a kind, sincere individual who, through this relationship, has developed a warmth beyond words. I have watched [the boys] grow and broaden their respect for each other. (José's Mom)

This friendship has been beneficial for all. The children are eager to help each other in any way possible. They seem to have learned compassion and understanding at a very young age. I think it's great that children learn that there is diversity in the world and have the opportunity to be friends. My son has learned to accept his own problems much more. (Zach's Mom)

The good thing about the friendship is that it is strong enough to concentrate on the positive so the negative things don't seem so large. The interacting of these kids is beneficial because it gives both kids a chance to relate to the things they have in common. Mark has learned that Jaime is really no different from himself, with feelings and needs. (Mark's Mom)

I knew it was important for Jaime to have friends who didn't have the same problems that he had. I didn't think that it was going to happen—but it did! The friendships go both ways, he cares about his friends, and they care about him. Jaime's friends are a very special part of his life. (Jaime's Mom)

Jaime's special education teacher was thrilled with the social changes and academic achievements accomplished over the course of the year. Her hope is that next year she will have more opportunity to support all of the students in her special day class in full-inclusion settings. She hopes that Jaime's success will encourage other general and special education teachers to work collaboratively to support the needs of all students in a shared environment.

Jaime's 6th-grade teacher admitted to being "more than just a little bit worried about the whole idea" when she was first approached. She agreed to give it a try because "she had seen Jaime around campus, had a good relationship with the special education teacher, and is always up for something new and different." By the end of the year she was so impressed with the positive impact that Jaime had on her students that she was trying to find out who she could include in her class the following year. In her words, "Jaime created challenges for everyone in Room 17 to recognize our roles as members of a caring community and realize the rewards that come with supporting one another and making sure everyone in our classroom is a success."

Transcending the IEP

Jaime's successes at the end of the year extended beyond meeting his IEP objectives. Jaime ran for a student council office and, with the help of his friend Zach, gave a speech in front of the whole student body. All day, students were popping into the classroom to say that they had voted for Jaime, and sure enough by the end of the day the votes were tallied and Jaime had been elected Commissioner of the Environment! Jaime was also coached, prodded, and cheered by his friends and received the President's Physical Fitness Award and was handed his certificate along with Zach, Mark, and José at the award ceremony. And finally, Jaime had a graduation party that included not only his family, but also friends who had stories to tell and secrets to share and memories to treasure. By June, Jaime had made friends.

Planning for Transition

Jaime and his friends would be attending different junior high schools, because he was moving out of the district. To facilitate the transition to junior high school, Jaime's special education teacher took him and a few of his friends to visit the new campus. The special education teacher, program specialist, and site principal came to observe Jaime in his 6th-grade class and meet with his teacher and friends so that a smooth transition could be accomplished. Jaime's mother helped him make plans to meet with his friends as much as possible over the summer so that the relationships might continue to grow and in hopes that they would help Jaime meet new friends in the neighborhood.

As the 6th-grade students were being prepared for the transition to junior high school, they were asked to write about the good things and the scary things they thought about junior high. Jaime's friends helped come up with the following list for him:

1. What are some good things about Jaime going to junior high?
   - He will meet new friends.
   - He might have a new girlfriend.
   - There will be a lot of people to help him.
   - He will be in regular classes.
   - He might have nice teachers.
   - He will learn a lot more.
   - There will be lots of sharing and co-operating.
   - There will be some good role models.
   - He will feel older.
   - He will get more respect.
   - He will have more responsibility.

2. What things about junior high might be scary for Jaime?
   - Bullies might harass him.
   - He might not have any friends.
   - There will be a lot of strange kids.
   - He might miss his old friends.
   - The kids might make fun of him.
   - He will need to change rooms each period.
   - He will have trouble seeing the numbers on the doors.
   - He will have trouble hearing the bells.
   - There will be a lot of hard work.
   - There might be mean teachers.
   - He might give in to bad influences.

3. What are some things we can do to help Jaime get ready for junior high?
   - Treat him like he's more mature.
   - Help him with his numbers.
   - Help him pay attention better.
   - Teach him to ignore hurtful remarks.
   - Give him more confidence.
   - Teach him to avoid peer pressure.
   - Show him who his friends are.

At the end of the 6th-grade year, it was time for another IEP meeting. This meeting also included the people who knew Jaime best: Zach, José, and Mark. They each contributed a goal for Jaime: That he would learn to say no to drugs, that he would avoid fights by walking away, and that he would keep working on his numbers so that he could tell time and call them on the telephone. Zach, José, and Mark signed as official participants at the IEP meeting, and on the IEP attendance sheet, under "role," they wrote, "Jaime's friend."

References

Falvey, M. (1989). *Community-based curriculum: Instructional strategies for students with severe disabilities.* Baltimore: Paul H. Brookes.

Forest, M., & Lusthaus, E. (1989). Promoting educational equality for all students: Circles and maps. In S. Stainback, W. Stainback, & M. Forest (Eds.), *Educating all students in the mainstream of regular education* (pp. 43-58). Baltimore: Paul H. Brookes.

Haring, T. G. (1990). Social relationships. In L. Meyer, C. Peck, & L. Brown (Eds.), *Critical issues in the lives of people with severe disabilities* (pp. 195-217). Baltimore: Paul H. Brookes.

Kennedy, C., & Itkonen, T. (1994). Some effects of regular class participation on the social contacts and social networks of high school students with severe disabilities. *Journal of The Association for Persons with Severe Handicaps, 19*(1), 1-10.

O'Brien, J., Forest, M., Snow, J., & Hasbury, D. (1989). *Action for Inclusion.* Toronto: Frontier College Press.

Stainback, S., Stainback, W., East, K., & Sapon-Shevin, M. (1994). A commentary on inclusion and the development of a positive self-identity by people with disabilities. *Exceptional Children, 60*(6), 486-490.

Strain, P. (1984). Social behavior patterns of nonhandicapped and developmentally disabled friend pairs in mainstream preschools. *Analysis and Intervention in Developmental Disabilities, 4*(1), 15-28.

Taylor, S. J., Biklen, D., & Knoll, J. (Eds.). (1987). *Community integration for people with severe disabilities.* New York: Teachers College Press.

Vandercook, T., & York, J. (1989). The McGill Action Planning System (MAPS): A strategy for building the vision. *Journal of the Association for Persons with Severe Disabilities, 14*(3), 205-215.

Update on Jaime: Since the time Jaime's story was first written many other students with disabilities have had the opportunity to develop friendships with peers in inclusive education settings. Jaime has continued to succeed both socially and educationally from his integrated experiences and this year completed the 8th grade receiving citizenship awards and a varsity letter in wrestling!

Children with Visual Impairments

Visual disabilities are common. Young children tend to have hyperopia (farsightedness) when their eyeballs are too small. After the growth spurt of adolescence, many students have myopia (nearsightedness) because their eyeballs are too long. In addition, many children have a degree of astigmatism. In this situation, one or both eyes have an irregular curvature of either the cornea or the lens, which blurs vision to some extent. All of these visual disabilities are easily corrected by wearing glasses, which can correct for length of the eyeballs or curvatures of the cornea or lens. Glasses can bring the visual image exactly where it needs to be on the retinal field.

Problems of vision involving other anatomical structures of the eye, especially the retina and the optic nerve, are not so easily corrected with glasses. Children with visual disabilities that cannot be corrected are the smallest group of children who qualify for special educational services through the Individuals with Disabilities Education Act (IDEA). In order to be assessed as visually disabled for purposes of receiving special educational services, a child must have low vision, which necessitates large print or magnification of print, or be blind, which necessitates use of hearing (audiotapes, records) or touch (braille, long cane) to be educated.

The educational definition of visual impairment focuses on what experiences a child needs in order to be able to learn. The legal definition of visual impairment is often given priority in assessment procedures. Legally, a child is considered to have low vision if acuity in the best eye, after correction, is between 20/70 and 20/180 and if the visual field extends from 20 to 180 degrees. Legally, a child is considered blind if visual acuity in the best eye, after correction, is 20/200 or less and/or if the field of vision is restricted to an area of less than 20 degrees (tunnel vision). These legal terms do not specify actual vision or accurately reflect a child's ability to see or read print. One must consider the amount of visual acuity in the worst eye, the perception of light and movement, the field of vision (a person "blinded" by tunnel vision may have good visual acuity in a very small field of vision), and the efficiency with which a person uses any residual vision.

The majority of children with visual impairments that necessitate special educational services have low vision rather than blindness. The wide variety of aids used to assist these children includes large print, magnifiers, computer software, wide-lined paper, felt-tip pens, and special typewriters. These can all be used in inclusive educational classrooms.

Children with visual impairments that prevent reading print are usually taught to read braille. Braille is a form of writing using raised dots that are "read" with the fingers. It takes many years to learn to read braille, and instruction should begin in preschool. Many children who are assessed as having low vision rather than blindness are also taught to read braille. This is especially true if the reason for their visual impairment is a problem with a poor prognosis (vision will deteriorate with age). In addition to braille, children who are blind are usually taught with Optacon scanners, talking books, talking hand-held calculators, closed-circuit television, typewriters, and special computer software.

All children with visual impairments should begin special educational services as soon as their problem of low vision or blindness is diagnosed. The amendments to IDEA provide for services from birth to age 21. In early childhood, many children with low vision are given instruction in use of the long cane. Although controversial for many years, the long cane is increasingly being accepted. A long cane improves orientation and mobility and alerts persons with visual acuity that the user of the now well-recognized cane has a visual disability.

The individualized educational programs (IEPs) of children with visual impairments reflect not only goals for using technological assistive aids but also goals for all of the academic subjects taught to children without visual impairments. Low vision or blindness does not impair learning ability unless the child concurrently has a learning disability or mental retardation. Many children with visual impairments are intellectually gifted.

The first article in this unit deals with the practice of starting orientation and mobility (O&M) training as soon after birth as the low vision or blindness is diagnosed. Many professionals believe that infants with limited vision should be allowed to crawl and walk at the same ages as infants with good visual acuity. What mobility devices are appropriate for visually impaired babies? When should precane activities begin? When should a cane be introduced? Susan Leong presents an extensive review of the literature on O&M training in infants, toddlers, and preschoolers. She documents the need for services and discusses several early approaches to O&M. Leong points out

the need for an expanded definition of O&M to include concept development, sensory and motor development, and skills such as using sighted guides, using a protective arm technique, and using range of mobility devices beyond the long cane.

The next unit article addresses the education of children who have hearing impairments in addition to visual impairments. Children who are deaf-blind have many special needs. This selection is concerned with teaching students who are deaf-blind to make choices and develop independence.

The last article in this unit presents case studies of three students who were intellectually gifted as well as visually and hearing impaired. The pros and cons of their inclusion in regular education programs are discussed, and the

authors give suggestions based on personal experience for more successful integration of such students in the future.

Looking Ahead: Challenge Questions

How early should O&M training start for infants and young children? Should a precane be introduced before a long cane? Why or why not?

How can choice making be taught to students who are deaf-blind?

How can students who are intellectually gifted but also visually and hearing impaired be successfully integrated into regular educational classrooms? What are the challenges to be faced? How can these challenges be met?

Preschool Orientation and Mobility: A Review of the Literature

Abstract: The past decade has witnessed the extension of orientation and mobility services to visually impaired children, aged birth to 6 years. These services have expanded rapidly despite the lack of a well-documented and thorough research base. This article presents a review of the literature on this topic, including its history and body of knowledge and research and suggests avenues for further research.

S. Leong

Susan Leong, M.A., teacher, Itinerant Teaching Service, Royal NSW Institute for Deaf & Blind Children, 361-365 North Rocks Road, North Rocks, New South Whales, 2151, Australia.

The increase in orientation and mobility (O&M) services for infants and preschool children who are visually impaired (both those with low vision and those who are blind) in the past 10 years occurred despite the lack of a well-documented and thorough research base (Ferrell, 1979; Joffee, 1988; Skellenger & Hill, 1991; Stack & Minnes, 1989; Warren, 1976). At the same time, practitioners have come to accept a broader definition of O&M for young children. As yet, no attempts have been made either to trace the history of this movement or to examine the body of knowledge in this area. This article attempts to redress this situation by presenting a comprehensive yet concise account of the background and related literature on this topic.

Need for services

O&M training for preschool children should involve activities that help young children who are visually impaired to move purposefully and safely in the environment. The importance of early O&M training for the independence and orientation of blind preschoolers to their environment has been postulated by many authors (Baird, 1979; Campbell, 1970; Cratty, Peterson, Harris & Schoner, 1968; DuBose, 1976; Eichorn & Vigaroso, 1967; Ferrell, 1979; Lord, 1969; Palazesi, 1986; Stack and Minnes, 1989; Warren, 1984; Webster, 1976). Most authors agree that this training should begin as early as possible, in most instances, before or in kindergarten (Benson, 1984; Bosbach, 1988; Pogrund & Rosen, 1989; Willoughby, 1979).

Without sight, the experiences of blind children must be channeled through the other senses, primarily hearing and touch. Without movement, the children's world is limited to the length of their arms. Therefore, any instruction in movement and mobility will extend the children's world and thus the children's knowledge about the world. Galloway (1981) described the cycle of learning that mobility training can set in motion: As children who are blind begin to master the environment and adequately move within it, they often grown cognitively and physically, their motivation to move and explore further increases; their greater motivation, in turn, ensures the continued expansion of their learning, control, and independence. In this regard, the importance of mobility and its interrelationship with other areas of learning has been noted by a number of authors, including Cratty (1970), Hapeman (1967), and Lowenfeld (1964/1981).

Studies (see, for example, Ferrell, 1979; Hill, 1970; Kephart, Kephart, & Schwarz, 1974; Mills & Adamshick, 1969) have substantiated the need of young visually impaired children for motor, concept, mastery, and body-image training. In addition, it has been observed that young blind children have motor problems, such as the lack of trunk and pelvic rotation, use of shuffling gait patterns, limited arm swing, dependence on a wide base of support for stability, and poor posture (Adelson & Fraiberg, 1976; Anthony & Gense, 1987; C. Brown & Bour, 1986; Campbell, 1970; Cratty, 1971; Eichorn & Vigaroso, 1967; Warren, 1976). If these essential elements on which walking is based are not corrected, atypical movement patterns become characteristic (C. Brown & Bour, 1986). Furthermore, as Clarke (1988) noted, many of these children do not move as independently as do their sighted peers for various reasons: nonexistent or ineffective walking patters (Holt, 1981); fixation at a low-level mode of movement (Elonen & Zwarensteyn, 1964); anxiety (Fraiberg, Smith, & Adelson, 1969); or an inability to monitor the changing environment visually, which results in the diminished ability and motivation to move within the environment (Sonksen, Levitt, & Kitsinger, 1984).

These problems may be alleviated when visually impaired children are given appropriate auditory, tactile-kinesthetic, and proprioceptive experiences and motor stimulation (Adelson & Fraiberg, 1976; Anthony & Gense, 1987;

Reprinted with permission from the *Journal of Visual Impairment & Blindness*, March/April 1996, pp. 145-153. © 1996 by the American Foundation for the Blind, 11 Penn Plaza, Suite 300, New York, NY 10001.

Butler, 1986; Cratty, 1971; Pereira, 1990). Such experiences include baby massage, kindergym, and sensory integration activities. Unfortunately, only anecdotal evidence has been presented on the benefits of these specific interventions.

But movement in itself is not enough. Rather, movement that is self-initiated, not passive, is what is essential for a variety of developmental achievements in early childhood (Ferrell, 1979; Olson, 1981). As Clarke (1988) summarized, active exploration by young children has been found to be related to higher levels of spatial knowledge (Hazen, 1982), to memory for spatial locations (Herman, Kolker, & Shaw, 1982), and to the ability to orient to external objects in the environment (Acredolo, 1982). Some practical suggestions for appropriate movement activities (precluding mobility aids) were published in the 1970s (D. Brown, Simmons, & Methvin, 1978; Cratty, 1971; Drouillard & Raynor, 1977; Raynor & Drouillard, 1975).

Early approaches

Early practitioners highlighted the significance of concept development, such as an adequate body image and good spatial awareness, for successful mobility but did not touch on any other areas of O&M instruction. Hapeman (1967) was concerned about the effect of the deficiencies of concept development on the mobility of a young blind child. He described the developmental concepts that need to be mastered by this age group, including body image, the nature of objects, terrain, and sounds and odors; the position of objects in space; distance and time; turning; and moving with and against objects. The importance of concept development to mobility, and indeed to learning in all areas, was later examined by Cratty and Sams (1968) and Lydon and McGraw (1973).

It was with the publication of two O&M assessment scales for blind children that aspects other than concept development were included. Lord (1969) used a developmental task approach to develop a scale for the appraisal of O&M skills in young blind children. The scales, field tested on 173 blind children aged 3–12 included self-help, precane O&M, movement in space, use of sensory skills, and use of directions

and turns. Harley, Merbler, and Wood (1975) produced the Peabody Mobility Scale, which covers four areas: locomotion, sensory training, concept development, and mobility skills. Although targeted to blind children with additional impairments, it can be argued with some justification that these scales would be equally applicable to preschool children who are blind and have no other impairments. It is important to note that these scales were the first documents to mention the use of any mobility devices. Since then, Harley, Long, Merbler, and Wood (1986) and Hill, Dodson-Burk, and Taylor (1992) field-tested and published screening tests that are targeted specifically for this population and are being used more and more by O&M instructors.

Expanded definition

Hill, Rosen, Correa, and Langley (1984) presented an expanded definition of O&M specific to the unique training needs of infants and preschoolers. To Ferrell's (1979) definition, which included sensory skill development, concept development, motor development, and formal mobility skills, they added environmental and community awareness and formal orientation skills, such as the use of the long cane or push-toy devices.

Hill, Smith, Dodson-Burk, and Rosen (1987) presented an O&M curriculum for visually impaired children, called the Preschool O&M Project (POMP), that incorporated formal orientation skills, formal mobility skills, gross motor skills, and fine motor skills. POMP includes a special section on teaching children to use mobility devices as bumpers for clearing and negotiating obstacles. However, it is important to note that the cane skills listed in the mobility section refer only to diagonal technique, probably because the project's initial sample was composed solely of blind children with multiple other impairments.

Mobility devices

Finnis (1975) recommended that children with physical impairments as young as 12 months should be encouraged to use mobility devices. Clarke (1988) discussed essential considerations for evalu-

ating and selecting mobility devices to encourage age-appropriate independent movement in children who are blind. Because every mobility device has certain enabling and hampering characteristics, she noted that instructors should choose a particular mobility device for an individual child on the basis of such factors as the child's motor skills and degree of residual vision; the device's level of social acceptance, appropriateness, safety, adaptability, and cost; and the availability of training. Clarke and others (Skellenger & Hill, 1991) suggested that a continuum of mobility aids, ranging from different push-toy devices to the long cane, may be more appropriate for this population.

Clarke's continuum of mobility devices is indeed broad and exhaustive, ranging from electronic travel aids to suspended movement devices to infant walkers to push-toys to precane instruments to the long cane. Pogrund, Fazzi, and Lampert (1992) grouped these devices in three broad categories: infant appliances, toys, and adaptive mobility devices. Both authors agreed that these devices should be used selectively with individual children at various developmental stages. A more detailed examination of the pros and cons of each category is warranted because of the increasing popularity of these devices.

Pogrund et al. (1992) urged that infant appliances should be used with caution and only after consultation with a physiotherapist to ensure that they are safe. For example, these appliances strengthen an infant's legs and provide some protection and opportunity for exploration, but they may reinforce inappropriate motor patterns and limit practice in crawling. Furthermore, some appliances may actually cause injury if an infant is not closely supervised while using them.

Toys, such as broom handles, hula hoops, shopping carts, lawn mowers, and golf clubs, are simple to use and are age-appropriate devices used by sighted children; they offer a degree of protection against obstacles and drop-offs, and some can even provide practice in centering the grip hand. On the other hand, they have a number of disadvantages; they are obtrusive and non collapsible, are not objects that children have with them all the time, and are not as tactilely sensitive as canes, and are not durable. In addition, children still need a transition period from their use to learning to use a long cane.

Adaptive mobility devices are specially designed apparatuses. Some researchers have reported the successful development and trial of various "precane" devices, including a two-pronged hooked cane (Foy, Kirchner, & Waple, 1991), a hula hoop (Bosbach, 1988; Ketterer, 1986), a swiveling wheeled cane (Kronick, 1987), and a T-bar bumper (Morse, 1980). But the positive reports of the use of these devices have been restricted to single case studies that have offered only subjective data. Adaptive mobility devices have many of the same advantages as toys, but they are more durable and tactilely sensitive. There disadvantages are that they can be obtrusive, are not common devices used by sighted children, may make the visually impaired child look more impaired than necessary because they may be confused with devices for physically disabled children, and required a transition period before the use of a long cane.

Long cane

Some authors (Pogrund & Rosen, 1989; Schroeder, 1989; Willoughby & Duffy, 1989; Wurzburger, 1990) see no need for training with these less sophisticated mobility devices and believe that the long cane should be the primary and sole mobility device. They contend that the long cane has all the same advantages of adaptive mobility devices with the additional advantages of being durable and collapsible and of offering much tactile and auditory feedback. Furthermore, since the long cane is the most likely mobility device that blind children will use as adults, they stress that its early introduction will avoid the necessary and often difficult transition period from one device to another. Finally, they note that the difficulty that older children may experience in being accepted by others will not occur if the long cane is introduced early because the children will have the opportunity to build its use into their self-image.

Pogrund and Rosen (1989) convincingly refuted the traditional arguments against introducing the long cane early. First, they claimed, using the long cane requires no more control or coordination than do skills that are usually termed "precane" skills (trailing and protective arm techniques) that are, themselves, separate and less efficient travel systems.

Secondly, cane skills can be refined gradually over time with improved coordination and muscle tone as are other skills (for example, scribbling leads to writing). Third, the environment, even the preschool environment, can be unstable and unpredictable. (In this regard, Wier, 1988, suggested that the long cane promotes travel in previously off-limits areas, so its use will actually increase the need for it.) Fourth, children can learn safety rules that will ensure that they use the long cane appropriately. Finally, the long cane, acting as a probe, actually offers more opportunities for hands-on experiences than do other travel techniques.

Despite these convincing arguments, Pogrund and Rosen offered no empirical evidence in support of their claims. Nor did Willoughby and Duffy (1989) and Schroeder (1989), who made similar proposals. Instead, they presented suggestions for lesson plans and teaching ideas for early long cane-travel sessions. Although both briefly mentioned that push-toy devices are excellent for promoting children's readiness for cane travel, they did so only on the basis of their personal observations and experiences. Furthermore, the fact that a search of the literature yielded no articles that questioned or refuted these authors' arguments suggests that although a thorough and well-documented research base is still to be established, the majority of O&M instructors seem to agree that the early use of the long cane is indeed the best practice.

Both Schroeder (1989) and Pogrund and Rosen stated that the term *precane skills* is a misnomer and that the term *basic skills* is preferable when referring to these techniques. Furthermore, Schroeder argued that the issue is not so much whether the long cane should be introduced to young children who are blind but how it should be introduced. The traditional methods of cane instruction, geared to adults who are adventitiously blind, are not sufficient for young congenitally blind children. Therefore, skilled O&M instructors will take full advantage of travel lessons to incorporate environmental awareness, sensory integration, concept development, and the technical refinement of cane skills within the same lesson.

Levels of O&M training

Two surveys (Dykes, 1992; Skellenger & Hill, 1991), limited in scope because of their small sample, were conducted in the early 1990s to determine the levels of O&M training provided to young children, as well as O&M instructors' opinions of the training. Both found that many O&M instructors were introducing the long cane to young children and that most responded favorably to this practice. Skellenger and Hill noted that, given the limitations of their survey (the small number of responses, the subjective nature of the feedback, and the small degree of consensus among respondents), the average age at which children were introduced to the long cane was 4–5 years. In addition, they found that the highest level of skill that the children attained was using an object other than a cane as a bumper (25%) and that only 13 percent of the children had learned the constant-contact technique or the touch technique.

Dykes (1992) discovered that the O&M instructors who responded to this survey favored the modified diagonal technique above all other techniques. Furthermore, the respondents agreed that teaching children all the precane skills before teaching them to use the long cane is an outdated idea. They also called for additional research to determine prerequisite skills, to develop curricula and training programs for the long cane, and to identify the developmental skills that are necessary for successful cane travel.

Pogrund et al. (1992) presented the first overview of early O&M intervention. Their compilation of ideas from various experienced practitioners offers a thorough introduction to the role and practice of O&M instructors with young children and a broad discussion of programs, goals, and strategies. It is particularly valuable for parents and practitioners who are entering the field.

In the latest published article that could be found in a literature search for this article, Clarke, Sainato, and Ward (1994) compared the effects of mobility training with a long cane and with a precane device (the Connecticut Precane; see Foy, Scheden, & Waiculonis, 1992). The results of their extremely small sample were as follows:

1. All the children used the precane more effectively than the long cane.

2. The precane was more effective than the long cane in preventing body contacts.
3. There were no differences in the speed of travel using the precane or the long cane.
4. Less intervention was necessary when the children used the precane.
5. There was no difference in the children's preferences for the precane and the long cane.

These results were probably to be expected: No one has suggested that the long cane is easier to learn to use than is any of the vast array of precane devices that are available. What was noteworthy was that all the children in the study were able to learn a modified diagonal cane technique, although some practitioners might question the priority given to this cane skill above that of the constant-contact technique. Also, Clarke et al. were correct in acknowledging that in their study, effectiveness applied to detecting obstacles and travel speed. Furthermore, since the study compared long cane travel to one specific precane device, generalizations to all precane devices should not be made.

Conclusion

This review of the literature on O&M instruction for visually impaired preschoolers has revealed many general findings. The value of O&M instruction in early intervention programs has been established. Meanwhile, the definition of O&M for young children has been expanded to include concept development; sensory development; motor skills; beginning formal skills, such as the sighted guide technique and the protective arm technique; and the use of a range of mobility devices of which the long cane is just one option. These developments have occurred more because of considerations about what is the best practice than because of the prevalence of overwhelming empirical evidence. It is hoped that the next 10 years will see the emergence of a rigorous empirical base to support these trends.

The publication of the study by Clarke et al. (1994) heralds the foundations of a solid research base and is to be welcomed. However, it leads to more questions than answers. To examine the benefits of both the use of the long cane and precane devices thoroughly, researchers need to conduct longitudinal comparison studies. However, given the difficulties of long-term projects and the low incidence of preschool children who are blind, these studies may be an unrealistic venture. Furthermore, in such studies, great care must be taken to specify both the particular long cane skill and precane device that are being used. Training methods for each device must be well documented, so that studies with small samples can be replicated.

The field of exploration is practically unlimited, for an examination of the "benefits" of early O&M instruction may include anything from better safety to improved self-esteem to increased concept development. There is still the question of whether it is valuable to introduce the precane before the long cane and whether doing so accelerates the acquisition of long cane skills, as Foy et al. (1992) discussed. Finally for all the O&M skills, teaching curricula with practical methods and successful strategies for this particular age group are urgently required. These are the directions that research must take in the future.

References

Acredolo, L. P. (1982). Spatial orientation in infancy. In J. C. Baird & A. Lutkus (Eds.). *Mind child architecture* (pp. 64–85). Hanover, NH: University Press of New England.

Adelson, E. & Fraiberg, S. (1976). Sensory deficit and motor development in infants blind from birth. In Z. S. Jastrzembska (Ed.)., *The effects of blindness and other impairments* (pp. 1–28). New York: American Foundation for the Blind.

Anthony, T. L. & Gense, D. J. (1987). Early intervention orientation and mobility programming: A developmental/habilitative approach/perspective. In *Proceedings of the Second International Symposium on Visually Handicapped Infants and Young Children* (pp. 31–34). Aruba, West Indies: International Institute for the Visually Impaired.

Baird, A. S. (1977). Electronic aids: Can they help blind children? *Journal of Visual Impairment & Blindness, 71,* 97–101.

Benson, S. (1984). *So what about independent travel?* Chicago: Catholic Guild for the Blind.

Bosbach, S. R. (1988). Precane mobility devices. *Journal of Visual Impairment & Blindness, 82,* 338–339.

Brown, C. & Bour, B. (1986). *A resource manual for the development and evaluation of special programs for exceptional students. Volume V-K: Movement analysis and curriculum for visually impaired preschoolers.* Tallahassee, FL: Bureau of Education for the Blind.

Brown, D., Simmons, V., & Methvin, J. (1978). *Oregon project for visually impaired blind children.* Medford, OR: Jackson County Education Service.

Butler, C. (1986). Effects of powered mobility on self-initiated behaviors of very young children with locomotor disability. *Developmental Medicine & Child Neurology, 28,* 325–332.

Campbell, L. F. (1970). Mobility for young blind children. In *Selected Papers from a Look at the Child* (pp. 79–84). New Orleans: Association for the Education of the Visually Handicapped.

Clarke, K. L. (1988). Barriers or enablers? Mobility devices for visually impaired and multihandicapped infants and preschoolers. *Education of the Visually Handicapped, 20,* 115–132.

Clarke, K. L., Sainato, D. M., & Ward, M. E. (1994). Travel performance of preschoolers: The effects of mobility training with a long cane versus a precane. *Journal of Visual Impairment & Blindness, 88,* 19–30.

Cratty, B. J. (1970). *Some educational implications of movement.* Seattle: Special Child Publications.

Cratty, B. J. (1971). *Movement and spatial awareness in blind children and youth.* Springfield, IL: Charles C. Thomas.

Cratty, B. J., Peterson, D., Harris, J., & Schoner, R. (1968). The development of perceptual-motor abilities in blind children and adolescents. *New Outlook for the Blind, 62,* 111–117.

Cratty, B. J. & Sams, T. A. (1968). *The body-image of blind children.* New York: American Foundation for the Blind.

Drouillard, R. & Raynor, S. (1977). *Move it!* Reston, VA: American Alliance for Health, Physical Education, Recreation, and Dance.

DuBose, R. F. (1976). Developmental needs in blind infants. *New Outlook for the Blind, 70,* 49–52.

Dykes, J. (1992). Opinions of O&M instructors about using the long cane with preschool age children. *RE:view, 24*(2), 85–92.

Eichorn, J. R. & Vigaroso, H. R. (1967). Orientation and mobility for preschool blind children. *International Journal for the Education of the Blind, 17*(2), 48–50.

Elonen, A. S. & Zwarensteyn, S. B. (1964). Appraisal of developmental lag in certain blind children. *Journal of Pediatrics, 65,* 599–610.

Ferrell, K. A. (1979). Orientation and mobility for preschool children: What we have and what we need. *Journal of Visual Impairment & Blindness, 73,* 147–150.

Fraiberg, S., Smith, M., & Adelson, E. (1969). An educational program for blind infants. *Journal of Special Education, 3,* 121–153.

Foy, C. J., Kirchner, D., & Waple, L. (1991). The Connecticut Precane. *Journal for Blindness & Visual Impairment, 82,* 85–86.

Foy, C. J., Scheden, M., & Waiculonis, J. (1992). The Connecticut Precane: Case study and curriculum. *Journal of Visual Impairment & Blindness, 82*(4), 178–181.

Galloway, A. (1981). Orientation and mobility readiness for the preschool deaf-blind child. *San Gabriel Valley School for Multiply-Handicapped Children,* 51–59.

Hapeman, L. B. (1967). Developmental concepts of blind children between the ages of 3 and 6 as they relate to orientation and mobility. *International Journal for the Education of the Blind, 17*(2), 41–48.

Harley, R. K., Long, R., Merbler, J. B., & Wood, T. A. (1986). The development of a program in O&M for multihandicapped blind infants. Final report. Nashville, TN: George Peabody College Press.

Harley, R. K., Merbler, J.B., & Wood, T. A. (1975). The development of a scale in orientation and mobility for multiply-impaired blind children. *Education of the Visually Handicapped,* **8,** 1–5.

Hazen, N. L. (1982). Spatial exploration and spatial knowledge: Individual and developmental differences in very young children. *Child Development,* **53,** 239–244.

Herman, J. F., Kolker, R. G., & Shaw, M. L. (1982). Effects of motor activity on children's intentional and incidental memory for spatial locations. *Child Development,* **53,** 239–244.

Hill, E. W. (1970). The formation of concepts involved in body position in space. *Education of the Visually Handicapped,* **2,** 112–115.

Hill, E. W., Dodson-Burk, B., & Taylor, C. R. (1992). The development and evaluation of an O&M screening for preschool children with visual impairments. *RE:view,* **23**(4), 165–176.

Hill, E. W., Rosen, S., Correa, V. I., & Langley, M. B. (1984). Preschool O&M: An expanded definition. *Education of the Visually Handicapped,* **16**(2), 58–71.

Hill, E. W., Smith, B. A., Dodson-Burk, B., & Rosen, S. (1987). O&M for preschool visually impaired children, in *AER Yearbook* (pp. 8–12). Washington, DC: Association of Education and Rehabilitation of the Blind and Visually Impaired.

Holt, K. S. (1981). Review: The assessment of walking in children with particular reference to cerebral palsy. *Child: Care, Health, and Development,* **7,** 281–297.

Joffee, E. (1988). A home-based orientation and mobility program for infants and toddlers. *Journal of Visual Impairment & Blindness,* **82,** 282–285.

Kephart, J. C., Kephart, C. P., & Schwarz, G. C. (1974). A journey into the world of the blind child. *Exceptional Children,* **40,** 421–427.

Ketterer, H. (1986). Mobility begins at birth: An early childhood orientation and mobility readiness program. In N. Neustadt-Noy, S. Merin, & Y. Schiff (Eds.), *Orientation and mobility of the visually impaired* (pp. 101–108).

Kronick, M. K. (1987). Children and canes: An adaptive approach. *Journal of Visual Impairment & Blindness,* **81,** 61–62.

Lord, E. (1969). The development of scales for the measurement of O&M of young blind children. *Exceptional Children,* **36**(2), 77–81.

Lowenfeld, B. (1981). The blind child as an integral part of the family and community. In B. Lowenfeld, *Berthold Lowenfeld on blindness and blind people.* New York: *American Foundation for the Blind.* (Original work published 1964).

Lydon, W. T. & McGraw, M. L. (1973). *Concept development of visually handicapped children.* New York: American Foundation for the Blind.

Mills, R. J. & Adamshick, D. R. (1969). The effectiveness of structured sensory training experiences prior to formal orientation and mobility instruction. *Education of the Visually Handicapped,* **1,** 14–21.

Morse, K. A. (1980). Modifications of the long cane for use by a multiply impaired child. *Journal of Visual Impairment & Blindness,* **74,** 15–18.

Olson, M. (1981). Enhancing the exploratory behavior of visually impaired preschoolers, *Journal of Visual Impairment & Blindness,* **75,** 373–377.

Palazesi, M. A., (1986). The need for motor development programs for visually impaired preschoolers. *Journal of Visual Impairment & Blindness,* **80,** 573–576.

Pereira, L. M. (1990). Spatial concepts and balance performance: Motor learning of blind and visually impaired children. *Journal of Visual Impairment & Blindness,* **84,** 109–110.

Pogrund, R. L., Fazzi, D. L., & Lampert, J.S. (Eds.). (1992). *Early focus: Working with young blind and visually impaired children and their families.* New York: American Foundation for the Blind.

Pogrund, R. L. & Rosen, S. J. (1989). The preschool blind child can be a cane user. *Journal of Visual Impairment & Blindness,* **83,** 431–439.

Raynor, S. & Drouillard, R. (1975). *Get a wiggle on!* Reston, VA: American Alliance for Health, Physical Education, Recreation, and Dance.

Schroeder, F. (1989). A step toward equality: Cane travel for the young blind child. *Future Reflections,* **8,** 3–8.

Skellenger, A. C. & Hill, E. W. (1991). Current practices and considerations regarding long cane instruction with preschool children. *Journal of Visual Impairment & Blindness,* **85,** 101–104.

Sonksen, P. M., Levitt, S., & Kitsinger, M. (1984). Identification of constraints acting upon motor development in young blind children. *Child, Care, Health & Development,* **10,** 273–286.

Stack, D. M. & Minnes, P. M. (1989). Aberrant motor development in three disabilities: Directions for research and practice. *Early Childhood Development,* **43,** 1–14.

Warren, D. H. (1976). Blindness and early development: What is known and what needs to be studied. *New Outlook for the Blind,* **70,** 5–16.

Warren, D. H. (1984). *Blindness and early childhood development* (2nd ed.). New York: American Foundation for the Blind.

Webster, R. (1976). *The road to freedom.* Jacksonville, IL: Katan Publications.

Wier, S. (1988). Cane travel and a question of when. *Journal of Visual Impairment & Blindness,* **82,** 197.

Willoughby, D. M. (1979). *A resource guide for parents and educators of blind children.* Baltimore: National Federation of the Blind.

Willoughby, D. M. & Duffy, S. (1989). *Handbook for itinerant teachers of blind and visually impaired students.* Baltimore: National Federation of the Blind.

Wurzburger, B. H. (1990). *Some ideas on O&M for preschool and early elementary school-aged visually impaired children.* Paper presented at the California Transcribers and Educators of the Visually Handicapped Conference, San Diego, CA.

TEACHING CHOICE-MAKING SKILLS TO STUDENTS WHO ARE DEAF-BLIND

Carole R. Gothelf, Daniel B. Crimmins, Caren A. Mercer, and Patricia A. Finocchiaro

Carole R. Gothelf *(CEC Chapter #45), Director, Education Services, The Jewish Guild for the Blind, New York, New York.* **Daniel B. Crimmins,** *Director, Department of Psychology, Westchester Institute for Human Development/University Affiliated Program, Valhalla, New York.* **Caren A. Mercer** *(CEC Chapter #45), Principal, Guild School, The Jewish Guild for the Blind, New York, New York.* **Patricia A. Finocchiaro,** *Coordinator, Day Treatment Program, The Jewish Guild for the Blind, New York, New York.*

The ability to make choices is an essential part of functioning independently and with dignity (Guess, Benson, & Siegel-Causey, 1985). Providing choice-making opportunities for students with the most severe disabilities (e.g., students who are deaf-blind with cognitive disabilities), who often do not communicate independently, presents a major challenge to educators. For example, Shevin and Klein (1984) have stressed that choice-making should be a "teaching target" (p. 60), yet there are few guidelines available for educators on

TABLE 1. CHOICE-MAKING INSTRUCTION

	STEP 1	STEP 2	STEP 3
PRINCIPLE	People typically make choices in the environments in which the outcomes of their choice are available.	The boundaries in which the choice-making activity takes place should be defined through the use of appropriate aids and cues. Providing boundaries minimizes the visual/motor and cognitive requirements of orienting and reaching.	Individual preferences play an important role in enhancing motivation for the activity.
PROCEDURE	Choosing what to eat should take place where the student normally eats. Teaching choice-making in an artificial environment removes many of the naturally occurring cues to the event.	A dycem placement can be used to secure a cafeteria tray on a table or on the lap tray of a student's wheelchair. A second dycem mat can be used to secure the plates and glasses on the tray. (Dycem is a nonslip plastic that is helpful in stabilizing objects on surfaces. It comes in reels or sheets that can be cut to size. It is portable, easily cleaned, inexpensive, and available from adaptive aids catalogs.)	The student is presented with two entree samples, one at a time. The items from which the student is choosing should be two foods that he or she is likely to want to eat.
SPECIAL CONSIDERATIONS	Administrative policies and procedures should ensure that the choice-making process can take place. This may involve working with the cafeteria staff or revising lunchtime schedules.	If cafeteria trays are not available or necessary, the plates of food can be placed on a dycem mat directly on a table. For students with vision, the color of the dycem should be selected to provide contrast with the tray or table and the plates.	Administrators should work with cafeteria staff to ensure that appropriate alternatives are made available. (E.g., if two hot meals are not available, a choice between a hot meal and sandwich or between two sandwiches should be substituted.) Staff should be aware that food preferences are influenced by a student's cultural and family background.

(table continues on next page)

From *Teaching Exceptional Children*, Vol. 26, No. 4, Summer 1994, pp. 32-35. © 1994 by The Council for Exceptional Children. Reprinted by permission.

(United Nations/O. Monsen)

When children have multiple disabilities, it is important to teach them about making choices.

	STEP 4	STEP 5	STEP 6	STEP 7
PRINCIPLE	Choices should be presented consistently in order in reinforce the physical structure within which choosing occurs. Placing the choices in the same locations in relation to the student's body each time helps the student to anticipate where the sample is likely to be.	The student is made aware of the food through tactile/kinesthetic cues (guided or paired movements between the teacher and the student) and/or visual, verbal, gestural, and object cues. The teacher must assess the conditions that facilitate comprehension (e.g., with gestures, without gestures, etc.)	Establishing routines within instructional sequences enables the student to anticipate the next step and encourages self-initiated choice-making. A pause or time delay in a sequence (hands in the lap) may serve as a prompt to the student to initiate an interaction or make a selection (Siegel-Causey & Ernst, 1989).	Reliable communication of preference depends upon a foundation of consistent responses to the student's nonverbal behaviors. Nonverbal behaviors need to be acknowledged by the teacher on the assumption that the individual is attempting to communicate meaningful dialog. This provides a basis for communicating shared meanings (Guess, et al., 1985; Williams, 1991).
PROCEDURE	The first sample is presented on the student's left, tasted with the left hand, and then removed. The second sample is then presented on the student's right, tasted with the right hand, and then removed. Care must be taken to ensure that the individual is not always choosing the sample on the right or the sample on the left.	For each sample of food, the student is guided through touching the plate, touching the food, smelling the food, and tasting the food. A staff member says the name of the food, signs it, and shapes the student's hands to sign the name of the food.	Both samples are then presented to the student. The student touches the left plate with the left hand and the right plate with the right hand. As the student touches each sample, he or she is reminded of its name. The student is then directed to place both hands in his or her lap (using verbal and/or physical prompting as needed). The student is then instructed, "It is time to pick what you want for lunch." Language input should be provided at a level and in a mode that the student can comprehend.	The student chooses the desired food by touching one of the samples, looking or making facial gestures, starting to eat, making vocal sounds and/or body movements, signing, or in any other way that indicates his or her preference.
SPECIAL CONSIDERATIONS	The student's ability to reach, grasp, and manipulate utensils or the food itself may be influenced by poor muscle tone, stability, or coordination, as well as limited visual functioning. Generally, proper postural alignment can be attained through the use of adaptive positioning equipment. Grasping and manipulating utensils can be assisted through the use of adaptive aids such as special spoons, plates with lips, or slant trays.	The student's receptive vocabulary may be limited. Natural routines should be maintained within the normal context of mealtime in order to help the student comprehend the expectancies for his or her behavior.	If the student does not respond when the question is repeated, the teacher says, "That's OK. If you don't want the meat or the rice, I'll ask you again soon." The teacher should always return and provide the student with another opportunity and additional prompting if necessary.	If the student reaches for both or neither, the teacher must repeat the previous procedure and reinforce that the student must choose one sample. The teacher must acknowledge any form of communication. If the student repeatedly reaches for both, he or she should be given some of each for lunch.

(table continues on next page)

how to do this. As a result, the systematic instruction necessary to teach students with severe disabilities how to make meaningful choices remains largely absent from the curricular content and daily routines of these students' educational programs.

◼

PROGRAM DESCRIPTION

This article offers a set of principles, procedures, and special considerations for teaching students who are deaf-blind with cognitive disabilities to make their own choices during mealtimes. It is intended to show teachers how a typical daily activity can be used to teach choice-making and how this skill can be increased in complexity as the student progresses.

Mealtime is ideal for such instruction because it naturally occurs on a consistent, daily basis in school, at home, and in community environments. The act of choosing what to eat or drink results in natural consequences that are generally self-reinforcing. Instruction centers on providing the student with structured opportunities for selecting foods, by offering a series of choices among familiar, meaningful, and disparate options.

The instructional principles and procedures are described in Table 1.

The procedures were field tested by classroom teachers, teacher assistants, administrative personnel, and parents of students from 7 to 14 years of age who are deaf-blind with cognitive and physical disabilities. Once the procedures were found to work, they were structured to make them understandable to virtually anyone who might be called on to offer a meal to a student, including his or her parent(s) and group home staff. As a follow up, the procedures were replicated and fine-tuned by the instructional staff of a day-treatment program serving adults with cognitive disabilities who are visually impaired or who are deaf-blind.

◼

IMPLICATIONS

The instructional procedures teach students about making choices and give them increased opportunity for control over one portion of their day. This provides several potential benefits. First, choice-making instruction allows students to take control of an aspect of their environment that is meaningful and motivating to them. This is significant in itself, because these students often have few opportunities for exerting such control. Second, there is evidence that student-selected tasks and reinforcers yield better performance than teacher-selected ones (Meyer & Evans, 1989; Parsons, Reid, Reynolds, & Bumgarner, 1990). Third, this finding has also been observed for challenging behaviors, with fewer challenging behaviors occurring when students select their activities than when the teacher assigns the activity (Crimmins & Gothelf, in press; Durand, 1990; Dyer, Dunlap, & Winterling, 1990).

A curricular approach that encourages students to exercise their own initiative requires both systematic teaching of choice-making and provision of opportunities to practice choosing. While this article provides examples of choice-making during mealtime, similar opportunities can be built into a variety of daily routines that promote the use of

STEP 8	STEP 9	STEP 10
omponents of everyday routines hould be employed to establish orrespondence between words and heir meanings. Routines enable tudents to take an active part in the ctivity and to communicate with the eacher.	In addition to establishing correspondence between words and their meanings, the process of systematically using routines in the choice-making process must be established.	Contingent communicative behavior is reinforced by getting the requested item. The student communicates through an action or a signal to indicate his or her preference.
he staff signs "Finished" for the ndesired plate, guides the student hrough the sign for "Finished," and rompts the student to move the late away.	The teacher signs "Eat" and the name of the desired food and prompts the student to do the same. This procedure must follow the previous one.	The student is served a full portion of the food that was selected.
itially, the student may require the eacher to move the hands for him r her. Subsequently, the teacher nd the student should move their ands together cooperatively, the tudent's hands riding on top of the eacher's. The teacher should pause n the pushing action, and allow the tudent to communicate a desire to ontinue by moving the teacher's ands.	The teacher may choose other ways to communicate the same message, such as signing the student's name followed by the signs for "Wants to eat" and the name of the food. Language input should be provided at a level and in a mode that the student can comprehend.	The student must join the cafeteria line to obtain the full portion of food.

this skill. Teachers are encouraged to provide choices in the context of natural routines that can be made increasingly more complex.

REFERENCES

Crimmins, D. B., & Gothelf, C. R., (in press). Examining the communicative purpose of behavior. In *American Foundation for the Blind: Deaf-Blind Project*. New York: AFB.

Durand, V. M. (1990). *Severe behavior problems: A functional communication training approach.* New York: Guilford.

Dyer, K., Dunlap, G., & Winterling, V. (1990). Effects of choice-making on the serious problem behaviors of students with severe handicaps. *Journal of Applied Behavior Analysis, 23,* 515–524.

Guess, D., Benson, H. A., & Siegel-Causey, E. (1985). Concepts and issues related to choice-making and autonomy among persons with severe disabilities. *The Journal of the Association for Persons with Severe Handicaps, 10,* 79–86.

Meyer, L. H., & Evans, I. M. (1989). *Nonaversive intervention for behavior problems: A manual for home and community.* Baltimore: Paul H. Brookes.

Parsons, M. B., & Reid, D. H. (1990). Assessing food preferences among persons with profound mental retardation: Providing opportunities to make choices. *Journal of Applied Behavior Analysis, 23,* 183–195.

Parsons, M. B., Reid, D. H., Reynolds, J., & Bumgarner, M. (1990). Effects of chosen versus assigned jobs on the work performance of persons with severe handicaps. *Journal of Applied Behavior Analysis, 23,* 253–258.

Shevin, M., & Klein, N. K. (1984). The importance of choice-making skills for students with severe disabilities. *The Journal of the Association for Persons with Severe Handicaps, 9,* 159–166.

Siegel-Causey, E., & Ernst, B. (1989). Theoretical orientation and research in nonsymbolic development. In E. Siegel-Causey & D. Guess (Eds.), *Enhancing nonsymbolic communication interactions among learners with severe disabilities* (pp. 17–51). Baltimore: Paul H. Brookes.

The preparation of this manuscript was supported in part by a grant from the New York State Department of Education (NYSED), Office for Special Education, Title VI-C. The information does not necessarily represent the policy of NYSED, and no official endorsement should be inferred.

The Success of Three Gifted Deaf-Blind Students in Inclusive Educational Programs

C.L. Ingraham, K. M. Daugherty, S. Gorrafa

Abstract: This article examines the challenges and successes of three academically gifted students in inclusive educational programs over four years and presents recommendations for teachers and parents who are contemplating the placement of students with similar needs in inclusive programs.

Since the enactment of the Education of the Handicapped Act (EHA), P.L. 94-142, an increasing number of students with combined vision and hearing impairments have been attending public school programs (Conlon, 1991; Roe & Roe, 1993; Tweedie & Baud, 1981; Zambone & Huebner, 1992). Each year, an estimated 1,100 students who are deaf-blind exit special education programs (Everson & Goodall, 1991), but it is not known how many of these students are gifted, of average intelligence, or have cognitive disabilities.

Like the EHA, the Individuals with Disabilities Education Act (IDEA), P.L. 101-476, states that students who are deaf-blind are entitled to a free and appropriate education in the least restrictive environment. Unlike the EHA, IDEA mandates the provision of effective transition services for deaf-blind students that are to be coordinated with appropriate educational and adult services agencies that reflect the needs of individual students.

Background

DEFINITION OF THE POPULATION

The exact number of gifted deaf-blind students who receive educational services from public school programs is not known, partly because of the various definitions of the population. For example, IDEA does not provide a clear, concise definition of *deaf-blind* or account for the various etiologies associated with deaf-blindness that may be progressive. However, the definition that appears in the 1992 amendments to the Rehabilitation Act is more inclusive and specific:

A. Congenitally Deaf-Blind—legal blindness and severe chronic hearing impairment that is present at birth

B. Adventitiously Deaf-Blind—legal blindness and severe chronic hearing impairment that occurs later in life

C. Congenital Vision Loss—Adventitious Hearing Loss— significant loss of vision (at least 20/70) and a hearing loss in at least the moderate range

D. Congenital Hearing Loss—Adventitious Vision Loss

E. Ill-defined, unspecified or unknown etiology—individual functions deaf-blind despite the inability to properly assess

THE STUDENTS

The case studies of the three students discussed in this article illustrate that whereas services can be mandated and coordinated, peer instruction and a sense of "belonging" cannot. The three students, two from Pennsylvania and one from Delaware, were successful academically, but each student was faced with his or her own challenges with respect to interaction with and acceptance by their peers.

Although the three students are deaf-blind because of two disorders—Leber's congenital amaurosis and retinal blastoma—the manner in which the disorders affected each of them was different. As a result, these students were not consistently viewed as deaf-blind. Often acknowledgment was given to the sensory impairment that presented the greatest challenge to the student or the teacher.

INTERVENTION

During the course of educational programming for the three students, the students' educational programs consulted with the Helen Keller National Center (HKNC)—a comprehensive short-term rehabilitation center that provides summer evaluations for deaf-blind

Reprinted with permission from the *Journal of Visual Impairment & Blindness,* May/June 1995, pp. 257-261. © 1995 by the American Foundation for the Blind, 11 Penn Plaza, Suite 300, New York, NY 10001.

students—to obtain information on the specific needs of deaf-blind students. It should be noted that this contact occurred both when the students were in residential programs for deaf or blind students and when they were enrolled in public school programs.

Three students were followed by the HKNC regional representative to determine the specific criteria that were needed to devise suitable individualized programs and to assess their skills when suitable programs were not present in the student's home state. Although not all deaf-blind students require an eight-week comprehensive evaluation at HKNC to determine their educational potential, in all of the cases this option was the most feasible. For those students whose age precluded their participation in the HKNC summer evaluation program, consultation was provided by the HKNC regional representative in the students' home communities until the students were able to participate in the HKNC evaluation program.

Services in Pennsylvania

In Pennsylvania, students with disabilities are often provided educational services through extended supported services called Intermediate Units (IUs), as well from segregated programs apart from regular education services. The two students from Pennsylvania received early educational intervention, including exposure to braille and sign language, in a residential school for the blind.

These two students were soon identified as two of the few cognitively gifted students in the residential school, and their need for peer interaction and an educational program better suited to the talents of such students was considered. With support from the supervisor of vision programs in the Pittsburgh Public School programs, the first deaf-blind student (Student A) was transitioned from the residential program to the Gifted and Talented Program at a nearby junior high school. The supervisor coordinated the services of the local technical support center, the IU, and the HKNC regional representative. The initial instruction equipped these two students with the necessary tools to enter the Gifted and Talented Program.

Student A had a moderate to severe hearing loss and a total loss of vision as a result of retinal blastoma. At the age of 13, he began participating in all classes in the junior high school with his nondisabled classmates and received support from both the vision and the hearing resource instructors. The overwhelming volume of educational materials that had to be transcribed into braille for him made the initial year of inclusion taxing for all who were involved. Student A typed homework assignments on a laptop computer and printed the

information out on a standard dot matrix printer for his sighted instructors to read.

Because of the vast knowledge of computer technology that Student A required, extensive computer instruction had to be provided. To accommodate his technological needs, the supervisor of vision programs wrote a grant to purchase comprehensive equipment (a character recognition scanner, an ink-print printer, a laptop computer with a refreshable braille display, a braille embosser, and a telecommunication device for deaf-blind users) that would enable Student A to gain independent access to all printed information.

Since Student A could comprehend spoken language with a hearing aid if he was positioned in the front of the classroom and could express himself verbally, he did not need extensive support services for communication. Furthermore, since his speech was clearly understood by his instructors and peers, he did not need a sign language interpreter.

The resource instructor was a valuable support person in Student A's educational program. With support from the resource instructor and itinerant vision consultants, Student A was able to participate in numerous academic competitions. Academically, his program was comparable to that of his nondisabled classmates except that the teachers were required to prepare lessons and assignments several days in advance to enable resource personnel or the student to transcribe information into an accessible format.

At the age of 12, Student B entered the Gifted and Talented Program at the same junior high as Student A. In addition to her vision and hearing losses caused by Leber's congenital amaurosis, Student B had a physical disability and required a walker to move to and from class. Because moving through the hallways and up and down stairs presented a hazard to her and her schoolmates, she used the elevator or a ramp, rather than the stairs, and was dismissed from class 5–10 minutes early to avoid possible collisions with the other students. Unlike Student A, Student B did not have sufficient hearing to comprehend spoken language, so her primary means of receptive communication was through the tactile signs of an interpreter assigned to her for each class. However, like Student A, her speech was intelligible and she could express herself verbally.

All the classroom material for Student B was brailled. In addition, she obtained equipment similar to the equipment that was purchased for Student A, but received training in the independent operation of the equipment from a local rehabilitation and adjustment training program for the blind, not from the school.

As is often the case with blindness agencies,

... the staff at this facility were either visually impaired or did not have sign language skills. Therefore, the HKNC recommended that both training on the equipment and interpreter services during training should be incorporated into the student's Individualized Educational Program (IEP), and financial support from the state rehabilitation agency covered the additional cost of using the interpreter. The commitment from the vocational rehabilitation agency to cover the cost of interpreter services is an excellent example of how vocational rehabilitation counselors can work cooperatively and establish a preliminary relationship with the educational program before a student leaves the school system (Ingraham, Carey, Vernon, & Berry, 1994).

In line with Murray's (1981) statement that each student in an inclusive setting should be viewed individually, it was realized that although these two students both met the definition of deaf-blind, they had different needs, and etiological factors were taken into consideration in placing them. The home school districts of both students were also supportive. Furthermore, as Thousand and Villa (1990) pointed out, transition planning should take place ahead of major moves from one educational program to the next. For these students, collaboration between the home school district and the host educational program was crucial to minimize the students' frustration and maximize their level of success.

Services in Delaware

Student C was totally deaf-blind as a result of Leber's congenital amaurosis and thus required extensive support services. Unlike the students in Pennsylvania, she received comprehensive educational support services outside a residential school program much earlier and had received sign language instruction at age 3 and braille instruction at age 4. In addition to speech therapy and occupational and physical therapy, she received mobility instruction and braille and sign language instruction continuously while she attended the state residential school for the deaf until she was 8 years old.

At the request of her parents, Student C was removed from the residential school program at the age of 8 and placed in a private program in her community because her parents believed that the inclusive environment provided greater challenges and a superior quality of education. Interpreter services from the school district and support from an itinerant instructor from the state rehabilitation agency were supplied when Student C was admitted to the inclusive program.

Much like the collaboration that occurred with Students A and B in Pennsylvania, many agencies came together to develop a comprehensive intervention team for Student C. Equipment that she would need for high school and for college was purchased with funds from the educational system that were funneled through the vocational rehabilitation program. This creative arrangement was made to enable Student C to keep the equipment after she would graduate from high school and college. An optical character recognition scanner, ink-print printer, braille embosser, Optacon, typewriter, desktop computer, refreshable braille display, and telecommunication device for the deaf-blind users were purchased with these combined funds.

In addressing the transition needs of this student, the educational team determined that she would need exposure to vocational and habilitation training. Because these services could not be provided by her current educational program, Student C was referred to HKNC for a comprehensive evaluation and subsequent training. Many students who attend HKNC for a summer evaluation return to their educational programs to receive training based on the findings of the comprehensive evaluation. However, it was decided that Student C would receive an evaluation before her junior year in high school and would return to HKNC for training the following summer. This approach allowed her to remain in her educational program for the entire school year and yet to receive the needed vocational exposure to complete her academic program.

Interaction with peers

The chief concern of the parents and instructors in the three students' educational programs was that although the students were academically successful in the inclusive environments and received excellent accommodations, their level of interaction with peers was disproportionate to their level of academic success. In short, all three students felt isolated and disconnected from everyday interactions and socializing with their classmates. Ironically, the presence of interpreters had a damaging effect on the students' ability to socialize with their peers. Often the interpreters were viewed as scrutinizing adults, rather than as nonsubjective support persons and became the students' connection with and sole source of communication and information with both the other students and the teachers. All information that was not provided in an alternate format was "filtered" through the interpreters.

In addition, the students' participation in scholastic competitions was often complicated by the presence of the interpreters, whom the other students often viewed as an added advantage for the deaf-blind students, not as a necessity for communication. Nevertheless, the students commented that although they often felt removed from social opportunities, the quality of the education that they received from the inclusive programs far outweighed these obstacles.

Harley, Garcia, and Williams (1989) recommended that administrators and consultants should evaluate all factors before recommending the placement of a student in an inclusive setting and that a child's rural or urban origin should be considered. The location of the preferred school programs and the follow-up support from the itinerant instructors who had experience in working with students who are deaf-blind were invaluable for the students' successful placements. At HKNC, questions are asked of all parents, administrators, and students about four basic factors before recommendations are made about the type of placement that would be most appropriate for a student who is deaf-blind. These four factors are etiology, age of onset, severity, and previous educational intervention. For example, Student C received a high-quality comprehensive program during the critical stages of maturation and language development, and her innate ability contributed greatly to the level of success that she achieved.

For all three students, preparation by the parents, support professionals, teachers, and the students themselves proved to be fundamental. Whether a student was participating in a class discussion of current events or an upcoming field trip or was reviewing vocabulary for a foreign-language class, the instructor had to be cognizant of the information that would be shared and whether it was indeed in an accessible format for a deaf-blind student. When an interpreter was involved, his or her background had to be considered as well. Furthermore, the interpreter would often take on the dual role of interpreter and tutor in that information that was supplied to the itinerant instructor to be transcribed was also given to the interpreter to review and to become familiar with.

The three students had above-average intelligence and achieved great academic success. Because the inclusive programs were not accustomed to accommodating deaf-blind students who functioned at such an advanced level, numerous meetings were held to discuss the specific services the students needed throughout their educational programs. Regular contact with the HKNC regional representative was maintained to ensure that the transition from each educational level and site to the next was as smooth as possible. Understanding of the individual students and their desired goals was crucial to the effectiveness of the collaboration

---

Checklist of Recommendations for Considering Inclusive Educational Placements

Etiology of the Disability
What was the cause of deaf-blindness? Often the cause of the disability will have an effect on how the student functions in various settings and under specific circumstances. For example, students with Usher syndrome may appear to be withdrawn and nonengaging with other students, partly because of their inability, as a result of visual field restrictions, to understand or perceive all information that is communicated (Vernon, Boughman, & Annala, 1982).

Age of Onset
At what age did the student's disability manifest itself? Disabilities that create barriers to communication are less complicated to address if the student acquired language before their onset.

Severity of the Disability
How severe is the student's disability? Often a student who is considered deaf-blind possesses some residual hearing or vision or both. The focus of the intervention for the student depends on how well the student uses his or her remaining sensory modalities.

Educational Background
What type of educational intervention did the student receive in the past? Students who have been exposed to language, either functional or conversational, have a greater language repertoire to draw from than do those students who have received no language intervention.

Support Services
What types of support services are available? Often students who are deaf-blind can effectively use services for the deaf or services for the blind. Depending on the severity of the student's sensory impairment and background, single-disability support services may be beneficial.

Box 1.

among the various agencies. It is important for administrators to support this type of collaboration (Thousand & Villa, 1989).

Recommendations for service providers

In providing support to and on behalf of these three students since 1981, the HKNC regional representative developed the checklist of recommendations presented in Box 1 that have proved practical for other cognitively gifted deaf-blind students in similar inclusive educational placements. However, it should be stressed here that each student must be looked at individually and that the impact of the placement on the student must be given serious consideration. The effects of possible isolation and efforts to address this potential barrier must be explored before placement. Because each new semester brings greater challenges socially as well as academically, the student's peer group and network of friends should be monitored closely. Often a minor misunderstanding can escalate into a major issue that can have devastating effects on the student's ability to perform academically. Each student discussed here was provided with a strong foundation from a segregated program. Although such support does not necessarily have to occur in a segregated setting, the comprehensive needs of the student must be fully addressed when the IEP is developed.

References

Conlon, S. (1991). The federal government's role in educating people with dual sensory impairments. *American Speech-Language-Hearing Association,* **32,** 42–45.

Everson, J. & Goodall, D. (1991). School work transition for youth who are both deaf and blind. *American Speech-Language-Hearing Association,* **33,** 45–47.

Harley, M., Garcia, M., & Williams, M.F. (1989). The educational placement of visually impaired children. *Journal of Visual Impairment & Blindness,* **83,** 512–517.

Ingraham, C.L., Carey, A., Vernon, M., & Berry, P. (1994). Deaf-blind clients and vocational rehabilitation: Practical guidelines for counselors. *Journal of Visual Impairment & Blindness,* **88,** 117–127.

Murray, J. (1981). Comments on the least restrictive environments for deaf-blind severe and pro-foundly handicapped children. *Journal of School Education,* **13,** 8–13.

Roe, C.E. & Roe, D. (1993). The dismantling of a culture: P.L. 94-142 and its effects on the education and future of deaf children. *Deaf American Monograph,* **2013,** 143–148.

Thousand, J. & Villa, R. (1989). *Accommodating for greater student variance in local schools.* Paper presented at the 1989 Convention of the Council for Exceptional Children, San Francisco.

Thousand, J. & Villa, R. (1990). Strategies for educating learners with severe disabilities within their local home schools and communities. *Focus on Exceptional Children,* **23,** 1–24.

Tweedie, D. & Baud, H. (1981). Future directions in education of deaf-blind multihandicapped children and youth. *American Annals of the Deaf,* pp. 829–834.

Vernon, M., Boughman, J., & Annala, L. (1982). Considerations in diagnosing Usher's syndrome: RP and hearing loss. *Journal of Visual Impairment & Blindness,* **76,** 258–261.

Zambone, A.M. & Huebner, K.M. (1992). Services for children and youth who are deaf-blind: An overview. *Journal of Visual Impairment & Blindness,* **86,** 287–290.

Cynthia L. Ingraham, M.S., representative, East Central Region, Helen Keller National Center for Deaf-Blind Youths and Adults, 6801 Kenilworth Avenue, Suite 100, Riverdale, MD 20737; *Kathryn M. Daugherty, Ph.D.,* supervisor, Division for Exceptional Children, St. Francis Medical Center Pittsburgh Public School Program, 4 East, 45th at Penn Avenue, Pittsburgh, PA 15201; *Sheila Gorrafa, M.Ed.,* former state coordinator of the Delaware Program for the Deaf-Blind, E4F Coffee Run, 614 Loveville Road, Hockessien, DE 19707.

Children with Physical and Health Impairments

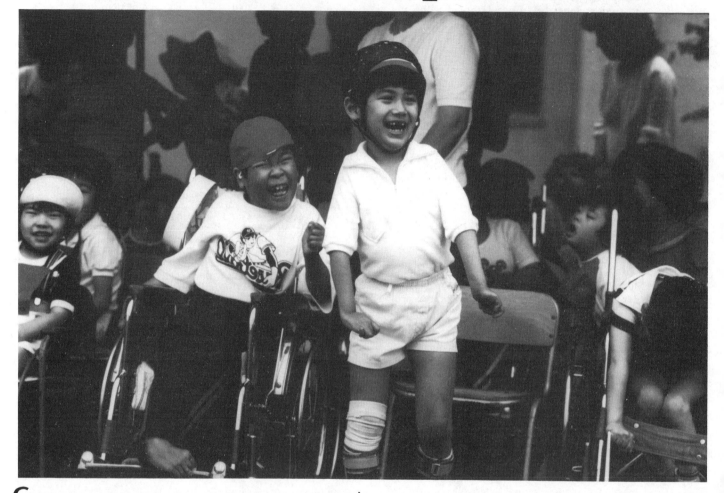

Children with physical and health impairments can be divided into classifications of mild, moderate, and profoundly disabled. Within most impairments, the same diagnosis may not produce the same degree of disability. For example, children with cerebral palsy may be mildly impaired, moderately impaired, or profoundly impaired. Physical impairments are usually defined as those that impair physical mobility and/or the ability to use one or more parts of the skeletomuscular system of the body. Health impairments are usually defined as those that impair stamina, and they predominantly affect one of the other systems of the body: cardiovascular, respiratory, gastrointestinal, endocrine, lymphatic, urinary, reproductive, sensory, or nervous systems. Physical and health impairments are not always mutually exclusive. Many times a child with a physical impairment also has a concurrent or contributing health impairment, and vice versa. In addition, children with physical and health impairments may also have multiple handicaps (e.g., the addition of one or more other disorders such as learning disability, mental retardation, behavioral disorder, communication disorder, or sensory disorder).

Some children with physical and health impairments have only transitory impairments; some have permanent but nonworsening impairments, and some have progressive impairments that make their education more complicated as the years pass and may even result in death before the end of the developmental/educational period.

Each of the dimensions defined in the preceding paragraphs makes educational planning for children with physical and health impairments very individualistic. The Individuals with Disabilities Education Act (IDEA) and its amendments mandate a free and appropriate public school education in the least restrictive environment for all children with physical and health impairments from the age of diagnosis until age 21, if needed. This may require only minimal special education, as in the cases of children with mild impairment, or with only one problem, or with a transitory disability. On the other end of the spectrum, children with profound or multiple or progressively worsening disabilities may need maximal special education services over a very long period of time. Between these two poles lie the majority of children with physical and health impairments. They have widely differing needs (qualitatively and quantitatively), depending on the nature of their impairments.

Physical (skeletomuscular) problems may have a neurological etiology (injury or dysfunction of the brain or spinal cord) or an orthopedic etiology (injury or dysfunction of an area of the muscles or skeletal bones). Regardless of etiology, the child with a physical impairment usually has a problem with mobility. A child with a mild impairment may be able to walk alone. A child with a moderate impairment may need crutches or other assistive aids to walk. A child with a more profound physical disability will probably be in a wheelchair.

Children with health impairments usually have to take medicine or follow a medical regimen in order to have the energy or salubrity required to attend school. The degree of impairment assessment (mild, moderate, profound) is usually based on limitations to activity (none, many), duration of problem (temporary, chronic, progressive), and extent of other problems (none, many).

When physical or health impairments are diagnosed in infancy or early childhood, an interdisciplinary team usually helps plan an individualized family service plan (IFSP) that includes working with parents, medical and/or surgical personnel, and preschool special education providers. When the physical or health impairment is diagnosed in the school years, the schoolteachers in regular and special education often collaborate with outside agencies, but more of the individualized educational programming (IEP) is in their hands. Children who have enjoyed normal physical and health status for years before becoming disabled often need more psychological support. Their self-esteem and self-confidence need to be supported as well as their academic progress. Teachers need to help them in their peer interactions and encourage their friendships

to continue. Teachers should also work closely with parents and significant others in the lives of children with sudden-onset physical and health impairments to ensure a smooth transition toward a more dependent lifestyle that also fosters independence and self-reliance.

The first article in this unit is a well-written, concise description of three fairly common reasons for physical and health impairments in children: (1) at-risk birth status (prematurity, low birth weight), (2) cancer, and (3) medical fragility (chronic, progressive illnesses that are profoundly disabling). Each of these conditions is described in enough detail to give the reader a grasp of the educational problems they pose. Not only are the natures of the conditions described, so too are the natures of their treatments. The authors have been praised for their clarification of the impairment categories and for their discussion of the educational implications of each category.

The second unit article deals with the human immunodeficiency virus (HIV) and AIDS. Two of the most rapidly growing populations of persons infected with HIV are infants (from prenatal exposure) and adolescents. Children and adolescents with HIV/AIDS have a progressively worsening and profoundly disabling impairment. The knowledge that they will die is not an excuse for refusing them the most appropriate education possible in the least restrictive environment. In addition, AIDS education should be given to all noninfected children. This essay discusses ways and means of such education.

The third and fourth unit articles present information about inclusive educational programming for children with physical and health impairments. The third article discusses how team teaching can help overcome some of the problems of placing children with multiple disabilities in regular education classes. The fourth article suggests using parents as a resource to help design the most appropriate IEPs for each child with physical and health impairments.

Looking Ahead: Challenge Questions

What are the education problems of children who survive high-risk birth, or cancer, or chronic debilitating diseases?

What should AIDS education entail?

How does team teaching benefit children with multiple disabilities? How can school-home partnerships assist children with disabilities?

Medical Treatment and Educational Problems In Children

NETTIE R. BARTEL AND
S. KENNETH THURMAN

NETTIE R. BARTEL (Temple University Chapter) and S. KENNETH THURMAN are professors in the Special Education Program, Department of Psychological Studies in Education, Temple University, Philadelphia.

Educators, in conjunction with the medical profession and parents, must respond to the special physical and cognitive needs of children who are alive today only because of advances in medical technology, Ms. Bartel and Mr. Thurman suggest.

JANET IS a 13-year-old who attends a junior high school. She is shorter and heavier than most of her classmates, and her physical development seems more suited to an elementary school. Although she is well-motivated and has two supportive parents, Janet is barely getting by in her school program. In elementary school, she was labeled "learning disabled" and received assistance in arithmetic and reading comprehension in a resource room. Her homeroom teacher describes Janet as industrious and earnest but indecisive and easily discouraged. Her mother states that Janet needs a structured home environment to enable her to function successfully in such everyday situations as getting herself ready for the school bus in the morning or completing her homework and household chores in the evening.

Janet's functioning is like that of many other students with learning disabilities. But there is one major difference. Janet was once precocious and lively. At age 5 she suddenly became anemic and sickly. Her pediatrician administered some blood tests and diagnosed her as having acute lymphocytic leukemia. She was taken to a major children's hospital in a nearby city and given treatment that saved her life. That treatment included cranial radiation.

Janet is one of thousands of children whose lives have been saved by aggressive medical treatment. Only later was it discovered that the very treatment that saved their lives also reduced the quality of their lives. These children provide poignant evidence that the miracles of modern medical technology sometimes come with unanticipated costs — costs that often must be borne by the very children whose lives are saved. These costs include the educational difficulties that can result from treatment.

We will consider the educational implications for three groups of children whose health conditions are such that they would not survive without medical intervention. Some of these children are like Janet: after a period of normal, healthy life, they contract a disease (often cancer) that would be fatal without medical treatment; yet the side effects of the treatment may cause school problems.

Other children seem normal at conception and during fetal development but have difficulties that can be attributed to the fact that they were born "too soon" or "too small." That is, they were born prematurely or born with low birth weight. Years ago, these babies would simply have died; today, many survive, sometimes with significant developmental problems.

A third group of children are those whose difficulties apparently go back to the prenatal period. These children (sometimes referred to as "medically fragile") are born with complex medical needs and remain alive only because of

From *Phi Delta Kappan*, September 1992, pp. 57-61. © 1992 by Phi Delta Kappa, Inc. Reprinted by permission.

intensive medical care that often continues throughout their lives. A few years ago, these children, too, would not have survived. But today they are found in significant numbers in our infant, preschool, and school programs.

CHILDREN TREATED FOR CANCER

There are a number of potentially lethal childhood diseases. However, because of their prevalence and the success with which they are being treated, we will concern ourselves here only with childhood cancers.

Nature of the condition. Cancer is a disease in which one or more cells of the body divide more rapidly than is healthy. The most common childhood cancer, acute lymphocytic leukemia (also known as acute lymphoblastic leukemia) is a cancer of the blood-forming organs of the body, including the bone marrow, the spleen, and the lymph nodes. Eighty percent of all cases of acute lymphocytic leukemia are seen in children, where it accounts for approximately one-third of total childhood cancers. In this disease, the body produces a large number of immature white blood cells that are unable to develop into normally functioning parts of the immune system. These immature cells proliferate rapidly, crowding out and interfering with the manufacture of other crucial blood cells, including red cells and platelets.

Taken together, leukemias and malignancies of the brain and nervous system account for more than half of all childhood cancers. Current statistics indicate that at least one child in 800 to 1,000 is a cancer survivor. This suggests that most schools have at least one survivor of childhood cancer in the student body.

The causes of these cancers are not known. As with other cancers, a number of factors appear to trigger the disease — including viruses, a genetic propensity, and exposure to radiation or other environmental factors.

The early symptoms of cancer in children are vague and frequently include headache, fatigue, a low-grade fever, easy bruising, and pallor. Bleeding, irritability, frequent infections, lowered resistance to infections, loss of appetite, weight loss, and facial puffiness are also seen. Diagnosis of acute lymphocytic leukemia is made by a complete blood count and an examination of a blood marrow sample. In the case of brain tumors, diagnostic imaging techniques — including x-rays, CAT scans, and NMRI (nuclear magnetic resonance imaging) — are often used.

Nature of the treatment. The treatment goal for acute lymphocytic leukemia is to eliminate all leukemic cells and to induce a remission. This goal is achieved by various combinations of radiation, chemotherapy, and systemic drug therapy. Treatments are given at the time of diagnosis and as a prophylaxis following initial treatment. Cranial radiation is also given prophylactically in an effort to prevent central nervous system disease later.

Treatment for brain tumors usually includes a combination of surgery, radiation, and chemotherapy. The use of cranial radiation has been suspected as a major cause of cognitive dysfunction. Because brain-tumor therapy requires much higher doses of radiation than does leukemia therapy, children with brain tumors may be at higher risk for subsequent learning problems than children with leukemia.

As recently as the 1950s a child diagnosed as having leukemia had an average life expectancy of three months. Today, almost 90% of such children achieve initial remission, and almost 80% are symptom-free five years after diagnosis. Patients with a poorer prognosis — boys, blacks, those younger than age 2 or older than age 10, and those with complications — require more aggressive treatment. The survival rate for brain cancer and nervous system cancer is not as high, hovering just above 50%.

Families of children with cancer frequently experience a roller coaster of emotions in which the initial shock of the diagnosis of a life-threatening disease is followed by relief at the apparently successful medical treatment. In cases in which the diagnosis calls for cranial radiation, this feeling may be followed by increasing concern on the part of the family as it becomes apparent that the child is manifesting learning difficulties that were not present previously. Many parents, in an attempt to avoid having the child stigmatized, may try to minimize the seriousness of the child's condition to school personnel. Yet, when learning problems become more pronounced, families and schools need to work closely together to address the special learning needs of the child.

Educational implications. Overall, children who survive leukemia or brain tumors show a decline in cognitive functioning and academic ability, with more severe problems evidenced by the latter group. While it is believed that acute lymphocytic leukemia does not in and of itself cause learning problems, the situation is more complicated in the case of brain tumors. It is difficult to separate the effects of the tumors themselves from the effects of the treatment. Recent studies have attempted to delineate the exact nature, severity, and possible cause or causes of adverse aftereffects of childhood cancers. It has been proposed that children treated at an early age (4 or younger) are more vulnerable to serious effects than are children treated when they are older. This suggestion is based in part on the theory that, because it is rapidly developing, the immature brain is more susceptible to adverse influences than the mature brain.

One major study reported intellectual and neuropsychological dysfunction over time in a group of children whose acute lymphocytic leukemia had been treated with cranial radiation.[1] This study is especially significant because it evaluated children both at the time of diagnosis and every six months for three years afterward. Three years after being treated with radiation and methotrexate, this group's average I.Q. score was 89, as compared to 109 at their first evaluation. The researchers concluded that the cognitive decline was not apparent until at least three years after treatment, that the children who were younger at diagnosis suffered greater adverse effects, and that children who received radiation experienced more adverse effects than children treated with methotrexate in the absence of radiation. The results of this study are typical of a number of similar studies, most of which have found an I.Q. decline of 12 to 20 points, with specific types of intellectual and academic deficits most frequently seen.

Between one-half and two-thirds of children who survive acute lymphocytic leukemia have been found to require some kind of special academic help, as compared to 15% of their siblings (about average for the school population as a whole). Teachers and parents report that these survivors take longer to complete tasks, have difficulty following multiple commands, and learn more slowly. They also describe them as less active, less expressive, and less able to concentrate.

A higher percentage of leukemia survivors than of the general student population attend special education classes or receive some form of specialized instruction; a higher than usual percentage of these children repeat grades. The reports of teachers and parents suggest that the specific areas in which these children experience the greatest difficulties include attention/concentration, mathematics, motor speed, visual/motor integration, timed performance, comprehension, spelling, planning ability, fine motor skills, and abstract thinking.

Of children successfully treated for brain tumors, about two-thirds are found in special education programs, while many of the rest require some specialized school help. Declines of 25 I.Q. points are common, and the school achievement of children who survive brain tumors is markedly below that of the general population. Learning disabilities are common. In one study in which none of the children with brain tumors had been in special education prior to diagnosis, at six months after treatment 50% of those under age 6 and 11% of those over age 6 were in special classes.

The specific learning problems of children who have been treated for brain tumors include attention deficits, problems with arithmetic, difficulty in self-organization, and reduced speed and dexterity. In addition to cognitive dysfunction and problems with school achievement, children treated for brain tumors often exhibit problems with emotional adjustment, shortened stature, and poor peer relations that stem from hair loss and otherwise feeling "different." Factors that seem to affect cognitive and academic functioning include amount of radiation, pre- and postoperative mental status, postoperative central nervous system infection, and how much of the head is irradiated.

Current treatment protocols for children with acute lymphocytic leukemia emphasize reducing or eliminating the use of cranial radiation whenever possible without reducing the child's survival chances. And fewer children with leukemia are receiving cranial radiation today than five years ago. Nevertheless, a significant number of such children still need this treatment if they are to have a chance of surviving. This means that educators will continue to see children with the specific cognitive deficits described above. The very success of treatment for these two most common childhood cancers is creating a population of children at risk academically and is presenting educators with the unique challenge of developing and implementing interventions

that may spare these children from failure in school. Improved medical interventions in the future will no doubt increase the rate of survival even more and result in the presence of more cancer survivors in our nation's schools.

LOW BIRTH WEIGHT AND PREMATURITY

Nature of the condition. Low birth weight is defined as weighing less than 2,500 grams or 5.5 pounds at birth. Very low birth weight refers to infants who weigh less than 1,500 grams or 3.3 pounds at birth, and extremely low birth weight is defined by a weight of 1,000 grams (or 2.2 pounds) or less at birth. In 1986 the National Center for Health Statistics reported that 6.8% of all infants born were classified as low birth weight. Given that there are between 3.5 and four million births each year in the U. S., this means that every year about 255,000 infants are born who can be classified as low birth weight. Sixty percent of all neonatal deaths (i.e., death within the first 28 days of life) can be accounted for by low birth weight, and 20% of babies who die in the first year of life were low weight at birth.

Typically, low birth weight is the result of premature birth or of intrauterine growth retardation. Birth is deemed premature when an infant is born after less than 37 weeks of gestation. Prematurity occurs in about 11% of all births, according to 1986 data from the National Center for Health Statistics. This means that about 412,000 infants are born prematurely each year. A number of factors are related to increased risk of premature birth, including adolescent pregnancy, maternal age greater than 35 years, poverty, poor nutrition, poor prenatal care, and drug use.

Retarded intrauterine growth is the other major contributor to low birth weight. This condition often results from decreased blood flow to the fetus that may be related to incomplete placental development, the effects of drugs, high altitude, or multiple births. It may also be related to certain chromosomal abnormalities. Babies whose growth was retarded in utero are referred to as small for gestational age. Unlike babies who are premature, babies who are small for gestational age are most often carried to full term. However, babies who are born prematurely may also be considered small for gestational age if their birth weight is more than 90% below the weight

that would be expected for their particular gestational age.

Both low birth weight and prematurity place infants at increased risk of poor development. Examining the literature since the early 1970s reveals an improving prognosis for low birth weight infants, especially those weighing less than 1,500 grams. In the early 1970s only about 20% of infants weighing less than 1,000 grams survived. By the early 1980s about 40% of these infants were surviving. A recent study also suggests that these infants are surviving with a lower incidence of developmental problems.[2] The data indicate that, by age 5, 80% of children who weighed 1,000 grams or less at birth showed either slight or only minor neurodevelopmental difficulties.

The prognosis for a low birth weight or premature infant can be influenced by a number of factors. The treatment of these infants in neonatal intensive care units may require physicians to deal with such complications as brain hemorrhages, lung damage, infections, and damage to sensory systems. Multiple complications may affect one infant, while another of equal birth weight or gestational age goes unaffected. Unfortunately, there is no way to tell at the onset which infant is more likely to experience such complications and to need extraordinary treatment.

The ultimate prognosis for these infants is most clearly mediated by environment. Studies have consistently demonstrated that infants of low birth weight and premature infants who are reared in enriched environments fare better than their counterparts who are reared in poverty or without the proper types of nurturance and stimulation from caregivers.

The birth and subsequent hospitalization of a premature or low birth weight infant can have significant impact on a family. The uncertainty experienced by the family during hospitalization can create stress. As one mother recalled:

> After I got over the initial shock of Julia's appearance it got easier to visit her. . . . I couldn't feel comfortable in the NICU [neonatal intensive care unit]. . . . Hospitals are intimidating; NICUs are even more so. I felt I had no control; I was just a bystander. Meanwhile, my poor husband was run ragged. [He] would work all day, and then drive to the hospital, which was a three hour round trip. [He] was also assembling furniture, painting her room, and scouting around for very tiny baby clothes.[3]

Once the infant has been brought home, the family remains under stress since the baby's course of development is not yet clear. In addition, prematurity alters the patterns of interaction between infants and their caregivers. Premature infants tend to be more irritable, less regular in their sleeping and eating patterns, and more ambiguous in the social cues that they emit. As a result, parents of these infants may tend to feel frustrated and less than competent.

Educational implications. Infants who survive low birth weight or prematurity need early intervention. At a minimum, these infants should be evaluated periodically to help make certain that they are developing properly. Early intervention should stress cognitive, language, and motor development and should focus on providing the necessary supports to the family to reduce stress and maximize the development of the child. The passage and implementation of P.L. 99-457 and its recent reauthorization with the passage of the Individuals with Disabilities Education Act Amendments (P.L. 102-119) provide the framework within which this early intervention can take place.

The need for special education services for these children as they get older is very much a function of the individual child. It is important to keep in mind that the largest percentage of children who experience low birth weight or who are premature function well within normal limits by the time they reach school age. Thus, while many children who begin life in neonatal intensive care units do manifest developmental and learning problems when they reach school age, it would be unwise to conclude that any child whose life begins under these trying circumstances is predestined to require special educational services.

THE MEDICALLY FRAGILE

Nature of the condition. The term *medically fragile* refers to children whose medical needs are complex and encompasses a wide range of conditions that affect the health and subsequent education and development of the children. Most often, the problems experienced by these children are chronic and require ongoing — frequently daily — treatment and monitoring (sometimes in a hospital setting) if the children are to survive. These children have conditions that are "extremely disabling or life-threatening. Usually such [children] are dependent on life-

support equipment such as ventilators, feeding tubes, or apnea (i.e., breathing) monitors for survival."[4] However, children with such conditions as diabetes, sickle-cell anemia, cystic fibrosis, and hemophilia may also on occasion manifest acute symptoms and have medical needs that significantly interfere with their education.

It is difficult to determine the incidence and prevalence of medically fragile children because the term is rather broad and because those children with multiple disabilities can end up being classified under some other label. The U.S. Department of Education estimates that, during the 1988-89 school year, there were 50,349 children between the ages of 6 and 21 who were classified as health-impaired and who were being served in special education programs across the nation.[5] Keep in mind that this low figure does not include any children who fall into another classification.

Because their conditions vary greatly, the exact prognosis of children with complex medical needs is difficult to determine. Many have decreased life expectancies. Some children with complex medical needs can experience relatively long periods of stability, though constant monitoring of their conditions remains necessary. For example, a child who has a tracheostomy and is dependent on a ventilator for assistance with breathing may be able to function reasonably well from day to day with proper suctioning, cleaning, and maintenance of the tubes that connect him or her to the ventilator. However, that situation may change rapidly if the child acquires an upper respiratory infection.

Families of medically fragile children often experience stresses that go beyond those of other families. They must adapt to the special needs of their child and often must learn how to maintain the equipment and use specialized devices and therapeutic techniques. Moreover, they must cope with the uncertainty of when their child's condition may suddenly become acute, requiring emergency treatment or hospitalization. At the same time, they may need to provide additional emotional support to help the child cope more easily with the medical condition. The constant care required by children who have complex medical needs can lead to parental fatigue and can create the potential for burnout. Such effects can adversely affect the relationships in the family.

Educational implications. Children with complex medical needs can be unique challenges to the education system. On occasion, these children will require homebound or hospital-based instruction. When they are attending school, these children may tire more easily and thus need periods of rest or inactivity between instructional sessions.

Nor is it uncommon for these children to require the services of a nurse or of a physical or occupational therapist in order to render treatment or to help them gain the most benefit from their learning experiences. Frequent or prolonged periods of hospitalization can further disrupt the educational process and frustrate the teacher, the child, and the family. Finally, it may be necessary to modify classroom space and routines in order to accommodate the equipment to maintain a child with complex medical needs. The effective education of these children depends on a flexible, interdisciplinary approach that can be equally responsive to their medical, psychological, and educational needs.

Educators, in conjunction with the medical profession and parents, must respond to the issues raised by the presence in our schools of children who are alive today only because of advances in medical technology. As we learn more about the physical and cognitive needs of these children and as their numbers increase with the use of new medical procedures, we must work to see that the quality of their lives remains at the highest possible level. Only as parents and educators are trained to help children overcome the cognitive problems brought about by their medical conditions and treatments can this goal be achieved.

---

1. Ann T. Meadows et al., "Declines in I.Q. Scores and Cognitive Dysfunction in Children with Acute Lymphocytic Leukemia," *Lancet*, vol. 2, 1981, pp. 1015-18.
2. William H. Kitchen et al., "Children of Birth Weight <1,000 Grams: Changing Outcome Between Ages 2 and 5 Years," *Pediatrics*, vol. 110, 1987, pp. 283-88.
3. Jean D. Rapacki, "The Neonatal Intensive Care Experience," *Children's Health Care*, vol. 20, 1991, p. 16.
4. Beverly A. Fraser, Robert N. Hensinger, and Judith A. Phelps, *Physical Management of Multiple Handicaps: A Professional's Guide*, 2nd ed. (Baltimore: Paul H. Brookes, 1990), p. 5.
5. *Thirteenth Annual Report to Congress on the Implementation of the Individuals with Disabilities Education Act* (Washington, D.C.: Office of Special Education and Rehabilitative Services, U.S Department of Education, 1991).

HIV/AIDS EDUCATION FOR STUDENTS WITH SPECIAL NEEDS

Examines how special educators can impact the spread of AIDS through appropriate and effective teaching

Steven E. Colson and Judith K. Carlson

We have moved into the second decade of a society living with Acquired Immune Deficiency Syndrome (AIDS). Research and education have focused our attention on this health crisis, but AIDS still remains a major epidemic with limited treatment options. Children and adolescents have not escaped the impact AIDS has had on our society. No longer is AIDS isolated to distant Hollywood figures or persons with alternative lifestyles. With greater frequency, today's youth are experiencing their personal heroes, their immediate families, and even their own peer groups infected with the Human Immunodeficiency Virus (HIV). Infants and teenagers represent two of the fastest growing populations at risk for contracting HIV (Simonds & Rogers, 1992).

As educators, most of us will not have the opportunity to influence the direction of medical research and intervention; however, we can still have a significant impact on the spread of this disease. Through education we have the power not only to teach the facts about AIDS but also to influence behavioral change through a winning combination of knowledge and decision-making skills. Research has

shown how educational efforts can influence attitudes and behavior with issues as diverse as cancer and sexually transmitted diseases (Ross, 1980). Education is our only effective inoculation against the spread of HIV disease, and educators are our key resource in meeting this challenge.

The challenge increases in the provision of HIV/AIDS education for children and adolescents with special needs. Mild to moderate cognitive and behavioral disabilities can influence critical thinking skills needed to make safe and effective decisions. Without these skills, students with disabilities are at even greater risk for HIV infection. Although some materials have been developed to teach AIDS education, few current curricula address the diverse needs of special populations. Failure to plan for these individual differences can result in life-threatening risks.

This article will examine how special educators can impact the spread of AIDS through appropriate and effective teaching. Included will be a brief overview of HIV disease, a description of the role of education as a prevention tool, and a rationale for the inclusion of students with special needs in AIDS education. A scope and sequence of

skills related to HIV/AIDS will be highlighted along with suggestions for implementing objectives across curricular areas. An extensive listing of multimedia resources includes hotlines, books, data banks, videos, and annotated bibliographies.

The Facts about HIV/AIDS

Educators cannot begin to adapt or teach an AIDS curriculum without first having a clear understanding of the facts regarding the history, prevalence, and transmission of this disease. Being committed to the importance of AIDS education as a prevention tool is only the first step. Teachers must make certain they do not communicate misinformation about AIDS or provide only limited information that could result in inadequate understanding. For this reason, AIDS education training programs for teachers, as well as students, should include sessions on basic AIDS information, with adequate time devoted to questions. This training piece is often referred to as "AIDS 101." The following section highlights aspects about HIV/AIDS that should be included in a comprehensive "AIDS 101" curriculum.

From *Intervention in School and Clinic*, May 1993, pp. 262-274. © 1993 by PRO-ED, Inc. Reprinted by permission.

Resource List

Hotlines

AIDS Crisisline	1-800/221-7044
National AIDS Information Line:	
English	1-800/342-AIDS
Spanish	1-800/344-SIDA
Hearing-impaired	1-800/AIDSTTY
National Drug Abuse Hotline	1-800/662-HELP
Sexually Transmitted Diseases National Hotline:	1-800/227-8922
Teen Tap Hotline	1-800/234-TEEN

Data Bases

AIDS School Health Education Database (CHID)	1-800/345-4277
National Institutes of Health	1-301/468-2162
ETR Associates/Network Publications	1-800/321-4407

Agencies and Organizations

National AIDS Information Clearinghouse
PO Box 6003
Rockville, MD 20805
1-800/458-5231

American Foundation for AIDS Research (AMFAR)
1515 Broadway, Suite 3601
New York, NY 10036
212/719-0033

AIDS Resource Center/National PTA
700 North Rush St.
Chicago, IL 60611
312/787-0977

Sex Information and Education Council of the U.S. (SIECUS)
New York University, 32 Washington Pl., Suite 52
New York, NY 10003
212/673-3850

History

In June of 1981 the Centers for Disease Control began to receive reports of cases of severe immune system suppression in otherwise healthy young adult men (Centers for Disease Control, 1981). Simultaneously, physicians began reporting opportunistic infections in young men such as Kaposi's sarcoma (a malignancy) and pneumocystis pneumonia, which would normally be diagnosed only in older and geographically isolated patients. Within 1 year, 355 serious cases of these infections were tallied. It was soon hypothesized that there could be a relationship between these cases and that a new syndrome was emerging that involved an infectious agent (Centers for Disease Control, 1982).

This new cluster of diseases was called by several names initially, but soon researchers agreed on the term "Acquired Immunodeficiency Syndrome" (AIDS). This term denoted that AIDS was a noninherited group of symptoms or conditions that together referred to a lack of, or disorder in, the body's system for fighting infection (Anderson, 1990). In 1984, both French and American researchers isolated the virus that caused AIDS and eventually this virus was referred to as HIV.

The AIDS virus is a retrovirus that permanently integrates itself into the genetic material of cells. A person can be infected by the virus and not appear to have any symptoms for many years (Anderson, 1990). This is a crucial part of AIDS information as many people still erroneously believe that if a person appears healthy he or she cannot be infectious. Originally, the lack of knowledge about the time between infection and the beginnings of specific symptoms created a silent epidemic where many thousands were unknowingly infected.

In the United States alone more than 230,000 persons have been diagnosed with AIDS and over 66% of these individuals have already died from AIDS-related illness (Kansas Department of Health and Environment, 1992).

Although there are several theories as to the origin of HIV disease, no single theory has been proven. HIV infection was first documented in countries with advanced medical technology; however, it is likely to have been prevalent in underdeveloped areas as well. Currently, HIV infection is a worldwide phenomenon affecting 5 to 10 million individuals (Anderson, 1990).

AIDS is often used incorrectly as a synonym for infection with HIV; however, people with HIV infection do not necessarily have AIDS. AIDS is just one stage in the progression of HIV disease. When people are first infected with HIV, they show no obvious symptoms and are classified in the asymptomatic stage. When they begin to show evidence of a weakened immune system, they are in the AIDS-related complex stage (ARC). When the immune system becomes so weakened that certain opportunistic infections and tumors are diagnosed, then the person is classified as having AIDS (Bartlett & Finkbeiner, 1991).

Prevalence

It is virtually impossible to have current, accurate statistics of the number of individuals affected by HIV/AIDS. The figures change daily and frequently underestimate actual occurrences of infection. Many individuals do not seek treatment until they experience symptoms related to immune system suppression.

Even the number of cases of AIDS attributed to individual states is misleading. When a person is identified as having AIDS, the case is counted on the state statistics where the individual lived at the time of diagnosis. However, many people with AIDS return home for care and treatment in the final stages of their illness. Therefore, funding based on diagnosis statistics results in states with large rural communities receiving unrealistically small resources in proportion to the true numbers of persons living with AIDS in their states.

Children under the age of 13 account for 2% of the reported cases of AIDS. These children are most frequently infected from mothers who were HIV positive. A disproportionate number of minority children, primarily black and Hispanic, are represented in this total (Centers for Disease Control, 1989). In New York and New Jersey, HIV/AIDS was surpassed only by accidents as the leading cause of death among black children under the age of 4 (Simonds & Rogers, 1992).

Less than 1% of current AIDS cases (872) have been reported in adolescents between the ages of 13 and 19. This statistic, however, can be misleading. Over 44,000 cases of AIDS are reported in the 20 to 29 age bracket. If the normal gestation period for HIV infection is 8 to 10 years, this means that the majority of these individuals were infected during adolescence.

Transmission

A core focus of any AIDS curriculum should be how AIDS is transmitted and when an HIV positive person can infect someone else. It should be made clear that AIDS is not transmitted through any ordinary activity of daily living. Hugging, kissing, or the sharing of eating utensils, glasses, and toilet facilities will not spread HIV. There is no evidence that HIV has ever been contracted in a swimming pool, from a mosquito bite, in a classroom, or in the workplace. Fortunately, AIDS is a basically weak virus that does not survive long outside of the body and it is difficult to contract (Anderson, 1990).

Rogers et al. (1990) reported on groups of children living in the same households, some with HIV infection and some without. These children shared common objects (e.g., toys, toothbrushes, kitchen utensils), bathed together, hugged, kissed, and slept in the same bed. Not one of the HIV-negative children became infected. The authors also reviewed 743 contacts in the medical literature and found no support that HIV could be transmitted by close, nonsexual contact or that casual contact constituted a risk.

There are, however, well-established, common ways in which the AIDS virus can be transmitted. These ways account for over 99% of all reported cases of HIV disease. HIV is most frequently transmitted through sexual activity or drug use that involves exposure to infected blood, semen, vaginal/cervical secretions, or breast milk. There are no known cases of HIV transmission by urine, feces, vomitus, sweat, tears, or saliva from infected persons. Body fluids that contain large numbers of white blood cells, especially blood and semen, are the most dangerous. Once infected with HIV,

persons must consider themselves infectious throughout the entire course of the disease (Bartlett & Finkbeiner, 1991).

A mutually monogamous relationship between two uninfected persons is the best assurance that HIV will not be spread sexually. The risk of HIV infection can be reduced with consistent,

---

"As educators, most of us will not have the opportunity to influence the direction of medical research and intervention; however, we can still have a significant impact on the spread of this disease."

---

proper use of latex condoms and a water-based spermicidal gel, preferably one containing the chemical nonoxynol-9. Individuals who are intravenous drug users must not share needles and are encouraged to use disposable needles or, as a less preferable option, to flush the needle and syringe with a 1:10 part chlorine bleach–water solution. Only abstinence from sexual intercourse and intravenous drug use can guarantee an absolutely safe environment for avoiding HIV infection.

Ninety percent of the young children with AIDS acquire their infection from their mothers. For infants, the primary means of transmission is through intrauterine exposure to the virus. The mother's infection frequently results from intravenous drug use. In one third of the cases, the mother is not a drug user herself, but has been infected by an HIV positive sexual partner who was exposed as a result of substance abuse (Anderson, 1990). Less frequent means of transmission to children include blood transfusions or exposure to infected breast milk.

HIV can also be transmitted through parenteral exposure to infected blood, blood products, or tissues. This type of transmission has occurred in cases involving transfusion of blood products

Facts About AIDS In Children

- Transmission from mothers infected with HIV accounts for nearly 85% of all pediatric AIDS cases (Simonds & Rogers, 1992).

- Perinatal infant infection can occur in utero, during labor or delivery, or through breast feeding (Oxtoby, 1988).

- Not all babies born to women with HIV infection will contract the virus. The transmission rate ranges between 9% and 65% (European Collaborative Study Group, 1988).

- Testing for HIV infection is difficult in children under 15 months of age since antibodies may not yet be measurable (Simonds & Rogers, 1992).

- In children the incubation period from infection to illness appears to be much shorter than in adults (Oxtoby, 1991).

- Ninety percent of children infected in utero will develop symptoms by age 4 (New York State Department of Health, 1990).

- Most children with AIDS die, and deaths related to HIV infection represent an increasing proportion of childhood deaths (Simonds & Rogers, 1992).

- Postmortem examination reveals that in a majority of pediatric AIDS cases brain mass is significantly reduced in the form of either microencephaly or brain atrophy. This brain involvement usually results in a chronically ill, often profoundly retarded child who may live for several years and require ongoing long-term care (Kozlowski, 1992).

- By 1995, HIV may become the largest infectious cause of mental retardation and encephalopathy in children under the age of 13 (Crocker & Cohen, 1990).

and clotting factors, organ or tissue transplantation, artificial insemination, and the sharing of needles or other sharp instruments used for activities such as tattooing or ear piercing.

Beginning in 1985, all donated blood was routinely screened for antibodies to HIV. This action has all but eliminated the spread of HIV through blood products. Currently, the risk of being exposed to HIV through a blood transfusion is estimated at only 1 in 40,000 transfused units (Ward et al., 1988). Since all blood is drawn with disposable needles, there is no risk of HIV-infection involved in donating blood.

Individuals can lower their risk of contracting HIV through blood products by following some specific procedures. Protection against parenteral exposure to the HIV virus is best achieved by reducing exposure to contaminated blood. To counteract growing fear and misinformation about how HIV is spread, the Centers for Disease Control and the Food and Drug Administration recommend all public and private sector workplaces enact the mandatory use of universal precautions. Universal precautions require treating all body fluids as potentially dangerous and offer solid protection for health care workers, teachers, day care providers, or others who may come in contact with HIV-infected individuals. Figure 1 summarizes the basic steps to implementing universal precautions.

The Role of Education as a Prevention Tool

Social reformers in the early part of this century believed that forthright education would end problems of sexually transmitted infection (Brandt, 1988). Education focused on hygiene and the majority of programs discussed only abstinence. These programs unrealistically hoped to end sexual activity outside of monogamous marriage.

Even though these reforms were not totally successful, they are still seen as the basic tenets of many sex education programs today. Lack of explicit information and discussion about safer sex alternatives are often left out of curricula due to conflicts of values and moral training. Although teaching students to "just say no" can be an effective prevention tool if practiced, many adolescents are not selecting abstinence. Data support this alarming lack of behavior change in adolescents, even

when they are exposed to education efforts (Reamer, 1991).

National, State, and Local Directives

Parents, educators, physicians, and health care providers are increasingly concerned that American children and youth are less healthy and less prepared to assume their responsibilities in society. Federal and state initiatives have addressed this concern resulting in comprehensive health care reform.

In 1990, the Centers for Disease Control (CDC) developed an operational definition of comprehensive school health education. They identified six categorical areas in which activities should be provided to help young people develop the skills needed to avoid an unhealthy lifestyle. These areas include (1) behaviors that result in unintentional and intentional injuries; (2) drug and alcohol abuse; (3) tobacco use; (4) inadequate physical activity; (5) imprudent dietary patterns; and (6) sexual behaviors that result in HIV infection, other sexually transmitted diseases, and unintended pregnancies.

Careful planning is essential to address all of these needs in an integrated

format. Becker and Joseph (1988) have documented that explicit programs that provide information about AIDS do produce significant changes in behavior. Individual groups have reduced the incidence of unprotected sex and the sharing of needles. There can be, though, a high incidence of recidivism as well as newcomers to unsafe behaviors, necessitating continuing educational efforts for all students at all grade levels.

The CDC and individual state departments of education have combined their expertise in developing AIDS guidelines, policies, and suggested curricula. Currently, nearly all states provide technical assistance to local education agencies to develop programs related to AIDS issues (Katsiyannis, 1992).

Inclusion of Students with Disabilities

Students with disabilities have the right to participate in a comprehensive health education program delivered by the public schools. They should be allowed to achieve their highest reasonable potential on the continuum of human sexual development. However,

---

The Centers for Disease Control and the Food and Drug Administration (1988) published guidelines designed to protect health care workers and to ensure the confidentiality of patients with HIV infection. These guidelines include the following information that is useful for classroom teachers.

- Blood should always be handled with latex or nonpermeable disposable gloves. The use of gloves is not necessary for feces, nasal secretions, sputum, sweat, saliva, tears, urine, and vomitus unless they are visibly tinged with blood. Handwashing is sufficient after handling material not containing blood.
- In all settings in which blood or bloody material is handled, gloves and a suitable receptable that closes tightly and is child-proof should be available. Although HIV does not survive well outside the body, all spillage of secretions should be cleaned up immediately with disinfectants. This is particularly important for cleaning up after a bloody nose or a large cut. Household bleach at a dilution of 1:10 should be used. Only objects that have come into contact with blood need to be cleaned with bleach.
- When intact skin is exposed to contaminated fluids, particularly blood, it should be washed with soap and water. Handwashing is sufficient for such activities as diaper change; toilet training; and clean-up of nasal secretions, stool, saliva, tears, or vomitus. If an open lesion or a mucous membrane appears to have been contaminated, AZT therapy should be considered.

Figure 1. Universal precautions for prevention of HIV, hepatitus B, and other blood-borne pathogens.

individuals with disabilities have been victimized by discriminatory myths for centuries. Many educators believed that if persons with developmental disabilities were taught about sex they would be bothered by it or, even worse, would be encouraged to engage in sexual activity. Even men and women with disabilities were treated differently, invoking age-old sexist stereotypes. Women were thought to have no interest in sex at all, while men were believed to have sexual feelings that were deviant in nature (Walker-Hirsch & Champagne, 1988).

Today, a comprehensive sexuality education program should include goals for relieving persons with disabilities of unnecessary guilt and anxieties emerging from these myths and negative attitudes. Information, carefully planned and evaluated, can help all students develop comfortably as sexual beings.

A Classroom HIV/AIDS Curriculum

It is important to remember that the most effective AIDS education will take place within the broader context of human sexuality education. How we feel about ourselves, our peers, and our social–emotional environment combines with our basic knowledge to determine our behavior. It is impossible to isolate one segment, such as HIV/AIDS prevention, and deal with it in a vacuum away from other aspects of psychosocial development.

HIV/AIDS Scope and Sequence

A primary component in a comprehensive AIDS curriculum must be a well-developed scope and sequence of skills. The following details a suggested scope and sequence highlighting critical concepts about HIV/AIDS education through eight skill areas: general knowledge ("AIDS 101"), affective development, sexuality and physical growth, positive self-esteem, personal relationships, sexual abuse, drug abuse, and sexual responsibility/safer sex practices.

The objectives in this scope and sequence were developed through personal experience and extensive reviews of model curriculum projects, including those from the Kansas State Department of Education and the South Dakota Department of Public Instruc-

Books

Books for Children

Blair, M. (1989). *Kids want to know about AIDS*. Rockville, MD: National AIDS Information Clearinghouse.

Fassler, D., & McQueen, K. (1990). *What's a virus anyway?: The kids' book about AIDS*. Burlington, VT: Waterford Books.

Hausherr, R. (1989). *Children and the AIDS virus: A book for children, parents, and teachers*. New York: Clarion Books.

Merryfield, M. (1990). *Come sit by me*. Toronto: Women's Press.

Quackenbush, M. (1988). *Does AIDS hurt?: Educating young children about AIDS*. Santa Cruz, CA: Network Publications.

Sanford, D. (1989). *David has AIDS*. Portland, OR: Multnomah.

Books for Adolescents

Hein, K., & DiGeronimo. (1989). *AIDS: Trading fears for facts: A guide for teens*. New York: Consumer Union of the United States, Inc.

Hubbard, B. (1991). *A disease called AIDS*. Reston, VA: American Alliance for Health, Physical Education, Recreation, and Dance.

Johnson, E.M. (1992). *What you can do to avoid AIDS*. New York: Random House.

Madaras, L. (1989). *Lynda Madaras talks to teens about AIDS*. Santa Cruz, CA: Network Publications.

National Joint Committee on Health and Safety. (1990). *Straight talk: A magazine for teens about AIDS*. Emmaus, PA: Custom Publishing, Rodale Press, Inc.

Yarber, W. (1991). *AIDS: What young adults need to know*. Reston, VA: American Alliance for Health, Physical Education, Recreation, and Dance.

Books for Parents and Professionals

Alyson, S. (1990). *You can do something about AIDS: New Edition*. Boston: The Stop AIDS Project, Inc.

Bayer, R. (1991). *Private acts, social consequences: AIDS and the politics of public health*. New Brunswick, NJ: Rutgers University Press.

Centers for Disease Control. (1989). *American responds to AIDS: A prevention guide for parents and other adults concerned about youth*. Washington, DC: Author.

Douglas, P.H., & Pinsky, L. (1992). *The essential AIDS fact book*. New York: Pocket Books.

Hitchens, W. (1992). *Fifty things you can do about AIDS*. Los Angeles: RGA Publishing Group.

Hooker, T., & Bryant, L. (1992). *HIV/AIDS: Facts to consider*. Denver: National Conference of State Legislatures (Phone: 303/830-2200).

Petrow, S. (1991). *Ending the HIV epidemic: Community strategies in disease prevention and health promotion*. Santa Cruz, CA: Network Publications.

Post, J., & McPherson, C. (1991). *Learning about AIDS*. Santa Cruz, CA: Network Publications.

Ralston, A. (1988). *What do our children need to know about AIDS? Guidelines for parents*. San Rafael, CA: HIV Education.

Books of Special Interest to Educators

American Foundation for AIDS Research. (1991). *Learning AIDS. An information resources directory*. New York: Author.

Bao, D., & Thorn, B. (1991). *Condom educator's guide*. Oakland, CA: The Men's Support Center (Phone: 510/891-0455).

Byron, E., & Katz, G. (Eds.). (1991). *HIV prevention and AIDS education: Resources for special educators*. Reston, VA: Council for Exceptional Children.

Collins, J.L., & Britton, P.O. (1990). *Training educators in HIV prevention: An inservice manual*. Santa Cruz, CA: Network Publications.

Kirp, D.L. (1989). *Learning by heart: AIDS and school children in American communities*. New Brunswick, NJ: Rutgers University Press.

Matiella, A.C. (1990). *Getting the word out: A practical guide to AIDS material development*. Santa Cruz, CA: Network Publications.

National Association of State Boards of Education. (1990). *Someone at school has AIDS: A guide to developing policies for students and school staff members who are infected with HIV*. Alexandria, VA: Author.

Quackenbush, M., Nelson, M., & Clark, K. (1991). *The AIDS challenge: Prevention education for young people*. Santa Cruz, CA: Network Publications.

Quackenbush, M., & Sargent, P. (1991). *Teaching AIDS: A resource guide on acquired immune deficiency syndrome*. Santa Cruz, CA: Network Publications.

(continues)

Books

Annotated Bibliographies
AIDS: Looking Forward/Looking Back
(AIDS-related resources for the general public)
SIECUS Publications Department, 32 Washington Pl., Suite 52
New York, NY 10003

Adolescents, AIDS, and HIV: Resources for Educators
(Print and audiovisual materials for HIV/AIDS education and prevention)
Center for Population Options, 1025 Vermont Ave., Suite 210
Washington, DC 20005

Working with AIDS
(Available print material for professionals)
SIECUS Publications Department, 32 Washington Pl., Suite 52
New York, NY 10003

---

tion. It is important to realize that these objectives represent only the most basic concepts related to HIV/AIDS education. They are by no means a comprehensive listing of all the skills that fall under the rubric of sexuality education.

As special educators, we are well aware how traditional scope and sequence information rarely addresses the diversity found in our classrooms. Traditional curricula, broken into linear age or grade brackets, have little meaning when applied to students whose splinter skills and inconsistent performance patterns jump between grade levels even within a given skill concept.

To address the needs of these special learners, this scope and sequence has been divided not into age or grade levels but into a loose hierarchical continuum ranging from readiness to advanced levels. This hierarchy provides a guideline for objectives to be presented early in a child's education on through more sophisticated concepts to be presented at later developmental levels. The exact point at which a given child is ready for a specific objective should be determined by a combination of prerequisite knowledge and the developmental stage of the child. The following descriptions differentiate the levels used in this scope and sequence:

Readiness Level: This is the awareness stage for each skill area. Readiness objectives expose the student to the existence of the basic concept and provide a frame of reference.

Beginning Level: These are the basic introductory concepts within a skill area. Beginning objectives provide recognition or rote learning of the concept.

Intermediate Level: This refers to higher-order concepts within a skill area. At this level the student is beginning to create linkages between pieces of information and apply cursory analytical abilities.

Advanced Level: These are the most sophisticated concepts within a skill area. The student is expected to synthesize information and apply evaluatory concepts to problem-solving and decision-making outcomes. At this level, the student must be able to generalize information to a variety of unique situations.

Keep in mind that a student may cycle back to lower developmental levels within or between skill areas. For example, he or she may be at the intermediate level in factual information but still at the readiness level in personal relationship development.

Specific Skill Areas

Although this scope and sequence is designed for HIV/AIDS education, you will see many objectives that do not directly address this issue. Sexuality development is a complex series of interconnecting concepts ranging from factual knowledge through independent decision making. Students need many prerequisite skills to interpret and utilize AIDS information. Disregarding these necessary prerequisites will limit the usefulness of the scope and sequence as well as exposing students to concepts for which they are not prepared.

As you teach these objectives, many other important concepts will arise that can and should be included in your personal curriculum. Some objectives will spill over into more than one category, and all objectives will be most effectively taught when integrated into the student's existing curriculum.

Skill Area 1: General Knowledge (AIDS 101)
Overall Goal: *To provide the student with factual information about identification, transmission, causes, and risk factors of HIV/AIDS*

Readiness level
The student will:

• Know the difference between being sick and being well
• Understand that some illnesses are "caught" and others are not "caught"
• Understand the concept of being healthy
• Identify health helpers

Beginning level
The student will:

• Understand the difference between infectious and noninfectious
• Know that disease is spread by germs
• Understand how our bodies fight disease
• Know the value of good personal hygiene habits
• Describe ways in which simple communicable disease is spread
• Understand personal responsibility in preventing and controlling disease
• Understand that you cannot get AIDS from a shot at the doctor
• Understand that you cannot get AIDS from playing with someone who has AIDS

Intermediate level
The student will:

• Define *virus* and *bacteria*
• Understand how the immune system helps protect the body

8. CHILDREN WITH PHYSICAL AND HEALTH IMPAIRMENTS

- Describe the domino effect of spreading disease from one person to another
- Identify and practice behaviors that help keep you healthy
- Understand what AIDS means
- Understand what HIV disease means
- Know different ways AIDS can be transmitted
- Describe behavior to avoid infection with HIV
- Understand how children can get AIDS

Advanced level
The student will:

- Develop a plan for rewarding self for positive health behaviors
- Explain how AIDS affects the immune system
- Understand that currently AIDS is considered a fatal disease
- Understand the basic structure of AIDS testing
- Know how to contact local health resources for AIDS information or testing
- Know what medications are used to treat AIDS
- Describe the phases of HIV infection
- Distinguish between facts, myths, and opinions about AIDS
- Demonstrate the ability to interpret media messages about AIDS
- Identify and practice behaviors that reduce the spread of AIDS

Skill Area 2: Affective Development
Overall Goal: *To understand the social and emotional impact of AIDS on the individual, the family, and/or the community*

Readiness level
The student will:

- Discuss how being sick can make you feel
- Understand that sick people still need friends
- Understand how being sick makes your family and friends concerned

Beginning level
The student will:

- Understand the basic concept of stress
- Identify how different body parts feel when you are experiencing stress

- Understand what it means for someone to die
- Realize that you can't get AIDS from playing with someone who is sick
- Understand that people don't get AIDS from being bad

Intermediate level
The student will:

- Practice different techniques for managing stress
- Identify forces that affect emotions and feelings
- Comprehend the finality of death

- Identify reasonable and unreasonable reactions to persons with AIDS

Advanced level
The student will:

- Refine skills in stress management and apply them to daily living
- Express personal fears about issues such as illness, AIDS, and death
- Examine the social and financial impact of AIDS on individuals, families, and communities
- Analyze public and media reactions to persons living with AIDS

Videos

Videos
Please preview before showing.

Thumbs Up for Kids (preschoolers)
AIMS Media
6901 Woodley Ave.
Van Nuys, CA 91406-4878
1-800/367-2467

Teen AIDS in Focus (adolescents)
San Francisco Study Center
PO Box 425646
San Francisco, CA 94142-5646
1-800/484-4173

It Can Happen to You: Adolescents and AIDS (adolescents)
Ohio Department of Health
35 East Chestnut St.
Columbus, OH 43215
1-614/644-1838

Time Out: The Truth About HIV, AIDS, and You (adolescents)
Magic Johnson and Arsenio Hall
Paramount Pictures Corp., 1992
Available at your local video store.

Mending Hearts (adolescents and adults)
Carle Medical Communications
510 West Main St.
Urbana, IL 61801
1-217/384-4838

We Bring a Quilt (adolescents and adults)
NAMES Project
PO Box 14573
San Francisco, CA 94114
1-415/863-5511

Common Threads (adult)
NAMES Project
Available at your local video store.

Saving a Generation: Successful Teaching Strategies for HIV Education in Grades 4–12 (Teachers and professionals)
Select Media
74 Varick St., Third Floor
New York, NY 10013
1-212/431-8923

- Examine ethical issues of AIDS such as confidentiality and discrimination

Skill Area 3: Sexuality and Physical Growth

Overall Goal: *To understand psychosocial and physical development as it relates to changes in the body and changes in sexual feelings*

Readiness level
The student will:

- Realize that boys and girls are different
- Describe how boys and girls are different
- Name and recognize body parts

Beginning level
The student will:

- Understand normalcy and health of genitalia
- Understand that certain personal activities are private (e.g., toileting, masturbation)
- Know where babies come from

Intermediate level
The student will:

- Realize that each person has sexual feelings
- Understand that sexuality is a natural and healthy part of personality
- Explain basic human reproduction and the concept of birth
- Explain the basic concept of death

Advanced level
The student will:

- Realize the effects of hormones on behavior
- Understand parents' ability to affect healthy fetal development
- Know the basic structure and function of the human reproductive system
- Understand the basic life cycle and changes/adjustments in the human body throughout life

Skill Area 4: Positive Self-Esteem

Overall Goal: *To provide an understanding of self-perceptions and their effect on sexual behavior and life choices*

Readiness level
The student will:

- Know it is normal to feel happy sometimes and sad other times
- Demonstrate self-confidence about simple choices and behavior
- Know that behavior has consequences

Beginning level
The student will:

- Discuss the importance of good decision making
- Demonstrate self-confidence about more complex choices and behavior
- Accept differences in self and other people

Intermediate level
The student will:

- Review and practice decision-making skills
- Understand individual needs and feelings
- Explain the importance of self-responsibility and self-respect
- Demonstrate the ability to set realistic goals

Advanced level
The student will:

- Demonstrate the use of decision-making strategies that utilize alternatives, options, and consequences
- Develop an appreciation of self and respect for others
- Understand that you do not have to be sexually active to feel good about yourself or make others feel good about themselves
- Assess own attitude about risk taking

Skill Area 5: Personal Relationships

Overall Goal: *To understand the range of appropriate interpersonal interactions with peers, family, and community*

Readiness level
The student will:

- Describe what a friend is
- Understand that people can have different kinds of friends
- Understand that each of us is a part of a larger family

Beginning level
The student will:

- Develop skills in self-expression and listening
- Understand how our behavior can affect others close to us
- Describe the responsibilities of friendship

Intermediate level
The student will:

- Recognize the impact of peer pressure, both positive and negative
- Understand developing special friendships with members of the opposite sex
- Understand the terms "heterosexual" and "homosexual" (gay and lesbian)
- Understand the concept of dating
- Demonstrate ways to show caring for persons living with AIDS

Advanced level
The student will:

- Understand the importance of individuality and group membership
- Understand the concept of individual rights
- Recognize that there are a variety of lifestyle choices
- Understand the choices, responsibilities, and rights of parenting

Skill Area 6: Sexual Abuse

Overall Goal: *To understand identification, prevention, and intervention related to sexual abuse*

Readiness level
The student will:

- Realize that bodies have private parts
- Know the difference between good and bad touch
- Understand that strangers can equal danger

Beginning level
The student will:

- Realize that you are important and you can choose who touches you
- Identify persons to go to when hurt or frightened
- Know the importance of reporting sexual abuse

Intermediate level
The student will:

- Recognize the basic signs of sexual abuse
- Understand the concept of sexual abuse and exploitation
- Know how to access prevention and intervention programs

Advanced level
The student will:

- Understand the social significance of sexual abuse and exploitation
- Understand the concepts of rape and date rape
- Identify personal strategies to use in unsafe situations
- Understand the concept of sexual harassment
- Discuss how sexual abuse can expose children to HIV infection

Skill Area 7: Drug Abuse
Overall Goal: *To understand identification, prevention, and intervention related to drug abuse*

Readiness level
The student will:

- Realize that some drugs can help and others hurt
- Know who you should get drugs from
- Describe different ways people take medicine

Beginning level
The student will:

- Understand the importance of abstaining from drug abuse
- Practice saying no to peers or adults who offer drugs
- Understand the concept of IV drug use

Intermediate level
The student will:

- Know about basic drugs that are abused and what they can do to you
- Identify how drug and alcohol abuse can affect behavior
- Understand how drug-related behaviors put individuals at high risk for HIV infection
- Know where to turn for help if self or friends are involved in drug abuse

Advanced level
The student will:

- Recognize the social and financial impact of drug abuse on individuals, families, and communities

- Describe ways persons involved in IV drug use can protect themselves from HIV infection
- Develop a personal plan to confront social pressures related to drug abuse
- Apply refusal skills to turn down drugs in peer pressure situations

---

"Through education we have the power not only to teach the facts about AIDS but also to influence behavioral change through a winning combination of knowledge and decision-making skills."

Skill Area 8: Sexual Responsibility and Safer Sex Practices
Overall Goal: *To understand the basic constructs of responsible sexual choices and sexual behavior*

Readiness level
The student will:

- Follow basic family rules
- Follow basic classroom rules
- Make simple choices such as what toys to play with or what food to eat

Beginning level
The student will:

- Understand the difference between blind obedience and decisive rule following
- Make more complex choices such as selecting friends and activities
- Know that some adults have sexual intercourse

Intermediate level
The student will:

- Realize that being sexually active is a choice
- Discuss the benefits of delaying sexual intercourse
- Understand the consequences of unplanned pregnancy and parenthood

- Describe how AIDS can be transmitted through sexual intercourse
- List sexual behaviors that put an individual at high risk for HIV infection

Advanced level
The student will:

- Understand the consequences of sexual behavior (including pregnancy, AIDS, sexually transmitted diseases, and emotional reactions)
- Describe the differences between love, lust, and infatuation
- Understand the concepts of genital intercourse, anal intercourse, and oral sex
- Know appropriate expression and control of sex drive
- Deal actively with peer pressure to have sex
- Understand concepts and importance of abstinence and mutual monogamy
- Understand basic condom and spermicide use and its effect in avoiding transmission of AIDS
- Describe safer sex practices
- Apply HIV/AIDS information to personal sexual choices

Evaluating HIV/AIDS Curricula
Some major publishing companies offer prepared curricula for HIV/AIDS education. As with all preset curricula, special educators have to be aware of the modifications and alterations needed to make these materials applicable for students with special needs. The Association for the Advancement of Health Education (1989), in collaboration with the Council for Exceptional Children (CEC), provides a series of guidelines for special educators to assist in reviewing AIDS curricula. These guidelines detail nine areas that should be considered in the selection of an AIDS curriculum for exceptional learners:

1. The goals of the curriculum should be clearly stated and targeted for special learners. Goals should also be consistent with the Centers for Disease Control guidelines for AIDS education.
2. Objectives should be clearly established and include both cognitive and affective components.
3. Concepts should be relevant and geared for the specific developmen-

tal level of the ability and age group involved.

4. The scope and sequence of the curriculum should delineate prerequisite concepts and provide appropriate learning activities. These activities should follow a logical sequence, encouraging discussion and addressing the myths and fears associated with HIV/AIDS.

5. The curriculum should include an evaluation component to determine the extent to which objectives are met. An additional evaluation component should address implementation of the curriculum.

6. A staff development component should be included to address knowledge and skills needed by teachers and to provide suggestions for interacting with health educators.

7. The curriculum should allow for parent and community involvement and should be sensitive to the values of the community in which it will be implemented. The curriculum should be reviewed by parents, students, medical personnel, and educators prior to implementation.

8. The curriculum should promote interagency, interoffice, and interdepartmental cooperation.

9. The materials utilized should be easily accessible and usable, with information presented in an appealing format.

Implementing an HIV/AIDS Curriculum

Many factors will affect how you begin implementing HIV/AIDS education in your classroom. We are all influenced by our personal experience, knowledge, and comfort levels. Teachers and students must be assured of a safe environment to discuss the sensi-

tive issues of AIDS. A set of ground rules, prepared in advance, can establish this atmosphere of respect and security. Although ground rules are best prepared with student input and ownership, Figure 2 offers some general guidelines for beginning this process.

Once objectives have been developed and ground rules established, instruction can begin. Effective instruction techniques should be utilized when you are teaching students with disabilities. Depending on the individual needs of each special learner, modifications and adaptations must be made.

The following effective instruction techniques are intended to build on a student's strengths while compensating for weaker areas. They can be incorporated into lesson plans and activities in your AIDS curriculum.

Goal Setting

Goals should be explicit and matched to the objectives, as well as to the student's level of performance. Objectives should be reviewed and modified using a calendar or timeline.

Instructional Grouping

Whole groups should be used when you are introducing new skills and concepts. Smaller, heterogeneous groups should be used for practice and higher order thinking skills. Group rewards can be used; however, individual accountability is important. Grouping should be varied frequently. Peer tutoring or cooperative learning methods can be used to optimize time and assistance concerns.

Time Management

Classroom instruction should occur at a brisk pace, minimizing noninstructional time. Self-paced seatwork

should be provided to reinforce skills. Homework should review concepts already well established.

Routines

Routines for utilizing materials, completing assignments, and securing assistance should be planned and taught in advance. Transitions within activities should be smooth and there should be little or no "down time" between activities.

Expectations

Standards for behavior and performance should be clear and consistent, with equitable application of reinforcement. Teachers should maintain explicit, high expectations for all students. These expectations should be posted and frequently reviewed by the group. Behavior management should reinforce positive, prosocial behavior and focus on the behavior, not the student.

Instruction

Instruction should be clear and targeted, with lessons carefully planned. Effective questioning strategies should be used that give all students an equal opportunity to respond. Regular feedback, both positive and critical, should be given. Concepts should be reviewed regularly and retaught, when necessary, for mastery.

Assessment

Both formative and summative evaluation should be used throughout instruction. Assessment information should lead to instructional planning. Progress should be closely monitored and students should have input into their own evaluation.

There are other important considerations when you are determining your individual approach to educating students with special needs about AIDS (Quackenbush & Villarreal, 1988). In private discussions with an individual student, your approach should differ from that used with a group of students. Time constraints will play an important role and there should be adequate time to provide closure as well as time for questions and comments at the conclusion of the session. Your own sense of preparedness will influ-

---

- No preaching or put-downs
- No personal questions
- No question is "dumb"
- Speak for yourself (Use "I" messages)
- Everyone has the right to pass on activities or questions
- No talking about comments outside of the group
- Bring complaints directly to the teacher

Figure 2. Ground rules for discussing sexuality in the classroom.

Note. Adapted from Kansas State Department of Education. (1991). *Human Sexuality and AIDS Education for Special Populations, Regional Trainer Manual.* Topeka: Author.

ence the depth of each discussion. Spontaneous questions may be covered less completely than a planned agenda. If this is the first time the group has discussed a specific issue, you will need to provide time for desensitization and opportunities to develop a comfort level with the content.

Fielding Student Questions

Teachers should be able to answer student questions about sexual behavior or orientation without digressing into detailed information about techniques and practices. When you are answering questions about sensitive issues, personal values and ethics often surface. Teachers can reinforce certain universal values like the following: (a) It is wrong to hurt another person, (b) it is wrong to pressure another person to do something he or she doesn't want to do, (c) it is wrong for an adult to use a child for sex, and (d) rape is never justified (Shapiro, 1991a). For other questions involving ethical issues, students should be directed to examine their own values, as well as their family moral and religious beliefs.

One nonthreatening approach to addressing student questions is the Anonymous Question Box. With this technique, students are encouraged to write questions on any sexuality topic and place them in a designated container. The teacher then selects questions at random and answers them in front of the entire group. This format allows students to ask questions they would not feel comfortable posing as part of a group discussion.

Students' questions about sexuality generally fall into a few basic categories. Questions asking for factual information should be answered to the best of the teacher's ability. It is acceptable for a teacher to say, "I don't know that, but I will find the answer for you." Questions about what is normal require assurance that things such as wet dreams, growth in size of genitalia/breasts, and thoughts of sex are all part of adolescent development. Questions asking permission and questions about values are tricky to answer because they are directly linked to personal belief systems. Teachers may turn these questions into requests for factual information and, when necessary, refer the student back to his or her family for values discussion. Questions to shock, such as, "Can you get AIDS

from sex with your dog?" should be answered with factual information and the teacher should quickly move on to another question. It is important that the teacher does not reinforce this type of question by becoming visibly flustered or angry. Personal questions, such as, "How often do you have sex with your boyfriend?" are not acceptable from students or teachers. The group should be reminded of the ground rule prohibiting personal questions (Shapiro, 1991b). Figure 3 offers some philosophical guidelines for answering tough questions about sexuality.

It is critical that teachers present information in a way that students can grasp the meaning as well as the behavioral implications. Do not assume that a level of generalization will occur without setting the framework for such a transfer. Cognitive, physical, and psychological differences may limit the understanding of complex concepts and impact the student's ability to synthesize and apply information.

Conclusions

It is easy to get discouraged about the AIDS epidemic. The numbers of persons infected with HIV continue to grow, especially women, children, and people of color. Many youth do not feel vulnerable to AIDS and have yet to change their high-risk behaviors. Effective treatments remain illusive and research continues to be underfunded. The enormous fiscal and human resources needed to combat this disease are overwhelming an already inadequate health care system. More and more families are experiencing AIDS first hand, with certain communities particularly devastated.

Yet, there still remains a vocal minority who do not want AIDS education in the schools. These individuals continue to misrepresent the enormity of this epidemic and promote unsubstantiated fear and lack of compassion for people living with AIDS. These discriminatory practices make it even more difficult to provide the kind of united effort necessary to confront this crisis.

Educators, especially those working with children and youth with disabilities, must fight these challenges with a renewed sense of mission. We must continue to educate ourselves about the facts of HIV/AIDS and must struggle to eliminate the barriers to implementing AIDS education in every school. We must advocate for the allotment of more resources and work with our community members to attain an integrated commitment. We must strive to help our students and colleagues develop a caring and compassionate attitude toward persons living with AIDS.

We have much to do to insure that all students are prepared for healthy adult lives, adequately protected from HIV infection. Each of us has touched the lives of so many individuals with disabilities. Let us continue to meet this challenge to empower students to make life-saving decisions.

1. Always be respectful of the diversity of moral/religious beliefs.
2. Refer to family/church on questions of values. Support students in sticking up for their own values.
3. Assure students that they are normal and allay fears and worries.
4. Emphasize similarities and downplay differences.
5. Occasionally, it may be best to rephrase a question; however, no question should be discarded.
6. Don't give permission. Offer factual information and support for personal values.
7. It is acceptable to admit you don't know an answer or that a question makes you feel uncomfortable. You should seek appropriate answers or resources (individuals who can comfortably address the issue) for the student.
8. Allow students to use the language they know but teach them correct terminology.
9. Don't get into technique or "how to" explanations.

Figure 3. Basic philosophy for answering questions about sexuality.
Reprinted by permission from Marian Shapiro, certified sexuality educator.

Steven E. Colson is a courtesy assistant professor in the Department of Special Education at the University of Kansas Medical Center, where he also serves as the educational diagnostician for the Children's Rehabilitation Unit. **Judith K. Carlson** is a doctoral candidate in the Department of Special Education at the University of Kansas, specializing in learning disabilities and behavior disorders. Her current research interests focus on crisis intervention education. Address: Steven E. Colson, University of Kansas Medical Center, Department of Special Education, 4001 Miller Bldg., 3901 Rainbow Blvd., Kansas City, KS 66160-7335.

References

Anderson, G. (1990). *Courage to care: Responding to the crisis of children with AIDS.* Washington, DC: Child Welfare League of America.

Association for the Advancement of Health Education. (1989). *Summary of the National Forum on HIV/AIDS Prevention Education for Children and Youth with Special Education Needs.* Reston, VA: Author.

Bartlett, J.G., & Finkbeiner, A.K. (1991). *The guide to living with HIV infection.* Baltimore: Johns Hopkins University Press.

Becker, M., & Joseph, J. (1988). AIDS and behavioral change to reduce risk: A review. *American Journal of Public Health, 78,* 394–410.

Brandt, A. (1988). AIDS in historical perspective: Lessons from the history of sexually transmitted diseases. *American Journal of Public Health, 78,* 367–371.

Centers for Disease Control. (1981). Kaposi's sarcoma and pneumocystis pneumonia among homosexual men in New York and California. *Morbidity and Mortality Weekly Report, 30,* 305.

Centers for Disease Control. (1982). Unexplained immunodeficiency and opportunistic infections in children. *Morbidity and Mortality Weekly Report, 31,* 665.

Centers for Disease Control. (1988). Update: Universal precautions for prevention of transmission of Human Immunodeficiency Virus, hepatitis B virus, and other bloodborne pathogens in health-care settings. *Morbidity and Mortality Weekly Report, 37,* 377–387.

Centers for Disease Control. (1989). *HIV/AIDS surveillance.* Atlanta: Author.

Centers for Disease Control. (1990). *Operational definition of comprehensive school health education.* Atlanta: Division of Adolescent and School Health.

Crocker, A., & Cohen, H. (1990). *Guidelines on developmental services for children and adults with HIV infection.* Silver Spring, MD: American Association of University Affiliated Programs.

European Collaborative Study Group. (1988). Mother-to-child transmission of HIV infection. *Lancet, 11,* 1039.

Kansas Department of Education. (1991). *Human sexuality and AIDS education for special populations, regional trainer manual.* Topeka: Author.

Kansas Department of Health and Environment. (1992). *HIV/AIDS quarterly update: Diagnosed cases.* Topeka: Author.

Katsiyannis, A. (1992). Policy issues in school attendance of children with AIDS: A national survey. *The Journal of Special Education, 26,* 219–226.

Kozlowski, P.B. (1992). Neuropathology of HIV infection in children. In A.C. Crocker, H.J. Cohen, & T.A. Kastner (Eds.), *HIV infection and developmental disabilities: A resource for service providers* (pp. 25–32). Baltimore: Brookes.

New York State Department of Health. (1990). AIDS morbidity and mortality. *Epidemiology Notes, 10,* 1–2.

Oxtoby, M. (1988). Human immunodeficiency virus and other viruses in human milk: Placing the issues in broader perspective. *Pediatric Infectious Disease Journal, 7,* 825–835.

Oxtoby, M. (1991). Perinatally acquired human immunodeficiency virus infection. In P. Pisso & C. Wilfert (Eds.), *Pediatric AIDS: The challenge of HIV infection in infants, children, and adolescents* (pp. 3–21). Baltimore: Williams & Wilkins.

Quackenbush, M., & Villarreal, S. (1988). *Does AIDS hurt? Educating young children about AIDS.* Santa Cruz, CA: Network Publications.

Reamer, F.G. (1991). *AIDS and ethics.* New York: Columbia University Press.

Rogers, M.F. (1990). Lack of transmission of human immunodeficiency virus from infected children to their household contacts. *Pediatrics, 85,* 801–807.

Ross, C.P. (1980). Mobilizing schools for suicide prevention. *Suicide and Life Threatening Behavior, 10,* 239–243.

Shapiro, M. (1991a). *Answering tough questions in sex ed class.* Unpublished manuscript.

Shapiro, M. (1991b). *A word about values.* Unpublished manuscript.

Simonds, R.J., & Rogers, M.F. (1992). Epidemiology of HIV infection in children and other populations. In A.C. Crocker, H.J. Cohen, & T.A. Kastner (Eds.), *HIV infection and developmental disabilities: A resource for service providers* (pp. 3–14). Baltimore: Brookes.

Walker-Hirsch, L., & Champagne, M.P. (1988). *Circles III: Safer ways.* Santa Barbara, CA: James Stansfield & Co.

Ward, J., Holmberg, S., Allen, J., Cohn, D., Critchley, S., Kleinman, S., Lenes, B., Ravenholt, O., Davis, J., Quinn, M., & Jaffe, H. (1988). Transmission of human immunodeficiency virus by blood transfusions screened as negative for HIV antibody. *New England Journal of Medicine, 318,* 473–478.

Creating Inclusionary Opportunities for Learners with Multiple Disabilities:

A

Team-Teaching

Approach

Students with multiple disabilities often have severe learning delays combined with other difficulties. These students may have orthopedic or health impairments, visual impairments, or hearing or speech disabilities. They may use unconventional behavior to communicate a basic need or desire, or they may have any combination of disabilities. Because these students present numerous areas of need, many general educators express concerns about including learners with multiple disabilities in their classrooms. These concerns are realistic—the inordinate amount of time these learners take away from their peers without disabilities and the traditionally required high learner/teacher ratios (Schaffner & Buswell, 1991). Providing a least restrictive environment for students with multiple disabilities has often been problematic.

To alleviate some of these concerns and to increase and improve inclusionary practices for learners with multiple disabilities in our school, we devised a plan to use team-teaching and cooperative learning activities in a combined classroom. (One author is a special education teacher and the other is a general education teacher.) Our purpose was to teach learners with multiple disabilities alongside students without disabilities in a general classroom setting. In this article, we describe how we planned and initiated a successful inclusionary program.

The concept of using cooperative learning techniques with general education learners and learners with multiple disabilities was chosen because of the wide range of benefits to all learners, whether identified as having a disability or not. As described by Cohen (1986) and Putnam (1993), benefits include increased skills in conceptual learning, planning, individual accountability, creative problem solving, self-esteem, oral language proficiency, and socialization. In addition, cooperative learning as a teaching tool assists in stressing traditional areas of curriculum content. These outcomes are also often common goals shared by parents and special education teachers for learners with multiple disabilities. By using cooperative learning, teachers are able to identify individual learner needs and ability levels to establish teacher expectations for each learner.

■ Planning for Inclusion

In the beginning of the fall semester, we worked together to plan and facilitate an inclusionary cooperative learning program involving team teaching. Because we instituted this program in a previously

Melissa M. Jones • Laura Little Carlier

From *Teaching Exceptional Children*, Vol. 27, No. 3, Spring 1995, pp. 23-27. © 1995 by The Council for Exceptional Children. Reprinted by permission.

established classroom in a public school setting, it required no additional funding.

Planning began informally as we brainstormed ideas for lessons, scheduling, physical arrangement of the classroom, and teaching techniques. Planning became more formalized as we began to determine which of the learner goals and objectives on current individualized education programs (IEPs) and from the graded course of study would be best met in our program. As a result of this planning, we selected communication and behavior goals from the various IEPs and language arts objectives from the sixth grade course of study.

Learner Description

We planned activities for students with ranges in ability, from learners with multiple disabilities (IQ in low 50s) to sixth graders without disabilities (with a mean school ability index = 94). The school ability index, based on the Otis-Lennon School Ability Test, is used in this school district to predict a learner's achievement ability in school instead of a standard IQ score. A 94 on this scale roughly translates to a low-average ability level. The students with multiple disabilities are exempt from taking this standardized test from which the ability index is derived. The ages of all the learners range from 10 to 13 years.

Scheduling

The program was originally scheduled for a minimum of 1 hour per week. With increased success, we revised the schedule mid-year to 1 hour per day, four to five times per week. Often the learners become so involved in the group projects that they requested additional time to continue working on them. Emphasis quickly moved from the counting of minutes spent in the general education classroom to the amount of quality instruction in a particular subject area.

Program Goals

We identified two basic program goals before we designed our inclusionary program:

1. To increase the amount of time learners with multiple disabilities spend in the general classroom.

2. To improve the quality of functional instruction given to learners with multiple disabilities while in the general classroom.

Learner Goals

Before implementing our proposed lessons, we identified learner goals and objectives by reviewing current IEPs and the Sixth Grade Competency-Based Graded Course of Study for Language Arts developed by the County Office of Education. The primary focus of the program for the learner with multiple disabilities is the improvement of language development and social development. For the learner without disabilities, the focus is on improving language arts skills. We use language experiences during groupwork to implement specific learner goals and objectives (see box).

Although the general education learners are expected to accomplish the goals and objectives written in the graded course of study, each special education learner has an IEP. Therefore, goals and objectives may vary according to each learner's individual needs.

■ Inclusionary Activities

The activities designed for this inclusionary program center around language arts. Initially, the class is trained in basic groupwork concepts, such as the delineation and responsibility of specific roles within the groups.

Forming Groups

At the beginning of each activity, which might take 4–5 days to complete, learners are individually assigned the role of leader, recorder, presenter, facilitator, timekeeper, or participant. The *leader* is expected to keep the group members on task and to be sure the assignment gets completed. The *recorder* has the job of writing down everyone's ideas and providing a visual representation of the

---

Learner Goals and Objectives for Groupwork

1. The learner will learn appropriate communication skills for daily living. For example, the learner will:

   a. demonstrate verbal expression by independently using language to predict, describe, and/or give cause and effect.

   b. interact conventionally with others by interacting with one to one, peers, and/or in small groups.

   c. develop comprehension skills by following directions that apply to group activities.

2. The learner will demonstrate conventionally social behavior in the school and work environment. For example, the learner will develop interpersonal skills necessary to relationships and successful employment by maintaining conventional social distance, making only necessary body movements (if appropriate), respecting the rights and property of others, joining in group activities, initiating conversations, communicating clearly, and/or cooperating with peers and teachers.

3. The learner will participate in small-group discussions.

4. The learner will give an oral presentation.

5. The learner will speak to entertain. For example, the learner will retell a story and/or dramatize.

6. The learner will demonstrate attention to delivery. For example, the learner will use conventional eye contact; vary volume, rate, and pitch; and/or maintain an appropriate demeanor.

7. The learner will recognize characterization.

8. The learner will identify setting, mood, and plot.

9. The learner will write imaginatively. For example, the learner will write in the form of a narrative, description, and/or a short story.

group's progress. The *presenter* has the responsibility of sharing the group's final product with the rest of the class. The *participants* are those group members without a specific role and have the job to create new ideas and to help the group problem solve. The *facilitator*, for the purpose of this program, has the responsibility of making sure that the ideas of the learners with multiple disabilities are heard and used. The *timekeeper* keeps group members aware of how much time is available for the task.

In our classroom, the students are divided into six groups of five to six learners per group. Using strategies for composing groups from Cohen (1986), we chose to group heterogeneously by gender and by ability level. To start, we place one strong resource person in each group. A resource person is not necessarily someone who is successful according to academic criteria, but rather someone who may be successful in other areas. These areas may include being creative, articulate, a flexible thinker, or maybe even someone who has personal experience with the task or some feature of the task (Cohen). We then assign a special education learner to the group. We place other students in the various groups, depending on the students' social and problem-solving skills and needs.

Designing Lesson Plans

Each activity is designed with the sixth grade course of study in mind, concentrating on the story development and writing aspects of the course of study. We feel it is important not to water down the sixth grade curriculum in any way, but rather to present the material in such a way so that all the learners participate more actively during their learning experiences. Teacher expectations of learners vary per learner and even vary per activity depending on the amount of experience each person has had with the material presented. We devise lesson plans with these various expectations in mind. The tasks assigned to the groups vary from writing a sequel for a published story or book, to creating a story from a magazine picture, creating a play, or practicing storytelling skills.

An example of such an activity is writing a sequel to a trade book such as *Ju-*

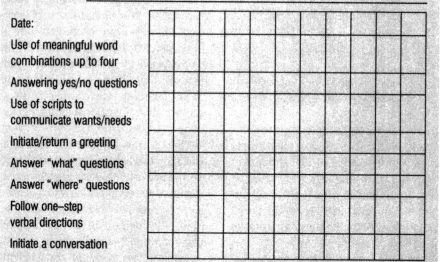

Figure 1. Sample Checklist

This checklist can be used for documenting changes in behavior of students with multiple disabilities during groupwork.

Learner's Name: _____

Date:											
Use of meaningful word combinations up to four											
Answering yes/no questions											
Use of scripts to communicate wants/needs											
Initiate/return a greeting											
Answer "what" questions											
Answer "where" questions											
Follow one–step verbal directions											
Initiate a conversation											

manji, by Chris Van Allsburg. After listening to one of the teachers read the book, students conduct a classwide brainstorming session to generate a variety of possibilities of successive events that could be used to create a sequel to the story. The learners then begin the small-group work, continuing the brainstorming process to discuss additional ideas for events that will be included in their sequel.

Once consensus within the individual groups has been reached as to which events to include, the actual writing of the sequel begins. Various groups may add illustrations. Some groups may choose to create a book, some may have a series of posters or smaller drawings, or some may develop a more elaborate method of publishing this work. The groups then orally share their sequels with the entire class.

Evaluating Groupwork

The teachers meet at least once a week to review the success of the previous activities, note problem areas, share in problem solving, and devise the activities for the succeeding lessons. To document changes in learner behavior during the inclusionary groupwork, we designed checklists for each of the students with

multiple disabilities. These checklists (see Figure 1 for an example) list individual IEP objectives used to document such changes. These checklists also demonstrate the various expectations teachers can have for each learner with multiple disabilities, aside from the expectations dictated by the graded course of study.

The teachers and speech therapist share the responsibility of observing and documenting language use and behavioral changes noted during the group processes, as stated in the learner objectives.

The general education learners are taught to monitor and evaluate their own progress in terms of the entire group process. Group members use an evaluation form to help them evaluate their work after they have completed the assignment. (See box for self-evaluation goals for the group process.)

In addition to self-evaluations by each group, we ask the class members to make positive remarks about each presentation. The general education teacher writes down all comments and compiles them for the group. She then includes these comments in a narrative evaluation, which is used in conjunction with the group's self-evaluation to derive a grade. The recorded grade is an average of the

Self-Evaluation Goals for the Group Process

1. Use the allotted time for completing a project of high quality.

2. Include everyone's ideas.

3. Resolve conflicts within the group.

4. Prepare a presentation that satisfactorily relays the ideas of the group.

5. Encourage full group participation.

two grades given, one from the teacher and one from the group.

After each activity, we evaluate the group processes as a whole. Sometimes we need to design an activity that might help to remediate any problem areas groups may have encountered during a particular activity. (See flowchart in Figure 2.)

For example, to help learners develop the skill of coming to consensus, we use an activity called "Shipwreck" (Cohen, 1986). This is a one-day activity in which the students are presented with a paragraph describing a hypothetical shipwreck. Within their groups, the learners must prioritize a list of items they will take with them to a nearby deserted island to assist them in their survival. Group members must also be prepared to state reasons for the choices they make as a group.

We have noted that each time an activity such as "Shipwreck" is done, the sophistication of the learner's knowledge about group processes increases, including that of some of the learners with multiple disabilities.

■ Outcomes and Conclusions

We originally thought that the learners with multiple disabilities would most likely keep the role of participant throughout the course of the school year. We noted, however, that the sixth graders without disabilities were not satisfied with such unequal distribution of duties. The special education learners are now serving as presenters and timekeepers as well. In fact, we no longer have to assign roles to students because the learners

share responsibilities, alternating roles to create an interdependence among group members.

We have found that team teaching of special educators with general educators, using cooperative learning techniques, helps to eliminate some of the common concerns teachers may have for placing special education learners in the general classroom. These techniques have resolved the issues of time being taken away from other learners and learner/teacher ratios that might be too high. Normally, the general education teacher involved in this program has 25 learners in the classroom. The special education teacher brings to the classroom 6–7 additional learners, as well as a teaching assistant, and thus actually lowers the learner/teacher ratio to 10:1. In addition, as we move from group to group, facilitating the group process and offering individual assistance as needed, we believe that quality time with all learners is enhanced instead of forfeited. This form of interdependency among teachers proves to be effective for including learners with multiple disabilities in the general education classroom, as well as being an effective cooperative model for learners to follow.

Through this experience, the special education teacher has the opportunity to see and better understand grade-level expectations for socialization and language development. This increased knowledge assists the special education teacher in determining goals and objectives relevant

to each learner's environment when writing IEPs for the following school year.

Individual learner gains were noted during the first year of this program's implementation. Students from the special education class showed progress by increasing the number of interactions they initiated or responded to, and by exhibiting increased confidence. Initially, the learners with multiple disabilities had an overall baseline average of initiating 0–2 interactions with peers during a 30-minute period and responding to peer questions an average of one out of five times during that same 30-minute period. After 5 months of participating in this program, the overall learner-initiated interactions with peers increased to 2–8 interactions during a 30-minute period. Responses to peers also increased to an average of three out of five responses. Learners with multiple disabilities who exhibited behavioral concerns showed a marked decrease in the number of less-conventional types of behavior, such as aggression and noncompliance, occurring during the groupwork process. One learner actually decreased her usual verbal outbursts to extinction during the groupwork activities and demonstrated a 25% increase in her attention to task.

We also observed gains in the sixth graders without disabilities as their confidence and ability levels improved. We attributed these gains not only to the groupwork activities, but also to the new relationships formed between these learners and the learners with multiple dis-

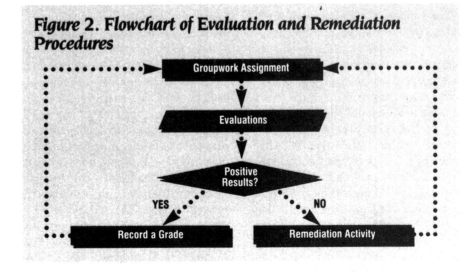

Figure 2. Flowchart of Evaluation and Remediation Procedures

Groupwork Assignment

Evaluations

Positive Results?

YES — Record a Grade

NO — Remediation Activity

abilities. We noted that the social attitudes of the sixth graders also changed over the course of the first year of this program. In the beginning, these children wanted to "help" the learners with disabilities; but during the year, they began to demonstrate an attitude of equality among learners, sharing the knowledge and resources that all learners possess. The children without disabilities now speak more often of likenesses between themselves and the children with disabilities, rather than looking for and responding to differences.

The successes we have realized for the learners in their classroom have not come without difficulty and some frustration. Communication between learners remains the biggest challenge to meaningful interactions. The teachers have had to problem solve ways to include the ideas of learners with autism who have poor expressive and receptive language skills, to intervene and redirect aggression used to communicate needs, and to encourage participation from learners who either verbally or nonverbally refuse to participate as a means of controlling their environment. By using a collaborative method of problem solving, these teachers feel they have been better able to find solutions to these difficulties than if they had been trying to problem solve alone.

■ Future Implications

As this program demonstrates, the thrust for including learners with disabilities in the general education classroom should not stop with learners who exhibit only mild disabilities. Learners with multiple disabilities can also benefit from programs that increase the amount of quality interactions they have with their peers without disabilities. Although current schoolwide involvement in this inclusionary program is still limited, additional possibilities for expansion to other classrooms and settings exist.

For expansion to be possible, it is essential that general and special educators work together to discover methods that can be used to teach all learners side by side in a productive setting. By doing so, not only will the learners with disabilities benefit by becoming active participants in the class activities, but so may other learners benefit who are deemed at risk for school success. Cooperative groupwork and team-teaching are efficient ways in which the individual needs of all learners can be met without sacrificing quality instruction.

Beyond the scope of the classroom, there exist sociocultural implications of inclusion. In our society, people often view learners with disabilities as needing help, always receiving and rarely giving. Through the use of cooperative learning and inclusion, the contrary can be realized as each member of the group contributes to the function and uniqueness of that group. With an increase in inclusionary practices, perhaps the next generation will learn to value all people as participating members in society instead of as separate groups of givers and receivers. To promote such social changes, future endeavors to create programs that destratify and desegregate current homogeneous classrooms should be encouraged.

■ References

Cohen, E. (1986). *Designing groupwork*. New York: Teachers College Press.

Putnam, J., (1993). *Cooperative learning and strategies for inclusion: Celebrating diversity in the classroom*. Baltimore, MD: Paul H. Brooks.

Schaffner, B., & Buswell, B. (1991). *Opening doors: Strategies for including all students in regular education*. Colorado Springs, CO: Peak Parent Center, Inc.

Melissa M. Jones *(CEC Chapter #11) was a Special Education Teacher for learners with multiple disabilities, Clermont Northeastern Intermediate School, and now supervises programs for learners with severe behavior handicaps, Clermont County Office of Education, Cincinnati, Ohio.* **Laura Little Carlier,** *General Education Teacher, Clermont Northeastern Intermediate School, Batavia, Ohio. The work the authors began, including learners with disabilities in general education, continues with the help of a team of exceptional general and special educators.*

Listening to Parents of Children with Disabilities

Linda Davern

Linda Davern is an Assistant Professor, Education Department, The Sage Colleges, Troy, NY 12180.

Interviews with parents of mainstreamed children shed light on building effective school-home partnerships.

A growing number of children with disabilities are becoming members of general education classes. As someone involved in teacher preparation, I am particularly interested in what teaching teams can do to build productive alliances, or strengthen existing relationships, with the parents or caregivers of these children.

To explore this issue, I conducted a series of in-depth interviews with 15 families (21 parents) whose children were fully included in general education programs—mostly at the elementary level. Many of these children needed a great deal of support and modification to participate successfully in general classes. Overall, these parents were extremely pleased with the impact that inclusion had on their children. They also offered suggestions for improving the quality of home-school relationships.[1] The following recommendations to teaching teams come from an analysis of these parents' perspectives.

■ *Convey a clear, consistent message regarding the value of the child.* How school personnel talk about children in both formal and informal interactions early in the school year has a significant impact on the development of relationships with their families. Several parents in this study valued the ability of teachers to see different aspects of a child's personality aside from academic achievement. As Gail put it.

> For teachers to say to me, "I really like your kid," or "You know, he really has a great sense of humor"... lets me know that they really care about him as a person.

These parents also commended personnel who focused on the individual child's progress, rather than using other children as a reference for comparison. As Anna said:

> So our child's not going to be the top of her class in gym. We understand that. Just take her for who she is. Find space for her.

Members of the teaching team need to convey clear, consistent messages that they are happy to have this child in the classroom and that they hold high expectations for the child's achievement.

■ *Put yourself in the shoes of the parent.* The parents I interviewed valued the efforts of school personnel to try to understand what it is like to have a child with a disability—for example, to have to negotiate both the general and special education bureaucracies in order to gain access to classes, accommodations, and support services. Several of these parents felt that some staff did not understand their anger and frustration with educational systems. While one mother felt more strongly than others I spoke with, she expressed the sense of detachment experienced by families of children in special education:

> Parents hate special ed.... Parents hate it because the kids hate it.... They hate the isolation of it.

Parents often felt they were viewed as impatient. They wanted staff to better understand their frustration with the slow pace of school improvement efforts related to inclusive practices. School staff who attempt to understand the parent's frame of reference are less likely to assume the judgmental attitudes that can be damaging to the home-school relationship.

■ *Expand your awareness of cultural diversity.* Building an awareness of cultural diversity will strengthen school personnel's ability to teach as well as connect successfully with families. Marguerite believed that "a lot of teachers have never had ... training in multiculturalism or diversity." Through effective staff development, schools can help personnel examine "the cultural base of their own belief system" in relation to children and families (Harry 1992, p. 23), and how these beliefs affect relationships.

Harry and colleagues emphasize that cultures are greatly influenced by generational status, gender, social class, education, occupational group, and other variables (1995, p. 106). Such an approach to professional development will help personnel be aware of the cultural lenses through which they make judgments about children and families.

■ *See individuals, challenge stereotypes.* A few parents felt that some teachers made assumptions about them and their parenting skills simply because their child had a disability. Doria saw some of these attitudes arising from a lack of understanding of some types of disabilities such as emotional disturbance. Marguerite felt that school personnel frequently "lumped parents together"—working from inaccurate assumptions about single parents and parents who were not of European heritage. School personnel need opportunities to explore the impulse to stereotype, and encouragement and support to challenge this tendency in themselves as well as their colleagues.

■ *Persevere in building partnerships.* While federal law requires school teams to invite parents into the planning process for their children with disabilities, the collaborative outcome envisioned by the legislation does not always materialize. Several parents thought that schools gave up too soon—that personnel were quick to dismiss parents who didn't attend meetings, and were cynical about the possibilities for change. Parents felt that building partnerships took commitment and vision over the *long* term. As one father stated, "The first year you make a decision to team with parents, maybe you're not going to get all the parents ... but give it a little time, nurture it along."

Parents suggested looking at how

Schools will not become proficient in building alliances with these families until general class membership, with adequate supports, is the norm for children with disabilities.

schools share information with parents, using more flexibility in setting up meeting times with them, and assisting parents in connecting with other parents who might share child care responsibilities to free one another to attend planning meetings.

■ *Demonstrate an authentic interest in the parent's goals for the child.* A first step in establishing dialogue is to connect with parents as individuals. Participants in the study commended some staff as very skilled in diminishing the psychological distance between parents and professionals. These teachers were able to create an atmosphere where parents did not feel that they had to "watch their p's and q's," as one parent put it. Staff did this through their choice of language, as well as their interaction styles. Their interest in parents' ideas felt authentic.

Parents also mentioned interactions that they viewed as evidence of an "expert syndrome." In these cases, parents felt that the attitude coming from staff was, "You couldn't possibly know what you're talking about." One parent described a critical distinction between those personnel who talk with parents as opposed to those who talk at them. Teachers can maintain their expertise as educators while fully acknowledging the information and insights held by parents. The interplay of these complementary roles can greatly enrich the outcome for students.

■ *Talk with parents about how they want to share information.* Successful collaboration requires effective ongoing communication between home and school. Some participants thought that having one school person as the primary contact would be helpful. Several parents in this study did not want their primary contact to

be a special educator, for fear that this would lessen the feelings of ownership on the part of the general educator for the child's progress. Yet consistent communication with a person who really knew the child and his or her unique learning characteristics was important.

Teachers need to ask parents which school representative they would like to communicate with, how frequently, and through which means (for example, combinations of meetings, phone calls, and written communication). Moreover, parents' preferences for involvement may change over time given a variety of factors such as the child's age and the family's circumstances.

Several families found home visits by school staff very helpful. Parents felt that opportunities to visit with children in their homes might give staff insight into children's capabilities that had not been demonstrated at school.

■ *Use everyday language.* Parents often felt excluded from the planning process when professionals used unfamiliar educational terms when discussing test results, staffing patterns, and ways of organizing and identifying services. One parent referred to this practice as "blowing all that smoke." As another put it:

> What does it mean "30 minutes three times a week," "one plus one," "parallel curriculum"?....When you do that stuff you just close out the parent. As soon as you use language that's exclusive of parents, they're gone.

It is an unfortunate irony that in order to graduate from many teacher preparation programs, preservice teachers must master a professional lexicon that ultimately creates significant barriers to being effective in their professions.

■ *Create effective forums for planning and problem solving.* Yearly review meetings, mandated by law, are held for each child with an Individualized Education Plan (IEP). During these meetings, school personnel and parents (and students at the secondary level) review assessments, make placement decisions, determine children's services, and identify individual goals. The parents I interviewed described these formal meetings as some of the most difficult interactions they experienced during the year. They used such phrases as "very intimidating" to describe them, adding that they felt at times like token participants in discussions about their children.

In contrast to these formal yearly reviews, at least six of the children involved in this study were the focus of regularly scheduled team meetings, composed of teachers, parents, related service providers, and occasionally teaching assistants. Although evaluations of these meetings varied greatly, parents indicated that, compared to the formal meetings, they felt more comfortable discussing their children in an atmosphere that recognized achievements, friendships, interesting stories, and humorous anecdotes. As one mother put it,

> When we go to team meetings, a lot of times it *is* a celebration. That's how it feels. By George, we're doing something *right* here—it's working!

The literature offers direction for districts interested in developing their expertise in the arena of team planning for individual children (Giangreco 1996, Giangreco et al. 1993, Thousand and Villa 1992).

Successful collaboration requires effective ongoing communication between home and school.

■ *Build long-term schoolwide plans that offer full membership to all children.* Several of the parents I interviewed had advocated extensively for a general class placement for their child. Schools will not become proficient in building alliances with these families until general class membership, with adequate supports, is the norm for children with disabilities. These findings reinforce calls from parents and others in the educational community for districts to develop long-term schoolwide plans to offer full membership to all students, not just set up programs for children in response to the requests of individual parents (Gartner and Lipsky 1987, Stainback and Stainback 1990). Teachers can actively support such restructuring (with appropriate safeguards to ensure adequate resources).

Such efforts will result in inclusive settings becoming available to those children whose parents are not in a position to pursue such extensive advocacy actions.

¹Parents' names are pseudonyms.

References
Gartner, A., and D. Lipsky. (1987). "Beyond Special Education: Toward a Quality System for all Students." *Harvard Educational Review* 57, 4: 367–395.
Giangreco, M. F. (1996). *Vermont Interdependent Services Team Approach: A Guide to Coordinating Educational Support Services.* Baltimore: Paul H. Brookes.
Giangreco, M. F., C. J. Cloninger, and V. S. Iverson. (1993). *Choosing Options and Accommodations for Children (COACH).* Baltimore: Paul H. Brookes.
Harry, B. (1992). *Cultural Diversity, Families, and the Special Education System.* New York: Teachers College Press.
Harry, B., M. Grenot-Scheyer, M. Smith-Lewis, H. Park, F. Xin, and I. Schwartz. (1995). "Developing Culturally Inclusive Services for Individuals with Severe Disabilities." *The Journal of The Association for Persons with Severe Handicaps* 20, 2: 99–109.
Stainback, S., and W. Stainback. (1990). "Inclusive Schooling." In *Support Networks for Inclusive Schooling,* edited by W. Stainback, and S. Stainback. Baltimore: Paul H. Brookes.
Thousand, J. S., and R. Villa. (1992). "Collaborative Teams: A Powerful Tool in School Restructuring." In *Restructuring for Caring and Effective Schools,* edited by R. A. Villa, J. S. Thousand, W. Stainback, and S. Stainback. Baltimore: Paul H. Brookes.

Children with Special Gifts and Talents

Children with special gifts and talents do not qualify for special educational services under the Individuals with Disabilities Education Act (IDEA). Are they to be considered disabled because of their gifts and talents? One might prefer to substitute the prefix *poti-* for *dis-* and refer to them as *potiabled*, suggesting their powerful abilities, or the prefix *super-* for *dis-* and call them *superabled*, suggesting their superior abilities. Since many textbooks on exceptional children include children with special gifts and talents, and since these children are exceptional, they should be included in this volume. Instructors who deal only with the categories of disabilities covered by IDEA may simply omit coverage of this unit. The question "dis-

abled or not disabled?" is less easily resolved. Many professionals would argue that simply by dint of their special gifts and talents, these children tend to be excluded from the mainstream. Their exceptionalities can, in fact, deprive them of some of the opportunities with which less exceptional children are routinely provided.

The first article included in this unit is a powerful argument by the director of the Gifted Education Policy Studies Program at the University of North Carolina, James Gallagher, who is in favor of providing special educational services to children with special gifts and talents. He calls forth the image of the practice within Chinese Communism of lopping off the heads of poppies that grow fast so that all poppies will be of a uniform size. Gallagher reports that studies of world-class tennis players, concert pianists, mathematicians, neurologists, and other high achievers reveal striking similarities in their childhoods. Their parents recognized their special abilities early and found tutors or mentors who would help them develop their skills faster. An educational program that refuses to find tutors or mentors, or provide special education in the skill areas of gifted students, is closer to using the Chinese Communist solution: Make them of a uniform size. Lop off their extra potential. Gallagher is a strong supporter of early recognition of children with special gifts and talents and providing them with early and continuing enriched education. He addresses the sex/ethnic difference question (a civil rights issue?) by advocating special exploration of talents in all youth (both sexes, minority-majority). He addresses the theory that "intelligence equals math and science aptitude" by citing Howard Gardner's work on multiple intelligences, including special skills in social sensitivity, music creativity, spatial perception, and body kinesthetics. He suggests we look for all "tall poppies of every hue" and help them grow taller.

The U.S. Omnibus Education Bill of 1987 provided modest support for gifted and talented identification and education. It required, however, that each state foot the bill for the development of special programs for children with special gifts and talents. Some states have implemented special education for the superabled. Most states have not.

The assessment of children with special gifts and talents, especially in the early childhood years, is fraught with difficulties. Should parents nominate their own children when they see extraordinary skills developing? How objective can parents be about their child's ability as it compares to the abilities of other same-aged children? Should measures of achievement be used (e.g., recitals, performances, art, reading levels, writings)? Do all parents want their children to have special gifts or talents? The evidence suggests that, to the contrary, many parents are embarrassed by their child's extraordinary aptitudes. They would rather have their child be more like his or her peers.

The second unit article emphasizes the importance of enriching the education of children with special gifts and talents as soon as they are identified. The author, Suzanne Foster, provides preschool teachers with many practical activities that can enrich the education of gifted and talented children and help them to develop their potentials before they begin regular education. She also gives hints on assessment, and she stresses the need for all children to learn through the medium of play.

Children with special gifts and talents often test the patience of their parents, their teachers, their peers, and even of special tutors or mentors asked to help them in their areas of exceptionality. Gifted children tend to ask a lot of questions and pursue answers with still more questions. They can be incredibly persistent about gathering information about topics that interest them and show no interest at all in learning about topics that do not. They may be very competitive in areas where they are especially skilled, competing even with teachers and other adults. They may seem arrogant about their skills, when they are only trying to be honest. Many children with special gifts and talents have extraordinary sensitivity to how other people are reacting to them. As they are promoted through elementary school into middle school and high school, many such children learn to hide their accomplishments for the secondary gain of being more socially acceptable or more popular. Because they have been underchallenged and/or discouraged from achieving at their highest potentialities, many gifted high-school students are underachievers. They have poor study habits bred of not needing to study in elementary school. They are unmotivated, intensely bored, and discouraged by the educational programs available to them.

The last article in this unit deals with the issues of females and mathematics. In elementary school, females are equal or superior to males in academic progress in arithmetic. However, by high school, females are seldom assessed as having gifts or talents in mathematics, and their performance drops, on the average, far below their male peers. This research-based article suggests that females learn that excelling in math is a masculine behavior. If females are given encouragement to work with mathematics and are explicitly told that they have the ability to excel, they will.

Looking Ahead: Challenge Questions

Should students with special talents be encouraged and helped to develop these valuable skills, or should they be assisted to fit in better and appear more like their nongifted peers?

How can preschool teachers encourage special gifts and talents?

Are females genetically inferior in mathematics, or have they learned not to excel in this area? Discuss your answers.

Education of Gifted Students
A Civil Rights Issue?

There are many students with high native abilities that remain uncrystallized because of a lack of opportunity, practice, and motivation. It is the responsibility of families, schools, and society to create a more favorable atmosphere for the full development of all students — including those with outstanding talents.

James J. Gallagher

THE TOPIC of civil rights has shaped many educational discussions and decisions during the past three decades. In the context of education, *civil rights* means the guarantee of equal opportunity and justice for all and the actions taken against those barriers that stand in the way of such equality.

How does the issue of civil rights bear on an area of special education such as the education of gifted students? There have been various suggestions that programs for gifted students may serve as a

JAMES J. GALLAGHER is Kennan Professor of Education and director of the Gifted Education Policy Studies Program, University of North Carolina, Chapel Hill.

haven for upper-middle-class white students and thus may qualify as a new and more subtle form of racial and ethnic discrimination. Such concerns emerge from one indisputable fact: the differential representation of the sexes and of racial and ethnic groups in classes for gifted students.[1] In advanced mathematics classes, we find more boys than girls.[2] In programs for gifted students at the elementary and middle school levels, there is a relative shortage of black and Hispanic students (less than half their proportion in the general population) and a relative surplus of Asian students (more than twice their proportion in the general population).[3] Some critics have advanced these findings as indicators that there must be unfair practices abroad that are intentionally reducing the opportunities for certain groups of students to participate in programs for gifted children.

But, we must ask, what model of child development — or of justice — are these programs following that would allow us to cry "foul" at the above figures? Why should the figures for student participation in programs for gifted students (or in athletics or in the school orchestra) match the proportions of gender, race, or ethnic origin in the society at large?

The Role of Genetics

One reason to expect proportional representation of various groups in these special programs for gifted students would be the belief that intellectual ability is determined at birth, that it unfolds in a regular maturational sequence, and that it is resistant to outside influences, so that environment and experience play no role in its

Point of View

development. Since few people can be found who accept the concept of an inherent difference between races, sexes, or ethnic groups in the ability to learn,[4] this would mean that there should be an equal distribution of these subgroups in programs for the gifted. A deviation from that equality would be interpreted as arising from some unfair practice, such as discriminatory tests for eligibility. Therefore, following this line of reasoning, someone's civil rights are being violated.

There is considerable evidence to suggest that genetics does play a significant role in the development of various intelligences. Studies of twins and adoptive children clearly indicate that some children are born with more potential for learning rapidly than others. These differences apply *within* various racial and ethnic groups, not between them.[5] But that is only part of the picture.

The rest of the story is that environment and sequential experiences play a significant role in the *crystallization* of native abilities. If a particular environment allows a child to have more experiences and to obtain more encouragement from adults and peers he or she considers important, then the child's abilities will flourish. Thus boys who are encouraged

From *Phi Delta Kappan*, January 1995, pp. 408-410. © 1995 by Phi Delta Kappa, Inc. Reprinted by permission.

to work with mathematics and are told (implicitly or explicitly) that excelling in math is a masculine trait will develop their native abilities beyond girls who are told that they are not supposed to be good in this subject and that math ability is gender-specific to males.[6]

In the end, it may be that educators and psychologists have been responsible for misleading the general public about some fundamental knowledge regarding intellectual development. The term *gifted* may even add to that misunderstanding by implying that native ability alone creates what we observe as giftedness in children.[7]

Differential Encouragement

Studies of academic progress in mathematics reveal few differences between males and females in performance at age 9, but huge differences are present — in favor of males — by age 17.[8] What has happened? The simplest, most parsimo-

nious answer is that the cultural values of the society have impinged on the genders differentially to create the disparities that the society expects.

A similar result could be expected in the field of language development. If there is differential encouragement by gender or by race or by ethnic group to achieve the full flowering of native ability in this domain, then one would expect different levels of reading performance for different groups. The older the children, the greater the difference.

I.Q. tests are merely one measure of the development of intellectual abilities at a given point in time. They cannot measure "native ability," but they can measure the current development of a child so that children can be compared with one another on such characteristics as their store of knowledge, reasoning ability, and ability to associate concepts — all of which are important predictors of academic success. It is this power of I.Q. tests to predict which students will do well in future

Certainly, the intellectually rich get richer because of their pyramidal structure of knowledge.

academic settings that has given them their reputation in education circles. Even though they are less than completely accurate when used alone, without regard to

Photo credit: Steve Miller/NYT Pictures

Intellectual ability is determined at birth, and society has the responsibility to create a more favorable atmosphere for the full development of all students.

motivational or social factors, I.Q. tests still remain the single most effective predictor of academic success that we have today.

A further question is whether such tests actually measure all of what we mean when we say "intelligence." Those who assert that there are multiple intelligences suggest that, by successfully measuring other ability domains — such as spatial perception, creative production, or social sensitivity — one could identify an expanded group of "gifted" students that might be more equitably balanced by ethnic or racial groups than are those served by the verbal- and mathematics-dominated programs that currently exist.[9]

Building a Knowledge Structure

What is often overlooked is that school and our other life experiences allow us to build a pyramidal structure of knowledge and understandings that will enable us to handle more and more complex systems of ideas. We expect, for example, high school students to understand the concept of representative government. Think of what other knowledge students must already have mastered before such understanding can take place. They must have learned about how various peoples have governed themselves or been governed in the past. They must be familiar with different types of government. They must know what various people have said about what government does for the people and is expected to do. To understand all of this, the students must have been able to read extensively. To fully understand the term *representative*, students must even be able to understand some fundamental arithmetic.

To see how the lack of past knowledge can hinder problem solving, consider a situation in which a group of our "brightest" students are asked the question, How can Australian farmers cope with the wild kangaroos that have been eating their crops? The initial reactions or suggestions from even the brightest of our students are not likely to be worth very much. However, the students who can read well can quickly come up to speed on the charactistics of Australian farming, the characteristics of kangaroos, and the farmers' past attempts to cope with this problem. They may also be able to draw associations from their own past knowledge of how farmers in this country have dealt with animal incursions. Thus the ability to gain new information rapidly, together with the ability to draw on past informa-

tion already stored, can allow some students to generate useful ideas much more effectively than other students who have fundamental deficits in skills or in stored information.

In short, future mastery of important knowledge rests heavily on past knowledge, and that is why the early development of one's basic abilities is so important in education. The particular case of Asian children has been remarked on by many observers.[10] Although living under disadvantaged environmental circumstances similar to other minority groups, many Asian students have shown a remarkable ability to achieve at high levels in many different forms of education.

The explanation most frequently given for this phenomenon is the intense focus on learning and education in Asian families and the insistence by Asian parents on high levels of academic performance from their children. Such an emphasis creates the conditions for the crystallization of abilities so that the various skills (verbal and mathematical) necessary for learning are mastered along with patterns of behavior (intensity of study and desire to achieve) that will serve the child well in later schooling. The child is building a knowledge structure that will be the foundation for further learning. Some refer to this as the Matthew Principle, referring to the Biblical phrase "The rich get richer." Certainly, the intellectually rich get richer because of their pyramidal structure of knowledge.

It should not be surprising that children with a rich structure of knowledge do well on achievement and aptitude tests (I.Q. tests) compared with other groups of children who come from families that place less emphasis on school and education. The long-term result of such early emphasis is that a future Olympic team of mathematicians, chosen on the basis of mathematical aptitude, would almost certainly contain a larger proportion of Asian students than of any other group.

The importance of a combination of experience and desire in crystallizing special abilities can be seen in the "Dream Team" in Olympic basketball. This team, representing the United States, did not have an even distribution of players by race or ethnic group. Not a single Asian player could be found on the team — or in the National Basketball Association. Does this mean that there are hereditary differences between blacks, whites, and Asians in native physical abilities? Hardly.

The easiest, most parsimonious explanation for the makeup of the team is that differential practice and motivation have caused some young people to excel in this special area. Therefore, we should direct our attention toward the differential opportunities, practice, and motivation — not toward the variations in aptitude scores. The retrospective study by Benjamin Bloom and his associates of the early life of world-class mathematicians, tennis players, neurologists, concert pianists, and so on confirmed the significant role played by parents in the full development — the crystallization — of their children's abilities.[11] Parents encouraged the special talent they perceived in their children by finding appropriate mentors or tutors who would help the children develop their valued skills. After a time, the students began to revel in their special skills and became motivated to continue to seek on their own those experiences that would further the development of their abilities.

What to Do?

In short, it is differential opportunities, practice, and motivation that appear to have been responsible for the differential proportions found in programs for gifted students. What action should education policy makers take in response to this situation? One solution is the "tall poppies" approach of Chinese Communism, which is based on the principle that poppies that grow more rapidly than others need to be lopped off so that there is a more even development of the flowers in a field. Eliminating programs for gifted students would be one practical application of the "tall poppies" approach to education. Indeed, the fact that so many gifted students complain about intense boredom with school shows that we have already chosen in many cases to neglect our tall poppies.[12]

A solution more in keeping with a society that purports to value individuality and to reward initiative would be to organize and institutionalize equal opportunities and experiences for talented students of both sexes and from all racial and ethnic groups. This approach would mean creating early programs for the stimulation of cognitive, mathematical, and perceptual abilities. These programs would be designed to find and encourage those students with special abilities — regardless of race, gender, or ethnic origin — while they are still in preschool or primary

> *Eliminating programs for the gifted would be one practical application of the "tall poppies" approach to education.*

school. In this way, all the poppies that can grow tall will be encouraged to do so.

Let us return to our original question. Is the differential representation of the sexes and of racial and ethnic groups in educational programs for gifted students a civil rights problem? It is a problem of equity, certainly, since the disproportions indicate that there have been differential sets of opportunities for different groups of children. The unfairness leading to the disproportions lies primarily in the imbalance of opportunities and environment, not in the selection process itself.

This situation provides American education with a major opportunity, because such disproportions should cause us to realize how far short we are of fully developing our students' and society's potential. There are many students with high native abilities that remain uncrystallized because of a lack of opportunity, practice, and motivation. It is the responsibility of families, schools, and society to create a more favorable atmosphere for the full development of all students — including those with outstanding talents.

One step in the right direction would be the creation of early and continuing enrichment programs that are directed at minority youths in particular. Advocacy for such programs arises partially out of a sense of justice but is also rooted in enlightened self-interest: the understanding that the full development of all our nation's talents will surely bring reward for all of us. Our tall poppies of multiple hues should cause us to rejoice in our rich and profitable diversity.

1. Mary M. Frasier, "Identification of Gifted Black Students: Developing New Perspectives," in C. June Maker and Shirley W. Schiever, eds., *Critical Issues in Gifted Education: Defensible Programs for Cultural and Ethnic Minorities* (Austin, Tex.: Pro-Ed, 1989), vol. 2, pp. 213-25; and Alexinia Y. Baldwin, "The Purpose of Education for Gifted Black Students," in ibid., pp. 237-45.

2. Julian C. Stanley, "An Academic Model for Educating the Mathematically Talented," *Gifted Child Quarterly*, vol. 35, 1991, pp. 36-42.

3. *The 1990 State of States' Gifted and Talented Education Report* (Augusta, Me.: Council of State Directors of Programs for the Gifted, 1991).

4. Arthur R. Jensen, *Bias in Mental Testing* (New York: Free Press, 1980).

5. Robert Plomin, "Environment and Genes: Determinants of Behavior," *American Psychologist*, vol. 44, 1989, pp. 105-11.

6. Sally Reis and Carolyn Callahan, "Gifted Females: They've Come a Long Way — Or Have They?," *Journal for the Education of the Gifted*, vol. 12, 1989, pp. 99-117.

7. James J. Gallagher, "The Gifted: A Term with Surplus Meaning," *Journal for the Education of the Gifted*, vol. 14, 1992, pp. 353-65.

8. James J. Gallagher, *Teaching the Gifted Child*, 3rd ed. (Boston: Allyn and Bacon, 1985).

9. Howard Gardner, *Frames of Mind: The Theory of Multiple Intelligences* (New York: Basic Books, 1986).

10. Harold W. Stevenson and Shin-ying Lee, *Contexts of Achievement*, Monographs of the Society for Research in Child Development, vol. 55 (Chicago: University of Chicago Press, 1990).

11. Benjamin S. Bloom, ed., *Developing Talent in Young People* (New York: Ballantine Books, 1985).

12. James Delisle and Sandra Berger, "Underachieving Gifted Students," ERIC ED 321 483, 1990.

MEETING THE NEEDS OF GIFTED AND TALENTED PRESCHOOLERS

Suzanne M. Foster

Suzanne M. Foster is a Doctoral Fellow in the Department of Elementary Education, Ball State University, Muncie, Indiana. She assists in the supervision of undergraduates who teach reading to local elementary school students.

Gifted preschool children are rarely served by special preschools for the gifted. There is a shortage of these kinds of programs in the United States. In 1982 there were only 18 such programs identified (Karnes & Johnson, 1991). If they are in preschool programs, gifted children may or may not be receiving enrichment. The current emphasis on inclusion makes it doubtful that preschool programs for the gifted will be publicly funded in the near future. Preschool teachers need to take responsibility for meeting the needs of this group, as well as the needs of other special needs children in their classroom. How can teachers help these children develop their potential? What kinds of things can be done in the regular preschool classroom?

Gifted preschoolers enjoy many of the same activities that non-gifted children enjoy but to a greater degree and in more depth and detail (Wolfe, 1989). If the preschool class is studying a unit on the human body, the teacher could go into more detail for the gifted children. This can be done through a learning center with models of the heart, brain and lungs. Many of the gifted and non-gifted children would love to see and touch the models. The gifted children would be able to understand the concepts in greater depth as their curiosity and thinking were stimulated. While these models would interest many of the children, they would also meet the needs of the gifted children.

Information Lovers

Many gifted preschoolers love to learn information. They are like sponges in their ability to absorb concepts and new ideas. Samantha, for example, loved dogs and focused for weeks on learning all about the different breeds. She loved to go to the grocery store and read the dog food labels and collect pictures of dogs. The teacher can provide enrichment by focusing on the special in-

terests of children like Samantha and integrating these interests into the curriculum. Through books, field trips, the arts and resource people, a teacher can expand gifted children's knowledge and introduce them to new ways of thinking about a subject they are interested in.

For example, gifted children who are interested in bees can be enriched by a unit on bees. The book corner could have books of various levels of difficulty on bees and related insects. The teacher could discuss wasps and help the children see the similarities and differences between bees and wasps. The teacher could stretch the children's knowledge through discussions, asking both higher and lower level questions. Materials such as empty wasp nests and honeycombs could be displayed on the science table. A beekeeper could be invited to the school to relate his/her experiences with the children. The gifted children would be fascinated by all the details as the other children benefited as well.

Many gifted preschoolers are very verbal; they easily absorb new vocabulary and are often interested in learning to read. Many show a fascination with books and some gifted

From *Children Today*, Vol. 22, No. 3, 1993, pp. 28-30. Reprinted by permission of *Children Today*, a publication of the Administration for Children and Families, U.S. Department of Health and Human Services.

children teach themselves to read before they enter kindergarten. Activities that introduce advanced vocabulary would be an excellent source of enrichment for gifted preschoolers. A unit on the oceans could be expanded for the gifted children by showing all the children a video of coral reefs. The gifted children would enjoy learning the names of the animals that live in the reefs—names like banner fish, anemones and clown fish. The teacher could print word cards with the names of the animals that live in the reef so the gifted children could use them to make sentences and stories.

The Need For Play

Play is one of the best ways for children to learn. According to Johnson, Christie and Yawkey (1987) children need at least a 30- to 50-minute block of uninterrupted time during their free play period to enact an episode in dramatic or consecutive play. It takes time for them to organize themselves and their materials and work out their ideas. Gifted preschoolers especially need these longer time blocks because they often are able to create extensive sociodramatic play episodes and build complicated block structures. They may get so involved in their play that they are reluctant to stop and move on to something else. They need to play with their intellectual peers to experience the joys of playing with someone who can understand them and help create these dramatic play episodes.

For example, five-year-old Jane often played at home with Megan, a non-gifted friend. Megan was not as advanced in her dramatic play as Jane was and would play the same role again and again with little imagination or variation. Jane would try to involve Megan in more complicated roles but would give up and go off to read a book by herself when Jane didn't respond. When Jane played with Beth, her gifted peer, the dramatic play would last for hours, with both children playing joyfully. Dramatic play can be especially

enriching for gifted preschoolers who have the imaginations and concepts to carry out elaborate play episodes.

Thematic Units

Thematic units in science and social studies are an excellent way to meet gifted children's intellectual needs. The units, along with appropriate field trips, can provide much of the enrichment a gifted preschooler needs. The block and dramatic play areas, art, music and literacy centers can all be coordinated around the theme. Some possible themes are:
- Pioneers
- The Ocean
- Dinosaurs
- Space
- Animals and Habitats.

Depending on the children's interest levels, the thematic unit can be as much as a month long. The unit should allow for more detail for the gifted preschoolers. For example, if the class is studying space exploration, props such as pieces of dryer hose for breathing equipment, space helmets, walkie talkies, a refrigerator box for a space ship and food in plastic bags could be put in the dramatic play center. The gifted children in the center will probably be organizing the play and helping the others create more complicated story lines. If the children are absorbed in their dramatic play, extending the play time will benefit all the children while meeting the needs of the gifted children.

Reading the children such books as *The Magic School Bus Lost in the Solar System,* and then inviting all of them to dictate individual stories using this theme to make their own books is a way to extend this theme. Later, the teacher could read to the gifted children more of the details in this book, which has two levels. This activity suits the needs of the gifted child, who may dictate more elaborate stories and spend more time illustrating them.

A field trip to a planetarium would fascinate most children while it enriches the gifted preschoolers, who

would love learning the names of the stars and constellations. A visit from an aerospace engineer or an astronomer who could share how their occupations related to space would be another way to provide enrichment.

Activities For Gifted Preschoolers

There are many other activities teachers or parents can do with gifted preschoolers. Examples of these are:
- reading higher level books to the children. Gifted 4-year-olds might enjoy listening to such books as *The Trumpet of the Swan* by E.B. White. They often enjoy paging through books about science and nature. The book corner should have books reflecting different interests and reading levels.
- teaching the children to use computers. Some programs such as *Dinosaurs and Facemaker* are enjoyed by gifted young children (Alvino, 1988).
- introducing them to music appreciation by letting them listen to Vivaldi, Bach and Raffi.
- introducing them to art appreciation by teaching them about great artists and different art styles, taking them to the art gallery, and reading them picture books with high quality illustrations such as *Animalia* by Graeme Base.
- providing a variety of manipulative materials—such as parquetry blocks, peg boards and Jumbo Cuisenaire Rods—to encourage math development (Alvino, 1989).
- teaching critical thinking skills and problem solving by introducing them to simple logic puzzles and mazes.
- providing art activities rather than crafts. A craft activity can intimidate gifted children, who are perfectionists and become frustrated when their project doesn't look like the model.

Ideas From Parents

Parents of gifted preschoolers are an ideal source of ideas. Here is a list of activities collected from parents of gifted preschoolers:

- Teach them to play card games of all kinds, e.g. War, Slap Jack, checkers, *Monopoly, Chutes and Ladders* and chess. They learn to read words and numbers, count and reason from these activities.
- Immerse them in literature by having books in every room to encourage their desire to learn to read.
- Leave writing and drawing materials out at all times for them to use, and have a special drawer of "junk" materials that can be used to create projects.
- Let them be chemists: Give them your old spices, vinegar and baking soda and let them see what happens.
- Make a list with them of all the materials they would need if they were buying a pet; figure the costs with them and take them comparison shopping.

- Give them coupons and let them choose items they would like to buy.
- Let them plan a party of their choice, designing the invitations, making the guest list and arranging for the activities and refreshments. Then hold the party.

Conclusions

Gifted preschoolers provide a special challenge to teachers and parents alike. Child care specialists, childhood development workers and educators need to remember that although gifted preschoolers may think like 8-year-olds, they are still preschoolers. The key to enriching gifted preschoolers lies in knowing their interests and offering activities and materials to expand these interests. Gifted preschool children can test the patience of both parents and teachers. Interesting and challenging activities at home and in preschool will help channel their energy and intellectual curiosity in positive ways. It is the job of parents and teachers to see to it that these children receive appropriate educational experiences so that boredom and underachievement don't occur (Koopmans-Dayton and Feldhusen, 1987).

References

Alvino, J. (1989). *Parents' Guide to Raising a Gifted Toddler.* Boston: Little, Brown and Company.

Base, G. (1986). *Animalia.* New York: Harry N. Abrams, Inc.

Cole, J. (1991). *The Magic School Bus Lost in the Solar System.* New York: Scholastic.

Karnes, M.B. and Johnson, L.J. (1991). The Preschool/Primary Gifted Child. *Journal for the Education of the Gifted,* 14(3), 267-283.

Koopmans-Dayton, J.D. and Feldhusen, J.F. (1987). A Resource Guide for Parents of Gifted Preschoolers. *Gifted Child Today,* 10(6), 2-7.

White, E.B. (1970). *The Trumpet of the Swan.* New York: Harper & Row.

Wolfe, J. (1989). The Gifted Preschooler: Developmentally Different but Still 3 or 4 Years Old. *Young Children,* 44(3), 41-48.

Gifted Girls in a Rural Community: Math Attitudes and Career Options

ABSTRACT: This study was designed to determine the feasibility of improving gifted girls' attitudes toward mathematics. This study was conducted in three school districts in an isolated rural setting. Subjects were 24 gifted girls in Grades 4-7. A control group also contained 24 gifted girls at the same grade levels. On pretest, using the Mathematics Attitude Inventory *(MAI), no significant differences were found between groups in their attitudes toward math. The intervention program included problem-solving activities, math-related career options, and self-esteem issues. MAI posttest scores after the 18-week program indicated that the program was effective in changing attitudes toward mathematics of gifted girls in a rural environment.*

JULIE LAMB

ROBERTA DANIELS

JULIE LAMB (CEC #185), educator for gifted children, Paragould, Northeast Arkansas School District. ROBERTA DANIELS (CEC #345), Director of Gifted Education, Special Education Department, Arkansas State University, Jonesboro, Arkansas.

□ For many years, researchers (Armstrong, 1979; Boswell & Katz, 1980; Fennema & Sherman, 1977; Fox, 1980) have been interested in educational and career barriers between females and the field of mathematics. Early research (Fennema & Sherman) indicated that males outperformed females in math achievement at the junior high and high school level but also found significant differences in attitudes toward math between the two groups. More than 10 years ago, Armstrong concluded that the development of attitudes that affect females' math achievement begins around age 13. Armstrong's research included a survey of 1,452 13-year-old students and 1,788 high school seniors and offered strong evidence that stereotypical expectation of parents, peers, and teachers influenced females' decisions not to participate in math. Thus, females' lack of positive attitudes toward math has been attributed to stereotyping rather than a lack of ability.

More recently, Kerr (1988) contended that gifted girls are rewarded for intellectual achievement at early ages; but by adolescence, they are rewarded for social conformity, which may include seeing math as masculine. In a 1984 study, Flemming and Hollinger examined internal barriers for gifted girls, which may prohibit their success in mathematics. These barriers included the following:

1. An avoidance of math because it is not feminine.
2. An exhibition of a lack of ability in math due to the lack of social expectation.
3. A lack of seeing math as necessary for obtaining their educational and career goals.

Gifted girls in rural settings may be particularly influenced by social conformity which affects their attitudes toward math due to cultural beliefs of the community. The demise of the one-room schoolhouse has not eliminated traditional rural values, which include sex-role stereotyping that may discourage gifted girls' participation in math and science (Howley, Pendarvis, & Howley, 1988; Southern, Spicker, & Davis, 1987).

From *Exceptional Children*, Vol. 59, No. 6, May 1993, pp. 513-517. © 1993 by The Council for Exceptional Children. Reprinted by permission.

By limiting their academic choices in math at adolescence, gifted girls also limit their occupational choices. Boswell and Katz (1980) found that girls who had a deficiency in high school mathematics courses did not have an appropriate background to enter technical fields of study in college. Further, many gifted girls fail to realize the potential of their early years, settling for jobs well below their abilities (Shaffer, 1986). In a study of the lives of 22 women who had been identified as gifted girls, Shaffer found that only 3 women reported having challenging careers. Gifted women, who have not fulfilled their academic potential and do not have challenging careers, may be largely regretful (Kerr, 1988). Gifted females in rural societies are no exception to the need for fulfilling career potential that may likewise benefit the rural communities (Howley et al., 1988).

Fox and Tobin (1988) have offered suggestions for improving math attitudes of gifted females, based on research conducted with 24, mathematically talented, 7th-grade girls. The girls were involved in exploration of math-related careers through four minicourses pertaining to geometry, statistics, probability, and computer science. During the program, the girls met with women scientists and mathematicians to examine engineering, medical research, and space exploration. Results of pre- and postmeasures of attitude and career interest demonstrated the effectiveness of the model that had a positive impact on the gifted females' math attitudes and career awareness.

As gifted girls participate in programs to deter negative attitudes toward mathematics, there is an increased opportunity to maximize career options as young adults. Because research (Armstrong, 1979; Boswell & Katz, 1980; Kerr, 1988) has described a change in attitude beginning with adolescence, the present intervention program began at the elementary level. The purpose of this study was to determine if an intervention program implemented in an isolated rural setting and designed to improve gifted girls' attitudes toward mathematics would produce positive math attitudes.

METHODS

Subjects

Forty-eight girls identified as academically gifted ranging from 4th to 7th grade participated in this study. The numbers per grade for the experimental group were as follows: 6 fourth graders, 4 fifth graders, 6 sixth graders, and 8 seventh graders. The control group contained 5 fourth graders, 7 fifth graders, 4 sixth graders, and 8 seventh graders. The 48 girls were included in the gifted program (which is a cooperative program that exists in three isolated rural communities' schools), based on scores from standardized aptitude and achievement tests and teachers' recommendations. Twenty-four girls from one school comprised the experimental group that received the intervention program. The control group consisted of 24 girls from the remaining two schools.

Though gifted girls from only one rural school district comprised the experimental group, the schools are demographically close—within an 18-mile radius. Each school is located in a small community (i.e., 3,000 or less in population). Similarities in socioeconomic status of the three communities are consistent: Each contains small merchant businesses, small factories, and crop farming.

Procedures

A quasi-experimental design using a pretest, posttest, and control group was used for the study so that control for threats to internal validity of maturation and selection was established. To control for possible variations between the control and experimental groups, a pretest using the *Mathematics Attitude Inventory* (MAI) (Sandman, 1980) was administered to all 48 gifted girls.

The MAI is a 48-item, self-rating scale. According to Sandman (1980), the test reports attitude toward math teachers, anxiety toward math, value of math in society, self-concept in math, enjoyment of math, and motivation in math. Eight questions in each of the six categories comprise the self-rating scale. Each question was answered according to a 4-point Likert scale (strongly agree, agree, disagree, or strongly disagree). The possible maximum score was 192 points, with a possible minimum score of 48 points.

A statistical analysis using *t*-test scores revealed that there were no significant differences between the experimental and control groups' scores for all six categories on the pretests. The total mean scores for the pretests, as measured by the MAI, were 140.38 for the experimental group and 142.17 for the control group, resulting in a *t*-test score of .26.

The MAI reports a maximum score of 32 and a minimum score of 8 for each of the six subtests. Subtest scores for the experimental and control groups on the girls' attitudes toward their math teacher, anxiety toward math, value of math in society, self-concept in math, enjoyment of math, and motivation in math are shown in Table 1. It should be noted that a high score on the anxiety toward math subtest reports low anxiety. There were no significant differences between the scores of the experimental and control groups on any of the subtests of the MAI.

The experimental group received the intervention program, which consisted of an 18-week treatment. The gifted girls were told at the first class meeting that they would be involved in a

TABLE 1
Pretest Scores of Experimental and Control Groups of Gifted Girls

Math Attitude	Experimental		Control		t	p
	Mean	(SD)	Mean	(SD)		
Attitude toward math teacher	22.33	(8.13)	24.88	(5.34)	1.28	.207
Anxiety	24.67	(4.43)	25.08	(4.62)	.32	.751
Value of math in society	26.75	(3.12)	26.29	(3.29)	.49	.623
Self-concept in math	24.25	(4.07)	24.54	(4.13)	.25	.806
Enjoyment of math	21.83	(4.86)	20.75	(4.64)	.79	.434
Motivation	20.54	(5.75)	20.63	(4.54)	.06	.956
Total	140.38	(25.97)	142.17	(21.70)	.26	.796

Note: $N = 24$ in each group. Differences not significant.

special unit pertaining to math. They were informed that they would be doing some fun activities and were given an overview of the activities they would encounter. The experimental group discussed the importance of the career decisions that each would encounter and how math-related careers were one available option. However, the group was not told that the unit was being implemented to determine if their attitudes toward math would change.

The intervention program included attitude and career awareness activities based on *Just Around the Corner* (Roberts, 1982) and *Math for Girls and Other Problem Solvers* (Downie, Slesnick, & Stenmark, 1981). The gifted girls developed problem-solving strategies according to *Problem of the Week* (Fisher & Medigovich, 1981) and *Mental Math in the Middle Grades* (Hope, Reys, & Reys, 1987). These materials contain both individual and group activities dealing with attitudes about mathematical decisions, career information in the area of math, and problem-solving strategies. Activities for the experimental group, Grades 4-7, were grouped according to units, for approximately 2 weeks per unit. The gifted girls in Grades 4-6 met daily for 30 min for 18 weeks for the intervention program. The 7th-grade girls met 2 days per week for 1 hr each meeting during the semester to receive the intervention program.

According to Fox and Tobin (1988) and Kerr (1988), intervention programming should encourage gifted girls to obtain a positive self-concept pertaining to mathematical concepts. The present intervention included six units. Unit 1 included activities to enhance self-esteem, such as the following:

1. Making lists of "Things I Do and Don't Do Well" and ways to improve the areas of lesser confidence.

2. Participating in role play to demonstrate optimistic and pessimistic attitudes.
3. Debating the effects of self-perception as it relates to task commitment.

After exploring the importance of a positive attitude in all pursuits, students went on to Unit 2, which emphasized appreciating math as a useful tool in daily events. This unit, involving school peers and the community, began with a "Math Appreciation Day." Other activities examined the work of people who dealt with mathematical processes in their daily lives, explored the usefulness of mathematical knowledge for particular industries in the community, and developed budgets for the girls' families after investigating how money and math processes coincide.

Unit 3 was designed to improve girls' problem-solving abilities (Fisher & Medigovich, 1981). In Unit 4, the girls developed a math newspaper, *Math Rap*, for the school. The girls created math games, puzzles, comics, and news about activities in their math classes.

Though not all models developed to involve females in math to promote positive attitudes have incorporated the same strategies, all have reported the importance of career awareness in math-related fields (e.g., Boswell & Katz, 1980; Fox & Tobin, 1988; Shaffer, 1986). Therefore, Unit 5 dealt with occupations in math-related fields. Resources were made available by the school and community libraries, the school counselor, and community industries so that the girls could research different occupations. Female guest speakers with math-related occupations were invited from industries in the community.

While participating in Unit 6, the 24 girls in the experimental group provided a tutoring service for a variety of students, at which time they showed a high level of confidence. The final intervention strategies included problem-solving

TABLE 2
Posttest Scores of Experimental and Control Groups of Gifted Girls

Math Attitudes	Experimental		Control			
	Mean	(SD)	Mean	(SD)	t	p
Attitude toward math teacher	25.96	(6.45)	23.33	(5.17)	1.56	.126
Anxiety	29.49	(2.41)	24.71	(4.51)	4.55	.001*
Value of math in society	30.46	(1.77)	25.42	(3.94)	5.71	.0001*
Self-concept in math	28.83	(2.04)	23.96	(3.91)	5.42	.0001*
Enjoyment of math	28.13	(2.69)	21.13	(3.36)	7.96	.0001*
Motivation	26.17	(3.20)	21.00	(4.59)	4.53	.001*
Total	169.00	(14.77)	139.54	(21.85)	5.47	.0001*

Note: N = 24 in each group.
*p < .05.

RESULTS

Statistical differences at the .05 level of significance in math attitudes of gifted girls were found between the experimental and control groups for the posttest scores. The total mean score of the posttests for the experimental group was 169.00; the control group's mean score was 139.54. Differences between the total mean scores of the posttests for the experimental and control groups resulted in a *t*-test score of 5.47. There were statistical differences significant at the .05 level in five of the six subtests (i.e., anxiety, value of math in society, self-concept in math, enjoyment of math, and motivation in math) (see Table 2). The gifted girls' posttest scores did not significantly differ in their attitudes toward their math teacher. As regular classroom math lessons continued routinely throughout the duration of the intervention program, attitudes for the classroom teachers did not vary.

Although no statistical differences at the .05 level of significance were reported on the pretest scores for any of the six subtests, experimental group scores increased after participation in the intervention program. Based on the results of the statistical analysis of the posttest scores, it was concluded that the intervention program designed to improve the math attitudes of the gifted females from that isolated rural area made a significant difference in the 24 gifted girls' math attitudes as measured by the MAI (Sandman, 1980).

CONCLUSION

Armstrong (1979) and Boswell and Katz (1980)

have reported that sex differences in mathematics achievement were not due to ability but some attitudinal factors. Kerr (1988) asserted that stereotypical expectations placed on girls relative to math involvement were the most influential factor affecting girls' choices to participate in math. According to Howley et al. (1988), gifted girls from rural areas are even less likely to participate in math because of traditional values of a rural community that may view involvement in math and math-related careers as a "masculine" trait.

The concern of some researchers (Fox & Tobin, 1988; Kerr, 1988; Shaffer, 1986) has focused on the loss of career potential and future happiness of gifted females who limit themselves in math due to internal barriers (via attitude). If these contentions are true, this study provides evidence that systematic intervention programming can positively influence the attitudes of gifted females toward math.

Further research needs to be conducted on populations in other isolated rural areas. It might be noted that a cursory glance at the raw data of this study revealed that large gains were obtained in the 4th and 5th grade. Further analysis in future studies should consider comparing the attitudes of larger groups of gifted girls by grade level to determine at which level intervention programs should be implemented for the most benefit.

A limitation of this study exists in the selection process. Location and the number of available gifted girls prevented the subjects from being randomly selected. The gains made by the experimental group are very likely due to the variety and extent of activities provided in the intervention program. Another factor that cannot be statistically supported by this study but had a possible effect on the findings, may be linked to the researcher as a female role model. Thus, further research is likewise recommended concerning

activities to reinforce skills from Unit 3 and concluded with the administration of the MAI as a posttest.

female role models' effect on gifted girls' math attitudes, particularly in rural settings.

If young gifted girls are to reach their potential mathematically, they must possess positive attitudes. The evidence from this study indicates that math attitudes of gifted females can be influenced. Thus, gifted females (even those from rural areas) can develop potential that will broaden career choices.

REFERENCES

Armstrong, J. M. (1979). *Achievement and participation of women in mathematics.* (Report No. NIE-G-7-0061). Denver, CO: Education Commission of the States. (ERIC Document Reproduction Service No. ED 184878)

Boswell, S. L., & Katz, P. A. (1980). *Nice girls don't study mathematics.* (Report No. NIE-G-78-0023). Boulder, CO: Institute for Research on Social Problems. (ERIC Document Reproduction Service No. ED 188888)

Downie, D., Slesnick, T., & Stenmark, J. (1981). *Math for girls and other problem solvers.* Berkeley, CA: Dale Seymour.

Fennema, E., & Sherman, J. (1977). Sex-related differences in mathematics achievement, spatial visualization and socio-cultural factors. *American Educational Research Journal, 14*, 51-71.

Fisher, L., & Medigovich, W. (1981). *Problem of the week.* Palo Alto, CA: Dale Seymour.

Flemming, E. S., & Hollinger, C. L. (1984). Internal barriers to the realization of potential: Correlates and interrelationships among gifted and talented female adolescents. *Gifted Child Quarterly, 28*, 135-140.

Fox, L. H. (1980). *The problem of women and mathematics.* New York: Library of Congress, Department of Cataloging in Publication Data. (ERIC Document Reproduction Service No. ED 211353)

Fox, L. H., & Tobin, D. (1988). Broadening career horizons for gifted girls. *The Gifted Child Today, 11*(1), 9-12.

Hope, J., Reys, B., & Reys, R. (1987). *Mental math in the middle grades.* Palo Alto, CA: Dale Seymour.

Howley, A. A., Pendarvis, E. E., & Howley, C. B. (1988). Gifted students in rural environments: Implication for school programs. *Rural Special Education Quarterly, 8*(4), 43-50.

Kerr, B. A. (1988). Raising career aspirations of gifted girls. *Vocational Guidance Quarterly, 32*(1), 37-43.

Roberts, D. R. (1982). *Just around the corner.* Little Rock: Arkansas Department of Education.

Sandman, R. S. (1980). *Mathematics Attitude Inventory.* Minneapolis: Minnesota Evaluation Center, University of Minnesota.

Shaffer, S. M. (1986). *Gifted girls: The disappearing act.* Washington, DC: Mid-Atlantic Center for Sex Equity. (ERIC Document Reproduction Service No. ED 301 994)

Southern, W. T., Spicker, H. H., & Davis, B. I. (1987). The rural gifted child. *Gifted Child Quarterly, 31*(4), 155-157.

We would like to thank John Enger of Arkansas State University for assistance with the statistical analysis and Beverly Shaklee of Kent State University for assistance with revisions.

Manuscript received December 1991; revision accepted April 1992.

Early Childhood Exceptionality

The 1986 amendment to the Individuals with Disabilities Education Act (IDEA) provided for intervention for young children with disabilities much earlier than elementary school. This amendment, Public Law 99–457, calls for early childhood special education and family-child intervention at home. All services to be provided for any infant, toddler, or preschooler with a disability and for his or her family are to be articulated in an individualized family service plan (IFSP). The IFSP will be written and implemented as soon as the disabling condition is diagnosed. In some cases, an IFSP can be written and implemented without the actual fact of a diagnosed exceptional condition. Some children believed to be "at risk" of a disability can also receive early childhood services. At-risk conditions may be problems associated with prematurity, low birth weight, birth injuries, and early environmental

trauma. IFSPs, like Individualized Education Programs (IEPs) in public school, are written in collaboration with parents, experts in the area of the child's exceptional condition, teachers, home-service providers, and other significant service providers. They are updated every six months until the child enters public school and receives an IEP.

In the United States, an association called Child Find has the responsibility for identifying infants, toddlers, and young children who qualify for early childhood special education and family services. Assessment is usually accomplished in a multidisciplinary fashion. It can be very difficult. As much as possible, it is conducted in the child's home in a nonthreatening fashion. Diagnosis of exceptionalities in children who cannot yet answer questions is complicated. Personal observations are used, as well as parent reports. Most of the experts involved in the multidisciplinary assessment want to see the child more than once to help compensate for the fact that all children have good days and bad days. Despite the care taken, many children who qualify for, and would benefit from, early intervention services are missed. On occasion, diagnoses of need are also made for children who outgrow their problems or were not truly subject to a disabling condition.

A challenge to all professionals providing early childhood special services is how to work with diverse parents. Some parents welcome any and all intervention, even if it is not merited. Other parents resist any labeling of their child as "disabled" and refuse services. Professionals must make allowances for cultural, economic, and educational diversity, multiple caregivers, and single parenting. Regardless of the situation, parental participation is the sine qua non of early childhood intervention. Fathers and mothers, and/or significant others, should be included in the planning and implementation of any prescribed treatments in order to maximize their usefulness.

At-home services may include instruction in the use of any assistive aids (e.g., wheelchair, hearing aid, cane), ways of meeting the educational goals of the IFSP, and basic skills such as discipline, behavior management, nutritional goals, and health maintenance. At-home services usually also include counseling for parents, siblings, and significant others to help them deal with their fears, anger, and anxiety and to help them understand how to accept, love, and challenge their special child to become all he or she is capable of being. A case manager is always

named for the interdisciplinary team to help ensure that there is cooperation and coordination of services by all team members and family members.

Most children receiving early childhood services have some center-based or combined center- and home-based special education. Center care introduces children to peers and introduces family to other families with similar concerns. It is easier to ensure quality education and evaluate progress when a child spends at least a part of his or her time in a well-equipped educational setting.

The first article in this unit concerns the assessment of needs in young children. The authors suggest that real-life activities that occur in naturalistic, everyday settings be substituted for some of the more artificial tasks routinely used in assessment (e.g., putting pegs in a pegboard). Real-life tasks can facilitate parent involvement. Assessment can also be broken down into specific components tailored to the child. The article includes a valuable checklist for writing goals and objectives for the IFSPs of infants and young children with exceptional conditions.

The next unit article is concerned with the needs of all children for physical education. Public Law 99-457 included young children in the IDEA provisions that mandate physical education: fitness, motor skills, sports skills, games, aquatics, and dance. Children with disabilities have the right to physical education in the least restrictive environment suitable to their individualized needs. Program goals and objectives for preschool children with disabilities and a sample core curriculum are included in this report.

The last article in this unit presents an 11-step program that facilitates social interaction between preschool children with disabilities and their nondisabled peers. The program has been pretested and has won approval from teachers. It encourages children to work and play together as friends.

Looking Ahead: Challenge Questions

How can assessment of early childhood disabilities be made more age appropriate, more educationally meaningful, and more enjoyable for families and children?

What is an optimum physical education curriculum for preschoolers with disabilities?

How can preschool "Buddy Skills" training procedures enhance the interactions and friendships between children with and children without disabilities?

Putting
Real-Life Skills
into IEP/IFSPs for
Infants and Young Children

ANGELA R. NOTARI-SYVERSON
SARA LERNER SHUSTER

Angela R. Notari-Syverson *(CEC Washington Federation), Project Director, Experimental Education Unit, Child Development and Mental Retardation Center, University of Washington, Seattle, and Research Associate, Washington Research Institute, Seattle.* **Sara Lerner Shuster**, *Instructor, Department of Teacher Education, University of Dayton, Ohio.*

An ecological approach (Bronfenbrenner, 1979) to intervention with infants and young children (6 months to 3 years) takes into account the functionality and meaning of the child's behavior across a variety of daily contexts (Hobbs, 1975), as well as the interpretation of behaviors from the family's perspective and value system (Bernheimer, Gallimore, & Weisner, 1990). From an ecological viewpoint, assessment and intervention should focus on real-life situations. Skills assessed and taught should have functional meaning as part of practical activities that fit into a family's daily routines (Johnson, McGonigel, & Kaufman, 1989) and should be generalizable across different environments (Seibert, 1987). Intervention strategies should be activity based, with educational goals and objectives embed-ded in routine activities that occur in naturalistic, everyday settings (Bricker & Cripe, 1989).

Guidelines for Developing Educational Goals and Objectives

To assist early interventionists in developing and evaluating educational goals and objectives that reflect skills that are relevant to everyday functioning, we propose a comprehensive set of guidelines in the form of questions for early interventionists to pose when developing individualized education programs (IEPs) and individualized family service plans (IFSPs). The guidelines were derived from a rating instrument developed for a study that evaluated the quality of IEP goals and objectives written for infants and young children (Notari & Bricker, 1990). The indicators and components included in the guidelines are identical to those of the rating instrument.

The questions cover five general characteristics identified from the current literature as indicators of high-quality goals and objectives: functionality, generality, ease of integration within the instructional context, measurability, and hierarchical relationship between long-range goal and short-term objective. The first 4 indicators are broken down into 10 specific components.

Functionality

Functionality refers to the characteristics of skills needed for effective and independent coping within the daily environment (Brown, Nietupski, & Hamre-Nietupski, 1976; LeBlanc, Etzel, & Domash, 1978; Wolery, 1989). Functionality includes two components: (1) The skill will increase the child's ability to interact with people and objects within the daily environment, and (2) the skill will have to be performed by someone else if the child cannot do it. For example, sorting shapes to corresponding pictures of shapes is not a skill that a child is likely to use during daily activities, whereas the child *is* likely to use the skill of matching various shaped lids to corresponding containers. While both skills involve matching, recognizing, and sorting shapes, the use of

From *Teaching Exceptional Children*, Vol. 27, No. 2, Winter 1995, pp. 29-32. © 1995 by The Council for Exceptional Children. Reprinted by permission.

functional objects such as containers and lids enables the child to learn a necessary skill that will foster independence in real-life situations.

Generality

Generality consists of three components: (1) The skill represents a general concept as opposed to a particular task (Bricker, 1986; Brinker, 1985); (2) the skill allows for individual adaptations and modifications for a variety of disabling conditions

---

Children may be motivated to perform at higher levels when everyday objects and functional activities are substituted for less meaningful manipulative items often found on developmental assessment batteries.

(Robinson & Rosenberg, 1987); and (3) the skill can be generalized across settings, materials, and people (Seibert, 1987). For example, targeting the specific skill of placing balls, blocks, and triangles into a sort box excludes many opportunities for a child to practice other skills that represent the generic concept of placing objects in a defined space, such as putting shoes in a shoebox, books in a particular space in the book rack, soap in a soap dish, or caps on pens. By focusing on the underlying concept of a skill, adults can modify and adapt materials and expected responses to the individual characteristics of a child. An example would be using noise-making objects for a child with visual impairments (e.g., placing a receiver on a toy telephone, pushing a noisy car into a garage). The emphasis on a generic process facilitates generalization because the skill can be taught using different objects in a variety of settings.

Ease of Integration

From an ecological perspective (Dunst, 1981; Hobbs, 1975), the ease of integration of a skill within daily routines is essential for meaningful and naturalistic teaching (Johnson, 1982; Templeman, Fredericks, & Udell, 1989). Skills should be taught in a way that reflects use in daily environments and should be easily elicited within home and classroom activities. For example, the skill "Walks between parallel lines 8 inches apart" requires the arrangement of an artificial clinical or educational situation, whereas the skill "Walks avoiding obstacles" can be taught using naturalistic intervention strategies and gives the teacher many opportunities to integrate the skill within daily routines, taking advantage of naturally occurring antecedents and logical consequences.

Measurability

For reliability and evaluation purposes, a skill needs to be measurable. A skill is measurable if it can be seen and/or heard; it can be directly counted (e.g., by frequency, duration, or distance measures); and it lends itself to determination of performance criteria. Compare, for example, the objectives "Child will participate at circle time" and "Child will participate in group activities by requesting a turn." The latter objective reflects a specific level of participation (requesting a turn), is observable, and can be counted (i.e., number of times the child requests a turn), and performance criteria can be established for it (i.e., two out of the three opportunities during each daily group time over 3 consecutive days).

Hierarchical Relationship

Finally, long-range goals and short-term objectives should be conceptually related within a hierarchical progression by formulating consistent instructional sequences that will increase the complexity of a child's skills (Brinker, 1985; Darby, 1979; Garwood, 1982; Johnson, 1982; Seibert, 1987; Tymitz-Wolf, 1982; Wolery, 1989). Three categories have been defined to classify the relationship between long-range goals and short-term objectives (see Figure 1). It is important to note that a long-range goal, as well as a short-term objective, should represent a specific expectation or skill, as opposed to a vague, generic statement such as "Will participate at circle time" or "To improve social communication skills." Figure 1 presents a list of the 10 components and 5 categories, with additional clarifications and examples of appropriate skills and opportunities to elicit skills in specific environments and situations.

Evaluation

Data on content validity and interrater reliability of the guidelines were obtained by having seven experts in early childhood special education rate a total of 24 long-range goals and short-term objectives. Interrater reliability ranged from 75% to 88%, with a mean of 82% for the 10 components and the hierarchical relationship. The indicators were identified from the current literature and judged by all seven experts as appropriate and comprehensive.

Conclusion

Teachers can apply the guidelines presented in this article in a variety of ways. They can use them to select educationally relevant assessments by evaluating the appropriateness of assessment items to serve as curriculum goals and objectives. They can rephrase educationally inappropriate assessment items derived from normative developmental tests into functional and educationally meaningful skills by identifying the underlying general concept, then applying it to daily situations with common objects. For example, "Places pegs in pegboard" can be reworded to "Fits objects in defined spaces," and "Uncovers rattle hidden under a cloth" can be reworded to "Locates a hidden object."

The guidelines may also be used as part of the IEP/IFSP process to facilitate parent involvement and integration of goals and objectives within family routines. For example, the guidelines may be given to parents to help identify functional goals for their child. They may be used together with the teacher to evaluate how well IEP/IFSP content optimizes active participation of the child within family, school, and community environments.

FIGURE 1. CHECKLIST FOR WRITING IEP/IFSP GOALS AND OBJECTIVES FOR INFANTS AND YOUNG CHILDREN

FUNCTIONALITY

1. **Will the skill increase the child's ability to interact with people and objects within the daily environment?**
   The child needs to perform the skill in all or most of the environments in which he or she interacts.
   Skill: Places object into container.
   Opportunities: Home—Places sweater in drawer, cookie in paper bag.
   School—Places lunch box in cubbyhole, trash in trash bin.
   Community—Places milk carton in grocery cart, rocks and soil in flower pot.

2. **Will the skill have to be performed by someone else if the child cannot do it?**
   The skill is a behavior or event that is critical for completion of daily routines.
   Skill: Looks for object in usual location.
   Opportunities: Finds coat on coat rack, gets food from cupboard.

GENERALITY

3. **Does the skill represent a general concept or class of responses? The skill emphasizes a generic process, rather than a particular instance.**
   Skill: Fits objects into defined spaces.
   Opportunities: Puts mail in mailbox, places crayon in box, puts cutlery into sorter.

4. **Can the skill be adapted or modified for a variety of disabling conditions?**
   The child's sensory impairment should interfere as little as possible with the performance.
   Skill: Correctly activates simple toy.
   Opportunities: Motor impairments—Activates light, easy-to-move toys (e.g., balls, rocking horse, toys on wheels, roly-poly toys).
   Visual impairments—Activates large, bright, noise-making toys (e.g., bells, drums, large rattles).

5. **Can the skill be generalized across a variety of settings, materials, and/or people?**
   The child can perform the skill with interesting materials and in meaningful situations.
   Skill: Manipulates two small objects simultaneously.
   Opportunities: Home—Builds with small interlocking blocks, threads lace on shoes.
   School—Sharpens pencil with pencil sharpener.
   Community—Takes coin out of small wallet.

INSTRUCTIONAL CONTEXT

6. **Can the skill be taught in a way that reflects the manner in which the skill will be used in daily environments?**
   The skill can occur in a naturalistic manner.
   Skill: Uses object to obtain another object.
   Opportunities: Uses fork to obtain food, broom to rake toy; steps on stool to reach toy on shelf.

7. **Can the skill be elicited easily by the teacher/parent within classroom/home activities?**
   The skill can be initiated easily by the child as part of daily routines.
   Skill: Stacks objects.
   Opportunities: Stacks books, cups/plates, wooden logs.

MEASURABILITY

8. **Can the skill be seen and/or heard?**
   Different observers must be able to identify the same behavior.
   Measurable skill: Gains attention and refers to object, person, and/or event.
   Nonmeasurable skill: Experiences a sense of self-importance.

9. **Can the skill be directly counted (e.g., by frequency, duration, distance measures)?**
   The skill represents a well-defined behavior or activity.
   Measurable skill: Grasps pea-sized object.
   Nonmeasurable skill: Has mobility in all fingers.

10. **Does the skill contain or lend itself to determination of performance criteria?**
    The extent and/or degree of accuracy of the skill can be evaluated.
    Measurable skill: Follows one-step directions with contextual cues.
    Nonmeasurable skill: Will increase receptive language skills.

HIERARCHICAL RELATION BETWEEN LONG-RANGE GOAL AND SHORT-TERM OBJECTIVE

Is the short-term objective a developmental subskill or step thought to be critical to the achievement of the long-range goal?
Appropriate: Short-Term Objective—Releases object with each hand.
Long-Range-Goal—Places and releases object balanced on top of another object.
Inappropriate: 1. The Short-Term Objective is a restatement of the same skill as the Long-Range-Goal, with the addition of an instructional prompt (e.g., Short-Term Objective—Activates mechanical toy with physical prompt. Long-Range-Goal—Independently activates mechanical toy) or a quantitative limitation to the extent of the skill (e.g., Short-Term Objective—Stacks 5 1-inch blocks; Long-Range-Goal—Stacks 10 1-inch blocks).
2. The Short-Term Objective is not conceptually or functionally related to the Long-Range-Goal (e.g., Short-Term Objective— Releases object voluntarily; Long-Range-Goal—Pokes with index finger).

References

Bernheimer, L. P., Gallimore, R., & Weisner, T. S. (1990). Ecocultural theory as a context for the individual family service plan. *Journal of Early Intervention, 14*(3), 219–233.

Bricker, D. (1986). *Early education of at-risk and handicapped infants, toddlers, and preschool children.* Glenview, IL: Scott Foresman.

Bricker, D., & Cripe, J. (1989). Activity-based intervention. In D. Bricker (Ed.), *Early education of at-risk and handicapped infants, toddlers, and preschool children* (2nd ed.) (pp. 251–274). Palo Alto, CA: Vort.

Brinker, R. P. (1985). Curricula without recipes: A challenge to teachers and a promise to severely mentally retarded students. In D. Bricker & J. Filler (Eds.), *Severe mental retardation: From theory to practice* (pp. 208–229). Reston, VA: The Council for Exceptional Children.

Bronfenbrenner, U. (1979). *The ecology of human development: Experiments of nature and design.* Cambridge, MA: Harvard University Press.

Brown, L., Nietupski, J., & Hamre-Nietupski, S. (1976). The criterion of ultimate functioning. In M. A. Thomas (Ed.), *Hey, don't forget about me* (pp. 2–15). Reston, VA: The Council for Exceptional Children.

Darby, B. L. (1979). Infant cognition: Considerations for assessment tools. In B. L. Darby & M. J. May (Eds.), *Infant assessment: Issues and applications* (pp. 103–111). Monmouth, OR: WESTAR.

Dunst, C. J. (1981). *Infant learning: A cognitive-linguistic intervention strategy.* Allen, TX: DLM Teaching Resources.

Garwood, S. G. (1982). (Mis)use of developmental scales in program evaluation. *Topics in Early Childhood Special Education, 1*(4), 61–69.

Hobbs, N. (1975). *The future of children.* San Francisco: Jossey-Boss.

Johnson, B., McGonigel, M., & Kaufmann, R. (Eds.). (1989). *Guidelines and recommended practices for the individualized family service plan.* Washington, DC: U.S. Department of Education and U.S. Department of Health and Human Services.

Johnson, N. (1982). Assessment paradigms and atypical infants: An early interventionist's perspective: In D. Bricker (Ed.), *Intervention with at-risk and handicapped infants: From research to application* (pp. 63–76). Baltimore: University Park Press.

LeBlanc, J., Etzel, B., & Domash, M. (1978). A functional curriculum for early intervention. In K. Allen, V. Holmes, & R. Schiefelbusch (Eds.), *Early intervention: A team approach* (pp. 331–381). Baltimore: University Park Press.

Notari, A., & Bricker, D. (1990). The utility of a criterion-referenced instrument in the development of individualized education plans for infants and young children. *Journal of Early Intervention, 14*(2), 117–132.

Robinson, C. C., & Rosenberg, S. (1987). A strategy for assessing infants with motor impairments. In I. C. Uzgiris & J. McV. Hunt (Eds.), *Infant performance and experience: New findings with the Ordinal Scales* (pp. 311–339). Urbana: University of Illinois Press.

Seibert, J. M. (1987). The Scales in early intervention. In I. C. Uzgiris & J. McV. Hunt (Eds.), *Infant performance and experience: New findings with the Ordinal Scales* (pp. 340–370). Urbana: University of Illinois Press.

Templeman, T. P., Fredericks, H. D., & Udell, T. (1989). Integration of children with moderate and severe handicaps into a daycare center. *Journal of Early Intervention, 13*(4), 315–328.

Tymitz-Wolf, B. (1982). Guidelines for assessing IEP goals and objectives. *TEACHING Exceptional Children, 14,* 198–201.

Wolery, M. (1989). Using assessment information to plan instructional programs. In D. Bailey & M. Wolery (Eds.), *Assessing infants and preschoolers with handicaps* (pp. 478–495). Columbus, OH: Merrill.

The preparation of this manuscript was supported in part by Grant No. G008715580 from the U.S. Department of Education to the Experimental Education Unit, Child Development and Mental Retardation Center, University of Washington.

A Physical Education Curriculum

for All Preschool Students

Gail M. Drummer

Fiona J. Connor-Kuntz

Jacqueline D. Goodway

Gail M. Dummer, *Professor, Department of Physical Education and Exercise Science, Michigan State University, East Lansing;* **Fiona J. Connor-Kuntz**, *Assistant Professor, School of Physical Education, Indiana University—Purdue University Schools at Indianapolis; and* **Jacqueline D. Goodway**, *Assistant Professor, Department of Health and Human Performance, University of Houston, Texas.*

The Individuals with Disabilities Education Act of 1990 (IDEA, 1990; "1991 Amendments," 1991) presents physical educators with the challenge of educating preschool-age children with disabilities. The early childhood provisions of IDEA apply to infants, toddlers, and preschool-age children who have disabilities, who are developmentally delayed, or who are at risk of substantial developmental delay.

The definition of physical education and the provisions for delivery of services under IDEA are similar in letter and spirit to the provisions of the Education for All Handicapped Children Act of 1975 (P.L. 94-142) and the Education of the Handicapped Act Amendments of 1986 (P.L. 99-457). According to IDEA, physical education includes the development of physical and motor fitness; fundamental motor skills; and skills in sports, games, aquatics, and dance. Physical education programs, including programs for preschool-age children, must be provided in the least restrictive environment. Furthermore, preschool programs, including physical education instruction, must be designed to facilitate transition into regular or special education programs for students in grades K through 12.

This article presents a physical education curriculum for preschool students that will help teachers and schools achieve the goals of IDEA. This curriculum was designed to facilitate the motor development of both typically developing preschool children (PS) and preschool children with disabilities (PPI) within an integrated, least restrictive physical education program. The goals and objectives for preschool children are linked to a prototype curriculum designed for K–12 students (Reuschlein, Haubenstricker, & Blauvelt, 1990), thereby facilitating transition to the K–12 program for regular and special education students. The curriculum's goals and objectives may be implemented in a variety of educational settings, including home-based, center-based, and school-based general education and physical education classes.

Curriculum Development Process

The PS/PPI curriculum presented in Figure 1 was developed using the procedures outlined by Vogel and Seefeldt (1988). There are eight steps involved in this process. Steps 1 through 5 were used to create an array of goals and objectives. In Steps 6 through 8 teachers determine

From *Teaching Exceptional Children*, Vol. 27, No. 3, Spring 1995, pp. 28-34. © 1995 by The Council for Exceptional Children. Reprinted by permission.

how and to what level of proficiency goals and objectives will be met.

Step 1

The potential contributions of physical activity to the well-being of PS and PPI children were defined and, where possible, documented via the research literature. During this step of curriculum development, careful attention was given to the physical growth, maturation, motor development, learning, and affective characteristics of PS and PPI children.

Step 2

The list of potential contributions was shared with university faculty members in motor development and adapted physical education, teachers of PS and PPI students, and the students' parents, each of whom rated the relative importance of the potential contributions to the physical education of young children. The feedback from this reference panel helped to ensure that the PS/PPI curriculum was relevant to local community values.

Step 3

The most important contributions of physical activity, as rated by the reference panel, were then categorized within the six program goal areas. Based upon suggestions from professionals in motor development and teachers of PS and PPI students, dance was specifically added as a component of the sports and games goal area. Eight students in a graduate-level course in adapted physical education generated lists of program objectives in each goal area that were consistent with the potential contributions of physical activity. These lists were subsequently discussed, combined, and refined as part of a class discussion. Skills that were not considered unique to physical education or that were deemed inappropriate for preschool children were deleted.

Step 4

University faculty members in motor development and adapted physical education and teachers and parents of PS and PPI students were invited to react to the proposed program goals and objectives. Their suggestions for additions, modifi-

cations, and deletions of selected statements were used to further refine the list of program objectives.

Step 5

The eight students rated the importance of each program objective using a five-point Likert-type scale, in which 5 corresponded to "extremely important" and 1 corresponded to "not at all important." To force discrimination among the objectives, students were instructed to use an equal number of 5, 4, 3, 2, and 1 ratings across the 160 program objectives. High-priority ratings were assigned to skills that were perceived to be developmental and/or functional, appropriately taught at the preschool level, unique to physical education, and consistent with local community values. Objectives that were retained at this point focus on the development of skills needed in activities of daily living and for participation in leisure activities that facilitate socialization and physical health and well-being. After computing an average rating for each objective, students were asked to defend individual ratings that were significantly higher or lower than the average. Using the rationales that emerged during this discussion, each student rerated each objective, and new averages were then computed. The priority ratings in the PS/PPI curriculum reflects these decisions.

Step 6

It is unlikely that any preschool program allocates sufficient instructional time to physical education to facilitate student attainment of all 160 program objectives included in the PS/PPI curriculum. Program personnel must construct a core curriculum that consists of high-priority objectives selected from the PS/PPI curriculum. The following procedure is recommended:

• Calculate available instructional time. For example, a physical education program that meets 3 times per week for 30 minutes per session, 36 weeks per year, for 2 years involves a total of 6,480 minutes of instruction.

• Determine the number of program objectives that can be taught in the available instructional time. Wessel and Kelly (1986) estimated that PS students require

an average of 210 minutes to achieve an objective and that PPI students require an average of 270 minutes to achieve the same educational gain (the actual time will vary by objective and for individual children). Using the example of available instructional time, PS students could be expected to achieve 31 objectives across a 2-year span. PPI students could be expected to attain 24 objectives in the same period.

• Select program objectives from the PS/PPI curriculum beginning with the objective that has the highest priority rating. Continue in descending order of priority ratings until the desired number of objectives have been selected. Figure 2 presents a sample core curriculum that includes the 31 highest-rated program objectives from the PS/PPI curriculum.

• Determine the desired sequence of teaching the program objectives across age/grade levels based upon developmental progressions and available personnel, equipment, and facility resources.

Step 7

Develop instructional objectives to operationalize each of the program objectives. Instructional objectives should specify the level of skill or knowledge required for successful completion of the task. For example, an instructional objective for a beginning-level vertical jump might require a 2-foot take-off and a 2-foot landing.

Step 8

Develop resource materials and activities that can be used as components of lesson plans to support instruction on program objectives. Resource materials should emphasize creative and fun ways of facilitating skill acquisition in gymnasium, classroom, and natural environments.

The process used to develop the PS/PPI physical education curriculum (Vogel & Seefeldt, 1988) can be generalized successfully to other situations. For example, the same process was used to generate program goals and objectives in adapted physical education for students with severe mental impairments (Dummer et al., 1990). Regardless of the population of interest, when the curriculum development process advocated by Vogel and Seefeldt is faithfully implemented, the resulting curriculum will include a reasonable number of defensible program goals and objectives that are relevant to community values and resources.

Characteristics of the PS/PPI Curriculum

The PS/PPI curriculum was designed to meet three specific educational needs of preschool children: motor development, age-appropriate functional skills, and integration of children with and without disabilities. Facilitating motor development was considered important because most PS and PPI students have tremendous potential for physical growth and the acquisition of motor skills. Teaching age-appropriate functional skills is important for all children, but especially for children with severe disabilities, to encourage active participation in activities of daily living. Integrating PS and PPI students in physical education activities contributes to a variety of important learning outcomes, including the development of positive social skills for all children. The PS/PPI curriculum is sufficiently flexible to accommodate students who require supportive services or alternate educational objectives and activities to meet these educational goals. Such modifications to the curriculum can be determined through the student's individual family service plan (IFSP) or individualized education program (IEP).

How Is the PS/PPI Curriculum Developmental?

During the first several months of life, the infant's movements are dominated by reflex and reaction patterns. Later in infancy, as a result of the continuing maturation of the central nervous system, the child develops the capability to perform early voluntary movements such as grasping, sitting, and crawling. Challenges in motor development for preschool children include the development of body management and fundamental motor skills, which in turn become the basis for the acquisition of sports, games, and dance skills by older children and adults.

The objectives included in the PS/PPI curriculum are consistent with this developmental model. In fact, there are 47 body management skills and 22 fundamental motor skills represented in the

curriculum. In addition, many of the objectives in the remaining goal areas are designed to facilitate the attainment, retention, and generalization of body management and fundamental motor skills. For example, the sports, games, and dance objective of "demonstrate ability to imitate or create movements during dance activities" facilitates the development of body management skills such as "move selected body parts" and "move the whole body or parts of the body in directional space."

During the first several months of life, the infant's movements are dominated by reflex and reaction patterns. Later in infancy, as a result of the continuing maturation of the central nervous system, the child develops the capability to perform early voluntary movements such as grasping, sitting, and crawling. Challenges in motor development for preschool children include the development of body management and fundamental motor skills, which in turn become the basis for the acquisition of sports, games, and dance skills by older children and adults. Because this pattern characterizes the sequence and rate of motor skill acquisition that is typical for most children, including most children with disabilities, general physical education programs will serve the needs of most children. However, some children with severe disabilities may require supplementary intervention from a physical or occupational therapist to get maximum benefit from instruction in physical education. The need for physical therapy (PT) or occupational therapy (OT) can be determined by (a) an absence of robust righting, protective extension, and equilibrium reactions; (b) inefficient sitting and standing posture; (c) limited ability to perform sensorimotor tasks such as the body management and fundamental motor skills in the PS/PPI curriculum; and (d) inadequate physical fitness for daily living activities. Preschool students who demonstrate difficulties in these areas should be referred for evaluation by a physical or occupational therapist.

How Is the PS/PPI Curriculum Functional?

A skill is functional for an individual if it (a) is regularly used in activities of daily

living; (b) is a prerequisite to the acquisition of another skill needed for daily living; (c) is used in more than one life environment; (d) is age appropriate; (e) contributes to personal independence; and/or (f) contributes to quality of life. According to these criteria, the skills included in the PS/PPI curriculum are functional for most preschool students. Some examples demonstrate this fact:

- The fundamental motor skill of "climbing up" is regularly used for a variety of activities in home, school, and community environments, for example, climbing into bed, climbing on playground equipment, and navigating stairs and curbs.
- The sports and games skill of "using playground equipment" is age appropriate for preschool children, and ability to use such equipment may lead to better quality of life in terms of socialization opportunities and physical fitness.
- Teachers must use common sense in determining necessary adaptations to curriculum objectives and associated instructional activities to ensure functionality for the individual students. Some children require assistive devices such as wheelchairs, walkers, or prostheses for locomotion, while others may benefit from special equipment such as beep balls or modified tricycles. In addition, children may need occasional assistance from another person to perform certain skills, especially during the initial stages of skill acquisition.

How Does the PS/PPI Curriculum Facilitate Integration?

Integration of students with disabilities and students who do not have disabilities requires careful attention to the nature of instructional objectives and activities, as well as the quality of social interactions. The objectives in the PS/PPI curriculum represent skill areas rather than specific ways of accomplishing a skill. Most preschool children, including those with disabilities, will be able to perform the movement skills from the PS/PPI curriculum in the usual manner described in motor development textbooks; however, other children may require modified or substitute objectives that are more functional for them. The IFSP/IEP process can be

Figure 1. Program Goals and Objectives in Physical Education for All Preschool Students
(Priority ratings are given in parentheses after each objective)

Goal 1: To Demonstrate Competence in Selected Body Management Skills

1. To demonstrate the ability to *move* selected body parts:
head (3.33), shoulders (3.22), back (3.44), elbow (3.58), hands (4.33), hips (3.33), knees (4.22), feet (4.22).

2. To demonstrate the ability to perform selected movements of the torso, arms (shoulder and elbow joints), and legs (hip and knee joints):
flexion (4.44), extension (4.22), abduction (3.33), adduction (3.33), rotation (3.00), swinging movements (3.00).

3. To demonstrate the ability to move the whole body or parts of the body in directional space:
forward (4.67), backward (4.33), sideways (3.56), over obstacles (3.89), under obstacles (3.89), between obstacles (3.44), around obstacles (3.67), through an opening such as a tunnel (3.00).

4. To demonstrate the ability to move the body into different shapes and sizes:
big-little (2.67), short-tall (2.33), fat-thin (1.89), straight-bent (2.00).

5. To demonstrate the ability to move objects:
carry-hold (3.44), lift-lower (3.67), pull-push (3.00).

6. To demonstrate the ability to perform selected static balance skills:
efficient sitting posture (3.67), efficient standing posture (3.67), stand on one leg (3.11), stand on toes (3.11), four-point balance facing the floor, e.g., "bear" position (2.78), four-point balance facing the ceiling, e.g., "crab" position (2.44).

7. To demonstrate the ability to perform selected dynamic balance skills:
walk forward on a line (3.22), walk sideways on a line (3.22), walk backward on a line (2.85), walk forward heel-toe (2.22), walk forward on a curved line (2.56), walk forward on a 4-inch floor-level balance beam (3.00), walk sideways on a 4-inch floor-level balance beam (2.44), walk backward on a 4-inch floor-level balance beam (1.98).

8. To demonstrate *beginning-level skill* on selected stunts and tumbling skills:
forward roll (2.11), log roll (4.22), side/egg roll (1.78), animal walks (2.56).

Goal 2: To Demonstrate Competence in Selected Fundamental Motor Skills

1. To demonstrate *beginning-level skill* in selected object-control skills:
roll a ball (4.56), throw/toss underhand (4.56), throw overhand (4.33), catch a rolling ball (4.78), catch a tossed ball (3.78), kick (4.67), bounce a ball (4.00), one-hand strike, e.g., using a paddle or racket (3.44), two-hand strike, e.g., using a bat (3.78).

2. To demonstrate *beginning-level skill* in selected locomotor skills:
walk (4.89), run (4.56), walk upstairs (3.29) walk downstairs (3.29), climb up (3.78), climb down (3.78), gallop (3.56), hop (3.78), vertical jump (3.89), horizontal jump (3.44), leap (2.89), skip (2.78), slide (2.56).

Goal 3: To Demonstrate Competence in Selected Games, Sports, and Dance Skills

1. To demonstrate the ability to follow the rules in low-organized games:
imitate the movements of the leader in follow-the-leader type games (3.67), follow the rules in low-organized games and activities, e.g., running the bases or participating in partner games (3.67).

2. To demonstrate the ability to play one's position in low-organized games and activities:
stay within assigned territory, e.g., behind the line, during games (3.11), participate in different roles, e.g., leader and player, within a game or activity (2.89).

3. To demonstrate ability to use selected equipment during games and movement activities:
soft sponge balls (3.56), playground balls (3.00), sport-like balls such as minibasketballs or Wiffle balls (2.11), lightweight, short bats, paddles, or rackets (2.22), scooter boards (2.78), tricycles (3.78), playground equipment such as swings, slides, and climbing apparatus (3.78).

4. To demonstrate competence in selected aquatic skills:
water adjustment (2.56), float with or without assistance (2.44), flutter kick (2.22).

5. To demonstrate ability to imitate or create movements during dance activities:
animal walks to music (3.33), imitate movements in dance activities (3.78), create movements in dance activities (2.22).

6. To demonstrate the ability to move the whole body or parts of the body to simple rhythms or music with *even* beats:
walk to simple rhythms or music with even beats (3.67), march to simple rhythms or music with even beats (2.82), run to simple rhythms or music with even beats (2.33), move the arms to simple rhythms or music with even beats (3.44).

7. To demonstrate the ability to move the whole body or parts of the body to simple rhythms or music with *uneven* beats:
move to simple rhythms or music with uneven beats (1.56).

Goal 4: To Demonstrate Competence on Selected Indicators of Physical Fitness

Indicators of physical fitness include: (a) ability of the various energy systems to do work; (b) flexibility of the major joints; (c) strength, endurance, and power in the large muscle groups; and (d) body composition. This curriculum does not include specific physical fitness objectives because most preschool-age children possess sufficient physical fitness to support participation in their daily living and play activities. Furthermore, the available instructional time in most physical education programs for preschool-age children is so limited that defining physical fitness as a goal separate from the development of fundamental movement skills such as those defined in Goals 1, 2, and 3 is not advised. Preschool-age children who have insufficient physical fitness for activities of daily living should be referred for physical therapy services as a supplement to instruction in physical education. Examples of inadequate fitness among children of preschool age include (a) insufficient joint mobility to reach objects on the floor or overhead, (b) insufficient energy to participate with peers in active play, and (c) insufficient muscular strength and power for the maintenance of sitting and standing posture or to enable the development of body management and fundamental motor skills.

Goal 5: To Demonstrate Knowledge of Selected Activity-Related Cognitive Concepts

1. To demonstrate the ability to *name* and *identify* (touch) selected body parts:
head (2.89), eyes (2.25), ears (1.88), shoulders (2.51), back (2.78), abdomen (2.67), arms (3.41), elbows (3.00), hands (3.67), hips (2.78), legs (3.33), knees (2.99), feet (3.44).

2. To demonstrate knowledge of simple movement terminology:
bend (3.44), straighten (2.89), stretch (3.22), twist (3.33), swing (2.22), sway (1.78), shake (1.57), clap (3.29).

3. To demonstrate knowledge of directions and positions in space:
forward-backward-sideways (3.44), near-far (2.22), together-apart (2.22), beside (2.00), right-left (2.22), up-down (2.67), high-low (2.89).

4. To demonstrate knowledge of different body shapes and sizes:
big-little (2.22), short-tall (2.00), fat-thin (1.22), straight-bent (1.67).

5. To demonstrate ability to follow directions in the physical education environment:
follow one-part directions (4.33), follow two-part directions (2.89), imitate simple movements that are demonstrated (3.33).

6. To demonstrate knowledge about safety in the physical education environment:
follow simple safety rules such as stay in the fenced playground area or walk on the pool deck (4.44), recognize and report safety hazards such as broken equipment, slippery surfaces, or sharp objects (3.22), recognize and report suspected injuries such as cuts, bruises, or pain (2.67).

7. To demonstrate basic knowledge about a healthy lifestyle:
states that exercise "makes me strong," "helps me grow," "is fun" (2.44).

Goal 6: To Demonstrate Competence in Selected Activity-Related Personal-Social Skills

1. To demonstrate enjoyment of physical activity:
show positive affects, e.g., smiling or laughing, during physical activity (3.22), participate willingly in physical education activities (3.44), indicate physical activity preferences (1.78).

2. To demonstrate a positive self-concept in the physical education environment:
attempt most activities suggested by the teacher (3.78), perform familiar activities with confidence (2.00), communicate satisfaction with one's abilities in physical activities, e.g., "I am good at catching the ball" (1.89), communicate satisfaction with one's body, e.g., "I am healthy" or "I look good" (1.33).

3. To demonstrate effort in games and physical activities:
follow directions related to intensity of physical effort, e.g., "run as fast as you can" or "throw as far as you can" (2.56), follow directions related to accuracy of physical effort, e.g., "walk on the line" or "roll the ball toward the target" (2.00).

4. To demonstrate ability to communicate with others in the physical education environment:
communicate needs such as teacher attention, water, equipment, and toilet (2.78), communicate choices such as preferences for activities, equipment, or activity partners (1.89), communicate feelings such as happy, proud, sad, or angry (2.11), communicate refusals such as inability or unwillingness to perform a skill (1.33).

5. To demonstrate ability to cooperate with others during low-organized games and activities:
share or exchange equipment when requested (3.11), take turns when requested (2.78), hold hands in a circle game (2.22), participate with a partner on a task requiring cooperative effort such as pushing partner on a scooter (2.22).

6. To demonstrate courage in movement activities that involve reasonable and safe physical or social risks:
participate in balance activities (2.22), participate in climbing activities (2.00), participate in aquatic activities (1.67), participate in games such as tag (2.78), participate in activities previously associated with perceived or real failure (2.00).

7. To demonstrate respect for others in the physical education environment:
appropriate use of personal and general space (3.67), courtesy including appropriate use of phrases such as "please" and "thank you" (3.11), support other students by offering physical assistance or verbal/nonverbal encouragement (1.44).

8. To demonstrate respect for equipment:
use equipment as directed (2.67), return equipment to storage area upon request (2.78).

9. To demonstrate self-control and personal responsibility:
listen to teacher directions (3.78), wait for turn (3.00), wait in line (3.69).

Figure 2. Sample Core Curriculum in Physical Education for All Preschool Students

Priority Rating	Program Objectives
4.89	1. Beginning-level skill in walking
4.78	2. Beginning-level skill in catching a rolling ball
4.67	3. Ability to move the whole body or parts of the body forward in directional space
4.67	4. Beginning-level skill in kicking
4.56	5. Beginning-level skill in running
4.56	6. Beginning-level skill in rolling a ball
4.56	7. Beginning-level skill in the underhand throw/toss
4.44	8. Knowledge about safety in the physical education environment
4.44	9. Ability to flex the torso, arms, and legs
4.33	10. Ability to follow one-part directions in the physical education environment
4.33	11. Beginning-level skill in the overhand throw
4.33	12. Ability to move the whole body or parts of the body backward in directional space
4.33	13. Ability to move the hands
4.22	14. Ability to move the feet
4.22	15. Ability to extend the torso, arms, and legs
4.22	16. Ability to move the knees
4.22	17. Beginning-level skill on the log roll
4.00	18. Beginning-level skill in bouncing a ball
3.89	19. Ability to move the whole body or parts of the body over obstacles in directional space
3.89	20. Ability to move the whole body or parts of the body under obstacles in directional space
3.89	21. Beginning-level skill in the vertical jump
3.78	22. Positive self-concept in the physical education environment
3.78	23. Beginning-level skill in climbing up
3.78	24. Beginning-level skill in climbing down
3.78	25. Ability to use playground equipment during games and movement activities
3.78	26. Ability to use tricycles during games and movement activities
3.78	27. Beginning-level skill in catching a tossed ball
3.78	28. Beginning-level skill in the two-hand strike
3.78	29. Ability to imitate movements during dance activities
3.78	30. Self-control and personal responsibility
3.78	31. Beginning-level skill in hopping

used to identify alternate objectives and suggested instructional activities. Block (1992) has provided some examples of ways in which instructional activities can be modified for children with disabilities:

• While most children in the class practice throwing, other students could push a ball down a ramp or practice grasping and releasing an object.

• While most students practice running, other children could practice keeping their head up while being pushed quickly in a wheelchair.

• While most children practice skills requiring visual-motor coordination, other students could track suspended objects or practice using switches that activate visually stimulating toys.

Integration is facilitated in these examples by designing instructional activities that permit all children to work toward the same objective (function).

The PS/PPI curriculum promotes so-cial integration through the deliberate inclusion of appropriate personal-social objectives such as "communicate needs, choices, feelings, and refusals in the physical education environment," "share equipment," "take turns," "participate with a partner on a task requiring cooperative effort," and "demonstrate respect for others in the physical education environment." Inclusion of such objectives in the curriculum encourages teachers to plan and implement specific activities designed to improve social skills and social integration, a practice recommended by many experts in early intervention.

In addition to promoting integration at the preschool level, the PS/PPI curriculum was designed to prepare young children for participation in typical physical education programs in regular elementary schools. The goal areas of the PS/PPI curriculum are consonant with the goals of most K–12 physical education programs. Children who master skills from the PS/PPI curriculum will possess the prerequisite skills needed for success in regular elementary school physical education programs. Thus, transition from a preschool program to an integrated elementary school program is facilitated.

Conclusion

The value and efficacy of this PS/PPI physical education curriculum can only be determined by the students, parents, teachers, administrators, and community groups associated with the schools and centers that actually incorporate these objectives into their curricular structure. Schools or centers that choose to use this curriculum as a starting point should redetermine priority ratings for the program objectives based upon input from parents, teachers, administrators, and community leaders who reside in their local community. Teachers can then select program objectives for inclusion in the physical education curriculum based upon the priority ratings, age/grade placements, estimates of the instructional time needed to teach the objectives, and available instructional time. Through the IFSP/IEP process, the curriculum may be personalized for a student with a disability by determining substitute or modified objectives that are functional for that child. The resulting physical education program will not include all objectives from the PS/PPI curriculum, but it will reflect selected high-priority objectives that are consistent with community values and individual student needs. More important, the children who are instructed on the objectives from this curriculum will have a head start on an active, healthy lifestyle.

References

Block, M. E. (1992). What is appropriate physical education for students with profound disabilities? *Adapted Physical Activity Quarterly, 9,* 197–213.

Dummer, G. M., DeYoung, L. L., Karakostas, T., Mattar, R., Neat, D. R., & Sochacki, K. M. (1990, Fall). Curriculum development in adapted physical education. *Michigan Journal of Health, Physical Education, Recreation and Dance,* pp. 8–10, 17.

1991 Amendments to the Individuals with Disabilities Education Act of 1990. (1991, October 22). *Federal Register,* pp. 54686–54705.

Individuals with Disabilities Education Act of 1990, 20 U.S.C. 1400–1485 (1990).

Reuschlein, P. R., Haubenstricker, J. L., & Blauvelt, C. (1990). *Michigan exemplary physical education programs project: A descriptive overview.* East Lansing: Michigan State University.

Vogel, P., & Seefeldt, V. (1988). *Program design in physical education: A guide to the development of exemplary programs.* Indianapolis: Benchmark. (ERIC Document Reproduction Service No. ED 292 803)

Wessel, J. A., & Kelly, L. (1986). *Achievement-based curriculum development in physical education.* Philadelphia: Lea & Febiger.

The physical education goals and objectives presented in this manuscript were developed as a project in a graduate-level course in adapted physical education at Michigan State University. The students who contributed to this project are Sue Cerny, Fiona J. Connor-Kuntz, Joseph A. Cook, Sherri L. Drayton, Jacqueline D. Goodway, W. Scott Hays, James V. Johnson, and Kihong Kim.

"Buddy Skills" for Preschoolers

Kris English
Howard Goldstein
Louise Kaczmarek
Karin Shafer

Kris English, *Project Coordinator;* Howard
Goldstein *(CEC Chapter #184), Professor; and*
Louise Kaczmarek *(CEC Chapter #961), As-
sistant Professor, Child Language Intervention
Program;* Karin Shafer, *Research Specialist, Al-
liance for Infants, University of Pittsburgh,
Pennsylvania.*

You have an inclusive preschool. You
have children with a wide range of abilities, including children with disabilities.
You want the children to work and play
together—to be friends. One way many
teachers encourage positive social relationships is by using the buddy system.

This article describes a buddy system
that helps children work—and play—together more cooperatively throughout the
day. It is child-tested and teacher-ap-
proved. Follow these 11 steps to
"preschooler peer 'preciation.'"

Figure 1 summarizes the sequence of
the 11 steps of the "Buddy Skills" training procedure. An explanation of each
step follows.

Step 1. Initial Assessment

Before you conduct Buddy Skills training,
make an inventory of the potential buddies in your classroom, weighing factors
like the maturity of the children without
disabilities, the social and communicative levels of the children with disabilities, and any shared interests in particular activities (e.g., playing similar games,

or using similar materials). We recommend matching genders when possible.
We also recommend that the pairing be
considered a long-term match (although
not necessarily exclusive); extended time
is needed for friendships to develop in
any situation.

Step 2. Pretraining/ Sensitization

Children without disabilities often fail to
notice or sometimes misinterpret the
communicative or play attempts of a
child with a disability (Goldstein & Kaczmarek, 1991; Goldstein, Kaczmarek, Pennington, & Shafer, 1992). The goal of the
first 20-min pretraining session is to sensitize children to these communicative attempts.

In a small group, lead a discussion
with peers without disabilities about different ways children in their class might
communicate: with voices, signs, or gestures, or with varying response times and
sometimes unclear intent. The use of
videotaped samples of classmates at play
can be used to help peers focus on, recognize, and interpret the intended meaning of subtle or ambiguous communicative acts.

Because it is difficult to generalize
about children's unique communication
strategies, we recommend that you use
videotapes of actual classmates rather
than unknown children. For example, the
teachers and peers might view a 2-min
videotape of a 4-year-old girl sitting on a
chair at a table. They observe that three
times she tries to get the attention of chil-

During the "Buddy Skills" training procedure, stickers can be used at the end of a
session to reinforce success. These reinforcers will be eliminated as social reinforcers
(friendship) take over.

From *Teaching Exceptional Children,* Vol. 28, No. 3, Spring 1996, pp. 62-66. © 1996 by The Council for Exceptional Children.
Reprinted by permission.

dren walking by, but is unintelligible and therefore is ignored. Finally, she gets up and pulls on the hand of an adult, leading her to the table. She points to a disassembled puzzle on the table.

The teacher discusses with the peers:
- What did the girl want?
- How did she try to get what she wanted?
- How did she tell other children?
- Why didn't other children answer her?
- How did she tell the adult what she wanted without using words?

The teacher and peers might go on to view another video segment of a classmate who throws a toy after trying unsuccessfully to participate in a play interaction. Each segment is discussed in the same manner.

If videotaping is not an option, demonstrate with role-playing some of the communicative and play behaviors observed in the classroom, and conduct the same type of discussion.

Learning how children use different abilities and strategies to communicate will help generate discussion on how to respond to those behaviors. Here are some questions for discussion:
- What should we do if we can't understand what our classmate is saying?
- What does it mean if he or she points or reaches for a toy?
- Will questions help, such as "Do you want this truck? Do you want to share this book with me?"

Explain to the children that responses to such questions from a child with a disability may be delayed or unclear. Discuss the need to take extra time to understand. During this pretraining session, take time to discuss what the concepts of "friendship" and "being a buddy" mean to the peers.

Step 3. Peer Training

Follow the sensitization session with two 20-min training sessions for children without disabilities, on two consecutive days, if possible. The training sessions will teach three Buddy Skills: to *STAY*, *PLAY*, and *TALK* with their buddy (a child with a disability). After the peers have learned the Buddy steps, show them how to apply the three steps with in-class guided practice. The following is a format for the two sessions.

Session 1. STAY and PLAY with Your Buddy

Teach the peers to maintain proximity with their buddy during free play, sit with them during snack and group activities, and participate in play activities with their buddy.

Teach the peers that to STAY with their buddy means to "stick close." When approaching a buddy for the first time, the peer is asked to get the buddy's attention by saying hello, using the buddy's name, tapping on the arm, and asking the buddy to play with them. If during free play their buddy moves from one activity to another, they are to follow.

Then show the peers that to STAY and PLAY with a buddy means: While "sticking close" to their buddy, they can join in the activity in which their buddy is participating, bring a toy over if the buddy is not playing, or ask the buddy to join in an ongoing activity. If the first suggestions do not appeal to the buddy, encourage the peer to think of other play activities, while maintaining proximity. During Buddy Skills training in our

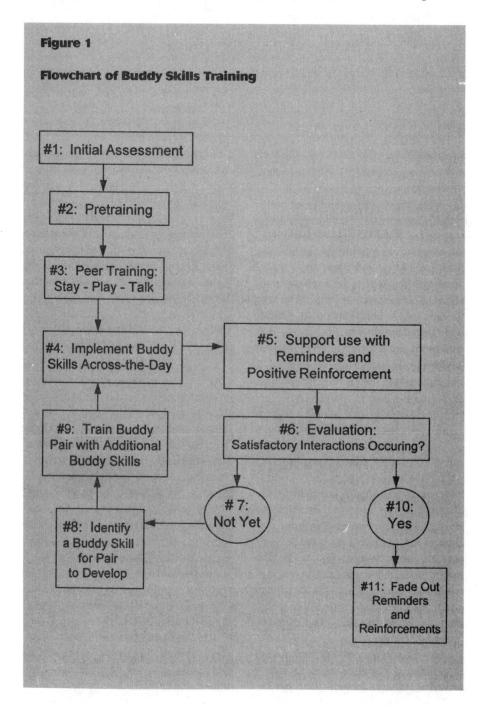

Figure 1

Flowchart of Buddy Skills Training

#1: Initial Assessment

#2: Pretraining

#3: Peer Training: Stay - Play - Talk

#4: Implement Buddy Skills Across-the-Day

#5: Support use with Reminders and Positive Reinforcement

#9: Train Buddy Pair with Additional Buddy Skills

#6: Evaluation: Satisfactory Interactions Occuring?

#8: Identify a Buddy Skill for Pair to Develop

#7: Not Yet

#10: Yes

#11: Fade Out Reminders and Reinforcements

What Does the Research Say About "Peer Interactions"?

As preschool programs continue to include children with disabilities, many educators contemplate how to promote friendships in their classrooms. Uditsky (1993) discussed the normative pathway to childhood friendship:

For children, the normative pathways of childhood support and encourage opportunities to play together informally and formally . . . sharing in the celebration of milestones, making discoveries together, and following each other's leads. These are the pathways that adults clearly need to support. (p. 94)

Physical placement in an integrated program alone, however, may not sufficiently *encourage opportunities to play together.* Without direction and support, children with disabilities are more likely to interact with adults and not with other children. In addition, children without disabilities are more likely to play together and not interact with children with disabilities (Beckman, 1983; Goldstein & Gallagher, 1992; Strain, 1984).

Educators have designed peer-mediated interventions that teach preschoolers a *set of initiation strategies* (Day, Powell, Dy-Lin, & Stowitschek, 1982; Odom, Hoyson, Jamieson, & Strain, 1985). Although research has been promising, there has been concern for the lack of generalization—that is, the inability of the peers to generalize the use of these strategies in activities across the classroom.

preschool classrooms, the peers practiced these steps with adult modeling, and received token reinforcement (e.g., stickers or stamps on a chart) for demonstrating competency. These may be replaced with whatever reinforcement systems are most successful within different classrooms and with different children.

Session 2. STAY, PLAY, and TALK with Your Buddy

Teach the peers to add a new step to "stay and play." STAY, PLAY, and TALK with a buddy involves additional interaction and communication, such as talking about the ongoing actions of the buddy or themselves, the toys (their colors, shapes, names, parts, or other attributes), or the actions and uses of the toys, as well as watching and responding to the communicative attempts of their buddy. In our classrooms, the peers again practiced all three steps with adult modeling, and received token reinforcement when mastery was demonstrated.

This phase of training ends when the peers are able to use these three steps in a chain without being told what to do, for at least two consecutive role-playing episodes. For some children, more than two training sessions may be required.

In-class Guided Practice

Allow the children without disabilities to try these Buddy Skills in class with a peer who has a disability. This practice serves as a transition activity from the controlled training situation to the classroom environment. During this time, help the peer stay on task and apply the steps to new situations.

Step 4. Implement Across the Day

Decide on three activities across the day (e.g., free play, snack time, and a structured activity) where the peer can be a buddy. To keep *"costs"* at a minimum, ask the peer to be a buddy for only a portion (4-5 min) of the activity, or share the role with other peers. This should reduce the possibility of peers losing interest or becoming anxious during interactions.

Step 5. Support Use with Reminders and Positive Reinforcement

You may find it useful to have a hierarchy of reminders or prompts. Friendships among children with and without dis-

abilities may require a great deal of support and encouragement. Simply teaching Buddy Skills will usually not ensure mutually satisfying interactions. *Reminders and reinforcements ("rewards") help children try new social skills* with a friend or in a new activity.

Initially, you may give a combination of verbal and visual prompts. Examples of verbal prompts include: "Tell me the Buddy Skills. Show me how to use them with Erica," or "Remember to talk to your buddy when you're playing." Examples of visual prompts include: a "thumbs-up" signal, or the sign for "friend." In our program, peers were positively reinforced with verbal praise or tokens for the way they "stayed, played, and talked" with their buddies during classroom activities across the day.

Step 6. Evaluation: Is Satisfactory Interaction Occurring?

Observe and evaluate the quality of the interaction resulting from the peers' use of the Buddy Skills. The first attempts at "being a buddy" usually do not result in social or communicative reciprocity. Following are typical early buddy behaviors, illustrated by Jacob (a child with a disability) and Erik (a peer without disabilities):

- Erik asks a question, but Jacob does not respond.
- Jacob asks for help, but Erik doesn't pay attention. Jacob does not repeat the request.

Through observations of these kinds, you may determine either that satisfactory interactions are "not yet" occurring (Step 7), or that the training has resulted in a relationship that is mutually enjoyable (proceed to Step 10).

Step 7. Not Yet

If you observe that mutually enjoyable interactions are not happening, make the determination that satisfactory interactions are "Not Yet" occurring, which leads to the beginning of a Buddy Pair training cycle (Steps 8 and 9, and repeating Steps 4, 5, and 6).

Step 8. Identify a Buddy Skill for the Pair to Develop

Choose a skill that will improve the give-and-take of the interaction between the buddies, based on your observation of the pair's interactions ("following each other's leads," Uditsky, 1993, p. 94). These skills may include using attention-getters (e.g., arm taps or verbalizations), responding to questions, and taking turns.

For example, in the Jacob-and-Erik example:
- If Jacob does not respond to a request from Erik, his new Buddy Skill will be to look when his arm is tapped, or look when his name is called. Erik in turn will be taught to respond with a smile, eye contact, and repetition of the request when Jacob responds to the arm-tap or the use of his name.
- If Erik doesn't pay attention to a re-

One strategy that will improve communication between buddy partners is eye contact and a friendly smile.

quest, Jacob's new Buddy Skill is to get Erik's attention with an arm touch or other attention-getter, and to "ask again" and point to the item of interest. Erik, in turn, is taught to look in the direction of the item, and ask questions to find out Jacob's intent.

The cycle of Buddy Training should convey to both members of the Buddy Pair that they have *mutual responsibility* in the interaction and that both are expected to understand and respond to each other.

Step 9. Teach Buddy Pair a New Buddy Skill

When you have identified the new Buddy Skill, teach the pair *together* so that both partners learn the new skill. This will help support a growing mutual investment in the developing relationship. Conduct this training across the day in various activities, and continue it over several days, until both children use the new skill.

Repeat Steps 4 and 5: Implement New Buddy Skill Across-the-Day

Once each member of the pair demonstrates the new skill, implement buddy interaction again across the school day. Continue to support the use of the Buddy Skills with the use of *reminders* and *reinforcers*.

What Are "Buddy Skills"?

We developed "Buddy Skills" to promote generalization of peer relationships across the day. The Buddy Skills program is an application of "social exchange theory" (Kelly & Thibaut, 1978), which states that the rewards of a potential relationship must outweigh the cost for each participant if the relationship is to be mutually satisfying.

- **Rewards** are the factors that reinforce behaviors, such as enjoyment, satisfaction, or task completion.
- **Costs** are factors that inhibit behaviors, such as embarrassment, anxiety, or excessive effort.

The Buddy Skills intervention attempts to *reduce the costs* and *increase the rewards* of relationship development between preschoolers with and without disabilities by teaching social-communication skills to both partners in a Buddy Pair. Each partner is asked to share responsibility for the relationship by developing a reciprocity in their social exchanges (Gaylord-Ross, Haring, Breen, & Pitts-Conway, 1984).

The Buddy Skills program was tested in three integrated preschool classrooms composed of one-third children without disabilities and two-thirds children with mild-to-moderate disabilities. Positive effects were noted in the relationships between each Buddy Pair, and teachers indicated that the training procedures were appropriate for class use. Anecdotal observations by teachers indicated that some generalization of the learned Buddy Skills occurred (e.g., Buddy Pairs held hands while walking to other activities, saved seats for the buddy partner for snack and calendar, and extended invitations to play without prompting). The program also was found to be socially valid by three panels of objective evaluators, who viewed randomly ordered videotapes and rated postintervention videos as displaying more and better interactions between Buddy Pairs.

Repeat Step 6: Evaluation: Is Satisfactory Interaction Occurring?

Again, observe the children to evaluate the effects of prior training. Initially, there may be room for much improvement, so it is likely that after one Buddy Skill is mastered by the Buddy Pair, another developmentally appropriate Buddy Skill may suggest itself. For example, after Jacob learns to look when his name is called, and Erik learns to respond with eye contact and a smile and a request to play, Jacob's next step is to provide a verbal or nonverbal response (such as a head nod or a verbal acknowledgment).

Typically, the peer may need to develop a new skill in response to the skill recently mastered by the child with a disability, and vice versa. If so, repeat the training cycle. Through these training cycles, both children can add to their repertoire of Buddy Skills. These common repertoires and shared experiences should facilitate social interactions.

Step 10. Yes

At some point, your observations may confirm that the quality of the interaction resulting from the use of the Buddy Skills has resulted in a fairly balanced, reciprocal relationship—a friendship is developing. Reduce adult intervention by proceeding to Step 11.

Step 11. Fade Out Reminders and Reinforcement

Decrease reminders and reinforcements. For example, if you have initially awarded stickers at the end of each session that the Buddy Skills are practiced (three times a day), you may delay these tokens and replace them with praise. Say, "Good job, you two! I like the way you're playing together. Keep up the good work—I'll hold on to these stickers now until the end of the day." Postpone the stickers until the end of the school day, and soon you will be able to delay them for 2 to 3 days, until you "extinguish" the use of stickers as social reinforcers take over. Friendship becomes its own reward.

During Step 2, students without disabilities observe a videotape to help them understand subtle or ambiguous communicative acts of students with disabilities.

References

Beckman, P. (1983). The relationship between behavioral characteristics of children and social interaction in an integrated setting. *Journal of the Division of Early Childhood, 7*, 69-77.

Day, R., Powell, T., Dy-Lin, E., & Stowitschek, J. (1982). An evaluation of a social interaction training package on mentally handicapped preschool children. *Education and Training of the Mentally Retarded, 17*, 125-130.

Gaylord-Ross, R., Haring, T., Breen, C., & Pitts-Conway, V. (1984). The training and generalization of social interaction skills with autistic youth. *Journal of Applied Behavior Analysis, 17*, 229-247.

Goldstein, H., & Gallagher, T. (1992). Strategies for promoting the social-communicative competence of young children with specific language impairments. In S. Odom, S. McConnell, & M. McEvoy (Eds.), *Social competence of young children with disabilities: Nature, development, and intervention* (pp. 189-213). Baltimore: Paul H. Brookes.

Goldstein, H., & Kaczmarek, L. (1991). Promoting communicative interaction among children in integrated intervention settings. In S. Warren & J. Reichle (Eds.), *Causes and effects in communication and language intervention* (pp. 81-111). Baltimore: Paul H. Brookes.

Goldstein, H., Kaczmarek, L., Pennington, R., & Shafer, K. (1992). Peer-mediated intervention: Attending to, commenting on, and acknowledging the behavior of preschoolers with autism. *Journal of Applied Behavior Analysis, 25*, 289-306.

Kelly, H., & Thibaut, J. (1978). *Interpersonal relations: A theory of interdependence.* New York: John Wiley.

Odom, S., Hoyson, M., Jamieson, B., & Strain, P. (1985). Increasing handicapped preschoolers' peer social interactions: Cross-setting and component analysis. *Journal of Applied Behavior Analysis, 18*, 3-16.

Strain, P. (1984). Social behavior patterns of nonhandicapped-developmentally disabled friend pairs in mainstream preschools. *Analysis and Intervention in Developmental Disabilities, 4*, 15-28.

Uditsky, B. (1993). Natural pathways to friendships. In A. Amando (Ed.), *Friendships and community connections between people with and without developmental disabilities* (pp. 85-95). Baltimore: Paul H. Brookes.

Preparation of this article was supported by U.S. Department of Education, Office of Special Education and Rehabilitative Services Grant #H023C10167 awarded to the University of Pittsburgh.

We thank Holly Polatas for her technical assistance in the development of this manuscript.

Address correspondence to Kris English, Child Language Intervention Program, 3600 Forbes, #500, Pittsburgh, PA 15213 (e-mail: english + @pitt.edu).

Transition to Adulthood

The 1990 amendment to the Individuals with Disabilities Education Act (IDEA) extended special educational services to students from the completion of their public school education through age 21. This extension of services is to prepare students with disabilities to make a successful transition from the dependent status of student to a more independent status as community member and participant in the world of work.

The implementation of this amendment, Public Law 101-476, is still in its infancy. Many teachers, special educators, vocational counselors, and employment mentors (job coaches) are not sure how much vocational preparation should be given in the public schools, or when. Should children with disabilities start planning for their futures in elementary school, in middle school, in high school, throughout their education, or just before they finish school? Should there be a trade-off between academic education and vocational education for these students? Should each student's vocational preparation be individualized according to his or her needs and abilities, with no general rules about the wheres and whens of transitional services?

These and other questions about implementation of transitional services for children with exceptionalities abound. The U.S. government defined transitional services as outcome-oriented, coordinated activities designed to move students with disabilities from school to post-school activities such as college, vocational training, integrated employment, supported employment, adult education, adult services, independent living, and community participation. Choices are not either/or, but rather multiple: to help students with disabilities move from school to successful adulthoods. While some students may only be able to achieve partial independence and supported employment, others may achieve professional degrees and complete self-sufficiency.

Public Law 101-476, the transition amendment, stipulates that every student have an individualized transition plan (ITP) added to his or her individualized education plan (IEP) by age 16. This mandate defines the upper limit for beginning transition planning, but not the lower boundary. Transition planning may begin in elementary school.

The transition from student to employee in the work world usually receives a great deal of attention. The transitions from child living at home to adult living away from parents, and from noncommunity participant to full participant in community activities should also be supported in an ITP.

The transition to the world of work may take the form of supported employment (i.e., mobile work crew, clustered or enclave placement, on-site training and supervision by a job coach, group providing a specific service product), or of sheltered employment (i.e., in a workshop). Many students with disabilities can make a transition from school to competitive employment. If they will eventually work side by side with nondisabled coworkers, they may need transitional services such as assertiveness training, negotiating skills, and personal empowerment counseling.

The transition to independent living requires careful planning, with goals and objectives as detailed as those for the transition to employment. Independent living may range from complete autonomy in a home or apartment, to partial autonomy with a spouse or roommate, to residence with a live-in aide or a part-time aide, to residence in a group home. Just a few years ago, adults with disabilities were expected to live with parents, siblings, or extended family members. This is no longer considered the most appropriate placement. Each individual with a disability should be encouraged to be as autonomous as possible in adulthood. Self-sufficiency is enhanced by providing education in life skills such as meal preparation and cleanup, home deliveries (e.g., mail) and delivery pickups (e.g., trash), using money and paying bills, making household repairs, and following home safety precautions.

The transition from noncommunity participant to fully participating member of society requires ITP modifications quite different from IEP academic goals. Students with exceptional conditions may need more than the usual amount of assistance in learning to drive a car or use public transportation. They need to know how to read maps and schedules. They need to be able to assert their right to vote in secret (e.g., ballot in braille or computerized for their software), and to marry, divorce, reproduce, sue, defend themselves, or even run for public office. They should know social conventions (greetings, conversation skills, manners), grooming fashions, and clothing styles. They deserve to have the same access to health settings, religious settings, social activities, and information services (e.g., telephone, television, computer nets) as do persons without disabilities. While much has been done since the passage of PL 101-476, much is still

left to be done to ensure a better life for adults with disabilities.

The first article included in this unit addresses the need to involve parents and students in the goals and objectives for transitional services. Special educators, teachers, and vocational counselors may know what they think a student should have in the way of preparation for adulthood, but their ideas are really secondary to the desires of the individual with a disability and his or her family. This essay reports on a study of four groups focusing on more effective ITP planning. All of the groups reported a need for more family input and support and for more student self-determination of adulthood roles.

The second unit article addresses the problems involved in fitting functional goals for transition into an inclusive educational setting. The next article, "Preparing Students for Transition: A Teacher Primer on Vocational

Education and Rehabilitiation," expands on the knowledge, attitude change, and teaching skills needed to help students with disabilities adapt to all the changes that accompany transition to adulthood. It provides useful tables on vocational assessments; on interviewing students, their parents, and their teachers; and on classroom vocational education preparation.

Looking Ahead: Challenge Questions

How much family involvement do students with disabilities want when planning for their futures?

How can ITPs be compatible with IEPs in inclusive educational settings? How does a functional curriculum improve compatibility?

What practical suggestions make transition planning easier for teachers, parents, and students?

What Do Students with Disabilities Tell Us About the Importance of Family Involvement in the Transition from School to Adult Life?

MARY E. MORNINGSTAR
ANN P. TURNBULL
H. RUTHERFORD TURNBULL III
Beach Center on Families and Disability
University of Kansas

ABSTRACT: *This qualitative study used focus groups to explore student perspectives on family involvement in the transition from school to adult life. Four focus groups, including students with learning disabilities, emotional and behavioral disorders, and mild mental retardation, identified pertinent issues concerning how families influence the development of a personal vision for the future, how students with disabilities perceive family involvement in transition planning, and how families influence the development of student self-determination. Results showed the importance to students of family input and support. Implications for transition planning, family roles for support during adulthood, and family-student-school partnership models are discussed.*

Families have a critical impact on the successful transition from school to adult life for young adults with disabilities (Everson & Moon, 1987). In fact, parent participation is considered to be one of the most important elements of transition programs (Sales, Metzler, Everson, & Moon, 1991; Schultz, 1986) that lead to positive outcomes for young adults with disabilities (Gardner, Chapman, Donaldson, & Jacobson, 1988). McNair and Rusch (1991) reported that, in the absence of special funding or special programs, parental involvement is the primary determinant of success in transition programs. In practice, however, parents and professionals experience difficulty in achieving collaborative working relationships (Goldberg & Kuriloff, 1991; Thornin & Irvin, 1992; Todis & Singer, 1991; Turnbull & Turnbull, 1990).

Although opportunities for parental involvement in planning educational programs has been mandated since 1975 (Public Law 94-142), the active involvement of students with disabilities is a relatively new concept. Research has shown that student involvement in educational planning is for the most part either nonexistent or passive (Van Reusen & Bos, 1990). Students who do not have the opportunities to learn to plan and manage their lives will leave school without the skills necessary to achieve positive adult outcomes (Martin, Marshall, & Maxson, 1993). In fact, Wehmeyer (1992a) concluded that one of the reasons for poor postschool outcomes is that students with disabilities leave school without self-determination.

Several recent models of student involvement in transition planning include creating a self-directed individualized education program (IEP) (Martin et al., 1993); student mastery of self-management skills (Mithaug, Martin, & Agran, 1987); and assisting students in learning

From *Exceptional Children*, December/January 1996, pp. 249-260. © 1996 by The Council for Exceptional Children. Reprinted by permission.

TABLE 1
Demographic Information of Focus Group Participants

Focus Group	*Geographic Location*	*No. in Focus Group*	*Disability Category and No.*	*Racial Breakdown and No.*	*Age of Participants (Years)*
Group 1	Rural	8	LD - 8	Caucasian - 7 Hispanic - 1	17-19
Group 2	Rural	15	LD - 6 BD - 2 MMR - 7	Caucasian - 15	13-19
Group 3	Suburban	11	LD - 4 BD - 5 MMR - 2	Caucasian - 8 Hispanic - 3	15-17
Group 4	Suburban	6	BD - 6	Caucasian - 5 African American - 1	13-16

Note. Abbreviations for disability categories are: LD, learning disabilities; BD, behavior disorders; MMR, mild mental retardation.

self-advocacy skills (Van Reusen & Bos, 1994). Though many of these new processes include the involvement of families, the primary focus is on skill development for students.

This article presents the analysis from four focus groups regarding the perspectives held by students with disabilities about the importance of family involvement in transition planning. The information provided by the students is a data subset from a larger study that is seeking to develop a better understanding of the methods and levels of collaboration among all participants in the transition planning process. The data presented in this article, however, focus specifically on students with disabilities and their perspectives regarding (a) family influence on the creation of a vision for their future, (b) family involvement in the transition planning process, and (c) family impact on the student's self-determination.

METHOD

Qualitative Methodology

A qualitative method of inquiry was used for this study. Qualitative methods are especially useful for exploratory research where little is known about the phenomenon of interest (Stewart & Shamdasani, 1990). We used focus groups as the primary source for data collection. A focus group has been defined as a "carefully planned discussion designed to obtain perceptions on a defined area of interest in a permissive and nonthreatening environment" (Krueger, 1988, p. 18). What differentiates focus groups from other forms of

qualitative data collection is the presence of group interaction in response to researchers' questions (Morgan & Krueger, 1993).

Sample·

Using purposive sampling, we selected the focus-group participants. In contrast to the random-sampling methods in quantitative research, purposive sampling involves the selection of a small number of groups representative of the diverse characteristics of the study population (Lincoln & Guba, 1985). For this study, we organized groups to represent the viewpoints of students with disabilities in Kansas who should be involved with transition planning. The four focus groups were organized to allow for predominantly homogeneous groups with regard to the similarity of their backgrounds and geographic location. However, groups were mixed by the characteristics of age, knowledge base, experience with transition planning, and with respect to ethnic diversity. These procedures attempt to address the recommendations that groups be homogeneous, but with sufficient variation among participants to allow for contrasting opinions (Krueger, 1988; Stewart & Shamdasani, 1990). Table 1 provides an overview of sample characteristics of the students.

We recruited participants through personal contact or phone calls. When the researchers did not have direct access to possible focus-group members, groups were organized through contact with administrators and teachers. Students with disabilities who participated in the focus groups were identified as having learning disabilities, emotional and behavioral disorders, and mild mental retardation.

Procedures

The focus groups lasted approximately 2 hr. To make participants feel more comfortable, the research team provided either a pizza lunch prior to holding the focus groups, or McDonald's gift certificates after the focus group. In an attempt to create a more familiar and informal environment within which the students could talk freely, the focus groups included time for participants to talk about subjects important to them even if not directly relevant to the focus group questions, attempted to instill humor and good-natured bantering among participants and the moderator, and included frequent breaks and opportunities for the students to move about.

Focus Group Questions. The content questions for this research study were organized around the three broad research questions:

1. How have families impacted the development of a personal vision for the future?
2. How do students with disabilities perceive their family's involvement with the transition planning process?
3. How have families influenced the students' self-determination?

We generated the specific content of the questions from the review of the literature and previous research regarding student and family involvement in transition planning.

Once we had compiled an initial set of questions and developed a moderator's guide for facilitating the focus groups, we field-tested the focus group format with two groups of students with disabilities (the data from the field tests were not used in the final data analysis). In this way, we modified the questions and pacing of the focus group to elicit more appropriate and relevant responses.

Conducting the Focus Groups. A two-person research team conducted the focus group interviews. The team included a moderator who asked open-ended questions, probed for additional comments, and monitored group discussion; and an observer, who operated the audiocassette recorder, kept track of time, and took accompanying field notes.

The moderator's primary task was to facilitate or guide the focus group in order to collect rich and valid insights about student perceptions regarding family involvement in transition planning. The moderator for this research study was trained in techniques that are considered by researchers to be effective strategies (Lincoln & Guba, 1985; Morgan & Krueger, 1993) and have been used in past focus group research (Morningstar, Sarkesian, & Tisdale, 1993).

Data Collection

We used two primary methods to collect the focus group data. All focus groups were audiotaped. These tapes were then fully transcribed for later data analysis. In addition, the observer was responsible for keeping field notes during the discussion. These notes included the main themes that emerged during the focus group and the general atmosphere and emotional responses of the participants. Immediately after the focus group had ended, the moderator and observer met to summarize and compare notes.

Data Analysis

A qualitative summary of participant comments was the primary method of data analysis for this study (Morgan, 1988). This summary involved reviewing all field notes, summarized notes, and transcripts from each focus group. The moderator and a second researcher analyzed the data, using established ethnographic and content data analysis techniques (Johnson & LaMontagne, 1993; Kerwin, Ponterotto, Jackson, & Harris, 1993; Krueger, 1988; Stewart & Shamdasani, 1990). This procedure involved "cycling through" the transcripts and notes and marking all relevant passages related to each of the questions or emergent categories (Morgan, 1988). Relevant information was assigned as individual data units.

All data units were then sorted by category. These initial categories were expanded to include additional categories or themes that emerged from each of the focus group discussions. Once specific categories were identified, the relevant information and salient quotes from the transcripts were sorted by category using *Ethnograph*, a qualitative data analysis computer program.

Data from each focus group were examined separately, indexed by focus group, and compiled with data from all other groups. This allowed for comparisons of the themes that emerged both across and within groups.

Credibility Procedures. At the completion of each of the two phases of data analysis (i.e., 1st phase—identifying relevant data units; 2nd phase—categorizing data units), the two researchers met to compare notes. If there was disagreement between researchers regarding any data unit, it was discussed until consensus could be reached. This allowed for the final conclusions to be considered more "verifiable" in that another researcher could arrive at similar conclusions using the available documents and raw data (Krueger, 1988). In addition, the data trail procedures will allow for an outside expert to perform the necessary data audit once the final research is completed.

RESULTS

Although each of the focus groups was unique, all four groups shared common issues and similar experiences. The focus group data were collapsed into three broad categories that specifically related to family issues:

- Creation of a vision for the future.
- Family and student involvement in the transition planning process.
- Family involvement in facilitating self-determination.

Under each of these broad categories, several themes and subthemes emerged.

Family Influence on the Creation of a Vision for the Future

The focus group participants had definite dreams for their future. In fact, the majority of students saw their future as bright. Students were asked about their future job and career expectations, where they wanted to live, whether they planned to attend a postsecondary school, and about their plans for social relationships and marriage. The overarching vision was positive and could be described as "The American Dream"—or as one student encapsulated the sentiments of the majority of participants: "I want to go to college, get a job, and get married." Very few students viewed their future as negative, and when negative future expectations were expressed, they were not often shared by classmates. Probably the most remarkable aspect of the development of a vision for the future was the influence that families have had on their sons and daughters with disabilities, particularly in the areas of career aspirations and living on their own.

Careers. The students in the focus groups identified a wide array of careers and occupations as possibilities for their future. Some of the reasons for choosing their possible careers were practical ones such as money, or were based on school vocational experiences. The influence of families on career choices, however, was clearly evident by

the overwhelming number of statements that students made about their families.

I plan to move to Nevada and become a cosmetologist.

Why do you want to move to Nevada?

Because my aunt lives there and she's a cosmetologist.

For many of the students, the careers that they were considering were directly related to a family member with a similar career. The careers that students were interested in because of family connections included pediatrician, veterinarian, nurse, airline industry worker, restaurant worker, diesel mechanic, and cosmetologist. The family members that influenced these young adults included mothers, fathers, aunts, uncles, brothers, sisters, and cousins. What was surprising, however, was the informality with which the students had decided on possible careers. The majority of these students had not had any formal discussions with family members about their careers. They were interested in the career due to the *informal role models* that family members have played in their lives.

Living on Their Own. The first response to the question of "Where do you want to live after high school?" was to move to exotic places like Hawaii, France, Las Vegas, Liverpool, Africa, or just "a big city, a humongous city!" The second response was to move to a location where they would have family and social supports:

I'm gonna go to [the] Vo-Tech. I might not this year, not after senior year, but I'm going to wait a year and go with Janelle, she's another friend. . . . I'm going to live with my uncle.

In fact, the issue of family supports often influenced decisions about where a student might go for postsecondary education and training:

It's kind of a toss-up with a college I want to go to right now. I'm looking at Vo-Tech, I mean I could drive back and forth over there and live with my parents. . . . If I go to [the] Community [College] . . . . I've got grandparents that live up there. . . . I've got nobody to live with down there [different town with a second community college], it's just like moving to a new country and trying to live on your own. It's going to be a little different than what I'm use to, and that's what is scaring me right now.

Family Involvement in the Transition Planning Process

Within the category of "family involvement in the transition planning process," several subcategories emerged: (a) starting the planning process, (b)

Should families be involved in planning? (c) How have or should families be involved? (d) What barriers do families face in helping to plan for the future? and (e) involving student and family in IEP meetings.

Starting the Planning Process. The majority of students reported that they had not begun an identified or formal process of planning for their future. For many of the students, this was because they felt they were too young to be worrying about such matters, despite what some of their older classmates might tell them:

Can you think of any advice you would give us about how you would better prepare kids for the future?

Older student: *I think I would start by, you know like I said, starting out in the 7th-grade year, talking to them about what kind of things they like to do, kind of work on those things. Sit down and talk to them individually about what kind of things they're planning on doing and just let them know that you guys are there and you guys are supportive.*

Okay, now I want to ask you all who are 13 and 14. What do you think about what she says?

1st younger student: *It's kind of like you guys are getting a little too old for us.*

So you think they're too grown-up?

1st younger student: *We still got a little while.*

2nd younger student: *You should wait until the 9th grade before worrying about getting a job or anything, because you can't get a job until you're at least 14.*

A few students reported that their families had started some discussions regarding life after high school:

Have you had any meetings that have focused on planning for your future?

Well, not exactly, but my parents have been giving me some ideas and stuff, and some teachers here have been giving me some ideas and I've been thinking, because my cousin, my one cousin is in it and so was my dad, he was in heavy equipment. My cousin was a diesel mechanic, and I was thinking of going out for those two because I heard that you make a lot of money and it would really be good for me.

Overall, the students with disabilities who participated in the four focus groups did not appear to be actively involved in any systematic transition planning. The few exceptions were a few students who were in their senior year of high school and who had had been involved in a tran-

sition planning process facilitated by their school district. Among those students who indicated at least a minimal level of thinking about their future, it was evident that their families were involved in this in an informal way.

What is interesting to note is the lack of direct comments pertaining to the role of families as a deliberate catalyst for starting the planning process. The students did not mention their families urging or encouraging them to begin to think about the future. In a few cases where there was a clear and definite change approaching (e.g., their senior year, getting married, moving out of the house), then students talked about the role that their families have played in helping them to plan for these future changes. But again, the comments from these students indicated that the process was informal:

How about your family? Have they been involved?

Well, my mom . . . kind of because I told her once I turn 18 that I was thinking about moving out and she told me that once you move out, once you turn 18 and move out of your parents' house, you're dropped off the insurance and stuff so you have to get your own insurance. Can't go crawling back to mommy and daddy.

Should Families Be Involved in Planning for the Future? Students indicated that a variety of people were involved in helping them to plan for their future, including boyfriends, parents, siblings, extended family members, teachers, adult service providers, classmates and friends, and other community members (e.g., employers). The majority of students, however, indicated that their families were the primary source of future planning and that this planning was informal at best:

We really don't talk about like, we're talking about my future, you know . . . if I come home and have a bad day or something like that, she'll just kind of give me a pep talk, you know. . . . It's not really future, but she just like, she just gives me pep talks or something like that, pretty much she supports me.

Most students stated that they felt that their family should be involved in helping them plan for their future:

My mom wants us not to be like her, so she'll go do what she has to so we can get a good education and go to college and stuff like that. And she said she'll kick our butt if we drop out of school.

The majority of students identified their families as being involved. However, several students indicated the opposite. For these students, their families were not involved in their lives (students were in foster homes), or the students felt that they should assume full responsibility for planning for their own future.

How Have or Should Families Be Involved? Students identified a wide range of ways that family members have been involved or should be involved in helping them to plan for their future. The ways that families can and should be involved in planning ranged across all aspects of their current and future lives including (a) making sure that they stay in high school, (b) planning for and helping to pay for college, (c) helping them move out on their own, and (d) helping them find a job. The students identified a wide range of family members who should be or have been involved in various aspects of their lives. These included both immediate and extended family members. The students discussed both concrete ways that families should be involved, such as paying for college, as well as more informal methods, such as just spending time talking with them or helping them with their homework.

What Barriers Do Families Face in Helping Plan for the Future? Several issues were evident when the discussion turned to barriers to family involvement in transition planning. Probably the most pressing issue that students identified as a barrier to having their families involved was the conflicts and disagreements between the student and his or her family:

How about when you disagree? Do you and your parents or family always agree on what you think is best?

No. [My] parents think they're right and you think you're right so you get in a fight and then you always win anyway because you'll walk outside the house and do it anyway.

Tied into this issue were the frustrations the students felt because they didn't think that their families gave them enough responsibilities. Another issue that was raised in two of the focus groups was the concern that families were not thinking about their futures, because they did not see the immediacy of the impending future:

Why do you think it's hard for your family to think about you guys being on your own?

Because you've lived with them all your life and they're used to you being there all the time.

Student and Family Involvement in IEP Meetings. Students were asked about their involvement in IEP meetings since the Individuals with Disabilities Education Act (IDEA) autho-

rizes student and family involvement before a student begins the transition process and mandates it after the student is 16 or earlier, as appropriate, when transition planning is initiated as part of the IEP. The majority of students knew about their IEP meetings, and they indicated that at least one member of their family (usually their mother) attended these meetings. It was also clear, however, that several students did not know precisely what an IEP was, and of those students who knew what their IEP meeting was, few had actually attended their meetings. There were a variety of reasons for this lack of attendance, starting with the fact that they had never been invited to a meeting. One student stated that his mother and father would not allow him to attend meetings. When asked why they would not allow him to go, he stated:

I talked to my dad about my meetings but he told me [he] don't care about them anymore.

He's not interested? Does he still go?

He goes but he don't care.

Does your mom go?

She don't care either. I don't know what the deal is but my mom and dad don't like going to the meetings. . . they think they're so stupid.

The majority of those who had not been to their meeting, however, had been invited and had decided not to attend. The primary reasons for deciding not to attend was that IEP meetings were meaningless and not relevant to planning for their future. Other students described their negative experiences at meetings as the reason for not wanting to attend.

It should be noted that not all of the students perceived their IEP meetings as negative. However, it was clear that those students who went to their meetings and who reported that they were active participants in their meetings were the *only ones* who saw any value in the IEP process. This was a small minority among all of the focus group participants. Overall, none of the students related incidents that indicated that their families had discussed IEP goals with them prior to the meeting or that they went into meetings with a sense of agreement on certain issues. The students did not describe any examples of their families supporting them or advocating for them during difficult meetings.

Family Involvement in Facilitating Self-Determination.

Students were asked a series of questions pertaining to self-determination and the opportunities they have had to make decisions in their lives. It was evident that families either facilitated:

When I was 13 my parents said that I need to start learning my own responsibilities and my parents would say you know, at this age I can start learning what's ahead in the future, so they let me have my own responsibilities.

or hindered self-determination:

My mom and dad are very strict. I don't get to go to any parties. I want to control my own life.

While some students appeared to have more opportunities in making day-to-day decisions, most students were able to identify some areas where their parents made the decisions. These ranged from simple issues, such as having to do household chores, to more critical areas of their lives:

I have some control of my life. I mean, like I have control whether or not I come home on time or not and whether or not I walk out of the house when I get grounded, especially whether or not I walk out of the house in front of my parents or not. But you know my parents have a choice of whether or not I get put in [out of home] placement.

For some students, there was a real sense that they were responsible enough to make important decisions about their own lives. These decisions ranged along a continuum of risk such as deciding what activities they were involved in after school, to going to parties and staying out late, to drinking and doing drugs, to moving away from home. Many students who were able to make important decisions reported that they felt they possessed a level of responsibility that would be needed for adult life:

So how does that make you feel when you get to make decisions?

It makes me feel like I can do whatever I want right now. As long as I know that then I can correct my own mistakes. I mean if we get to make our decisions—if our parents are not making our decisions now, then we're getting pretty, you know what it should be like in adult life.

It appeared that the students who felt they had opportunities to make decisions usually were able to communicate with their parents and felt that their parents were supportive of their decisions:

[If] my parents don't like it and we usually have a seat in their living room and we'll talk it out and discuss it, and then we'll come up with another solution and do it a different way.

In other situations, students reported parental consequences when they made poor decisions. Many of the students discussed the fact that they respected and appreciated their parents' involvement in supporting them to make decisions:

I wanted to say parents [it seems as if we] don't like our parents, but really if you think about it, you know, they aren't that bad because they give you your own responsibility.

It is interesting to note that students overwhelmingly reported that the "big decisions" that they were making included: staying out late (past their curfew), drinking and driving, doing drugs, having sexual experiences, and moving away from home. However, students did not discuss any particular strategies that their families used to facilitate their self-determination. Clearly, this is an area that needs further exploration, particularly in light of the fact that these same students did not report any formal school curriculum or activities that were teaching these critical decision-making skills, and in some cases, the students realized how important these skills were.

DISCUSSION

A word of caution is in order related to the purpose and nature of qualitative research methodology. Using qualitative methods, the researcher inductively derives an understanding by attending to the participants' discussion rather than by testing or confirming hypothesis or theory (Krueger, 1988). The purpose of this focus group research, then, is not to broadly generalize the results to all students with disabilities, but to explore students' views concerning family involvement—perspectives that have been previously ignored. The issues that will be discussed in this section include: (a) family roles in creating a future vision; (b) family involvement in the planning process; and (c) family involvement in facilitating self-determination.

Family Roles in Creating a Future Vision

The students specifically described ways that families have helped them to develop a future vision related to career and lifestyle options. The finding that families influence career aspirations is not new (Super, 1990; Szymanski, 1994); however, it is the predominant means by which these students have begun to develop a career vision. The literature that does exist on family career influence, however, tends to focus on parental roles and does not include the contribution of extended family members. The comments from students in this study concerning the roles of grandparents, aunts, uncles, cousins, and siblings is extremely noteworthy, and data suggest that extended family might be considered as powerful partners in career preparation.

Equally striking is that relatively few students identified their school-based vocational training experiences as impacting career decisions. In some instances, a lack of a systematic and effective community-based vocational program was the cause; but in other cases, students' vocational experiences just were not as relevant to them as were their families'. Perhaps schools need to pay closer attention to the importance of including family careers as an aspect of a school vocational curriculum. The findings from these focus groups seem to indicate that emphasizing family careers is one area that might motivate students into developing career goals for the future.

The second component of developing a future vision focused on the students' having a concept of what supports might be needed for them to live on their own. Students expressed a preference to live close to their families so that they would have ongoing support. This is consistent with career literature that describes life-space considerations for transition (Super, 1990; Szymanski, 1994). Life-space issues refer to the different life roles (e.g., worker, community citizen, child, spouse, parent) and the ecological context within which those roles are carried out. These students clearly preferred ongoing contact with both the nuclear and extended family. This point raises the issue of how different family members could be involved in transition planning in terms of the supports that they can offer. It is noteworthy that very few students mentioned accessing professional support from the adult service system to assist them in their daily living needs.

Concerning career and lifestyle visions, parents and extended family members helped students shape their aspirations in an informal, almost implicit, manner with "families as role models." Based on the life-span perspective of transition (Hershenson, 1984; Szymanski, Hershenson, & Power, 1988), early childhood years provide a strong foundation for career development (and likely for lifestyle development as well). Because family roles appear to be highly implicit in providing a vision for the future, whether it would be advantageous or detrimental to encourage this contribution to be more explicit is a useful question. If family roles are made more explicit in terms of developing a vision for the future, one must consider the potential positive and negative impacts of early, structured future planning during childhood years.

Family Involvement in the Planning Process

A critical theme that emerged across all focus groups was lack of systematic attention to the process of planning for the future. It was clear from the students' responses that the majority of students (with the exception of those who were seniors and facing the inevitable) have had only a loose connection with future planning. Interestingly, several younger students did not think it necessary to begin the planning process before 9th grade, whereas other older students felt planning should begin as early as 7th grade.

Perhaps it is imperative to heed the warning from one young man, who stated: "If you start them so early, you're more or less training them to be adults." From this perspective, perhaps we need to consider what type of future planning is most appealing and relevant to students with disabilities and their families across the life-span. If schools start too soon and encourage families to do the same in a way that is not meaningful to the students and families, we may in the end lose students and families to the process because of our zeal to provide "early transition planning" training. It would be critical to avoid the pressures described by many parents in early intervention programs to constantly be "working" with their child to make developmental gains (Turnbull, Turnbull, & Blue-Banning, 1994).

The majority of students identified certain family members as being able to provide support during the transition process. It might be a grandparent they were going to live with, or their father who has helped them find a job. The students frequently mentioned the ongoing connections with family members after graduation from high school. This raises the issue of the importance of the family in the "long haul." Families and professionals must develop a more extensive understanding of the roles that families play throughout adulthood for people with disabilities. Perhaps a critical element of transition planning is the identification of both immediate and extended family who will be involved in supporting the young adult after graduation from high school.

Of great concern is the finding that the majority of students reported the IEP process as irrelevant. The lack of student attendance at meetings is just the tip of the iceberg. More striking is the overall picture in which students are not actively engaged or involved in making decisions regarding their goals and objectives, including those involving life after high school. Disappointedly absent from the student descriptions of IEP meetings was any reference to a sense of family "solidarity" in participation. By family solidarity, we mean the partnership of students, parents, and extended family working in advance to formulate priority issues and attending the conference with a sense of unanimity in sharing their visions, goals, strengths, and needs for immediate and ongoing support.

Given the data shared from the students in the focus group concerning the potent role of parents and extended families in developing future visions related to career and lifestyle options, as well as in their preferences for receiving ongoing family support, it would appear that a major need for IEP model development would be preparation of family members to collaborate with their students. The most exciting work in this regard is from the person-centered planning literature regarding models such as the McGill Action Planning System (Forest & Pierpoint, 1992), Personal Futures Planning (Mount & Zwernik, 1988), Essential Lifestyle Planning (Smull & Harrison, 1992), and Group Action Planning (Turnbull, Turnbull, & Blue-Banning, 1994). All of these person-centered planning approaches place strong emphasis on creating connections among the person with a disability, nuclear and extended family, professionals, friends, and community citizens. Almost all person-centered planning has occurred outside of the formal IEP process, likely because of concern that the general atmosphere of IEP meetings would stifle the essence of person-centered planning. An issue for future research is why these processes seem to have benefits that the IEP transition planning process lacks.

Family Influence on Self-Determination

Wehmeyer (1992b) suggested that being self-determined, a primary causal agent in one's life, means that students act autonomously. Although there is a growing literature on self-determination (Sands & Wehmeyer, in press), researchers have not provided sufficient explication of the interaction between self-determination and a family systems orientation to ongoing family support. It was clear that a number of students from the focus groups are seeking autonomy in making certain kinds of decisions, but they are also seeking ongoing family support. Interestingly, no students indicated support for or training in self-determination for themselves or their families had been part of the transition preparation process. They also did not mention any explicit strategies that their families had used in addressing issues of evolving autonomy over the lifespan.

It is critically important for special education leaders from across the age span to collabo-

rate in the development of family-student-school partnership models. From the earliest ages, these models need to incorporate a much stronger emphasis on self-determination in enhancing students' autonomy, even during early childhood years, to express their preferences for activities and to assess their strengths and needs. In particular, family roles need to be conceptualized to ensure that parents and extended family have opportunities to be collaborators with their son or daughter in collective decision making. Thus, appropriate roles need to be delineated for students and families to experience self-determination at younger ages and for families to be involved in supporting their son or daughter's autonomy in planning meetings at older stages.

CONCLUSION

The findings reported here are the first phase of an ongoing research project designed to solicit the viewpoints and perceptions of secondary students with disabilities regarding their experiences with transition planning. Given the nature of qualitative research methodology, we emphasize that the purpose of this research is not to generalize broadly the results that we have obtained to all students with disabilities, but to give voice to students' perspectives concerning family involvement that has typically not been part of the professional literature. The findings of this research, therefore, can be used to generate additional research directions and demonstration models regarding the involvement of students with disabilities and families in the transition planning process.

REFERENCES

Everson, J., & Moon, S. (1987). Transition services for young adults with severe disabilities: Defining professional and parental roles and responsibilities. *Journal of the Association for Persons with Severe Handicaps, 12*(2), 87-95.

Forest, M., & Pierpoint, J. C. (1992, October). Putting kids on the MAP. *Educational Leadership*, 26-31.

Gardner, J. F., Chapman, M. S., Donaldson, G., & Jacobson, R. (1988). *Toward supported employment: A process guide for planned change.* Baltimore: Paul H. Brookes.

Goldberg, S. S., & Kuriloff, P. J. (1991). Evaluating the fairness of special education hearings. *Exceptional Children, 57*, 546-555.

Hershenson, D. B. (1984). Vocational counseling with learning disabled adults. *Journal of Rehabilitation, 50*, 40-44.

Johnson, L. J., & LaMontagne, M. J. (1993). Research methods: Using content analysis to examine the verbal or written communication of stakeholders within early intervention. *Journal of Early Intervention, 17*(1), 73-79.

Kerwin, C., Ponterotto, J. G., Jackson, B. L., & Harris, A. (1993). Racial identity in biracial children: A qualitative investigation. *Journal of Counseling Psychology, 40*(2), 221-231.

Krueger, R. A. (1988). *Focus groups: A practical guide for applied research.* London: Sage.

Lincoln, Y. S., & Guba, E. G. (1985). *Naturalistic inquiry.* London: Sage.

Martin, J. E., Marshall, L. H., & Maxson, L. L. (1993). Transition policy: Infusing self-determination and self-advocacy into transition programs. *Career Development for Exceptional Individuals, 16*(1), 53-61.

McNair, J., & Rusch, F. R. (1991). Parent involvement in transition programs. *Mental Retardation, 29*(2), 93-101.

Mithaug, D. E., Martin, J. E., & Agran, M. (1987). Adaptability instruction: The goal of transitional programming. *Exceptional Children, 53,* 500-505.

Morgan, D. L. (1988). Focus groups as qualitative research. *Qualitative Research Methods Series, 16.* London: Sage.

Morgan, D. L., & Krueger, R. A. (1993). When to use focus groups and why. In D. L. Morgan (Ed.), *Successful focus groups: Advancing the state of the art* (pp. 3-19). Newbury Park: Sage Publication.

Morningstar, M. E., Sarkesian, S., & Tisdale, C. (1993, July). *Report of the transition training needs in Kansas.* Lawrence: University of Kansas, Department of Special Education.

Mount B., & Zwernik, K. (1988). *It's never too early, it's never too late: A booklet about personal planning for persons with developmental disabilities, their families and friends, case managers, service providers, and advocates.* St. Paul, MN: Metropolitan Council. (ERIC Document Reproduction Service No. ED 327 997)

Sales, P., Metzler, H. M., Everson, J. M., & Moon, M. S. (1991, October). Quality indicators of successful vocational transition programs. *Journal of Vocational Rehabilitation, 1*(4), 47-63.

Sands, D., & Wehmeyer, M. (Eds.). (in press). *Self-determination across the lifespan: Theory and practice.* Baltimore: Paul H. Brookes.

Schultz, R. P. (1986). Establishing a parent-professional partnership to facilitate competitive employment. In F. R. Rusch (Ed.), *Competitive employment issues and strategies* (pp 289-302). Baltimore: Paul H. Brookes.

Smull, M., & Harrison, S. B. (1992). *Supporting people with severe reputations in the community.* Alexandria, VA: National Association of State Mental Retardation Program Directors.

Stewart, D. W., & Shamdasani, P. N. (1990). Focus groups: Theory and practice. *Applied Social Research Methods Series, 20.* London: Sage.

Super, D. E. (1990). A life-span, life-space approach to career development. In D. Brown, L. Brooks, & Associates (Eds.), *Career choice and development: Applying contemporary theories to practice* (2nd ed., pp. 197-261). San Francisco: Jossey-Bass.

Szymanski, E. (1994). Transition: Life-span and life-space considerations for empowerment. *Exceptional Children, 60,* 402-410.

Szymanski, E. M., Hershenson, D. B., & Power, P. W. (1988). Enabling the family in supporting transition from school to work. In P. W. Power, A. Dell Orto, & M. B. Gibbons (Eds.), *Family interventions throughout chronic illness and disability* (pp. 216-233). New York: Springer.

Thornin, E. J., & Irvin, L. K. (1992). Family stress associated with transition to adulthood of young people with severe disabilities. *Journal of the Association for Persons with Severe Handicaps, 16*(1), 31-39.

Todis, B., & Singer, G. (1991). Stress and stress management in families with adopted children who have disabilities. *Journal of the Association for Persons with Severe Handicaps, 16*(1), 3-13.

Turnbull, A. P., & Turnbull, H. R. (1990). *Families, professionals and exceptionality: A special partnership* (2nd ed). Columbus, OH: Merrill.

Turnbull, A. P., Turnbull, H. R., & Blue-Banning, M. J. (1994). Enhancing inclusion of infants and toddlers with disabilities and their families: A theoretical and programmatic analysis. *Infants and Young Children, 7*(2), 1-14.

Van Reusen, A. K., & Bos, C. S. (1990). IPLAN: Helping students communicate in planning conferences. *TEACHING Exceptional Children, 22*(4), 30-32.

Van Reusen, A., & Bos, C. (1994). Facilitating student participation in individualized education programs through motivation strategy instruction. *Exceptional Children, 60,* 466-475.

Wehmeyer, M. L. (1992a). Self-determination and the education of students with mental retardation. *Education and Training in Mental Retardation, 27*(4), 302-314.

Wehmeyer, M. L. (1992b). Self-determination: Critical skills for outcome-oriented transition services. *The Journal for Vocational Special Needs Education, 15,* 3-7.

ABOUT THE AUTHORS

MARY E. MORNINGSTAR (CEC KS Federation), Project Director; **ANN P. TURNBULL** (CEC #665), Co-Director; and **H. RUTHERFORD TURNBULL III** (CEC #665), Co-Director, Beach Center on Families and Disability, University of Kansas, Lawrence.

Is a Functional Curriculum Approach Compatible with an Inclusive Education Model?

Gary M. Clark

Gary M. Clark *(CEC Chapter #665), Professor, Department of Special Education, University of Kansas, Lawrence.*

A nagging question for many special education teachers at elementary, middle school, and high school levels is the question of what to teach. What is most important for students to know or be able to do both now and in the future?

Instruction has always involved deciding on what to teach (curriculum) and how to teach it (methods, materials, and activities). Special education in its earliest years was left to develop its own discipline around both of these areas. As a separate educational system, it went about this in a variety of ways, but most often it started with the general education curriculum as a base and modified it to fit the expected performance levels of the students. Most of the modifications were accomplished by adapting instruction; for example, devising new ways of teaching reading (Fernald method or the Gillingham approach) and mathematics (Cuisenaire rods, abacas, etc.) or new materials, and not by modifying the content itself.

Looking back, this approach to academics was a logical first step. Many of the children placed in special education classes during those early years had mild levels of learning and behavior disorders. Hopes were high that specialized methods and materials could

remediate their difficulties and help them achieve in the general education curriculum with other children, although at a slower pace. As special education identification and placement began to include children with moderate to severe disabilities, the next logical step was to consider some changes not only in *how* children with special needs are taught, but also in *what* they are taught. The term *functional academics* was used early on to reflect the shift away from traditional academics.

In the 1970s, the field of special education moved from being the sole provider of special education content and instructional strategies and techniques to being a system that would provide and support a continuum of educational options. Most of the options developed, however, placed the responsibility for curriculum back in the hands of general education. Before long those early questions regarding the generalizability and relevance of traditional academics for students with moderate and severe disabilities evolved into the current questions regarding functional outcomes for all students with disabilities.

Functional outcomes of education—that is, the ability to live and work as a part of the community satisfactorily—may or may not result from traditional academic curricula. What makes it so difficult for parents and educators to deal with this fact is that the idea of providing a more functional curriculum for more functional outcomes seems to preclude full inclusion, especially given today's increased emphasis on academics in public education. This special focus section of *TEACHING Exceptional Children* looks at a functional curriculum approach and how it might work within an inclusive education context.

What Is a Functional Curriculum Approach?

A variety of writers have defined functional curricula, or what is sometimes referred to as *life skills instruction* (cf. Brolin, 1991; Brown et al., 1979; Clark, 1991; Cronin & Patton, 1993; Falvey, 1989; Mithaug, Martin, & Agran, 1987). While there is a common theme imbedded in these and other perspectives described in the literature, there is still a possibility of miscommunication when the term *functional* is used.

The basic notion of functionality implies the usefulness of something or usefulness for somebody. Given that, it is clear that what is functional for one person is not necessarily functional for another person or what is a functional use for an object in one situation may not be functional in another situation. A cane may be functional for a person who needs support for mobility, but it has no usefulness for someone who does not need it. Likewise, the cane can be func-

From *Teaching Exceptional Children*, Vol. 26, No. 2, Winter 1994, pp. 36-39. © 1994 by The Council for Exceptional Children. Reprinted by permission.

tional as a support tool for walking but without function in swimming. For our purposes, functional curriculum must have a specific context and focus for children and youth with disabilities. The context and focus arise from the need of all persons with disabilities to have the life skills to make a successful transition from school to adult living (Brolin, 1991; Clark & Kolstoe, 1990; Halpern, 1985; Polloway, Patton, Epstein, & Smith, 1989). From this perspective, the concept can be defined as follows:

A functional curriculum approach is a way of delivering instructional content that focuses on the concepts and skills needed by all students with disabilities in the areas of personal-social, daily living, and occupational adjustment. What is considered a functional curriculum for any one student would be the content (concepts and skills) included in that student's curriculum or course of study that targets his or her current and future needs. These needs are based on a nondiscriminatory, functional assessment approach.

How Do You Determine What Is Functional Knowledge or a Functional Skill?

The answer to this question depends upon the answers to a variety of related questions:

- Is the instructional content of the student's current educational placement appropriate for meeting the student's personal-social, daily living, and occupational adjustment needs? That is,
- Does the content focus on necessary knowledge and skills to function as independently as possible in the home, school, or community?
- Does the content provide a scope and sequence for meeting future needs?
- Do the student's parents think the content is important for both current and future needs?
- Does the student think the content is important for both current and future needs?

- Is the content appropriate for the student's chronological age and current intellectual, academic, or behavioral performance level(s)?
- What are the consequences to the student of not learning the concepts and skills inherent in the current educational placement?

As these questions imply, the determination of functionality with a specific focus on transition to adult living does not depend on a particular point of view about where a student is educated. A student in a segregated, self-contained special school or class may not be receiving a functional curriculum any more than a student in an inclusive education model. This is not to say that there may not be positive benefits associated with various current placement alternatives. If those benefits do not include life skills instruction at all or in sufficient amount, however, the educational placement is not providing an appropriate functional curriculum. If parents and students choose general education as the desirable primary or even exclusive placement, a functional curriculum must be planned within that context. The Special Focus article by Field, LeRoy, and Rivera gives an example of a student-centered functional curriculum determination.

Current functional curriculum models focus directly on knowledge and skills that need to be taught and leave the delivery procedures and instructional environment decisions to users. Some of the better known models include the Community-Referenced Curriculum (Smith & Schloss, 1988), Community Living Skills Taxonomy (Dever, 1988), Hawaii Transition Project (1987), and Life Centered Career Education model (Brolin, 1991). Of these, the Life Centered Career Education (LCCE) model by Brolin is probably the best example of a comprehensive functional curriculum model across age levels and the most completely developed curriculum package for secondary school teachers (Brolin, 1992).

The LCCE model is organized around 22 competencies needed for adult living. The competencies are clustered across three basic domains: Daily Living, Personal-Social, and Occupa-

tional Guidance and Preparation. Each of the 22 competencies can be broken down into subcompetencies that may be appropriate for individualized education program (IEP) goals or short-term objectives. The curriculum content domains of the LCCE model, as well as the other models that are available, are directly on target for the planning of transition services mandated for students 16 years of age and older under Public Law 101-476 (IDEA), the Individuals with Disabilities Education Act of 1990.

When Do You Start a Functional Curriculum?

Special educators who value life skills education have long held the view that a functional curriculum for children with disabilities should begin formally when these children enter the public schools (Kokaska & Brolin, 1985; Clark, 1979). The Division on Career Development and Transition of The Council for Exceptional Children established its position on early beginnings with a formal policy statement reflecting the view that many concepts and skills must be introduced at the awareness and exploration stages for elementary school children in order to make the most of instructional efforts during the secondary school years (Clark, Carlson, Fisher, Cook, & D'Alonzo, 1991). The Special Focus article by Beck, Broers, Hogue, Shipstead, and Knowlton demonstrates the possibilities of this practice for elementary school children in grades two through four.

Who Needs a Functional Curriculum?

All children and youth in public schools today should be provided an education that is specific enough to provide them with the knowledge and skills they need to perform age-appropriate roles while in school and to meet the demands of being family members, citizens, and workers as adults. As early as 1979, the Carnegie Council of Policy Studies in Higher Education stated in an educational reform paper that the public education approach to teaching basic skills and academic content was successful with only about two-thirds of the school population. Few would argue that a large proportion of the population of students who are at risk and many students with disabilities have difficulties using what schools provide for successful adult adjustment. Follow-up studies of former special education students, including the majority of students referred to as having mild disabilities, support the Carnegie study contention that another approach should be considered.

Many teachers who are assigned to resource rooms or collaborative programs either do not consider their students as needing functional curricula or perform their roles within whatever curricular offerings exist without concerning themselves with curriculum alternatives. Some states using noncategorical teacher endorsements complicate the issue by differentiating mild/moderate teaching endorsements from severe/profound teaching endorsements according to the different curricula used with the students in the two groups. That is, a functional curriculum is typically identified with students with severe disabilities, and all other students (i.e., those with mild to moderate disabilities) are assumed to be able to benefit sufficiently from the general education curriculum.

Logic, research data, and now the IDEA mandate to at least address functional curriculum needs through transition planning for students age 16 and above all lead to only one answer to the question of who needs a functional curriculum: All students with disabilities need such a curriculum, but each must be determined individually.

How Do a Functional Curriculum and a Traditional Curriculum Relate to One Another?

For some people, the relationship between a functional life skills curriculum and academics is a practical question. For others, it is a philosophical question that might be phrased more directly as "What is the place of a functional curriculum approach in the context of the inclusive education movement?" It is easier to deal with these questions if a distinction is made between a functional curriculum and a functional curriculum approach.

The term *functional curriculum* suggests a document or written guide that is in place and used for all students in a particular setting. While this could be the case, the definition given earlier implies that it could also be a specified program of instruction or course of study for an individual student. It may be tied to a group instructional setting if, in fact, it is used for most or all of the students in that setting, but this is not necessarily the case. If it is tied to a self-contained or separate delivery alternative, a high degree of responsibility is placed on special education teachers to demonstrate that the outcomes are not only satisfying to the students and their families, but also acceptable and desirable outcomes of the school's commitment to providing quality, integrated educational programs.

A *functional curriculum approach*, on the other hand, suggests that functional content is prescribed on the IEP, but that it has no restrictions regarding the type or location of instructional delivery. This perspective permits educators and families to look first to what a child's instructional content should be before determining where and how it should be provided. The functional curriculum approach places a high degree of responsibility on both general and special educators to make sure that the instruction is delivered effectively and with integrity, regardless of the delivery environment(s).

At present, the relationship between a functional curriculum approach and the traditional academic curriculum is a tenuous one. A lot is going on in public education that sends both discouraging and encouraging messages. The discouraging message is that general education is moving toward a more rigorous academic model and that effective schools and outcomes-based/performance-based education will focus on fostering higher achievement scores in the traditional subject matter areas and increased skills in higher-order thinking and problem-solving. The encouraging message is that some educators are viewing outcomes-based education more broadly than as simply increasing academic achievement scores and higher-order thinking. They are advocating functional, generalizable skills for responsible citizenship as the ends and academic skills as the means to those ends. This broader view of outcomes for education provides special educators and families who want a functional approach a window of opportunity to choose to be a part of a single educational system that takes responsibility for *all* students.

How Can Schools Develop a Functional Curriculum Approach and Promote Inclusive Education?

Even a functional curriculum delivery system that is based on a special class model can incorporate many aspects of inclusion. The very nature of life skills instruction depends upon age-appropriate skills and experiences with age peers who do not have disabilities. A transition perspective of preparing students to leave school and assume adult roles depends upon real-life, community-based skills and experiences for learning and generalization. This means that a highly inclusive model can organize and present instruction together with students without disabilities, but it must meet the functional, community-based needs of all students. Functional skills instruction must be planned deliberately and implemented with families and general education teachers. Implementation of this type of planning and collaboration becomes increasingly more difficult and complex as students move from elementary to high school settings. This may affect both the nature and the quality of both functional skills acquisition and inclusion.

Three ways of developing and implementing a functional curriculum within an inclusive education philosophy are presented in the three Special Focus articles that follow. The three approaches reflect a "bottom-up" model, a student-centered model, and a "top-down" model. Each article illustrates not only what can be done but also what has been done in certain situations and settings. Each reflects a high degree of commitment to the notion of the importance of functional life skills and integration outcomes. Your task as a reader is to determine which one, if any, fits your situation and decide what you can replicate or adapt to suit your needs.

References

Brolin, D. E. (1991). *Life centered career education: A competency based approach* (3rd ed.). Reston, VA: The Council for Exceptional Children.

Brolin, D. E. (1992). *Life centered career education (LCCE) curriculum program.* Reston, VA: The Council for Exceptional Children.

Brown, L., Branston, M., Hamre-Nietupski, S., Pumpian, I., Certo, N., & Gruenwald, L. (1979). A strategy for developing chronological age-appropriate and functional curricular content for severely handicapped adolescents and young adults. *Journal of Special Education, 13*(1), 81-90.

Carnegie Council of Policy Studies in Higher Education. (1979). *Giving youth a better chance: Options for education, work, and service.* San Francisco: Jossey-Bass.

Clark, G. M. (1979). *Career education for the handicapped child in the regular classroom.* Denver, CO: Love Publishing.

Clark, G. M. (1991). Functional curriculum and its place in the regular education initiative. Paper presented at the Seventh International Conference of the Division on Career Development, The Council for Exceptional Children, Kansas City, MO.

Clark, G. M., Carlson, B. C., Fisher, S. L., Cook, I. D., & D'Alonzo, B. J. (1991). Career development for students with disabilities in elementary schools: A position statement of the Division on Career Development. *Career Development for Exceptional Individuals, 14*, 109-120.

Clark, G. M., & Kolstoe, O. P. (1990). *Career development and transition education for adolescents with disabilities.* Needham Heights, MA: Allyn and Bacon.

Cronin, M. E., & Patton, J. R. (1993). *Life skills instruction for all students with special needs: A practical guide for integrating real-life content into the curriculum.* Austin, TX: Pro-Ed.

Dever, R. B. (1988). *Community living skills: A taxonomy.* Washington, DC: American Association on Mental Retardation.

Falvey, M. (1989). *Community-based curriculum* (2nd ed.). Baltimore: Paul H. Brookes.

Halpern, A. S. (1985). Transition: A look at the foundations. *Exceptional Children, 51*, 479-486.

Hawaii Transition Project. (1987). Honolulu: Department of Special Education, University of Hawaii.

Kokaska, C. J., & Brolin, D. E. (1985). *Career education for handicapped individuals* (2nd. ed.). Columbus, OH: Merrill.

Mithaug, D., Martin, J. E., & Agran, M. (1987). Adaptability instruction: The goal of transitional programming. *Exceptional Children, 53*, 500-505.

Polloway, E. A., Patton, J. R., Epstein, M. H., & Smith, T. E. C. (1989). Comprehensive curriculum for students with mild handicaps. *Focus on Exceptional Children, 21*(8), 1-12.

Smith, M. A., & Schloss, P. J. (1988). Teaching to transition. In P. J. Schloss, C. A. Hughes, & M. A. Smith (Eds.), *Community integration for persons with mental retardation* (pp. 1-16). Austin, TX: Pro-Ed.

Preparing Students for Transition:

A Teacher Primer on Vocational Education and Rehabilitation

Provides an overview of the two programs and addresses the entry process, available services, and student preparation for entry into the programs

Carol A. Dowdy and Rebecca B. Evers

Carol A. Dowdy, EdD, is an associate professor of special education at the School of Education at the University of Alabama. **Rebecca B. Evers,** EdD, is an assistant professor of special education in the Center for Pedagogy at Winthrop University in Rock Hill, South Carolina. Address: Carol A. Dowdy, School of Education, University of Alabama, UAB Station, Birmingham, AL 35243.

The reauthorization of the Individuals with Disabilities Education Act (IDEA) of 1990 mandates the provision of a coordinated set of transition activities within an outcome-oriented process for all secondary students who have an Individualized Education Program (IEP). School should incorporate these services into each student's IEP through a process of formal transition planning that includes the designation of interagency responsibilities and/or linkages when appropriate. In the planning stage, educators and other agency and program personnel can coordinate secondary school coursework, related activities, work experiences, responsibilities at home, and community participation to maximize a student's readiness for postschool settings. Certainly, the degree to which students access and succeed in postsecondary settings is to a large extent a result of their secondary programming (DeStefano & Wermuth, 1992). The effectiveness of the secondary programming may depend on the teacher's ability to effectively collaborate with personnel from the community, other agencies, and vocationally oriented programs.

The purpose of this article is to provide information that will facilitate the special education teacher's linkages with two important employment-oriented programs: vocational education and vocational rehabilitation. We provide an overview of each program and address the referral process, eligibility, the range of services and programs available, preparation of students for entry into vocational education and vocational rehabilitation, and tips for interagency collaboration.

Program Overviews

Vocational education is a program available in public school settings to develop specific occupational skills for secondary students in general and special education. Vocational rehabilitation is a program that assists eligible adults with disabilities in employment and integration into society to the maximum extent possible.

Although differences exist between vocational education and vocational rehabilitation, both programs have much to contribute to the successful transition of students with disabilities. Teachers should know about these two programs so they can

- Refer students appropriately;
- Describe services and programs available to students;
- Prepare students to successfully participate; and

- Collaborate effectively with personnel in vocational education and vocational rehabilitation programs.

Next we describe the mission and goals of each program, the basic administrative patterns, and the current utilization of services and outcome data for students with disabilities.

Vocational Education

The purpose of vocational education is to provide opportunities for persons to develop occupational competencies through sequential educational instruction and training appropriate for their abilities and needs. Cobb and Neubert (1992) described the following five broad goals for secondary vocational education:

- (a) acquisition of personal skills and attitudes;
- (b) communication and computational skills and technological literacy;
- (c) employability skills;
- (d) broad and specific occupational skills and knowledge; and
- (e) foundations for career planning and lifelong learning. (p. 93)

The overall goal of placing students in vocational education is to develop fundamental, academic, and employability skills for the world of work in a vocational area of their interest. Traditionally, vocational educa-

 From *Intervention in School and Clinic*, March 1996, pp. 197-208. © 1996 by PRO-ED, Inc. Reprinted by permission.

tion has been seen as the most realistic method of assisting persons in making the transition from education to employment. Ensuring free and equal access to vocational education programs for individuals with disabilities has been incorporated in landmark legislation. The Education for All Handicapped Children Act of 1975, IDEA, and the Rehabilitation Act of 1973 (Section 504) mandate that educational programs and facilities, including vocational education and training programs at the secondary and postsecondary levels, may not discriminate against persons with disabilities solely on the basis of their disability. Further, institutions may not discriminate in recruitment and admissions practices or provision of reasonable support services, accommodations, and modifications to the course requirements and facilities.

Typically, vocational education in secondary public schools is administered by individual states through a department of vocational education. States may apply for funds through the U.S. Department of Education's Office of Vocational and Adult Education. The provisions of the 1990 Carl C. Perkins Vocational Education and Applied Technology Act eliminated previously set aside funds; now funds are directed to school districts where special populations are highly concentrated. For example, within school districts, 70% of the allocation is based on the number of economically disadvantaged students, 20% on the number of students with disabilities, and 10% on the overall number of students enrolled in vocational education. For postsecondary schools, the allocation is based on the number of economically disadvantaged students who are eligible under Pell Grants. The responsibility for determining how monies are spent falls to the local vocational and community college administrators.

Another important legislative action with a significant impact on the administration of vocational education programs is the reappropriation of the Perkins Act. Congress and the U.S. Department of Education are negotiating the renewal of the Perkins Act to take effect mid-1997. The U.S. Department of Education is attempting to increase the support services (e.g., Braille tests and teachers' aides)

provided to special populations in vocational education classes. Vocational education administrators, however, believe that an expansion of support services will deplete program improvement funds and reduce the overall quality of vocational education programs ("Congress Blocks," 1994). In addition, some members of Congress wish to combine vocational education and job training programs while converting them to state block grants ("House, Senate," 1995). The new laws would supersede the Perkins Act.

Despite federal policy aimed at increasing the participation of students with disabilities in vocational programs, local implementation has resulted in the shrinking of programs and services (Kochlar & Deschamps, 1992). Specifically, the results may be (a) the elimination of special needs positions at the state and local level, (b) a shift of vocational education dollars to academics, (c) the elimination of vocational assessment and evaluation services, and (d) a shift of secondary vocational education funds to postsecondary programs (where there is no legal requirement to provide special education services under IDEA). This trend is all the more alarming in view of the proposed conversion to state block grants of many programs that currently are federally funded.

Vocational Rehabilitation

The purpose of vocational rehabilitation (VR) is to empower individuals with disabilities to achieve gainful employment consistent with their strengths, priorities, concerns, resources, and informed choices. This purpose is stated in the Rehabilitation Act of 1973 (amended in 1992 and 1993), which guides vocational rehabilitation services much as IDEA guides the special education service delivery system. The purpose of the Act is to assist states to deliver a comprehensive, coordinated vocational rehabilitation program designed to empower individuals with disabilities to maximize employment, economic self-sufficiency, independence, and inclusion and integration into society. These goals are pursued through comprehensive, state-of-the-art vocational rehabilitation programs, inde-

pendent living centers, research, training, demonstration projects, and the guarantee of equal opportunity. The legislation focuses on promoting meaningful and gainful employment and independent living in individuals with disabilities, especially individuals with severe disabilities (see Section 2(b)(1)(2)).

The Act mandates the following principles:

- Individuals with disabilities are presumed to be capable of engaging in gainful employment and benefiting from VR services;
- Opportunities for employment must be provided in integrated settings;
- Individuals with disabilities must be active participants in their own rehabilitation programs, making meaningful and informed choices in the selection of personal vocational goals and VR services they receive;
- Families or other natural supports can play a significant role in the VR process;
- Individuals with disabilities and their advocates are full partners in the VR program and must be involved in a meaningful manner and on a regular basis in policy development and implementation. (Section 100 (a)(2))

The federal government provides VR leadership and technical assistance to the states. It also provides 78% matching funds to the states for program implementation. Each state agency offers direct assistance to individuals with disabilities through local VR offices and individual counselors assigned to specific geographical areas or specific areas of disability.

Anyone who is familiar with an individual with a disability—or the individual him- or herself—can make a referral to vocational rehabilitation. After the appropriate VR counselor is identified, an initial interview is held to gather information about the disability and the person's work history. This begins the process necessary to determine the individual's eligibility for VR services. The assessment process will be described later in more detail; however, it includes assessing the individual's education and training, strengths, interests, work history, vocational rehabilitation needs, and employment goals (Dowdy & McCue, 1994). When eligibility is approved, the counselor and the individual (or the representative of the individual) develop an Individualized Written Rehabilitation Program (IWRP). According to the 1992 amendments to the Vocational Rehabilitation Act, each IWRP shall

a. be designed to achieve the employment objective consistent with the unique strengths, resources, priorities, abilities, capabilities, and concerns of the individual;

b. include the long-term goals determined by assessment;

c. include the degree to which the goals can be accomplished in integrated settings;

d. identify the short-term rehabilitation objectives related to the long-term goals;

e. include the specific services to be provided by VR and the dates of services anticipated;

f. include technological services if appropriate;

g. include specific on-the-job and related personal assistance services to be provided;

h. include the need for post-employment services;

i. include how the services will be provided through cooperative agreements with other agencies or through VR personnel; and

j. include evaluation procedures and criteria for determining if the goals have been met.

The IWRP must also document that the individual was informed about choices and involved personally in determining goals, objectives, services, and service providers. The IWRP, which is signed by the individual or the individual's representative, must be reviewed and updated annually with any changes approved by all parties.

The 1992 amendments to the Act mandate collaboration with community agencies and specifically refer to special education services. Although there is no age criterion in the VR program, the typical age to begin services is 16. The 1992 amendments to the Act include the same definition of transition services as that used in IDEA, so VR counselors are also provided legislation to work with school personnel to agree on a coordinated set of activities needed for successful transition. Both agencies mandate that this program be based on the individual's choices, needs, and interests.

Referral and Eligibility

Vocational Education

Procedures for students to enter vocational classrooms and programs vary among school districts. Students may elect to take vocational courses or be so advised by guidance counselors in comprehensive high schools. In the case of students with disabilities, decisions regarding vocational programs may be part of the annual IEP meeting or written into the Transition Plan.

The legislative support for vocational education of students with disabilities provided through various federal acts may have affected the inclusion of students with disabilities in vocational education programs. Students with disabilities have had difficulty in completing high school as well as vocational education courses (U.S. Department of Education, 1994b; Wagner, 1991). However, these data should be interpreted carefully, because enrollment in general has decreased for vocational education (U.S. Department of Education, 1994a). More than half of the vocational teachers surveyed indicated that the status of vocational education was a serious problem in their school, and 47% responded that maintaining vocational enrollments was also a serious problem. This may be a direct result of increased pressure on nondisabled students to take more academically oriented high school programs. As states have raised graduation requirements to include more mathematics, science, and other academic classes, and as college admission standards have increased the requirements for foreign languages, mathematics, and science, the number of elective credit hours available for high school students to select vocational education has been reduced.

Further, gender and ethnic background appear to have an effect on accessibility to vocational education (Wagner, 1991). Although young men and women with disabilities were equally likely to have enrolled in vocational courses, young men spent significantly more time than young women in occupationally oriented courses (Wagner, 1991). These differences were apparent regardless of disability category. Similarly, Wagner (1991) found that White students were significantly more likely to have taken occupationally oriented courses than were African-American students.

Another major factor determining accessibility of vocational programs has to do with the structure of most secondary vocational programs. Enrollment in vocational programs at most high schools is reserved for juniors and seniors (Cobb & Neubert, 1992) and, in most secondary schools, the vocational education classes are considered electives (P.L. Sitlington, personal communication, September 16, 1994). If students with disabilities have dropped out in or before 10th grade (Wagner, 1991; Zigmond & Thorton, 1985) or have not had time in their programs for electives, then these programs are accessible too late in the students' school careers to have a beneficial effect on their school progress.

Vocational Rehabilitation

As noted, an individual with a disability can self-refer to a vocational rehabilitation agency, or any person familiar with the individual who has a disability can make the referral. High school teachers account for a large number of referrals to the VR agency. Each high school teacher should contact the local VR agency and determine the counselor assigned to the region or high school. It is helpful to keep an ongoing relationship with the VR counselor by inviting him or her into the classroom to meet all students. If possible, the teacher should hold an additional meeting where VR counselors can meet with parents of students with disabilities. As soon as the referral is made, the counselor will hold an interview to begin the assessment process. During this process, information is gathered to assist the counselor in determining eligibility.

Eligibility in the vocational rehabilitation system is different from the eligibility process in the vocational education system. In the VR system, the presence or diagnosis of a learning disability does not automatically entitle one for services (Abbott, 1987). However, the 1992 amendments to the Rehabilitation Act have made eligibility for VR services much more accessible to individuals with disabilities.

The amendments state that an individual must

(1) have a physical or mental impairment that results in a substantial impediment to employment;

(2) be able to benefit from vocational rehabilitation services in terms of employment; and,

(3) require vocational rehabilitation services to prepare for, enter, engage in, or retain gainful employment. (Section 102(a)(1))

The VR counselor is solely responsible for reviewing assessment data and determining eligibility for VR services. Counselors first look at the current assessment data available, and if those data are not sufficient, additional testing can be requested. Frequently, counselors rely on other agencies such as the education agency to obtain information. Important sources of information might include school history, medical and developmental history, psychological and neuropsychological testing, opinions from teachers and past employers, interviews with parents, vocational evaluations, and situational assessments (McCue, 1994).

The counselor is required to determine eligibility within 60 days after the individual has applied for services. The 1992 amendments to the Rehabilitation Act state that individuals are presumed to be able to benefit from VR services in terms of employment unless the state VR agency can demonstrate by clear and convincing evidence that the individual is not capable of benefiting. These changes in legislation have brought significant increases in VR acceptance rates. In the first 6 months of 1995, 75.7% of all applicants to VR were determined to be eligible. This represents a significant increase over the years prior

to 1992 (Mars, 1995). With this tremendous increase in eligibility, counselors may have increasingly large caseloads, which may create an impasse to service delivery in the system. If an individual feels that his or her rights have not been protected or that he or she has not been treated fairly by the vocational rehabilitation system, that person is entitled to a fair hearing by an impartial hearing officer, and/or assistance from the Client Assistance Program (CAP) located in each VR state agency.

In approximately half the states, the VR agencies have determined that all eligible individuals cannot be served due to limited funds, and agencies have initiated an order of selection that provides services first to those individuals determined to be most severely disabled. The criteria for determining severity are established by each state within the guidelines of the 1992 amendments to the Act. An individual with a severe disability is defined as an individual

(1) who has a severe physical or mental impairment which seriously limits one or more functional capacities such as communication, self-care, mobility, self-direction, interpersonal skills, work tolerance or work skills in terms of employment outcomes;

(2) whose vocational rehabilitation is expected to require multiple vocational rehabilitation services over an extended period of time;

(3) who has one or more physical disabilities resulting from such conditions as mental retardation, mental illness, Multiple Sclerosis, Muscular Dystrophy, Neurological Disorders (including strokes and epilepsy), paraplegia, quadriplegia, specific learning disabilities, or a combination of disabilities based on a valid evaluation of functional limitations and vocational potential. (Section 7(15)(a))

Once eligibility has been determined, the individual, the counselor, and family members or significant others get together to write the IWRP. Following is a discussion of the options

that might be available to an individual through the vocational rehabilitation agency and the vocational education programs.

Services/Curricula

Vocational Education

Assessment. One of the most important services available in vocational education is assessment. The purpose of a vocational assessment is to collect and analyze information that will facilitate the development of goals and objectives for transition planning, including vocational program planning. This assessment should be a comprehensive, ongoing process, and data should be collected throughout the student's high school career. To assure appropriate placement in 9th-grade programs, assessment should begin during the 8th-grade year. Additional assessments should be completed at other strategic decision-making times, such as the beginning of 10th grade. Assessment should include a comprehensive profile of the student's strengths and limitations as well as interests and transition goals. The following components should be included in a vocational education assessment of students with mild disabilities (see Table 1 for an outline of assessment tools for both vocational education and vocational rehabilitation).

1. *Cumulative Data Review:* To begin, information may be obtained by reviewing cumulative records kept in a student's special education folder: attendance records, transcripts, teacher observations, recent psychological and medical evaluations, and current IEPs and Multidisciplinary Staffing Reports.

2. *Career Interest Inventory:* The purpose of career interest inventories is to gain information about the activities a person does or does not like to do and to assess occupational preferences. Information can be obtained using normed interest tests or informal activities with commercially available workbooks that have self-report inventories and checklists (see Brolin, 1995, and Cronin & Patton, 1993, for comprehensive listings of publishers and products).

3. *Aptitude and Ability Testing:* In testing a student's aptitude, the purpose is to assess the person's capacity to learn a new activity. Certainly, information from psychological tests can be used here but, more importantly, tests designed to measure specific aptitudes such as mechanical and clerical should be administered.

To test a student's natural and/or acquired ability to perform various activities, assessment should include measuring the student's abilities in reading, mathematics, language, and daily living skills. Further, testing may include fine/gross motor coordination, dexterity, and tool usage. Again, information from psychological evaluations as well as the school district's group tests may be used. Situational evaluations and parent and teacher observations can provide valuable information regarding a student's ability to perform specific tasks. Finally, commercially prepared tests are available to test a student's ability to perform specific occupational skills.

4. *Interviews:* Interviews of the student, parents, and teachers can provide important information for planning. When talking with the student, the interviewer should collect information regarding current interests, hobbies, part-time or summer jobs held, and types of chores or tasks performed at home and school. Certainly, the classes and teachers liked the most and the least would provide insight regarding possible career interests. Students should be questioned about their ability to discuss how their disability affects their lives. Finally, the interview should include some discussion of future personal goals and dreams (see Figure 1 for a sample student interview form).

When interviewing the parents, the interviewer should collect information regarding the strengths, limitations, and educational needs of their adolescent (see the sample parent interview form in Figure 2). During the teacher interviews, questions should focus on the student's functioning in the classroom, including functioning in both the cognitive and affective domains. If a vocational placement is being considered, information regarding the student's work-related behaviors is critical, such as motivation, organizational skills, attention span, classroom conduct, and frustration

level (see Figure 3 for a sample teacher interview form).

The above activities will provide the foundation of information necessary for beginning transition planning for most students with mild disabilities. However, in some cases, students may have difficulty expressing or identifying their interests and abilities. Additional information may be collected by using instruments and inventories designed to assess learning styles, values, career maturity, and job readiness.

Also, for students who have severe academic deficits and moderate to severe physical/mental disabilities, work samples and work evaluation systems may be used. Such testing requires a person trained as a vocational assessment specialist or trained to use the instruments selected.

Finally, for students who have extremely limited mental, physical, or emotional abilities, for whom the appropriate placement might be day training in a community setting or supported and/or sheltered employment, interviews, paper-and-pencil assessment, and work samples may not present an accurate measure of competency. The assessment of these students should include evaluation of functional living skills and job simulations. Although the assessment of functional living skills can be conducted in a classroom, the job simulations and production work samples should be conducted outside the school setting.

After completing the assessments, a report should be prepared for the transition planning meeting. Presenting the information in a format that will facilitate the planning process is vital. In addition, this information will assist in planning service delivery to support the student who is enrolled in a mainstream vocation class.

Curricula. The curriculum of typical high school vocational programs usually encompasses several components. Specific skill instruction would include automotive, wood, or metal work; cooking, sewing, or childcare; and computer keyboarding or bookkeeping. Work-training programs are conducted in cooperation with local business, and student vocational organizations are there to provide needed assistance and support.

Vocational Rehabilitation

Assessment. The 1992 amendments to the Rehabilitation Act specifically state that the VR assessment process must be comprehensive enough to determine eligibility, provide a diagnosis, identify vocational rehabilitation needs, identify any needs for technology services, and develop the IWRP. For VR purposes, it is important to determine the strengths, abilities, resources, and needs of an individual. Assessment should also determine the need for supportive employment. To determine eligibility, the counselor must have a comprehensive assessment of all areas suspected to pose a vocational limitation. Areas of assessment might include interests, interpersonal skills, personality, education achievements, intelligence, and related functional capacities; vocational attitudes; personal and social adjustments; and employment opportunities. In addition, psychiatric and psychological records, medical information, and other information such as recreational, cultural, and environmental data pertinent to rehabilitation needs for employment must also be assessed (Dowdy, in press). The vocational assessment services described in the vocational education assessment process are equally important in assessment for VR purposes.

The 1992 amendments to the Rehabilitation Act specifically mandate the use of situational assessment to provide a realistic appraisal of work behavior. Situational assessment assesses an individual's work attitudes, work tolerance, work habits, and social behaviors while on a simulated or real job site. It is important for the evaluator to modify areas of difficulty or provide accommodations to facilitate success on the job during this assessment (McCue et al., 1994).

When the assessment is complete, other considerations are useful in preparing students for either vocational education or vocational rehabilitation. Students should be provided a thorough discussion of the results. Ultimately, students should be able to describe their strengths and limitations, as well as the accommodations they need for success in classroom and work environments. This preparation is particularly important in VR, where client choice is mandated. Cli-

Table 1. Description of Instruments Used in Vocational Assessments

Instrument	Type	Assessor	Population	Description
Wide Range Interest Opinion Test (Jastak & Jastak, 1979)	Interest	Teacher, teacher aide	Ages 5–Adult; all but most severe disabilities	150 questions, untimed & forced-choice; uses pictures; results provide both high- & low-interest choices
Janus Job Planner (Jew & Tong, 1987)	Interest	Student	High school to adult	Workbook; paper-&-pencil activities
Talent Assessment Program (TAP; Talent Assessment, Inc., n.d.)	Aptitude	Trained paraprofessional	Grade 8 to adult; all but multiply disabled	Scores given for visualizing structural detail; sorting skills (size/shape, color, texture); use of small/large tools; and memory
Armed Services Vocational Aptitude Battery (Department of Defense, n.d.)	Aptitude	School counselor	High school to adult; requires sixth-grade reading	Comprehensive data regarding aptitude for specific occupations
Practical Assessment Exploration System (PAES; Talent Assessment, Inc., n.d.)	Work sample	Teachers, paraprofessionals	Middle school to adult; all populations of disability	Simulated work situations; used for both evaluation and assessment of job-related skills
Vineland Adaptive Behavior Scales (Sparrow, Balla, & Cicchetti, 1985)	Functional skills	Parents, teachers	All populations with disabilities	Interview and survey format to determine skill level in four domains; communication, daily living skills, socialization, & motor skills
Prevocational Assessment & Curriculum Guide (Mithaug, Mar, & Stewart, 1978)	School & work skills	Teachers, paraprofessionals	All populations	Assesses 46 school & workshop expectations in 9 areas; curriculum guide assists writing instructional goals

ents should be able to communicate their goals and view professionals and their families as "consultants" as they make their life choices (Pramuka, 1994).

Services. Under the 1992 amendments to the Rehabilitation Act, vocational rehabilitation services are defined as any service or goods necessary to prepare an individual with a disability for employment. Services include but are not limited to the following:

1. Assessment for determining eligibility or vocational rehabilitation needs, including assessment of rehabilitation technology needs if appropriate;

2. Counseling and work-related placement services, including assistance with job search, placement, retention, and any follow-up or follow-along needed to assist in maintaining, regaining, or advancing in employment;

3. Vocational and other training services, including personal and vocational adjustment, books, or other training materials. Training in higher education institutions cannot be paid for unless maximum efforts have been made to obtain grant assistance from other sources;

4. Physical and mental restorative services such as corrective surgery, eye glasses, and diagnosis and treatment for mental and emotional disorders;

5. Occupational licenses, equipment, tools, and basic stocks and supplies;

6. Transportation needed to participate in any vocational service;

7. Technological aids and devices; and,

8. Supported employment services. (Section 103 (a))

Student Classroom Preparation

Vocational Education

Students with disabilities may experience difficulties in vocational classes that are similar to those they experience in academic classes. As in academic classes, students will be called on to use math, reading memorization, note-taking, and test-taking skills. In addition, students will need to maintain high levels of motivation and on-task behaviors in workshop settings. As much of the work in vocational classes must be completed in the workshop where special machinery and tools are available, students may have few opportunities to obtain help through traditional home, peer, or special education networks. Therefore, students with disabilities may

11. TRANSITION TO ADULTHOOD

DIRECTIONS: *Interview the student and record responses.*

A. ATTITUDE TOWARD DISABILITY
1. Tell me about your disability.
2. Are you in a special education program? Which one? Why?
3. How do you feel about this program? Is it helpful?

B. INTERESTS IN LEISURE ACTIVITIES
1. What do you do in your spare time? Sports? Hobbies? Church? Extracurricular clubs at school?
2. What chores do you do at home?
3. Do you have friends? What do you and your friends do together?
4. On a perfect Saturday, what would you do?

C. FAMILY RELATIONSHIPS
1. What do you like best about your family?
2. Who usually helps you with schoolwork or other problems?
3. Is there anything that causes difficulties for you at home?

D. FUNCTIONAL SKILLS
1. If you had a job, how would you get to work?
2. Who selects your clothes?
3. Do you shop alone for your personal things?
4. Do you have an allowance or personal money from a job?
5. If you were home alone at dinner time, what would you eat and what would you do to prepare this meal?
6. If you had $1000, what would you buy?

E. EDUCATIONAL INTERESTS
1. What classes would you like to take? Would you like to include vocational classes?
2. Of all the classes you have taken, which one(s) was the best? Why?
3. Do you want to go to school after high school? Where?
4. What do your parents want you to do after high school?

F. WORK AND CLASS PREFERENCES
1. What teachers do you like best? Why?
   Least? Why?
2. Do you like to work alone or in a group?
3. When you work, do you like to sit most of the time or move around?
4. Do you prefer to work inside or outside?
5. Do you like to work on a computer?
6. Do you like to help people? Or work with things?

G. OCCUPATIONAL AND CAREER AWARENESS
1. Name as many jobs as you can. (time limit: 2 minutes)
2. Where do you begin to find a job?
3. What are some reasons people get fired?
4. What should you do when you are going to be absent or late to work?

H. FUTURE PLANS
1. What will you be doing during the next year, in 5 years, in 10 years toward the following postschool outcomes?
   Employment:
   Education:
   Living arrangements:
2. Will you need help meeting your goals? Which one(s)?
3. Where would you get the help you need?
4. What concerns you most about the future?

Figure 1. Sample student interview form. (This form may be photocopied for noncommercial use only. Copyright © 1996 by PRO-ED, Inc.)

DIRECTIONS: *Interview the parent who is the primary caregiver and record his or her responses.*

A. ATTITUDE TOWARD CHILD'S DISABILITY

1. Tell me about your child's disability. What are your child's strengths? Limitations?
2. Is your child in a special education program? Which one? Why?
3. How do you feel about this program? Is it helpful?

B. FAMILY RELATIONSHIPS

1. What are your family's strengths?
2. Who usually helps your child with schoolwork or other problems?
3. Is there anything that causes difficulties for your child at home?
4. Tell me about your child's relationships with other family members.

C. EDUCATIONAL PLANS

1. What classes would you like your child to take? Would you like to include vocational classes in your child's program? Which ones?
2. What skills would you like your child to learn in school?
3. What area of your child's education needs the most improvement?
4. What do you see your child doing after high school? Select one and explain your rationale.

   College/junior college

   Military

   Trade school

   Skilled employment

   Semi-skilled employment

   Other

D. LEISURE ACTIVITIES

1. What does your child do in his or her spare time? Sports? Hobbies? Church? Extracurricular clubs at school?
2. What chores do you assign for your child to do at home?
   Does your child complete these chores to your satisfaction?
3. Does your child have friends? What activities do they do together?
4. On a perfect Saturday, what would you and your child do together?

E. FUNCTIONAL SKILLS

1. If your child had a job, how would he or she get to work?
2. Who selects your child's clothes?
3. Do you allow your child to shop alone for personal things? Gifts?
4. Does your child have money for personal use? From an allowance or a job? Is your child allowed to manage his or her personal money?
5. If your child were home alone at dinner time, could he or she prepare a meal?

F. FUTURE PLANS

1. What will your child be doing during the next year, in 5 years, in 10 years toward the following postschool outcomes?

   Employment:

   Education:

   Living arrangements:
2. Will your child need help meeting his or her goals? Which one(s)?
3. Where would you and your child get the help you need?
4. What concerns you most about your child's future?
5. Name three jobs that you think your child could succeed at and would enjoy.

Figure 2. Sample parent interview form. (This form may be photocopied for noncommercial use only. Copyright © 1996 by PRO-ED, Inc.)

DIRECTIONS: *Interview teachers who have had this student in their classroom or extracurricular activities.*

A. COGNITIVE DOMAIN

Ask the teacher to discuss the student's cognitive abilities as related to instructional demands and academic tasks in the classroom. For example, does the student's disability have an impact on his or her ability to complete academic tasks such as homework? To understand lectures? To participate in group discussions? Does the student require support from special education personnel to complete tasks?

B. AFFECTIVE DOMAIN

Ask the teacher to discuss the student's ability to cope with stressful situations within the classroom, how the student relates to peers, general level of confidence and demeanor, and attitude toward school.

C. STUDENT'S WORK AND/OR CLASSROOM BEHAVIOR

Ask the teacher to discuss the student's work habits. For example, is work handed in on time? Does student exhibit inappropriate behaviors that distract the classroom? Does the student work best in groups or alone? Is student able to concentrate and remain on task?

D. STUDENT'S LEARNING STYLE EXHIBITED IN CLASSROOM

Ask the teacher to discuss observations of the student's learning style. For example, does the student appear to learn better from demonstrations and models, from lectures, or from written text?

E. LIST THREE JOBS YOU THINK THE STUDENT WOULD ENJOY AND SUCCEED IN

1.

2.

3.

F. OBSERVED ATTITUDE TOWARD STUDENT

Ask the teacher to rate how the majority of students in the classroom relate to the student with disabilities.

____ Accepting

____ Accepting with reservations

____ Question placement of student in class

____ Would prefer not to work with student

____ Refuse to work with student

Figure 3. Sample teacher interview form. (This form may be photocopied for noncommercial use only. Copyright © 1996 by PRO-ED, Inc.)

benefit from instruction in independent learning strategies, including problem solving, time management, self-questioning, and mnemonic strategies.

Task analysis is known to be helpful in other learning situations and can be a "power tool" in vocational settings for students with disabilities. Some students can be overwhelmed by the size and scope of projects requiring several steps to complete. Helping students break the project into the tasks and subtasks for each class session will allow them to understand what is to be done daily in order to meet long-range deadlines. Further, in the workshop setting, requiring self-monitoring of on-task behaviors and adding a timeline to the task analysis will help students plan and manage their work. Finally, the task analysis should include a checklist for students to verify that they have completed all steps required in the correct sequence.

Support for the student can equal support for the vocational teacher as well, particularly if the special and vocational educators work together as a collaborative team. The special educator can perform a number of helpful tasks in the vocational workshop; examples include the following:

- Spend some time in the workshop setting, becoming familiar with the instructional and setting demands of the vocational class;
- Provide textual materials and worksheets in the format needed by students (e.g., taped lectures, Braille, highlighted passages);
- Videotape lectures and demonstrations so that students can review procedures for clarification;
- Review task analysis/timeline with students daily;
- Demonstrate procedures as the vocational teacher lectures;
- Write notes and outlines on the board or overhead while the vocational teacher demonstrates/lectures; and
- Circulate among students while they are working to monitor on-task behavior, offer assistance, and answer questions. This may be particularly useful when students are involved in the more academically oriented tasks of completing worksheets or taking tests.

In order to improve the opportunities for students with disabilities to access and be successful in vocational education courses, special educators should be aware of the situational factors that will affect students in these settings. *Instructional demands*, as defined by Evers and Bursuck (1993), are those prerequisite skills necessary for successful completion of a class. They include both academic skills (such as reading and math) and social behaviors (such as attending to task and working independently). Deshler, Putnam, and Bulgren (1985) defined *setting demands* as the teacher's expectations for students to effectively manage the information presented as well as the procedures the teacher uses to evaluate the students' academic progress. Table 2 briefly outlines the instructional and setting demands found in vocational classrooms.

Vocational Rehabilitation

Several areas of preparation are important for success in the vocational rehabilitation process. First, students must understand the reason they are being referred to a vocational rehabilitation counselor, the process for receiving services, and what services are available. For example, a student may antagonize a counselor by blunt demands such as "I want VR to pay for college" or "Find me a job!" They need a thorough understanding of the agency's mission and how they might benefit from working with the vocational rehabilitation counselor in terms of employment.

Students should also be trained in the area of metacognitive skills. It is important for students to compensate for their limitations and be able to state their strengths and limitations, plan, organize, set goals, and monitor progress toward their goals. VR counselors respect an individual's right to participate as a partner in the rehabilitation process. Self-advocacy and self-evaluation are important skills for this interaction. Counselors may ask an individual to visit a campus and obtain specific information or visit job sites and analyze job requirements in terms of their own strengths and limitations. Teachers must begin to foster these skills in self-determination as part of the secondary curriculum.

Students also need to know about the world of work. They need an understanding of what it is to be a good employee and of the job market in their area in order to match their skills with available job openings. Teachers can find creative ways to incorporate information and experiences in work and independent living into existing courses, for example, math and economics.

Collaboration

Collaboration between families and agencies or programs such as special education, vocational education, and vocational rehabilitation is mandated by legislation. These individuals must work together throughout the design of the transition component of the IEP; if one of the responsible parties fails to follow through as designated by the IEP, another service delivery agency must be identified. Some suggestions to facilitate this collaborative process include the following:

1. Personnel from these agencies should be educated regarding the key components for the transition process for school-age students with disabilities.
2. Personnel should be informed of the transition services available in the local district, including the referral and eligibility process for each.
3. A local resource manual should be developed and continually updated to provide ready access to program overviews and important telephone numbers.
4. Agency personnel should be encouraged to meet students and families early in the transition process, possibly through classroom visits or specially scheduled meetings.

Table 2. Instructional and Setting Demands in Vocational Classrooms

| Report | Demands | |
	Instructional	Setting
Greenan (1983)	28 mathematical 27 communication 20 interpersonal 40 reasoning skills	
Elrod (1987)	Basic math skills Reading ability of seventh to ninth grade	
Okolo (1988)		High level of independence: self-monitoring, appropriate work habits, ability to stay on task
Okolo & Sitlington (1988)	Teacher lecture; note taking needed; independent use of text and workbooks	Independent work in labs/workshops
Evers & Bursuck (1993, 1994)	Teacher lecture; note taking required; use of texts and workbooks; requires some basic math and some geometry skills; homework assignments given; tests/quizzes for 20%–30% of grade	High levels of independent work required; specific projects with a specific order of completion required; requirements for vocational education teachers identical to those of academic teachers

5. Procedures should be implemented to facilitate the authorized sharing between agencies of information on students. Too often, the "bureaucratic red tape" creates logjams in the transition process.

6. Agency personnel should suggest information that could be taught in the special education classrooms to facilitate the transition process. Special education teachers should share their goals and needs for students with agency personnel.

7. Agency personnel participating in developing IEPs should consult before scheduling IEP and other types of meetings.

8. Students and families should be encouraged to contact a transition team member regarding their relative satisfaction with services provided.

9. Team members should maintain regular contact with one another regarding student progress and the status of transition services.

Conclusion

With an understanding of the services available and the processes involved in vocational education and rehabilitation, teachers can serve as the critical liaison between these programs and the students and their families. To adequately prepare students for their interaction with these programs, teachers may add employment-related and living skills to their existing curriculum or incorporate the teaching of these skills into more traditional high school content areas. Equally important for special education teachers is building a partnership with professionals in these programs to facilitate the transition process for their students with disabilities.

References

Abbott, J. (1987, February). *Accessing vocational rehabilitation training and employment programs.* Paper presented at the annual meeting of the ACLD, San Antonio, TX.

Brolin, D. E. (1995). *Career education: A functional life skill approach.* Englewood Cliffs, NJ: Merrill.

Carl Perkins Vocational Education and Applied Technology Act Amendments of 1990, Pub. L. 101-392.

Cobb, R. B., & Neubert, D. A. (1992). Vocational education models. In F. R. Rusch, L. DeStefano,

J. Chadsey-Rusch, L. A. Phelps, & E. Szymanski (Eds.), *Transition from school to adult life* (pp. 93–113). Sycamore, IL: Sycamore.

Congress blocks ED changes to Perkins Rule. (1994, September 29). *Vocational Training News,* pp. 3–4.

Cronin, M. E., & Patton, J. R. (1993). *Life skills instruction for all students with special needs: A practical guide for integrating real-life content into the curriculum.* Austin, TX: PRO-ED.

Deshler, D. D., Putnam, M. L., & Bulgren, J. A. (1985). Academic accommodations for adolescents with behavior and learning problems. In S. Braaten, R. B. Rutherford, Jr., & C. A. Kardash (Eds.), *Programming for adolescents with behavioral disorders* (Vol. 2, pp. 22–30). Reston, VA: Council for Exceptional Children.

DeStefano, L., & Wermuth, T. R. (1992). Chapter 29: IDEA (P.L. 101-476): Defining a second generation of transition services. In F. R. Rusch, L. DeStefano, J. Chadsey-Rusch, L. A. Phelps, & E. Szymanski (Eds.), *Transition from school to adult life* (pp. 537–549). Sycamore, IL: Sycamore.

Dowdy, C. A. (in press). Vocational rehabilitation and special education: Partners in transition for individuals with learning disabilities. *Journal for Learning Disabilities.*

Dowdy, C. A., & McCue, M. (1994). Crossing service systems: From special education to vocational rehabilitation. In C. A. Michaels (Ed.), *Transition strategies for persons with learning disabilities* (pp. 53–78). San Diego: Singular.

Education for All Handicapped Children Act of 1975, 20 U.S.C. § 1400 *et seq.*

Elrod, G. F. (1987). Academic and social skills prerequisite to success in vocational training. *The Journal of Special Needs Education, 10,* 17–21.

Evers, R. B., & Bursuck, W. B. (1993). Teacher ratings of instructional and setting demands in vocational education classes. *Learning Disability Quarterly, 16,* 82–92.

Evers, R. B., & Bursuck, W. (1994). Literary demands in secondary technical vocational education programs: Teacher interviews. *Career Development for Exceptional Individuals, 17,* 135–144.

Greenan, J. P. (1983). *Identification of generalizable skills in secondary vocational programs: Executive summary.* Springfield: Illinois State Board of Education.

House, Senate make kill off longtime voc-ed law. (1995, March 16). *Vocational Training News,* pp. 1–3.

Individuals with Disabilities Education Act of 1990, 20 U.S.C. § 1400 *et seq.*

Jew, W., & Tong, R. (1987). *Janus job planner: A guide to career planning* (2nd ed.). Belmont, CA: Fearon/Janus/Quercus.

Kochlar, C. A., & Deschamps, A. B. (1992). Policy crossroads in preserving the right of passage to independence for learners with special needs: Implications of recent changes in national, vocational,

special education policies. *Journal for Vocational Special Needs Education, 14* (2-3), 9–19.

Mars, L. I. (1995). [Case services report-RSA-911 raw data. Persons rehabilitated in state agencies. October 1, 1994-April 1, 1995] Unpublished raw data.

McCue, M. (1994). Clinical, diagnostic, and functional assessment of adults with learning disabilities. In P. J. Gerber & H. B. Reiff (Eds.), *Learning disabilities in adulthood: Persisting problems and evolving issues* (pp. 55–71). Boston: Andover Medical Publishers.

McCue, M., Chase, S. L., Dowdy, C. A., Pramuka, M., Petrick, J., Aitken, S., & Fabry, P. (1994). *Functional assessment of individuals with cognitive disabilities: A desk reference for rehabilitation.* Pittsburgh, PA: Center for Applied Neuropsychology Associates.

Mithaug, D. E., Mar, D. K., & Stewart, J. E. (1978). *Prevocational assessment curriculum guide.* Seattle: J. E. Stewart.

Okolo, C. (1988). Instructional environment in secondary vocational education programs: Implications for LD adolescents. *Learning Disability Quarterly, 11,* 136–148.

Okolo, C., & Sitlington, P. L. (1988). Mildly handicapped learners in vocational education: A statewide study. *The Journal of Special Education, 22,* 220–230.

Practical assessment exploration system. (n.d.) Jacksonville, FL: Talent Assessment, Inc.

Pramuka, M. (1994). *Facilitating empowerment in students with learning disabilities: Guidelines for teachers.* Unpublished manuscript.

Rehabilitation Act of 1973, 1992 Amendments, 29 U.S.C. § 701 *et seq.*

Sparrow, S. S., Balla, D. A., & Cicchetti, D. V. (1985). *Vineland adaptive behavior scales.* Circle Pines, MN: American Guidance Service.

Talent assessment program. (n.d.) Jacksonville, FL: Talent Assessment, Inc.

U.S. Department of Education. (1994a). *Public secondary school teacher survey on vocation education: Contractor report.* Washington, DC: National Center for Education Statistics.

U.S. Department of Education. (1994b). *Sixteenth annual board of education report to Congress on the implementation of the Individuals with Disabilities Education Act.* Washington, DC: Office of Special Education Programs.

Wagner, M. (1991, April). *The benefits of secondary vocational education for young people with disabilities: Findings from the National Longitudinal Transition Study of special education students.* Paper presented at the annual meeting of the American Educational Research Association, Chicago.

Zigmond, N., & Thorton, H. (1985). Follow-up on postsecondary age learning disabled graduates and drop-outs. *Learning Disabilities Research, 1*(1), 50–55.

Credits/Acknowledgments

Cover design by Charles Vitelli

1. Inclusive Education
Facing overview—New York Times Pictures photo by Therese Frare.

2. Children with Learning Disabilities
Facing overview—United Nations photo by L. Solmssen.

3. Children with Mental Retardation
Facing overview—United Nations photo by L. Solmssen.

4. Children with Behavioral Disorders and Autism
Facing overview—WHO photo by K. Kalisher. 95—Graphics by Jared Schneidman Design.

5. Children with Communication Disorders
Facing overview—United Nations photo by Marta Pinter. © 1979 by Interfoto MTI, Hungary.

6. Children with Hearing Impairments
Facing overview—WHO photo by E. Schwab.

7. Children with Visual Impairments
Facing overview—United Nations photo by S. Dimartini.

8. Children with Physical and Health Impairments
Facing overview—United Nations photo by Jan Corash.

9. Children with Special Gifts and Talents
Facing overview—Photo by Pamela Carley.

10. Early Childhood Exceptionality
Facing overview—United Nations photo by John Isaac.

11. Transition to Adulthood
Facing overview—United Nations photo by S. Dimartini.

PHOTOCOPY THIS PAGE!!!

ANNUAL EDITIONS ARTICLE REVIEW FORM

■ NAME: _____ DATE: _____

■ TITLE AND NUMBER OF ARTICLE: _____

■ BRIEFLY STATE THE MAIN IDEA OF THIS ARTICLE: _____

_____

■ LIST THREE IMPORTANT FACTS THAT THE AUTHOR USES TO SUPPORT THE MAIN IDEA:

_____

_____

_____

_____

■ WHAT INFORMATION OR IDEAS DISCUSSED IN THIS ARTICLE ARE ALSO DISCUSSED IN YOUR TEXTBOOK OR OTHER READINGS THAT YOU HAVE DONE? LIST THE TEXTBOOK CHAPTERS AND PAGE NUMBERS:

_____

_____

_____

_____

_____

■ LIST ANY EXAMPLES OF BIAS OR FAULTY REASONING THAT YOU FOUND IN THE ARTICLE:

_____

_____

_____

_____

■ LIST ANY NEW TERMS/CONCEPTS THAT WERE DISCUSSED IN THE ARTICLE, AND WRITE A SHORT DEFINITION:

_____

_____

_____

_____

*Your instructor may require you to use this ANNUAL EDITIONS Article Review Form in any number of ways: for articles that are assigned, for extra credit, as a tool to assist in developing assigned papers, or simply for your own reference. Even if it is not required, we encourage you to photocopy and use this page; you will find that reflecting on the articles will greatly enhance the information from your text.

We Want Your Advice

ANNUAL EDITIONS revisions depend on two major opinion sources: one is our Advisory Board, listed in the front of this volume, which works with us in scanning the thousands of articles published in the public press each year; the other is you—the person actually using the book. Please help us and the users of the next edition by completing the prepaid article rating form on this page and returning it to us. Thank you for your help!

ANNUAL EDITIONS: EDUCATING EXCEPTIONAL CHILDREN, Ninth Edition

Article Rating Form

Here is an opportunity for you to have direct input into the next revision of this volume. We would like you to rate each of the 40 articles listed below, using the following scale:

1. **Excellent: should definitely be retained**
2. **Above average: should probably be retained**
3. **Below average: should probably be deleted**
4. **Poor: should definitely be deleted**

Rating	Article	Rating	Article
	1. Questions and Answers about Inclusion: What Every Teacher Should Know		21. Do You See What I Mean? Body Language in Classroom Interactions
	2. What Do I Do Now? A Teacher's Guide to Including Students with Disabilities		22. The Roles of the Educational Interpreter in Mainstreaming
	3. The Real Challenge of Inclusion: Confessions of a "Rabid Inclusionist"		23. Developing Independent and Responsible Behaviors in Students Who Are Deaf or Hard of Hearing
	4. Restructuring the Participation of African-American Parents in Special Education		24. By June, Given Shared Experiences, Integrated Classes, and Equal Opportunities, Jaime Will Have a Friend
	5. Peer Education Partners		25. Preschool Orientation and Mobility: A Review of the Literature
	6. Is Attention Deficit Disorder Becoming a Desired Diagnosis?		26. Teaching Choice-making Skills to Students Who Are Deaf-Blind
	7. Identifying Students' Instructional Needs in the Context of Classroom and Home Environments		27. The Success of Three Gifted Deaf-Blind Students in Inclusive Educational Programs
	8. Adapting Textbooks for Children with Learning Disabilities in Mainstreamed Classrooms		
	9. Mastery Learning in the Regular Classroom: Help		28. Medical Treatment and Educational Problems in Children
	10. Prenatal Drug Exposure: An Overview of Associated Problems and Intervention Strategies		29. HIV/AIDS Education for Students with Special Needs
	11. Integrating Elementary Students with Multiple Disabilities into Supported Regular Classes: Challenges and Solutions		30. Creating Inclusionary Opportunities for Learners with Multiple Disabilities: A Team-Teaching Approach
	12. What's Right for Rafael?		31. Listening to Parents of Children with Disabilities
	13. Helping Individuals with Severe Disabilities Find Leisure Activities		32. Education of Gifted Students: A Civil Rights Issue?
	14. They Can But They Don't: Helping Students Overcome Work Inhibition		33. Meeting the Needs of Gifted and Talented Preschoolers
	15. The Culturally Sensitive Disciplinarian		34. Gifted Girls in a Rural Community: Math Attitudes and Career Options
	16. Variables Affecting the Reintegration Rate of Students with Serious Emotional Disturbance		35. Putting Real-Life Skills into IEP/IFSPs for Infants and Young Children
	17. Autism		36. A Physical Education Curriculum for All Preschool Students
	18. Language Interaction Techniques for Stimulating the Development of At-Risk Children in Infant and Preschool Day Care		37. "Buddy Skills" for Preschoolers
	19. Distinguishing Language Differences from Language Disorders in Linguistically and Culturally Diverse Students		38. What Do Students with Disabilities Tell Us about the Importance of Family Involvement in the Transition from School to Adult Life?
	20. Toward Defining Programs and Services for Culturally and Linguistically Diverse Learners in Special Education		39. Is a Functional Curriculum Approach Compatible with an Inclusive Education Model?
			40. Preparing Students for Transition: A Teacher Primer on Vocational Education and Rehabilitation

(Continued on next page)

ABOUT YOU

Name _____ Date _____

Are you a teacher? ❑ Or a student? ❑

Your school name _____

Department _____

Address _____

City _____ State _____ Zip _____

School telephone # _____

YOUR COMMENTS ARE IMPORTANT TO US!

Please fill in the following information:

For which course did you use this book? _____

Did you use a text with this *ANNUAL EDITION*? ❑ yes ❑ no

What was the title of the text? _____

What are your general reactions to the *Annual Editions* concept?

Have you read any particular articles recently that you think should be included in the next edition?

Are there any articles you feel should be replaced in the next edition? Why?

Are there other areas that you feel would utilize an ANNUAL EDITION?

May we contact you for editorial input?

May we quote you from above?

ANNUAL EDITIONS: EDUCATING EXCEPTIONAL CHILDREN, Ninth Edition

BUSINESS REPLY MAIL

First Class   Permit No. 84   Guilford, CT

Postage will be paid by addressee

**Dushkin Publishing Group/
Brown & Benchmark Publishers**
Sluice Dock
Guilford, Connecticut 06437

No Postage
Necessary
if Mailed
in the
United States